Ernest Alfred Wallis Budge

First Steps in Egyptian

A Book for Beginners

Ernest Alfred Wallis Budge

First Steps in Egyptian
A Book for Beginners

ISBN/EAN: 9783337330279

Printed in Europe, USA, Canada, Australia, Japan

Cover: Foto ©Thomas Meinert / pixelio.de

More available books at **www.hansebooks.com**

FIRST STEPS IN EGYPTIAN

A BOOK FOR BEGINNERS

BY

E. A. WALLIS BUDGE, Litt. D.,

KEEPER OF THE EGYPTIAN AND ASSYRIAN ANTIQUITIES,

BRITISH MUSEUM

LONDON

KEGAN PAUL, TRENCH, TRÜBNER & CO., Ltd.

PATERNOSTER HOUSE, CHARING CROSS ROAD

1895.

PREFACE.

THE widespread interest in Egyptology which has sprung up during the last few years has produced an increased demand for books upon every branch of the science; Egyptologists have striven to meet this demand, and the wants of almost every class of student have been adequately supplied. Only the beginner has been somewhat forgotten. One of the chief obstacles to the study of the Egyptian language is the want of suitable material for elementary work, that is to say editions of texts of all periods of Egyptian history, which may be obtained easily and at a reasonable price. The main sources of information on ancient Egypt must always be such works as the *Description de l'Égypte*, the *Denkmäler*, the *Select Papyri in the Hieratic Character in the British Museum*, the editions of texts by Mariette, etc.; but these are only to be found in large libraries, and their great cost puts them out of the reach of all but the few. Moreover, many of the most important texts in them have been republished with corrections and emendations, and they have formed the subjects of special studies by various scholars who have issued the results of their labours either in the form of independent treatises or as contributions to serial archaeological periodicals. Thus there has grown up around the subject a large and scattered literature which the beginner cannot penetrate alone without loss of time.

The following pages have been drawn up with the view of helping the beginner to take his first steps in Egyptian. In brief, they contain a sketch of the commonest and most useful facts connected with the writing and grammar, short lists of the signs and determinatives which occur most frequently, a short vocabulary of about five hundred common words, a series of thirty-one texts and extracts, with interlinear transliteration and word for word translation, which belong to the period that lies between B. C. 4200 and 200, and a few untransliterated and untranslated texts, with glossary, to be worked out independently. The Introduction is intended to enable the beginner to use with advantage and with little loss of time any of the grammars which he will find in English, French and German, and it is hoped that the frequent examples of words in it will make him familiar with the use of the alphabetic and syllabic signs and determinatives. The hieroglyphic texts which follow the Introduction include examples of the chief divisions of Egyptian literature, historical, funeral, religious, moral, mythological, etc., and the aim has been to give passages which are at once interesting and complete in themselves. The translations have been made as literal as possible.

To learn the hieroglyphic characters and words the beginner is recommended to write them out frequently. Nothing will help him so much in this direction as copying inscriptions, and nothing will teach him the values of the signs and the meanings of determinatives and words so well as constant practice in writing and reading texts. He should note, too, that a few new words learnt correctly each day will, in a short time, enable him to read new texts.

E. A. WALLIS BUDGE.

London, August 31, 1895.

CONTENTS.

PAGE.

Preface V

PART I.

Introduction :—

Egyptian Writing 1

Alphabetic signs 6

Syllabic signs ... ... 8—11

Determinatives ... ... 11—22

Pronouns ... ... 22—24

Nouns ... ... 24—26

The Article ... ... 26—30

Adjectives ... ... 30—32

Numbers ... ... 32—34

Measures 34

Time, divisions of 35

The Year 35

The Verb ... ... 36—42

The Adverb 42

Prepositions and Conjunctions ... ... 43—46

Particles ... ... 46—48

A list of common words to be learnt ... ... 48—71

Egyptian Gods and Goddesses ... ... 71—75

PART II.

Texts with interlinear transliteration and word for word translation :—

1. Extracts from the Prisse Papyrus ... ... 79—85

See Prisse d'Avennes, *Facsimile d'un papyrus égyptien*

PAGE.

en caractères hiératiques, Paris, 1847; and Virey, *Études sur le Papyrus Prisse,* Paris, 1887.

2. Extracts from the pyramid texts of Unȧs and Tetȧ 86—94
See Maspero, *Recueil de Travaux,* tomm. III, IV and V, Paris, 1882, 1883, 1884.

3. Inscription from the tomb of Ḥeru-khuf at Aswân 95—98
See Schiaparelli, *Una tomba Egiziana* (*Atti della R. Accademia dei Lincei,* anno CCLXXXIX., Ser. 4[a], Classe di Scienzie Morali, t. X. Roma, 1893, pp. 22—53).

4. Inscription from the stele of Abu ... ... 99—102
See Maspero, *Recueil de Travaux,* tom. III, p. 115 f.

5. Inscription of Ȧṭa 103

6. Inscription from the tomb of Khnemu-Ḥetep at Beni-hasan ... ... 104—105
See Newberry, *Beni Hasan,* pt. 1. Lond., 1893, pl. 41.

7. Inscriptions from the tomb of Ȧmeni-em-ḥāt at Beni-Hasan ... ... 106—113
See Newberry, *op. cit.,* pll. 8, 11, etc.

8. Stories of the reigns of Seneferu and Khufu ... 114—125
For the hieratic text, transcript, etc., see Erman, *Die Märchen des Papyrus Westcar,* Berl., 1890, pll. 6, 7.

9. The Life of Amāsis, the naval officer, as told by himself ... ... 126—137
See Lepsius, *Denkmäler,* Abth. III, Bl. 11, and for the last translation by Brugsch see *Egypt under the Pharaohs,* vol. 1, p. 249 ff.

10. The Harper's Lament ... ... 138—140
See Stern, *Aegyptische Zeitschrift,* 1873, p. 60.

11. The Battle of Megiddo ... ... 141—155
See Maspero, *Recueil de Travaux,* tom. II, p. 51 ff.

12. Speech of Ȧmen-Rā to Thothmes III. ... ... 156—167
See Mariette, *Karnak,* Leipzig, 1875, plate 11; and Brugsch, *Geschichte Aegyptens,* Leipz., 1877, p. 352 ff.

PAGE.

13. Address of Thothmes III to Osiris (Book of the Dead, Chap. CLIV) ... ... 168—171
See Naville, *Todtenbuch*, Bd. 1. Bl. 179.

14. Specimens of the Maxims of Ani ... ... 172—178
See Chabas, *L'Égyptologie*, Chalons-sur-Saone, 1874; Amélineau, *La Morale égyptienne*, Paris, 1892.

15. Hymn to Osiris ... ... 179—188
See Ledrain, *Monuments Égyptiens*, Pl. XXII ff.; and Chabas, *Revue Archéologique*, 1857, p. 65.

16. Inscription from the Stele of Teḥuti-nefer ... 189—193
See Maspero, *Recueil de Travaux*, tom. III, p. 122, tom. IV, p. 125.

17. Inscription from the Stele of Tchanni ... ... 194—195
See Maspero, *Recueil de Travaux*, tom. IV, p. 130.

18. Inscription from the Stele of Sesh ... ... 196—199
See Maspero, *Recueil de Travaux*, tom. IV, p. 127.

19. Inscription from a sepulchral Stele ... ... 200—201
See Piehl, *Recueil de Travaux*, tom. I, p. 197.

20. Inscription from the Stele of Ȧmen-hetep ... 202—203
See Piehl, *Recueil de Travaux*, tom. II, p. 124.

21. Hymn to the god of the Nile ... ... 204—211
See Birch, *Select Papyri*, pl. XX f.; Maspero, *Hymne au Nil*, Paris, 1868.

22. Examples of the Proverbs of Tuauu-f-se-Kharthai 212—217
See Birch, *Select Papyri*, pll. XV—XX, CXXVIII—CXXXIV; and Maspero, *Du Genre Épistolaire*, Paris, 1872.

23. The Destruction of Mankind ... ... 218—230
See Lefébure, *Tombeau de Séti I*, part IV, pll. 15—18; Brugsch, *Die neue Weltordnung*, Berlin, 1881; Naville, *Trans. Soc. Bibl. Arch.*, vol. IV, p. 1 ff., vol. VIII, p. 412 ff.; Wiedemann, *Die Religion der alten Aegypter*, p. 32 ff.

PAGE.

24. The War of Rameses II. against the Kheta ... 231—234
See Guieyesse, *Recueil de Travaux,* tom. VIII, pp. 136, 139.
25. Hymn to Rā (Book of the Dead, Chap. XV) ... 235—238
See Naville, *Todtenbuch,* Bd. I. Bl. 16.
26. Numbers from the papyrus of Rameses III. ... 239—240
See Birch, *Facsimile of an Egyptian Hieratic Papyrus,* London, 1876.
27. The Legend of Rā and Isis ... ... 241—256
See Pleyte and Rossi, *Papyrus de Turin,* pll. 31, 77, 131—8; Lefébure, *Aegyptische Sprache,* 1883, p. 27; Wiedemann, *Die Religion,* p. 29 f.
28. From the Monument of Uaḥ-åb-Rā em khu ... 257
See Piehl, *Recueil de Travaux,* tom. III, p. 28.
29. Texts from the sarcophagus of Paṭepep ... ... 257—260
See Bergmann, *Recueil de Travaux,* tom. III, pp. 148—152.
30. The Legend of the Seven Years' Famine in Egypt 261—268
See Brugsch, *Die biblischen sieben Jahre der Hungersnoth,* Leipzig, 1891.
31. From an Inscription of Ptolemy V. ... ... 269—272
See Bouriant, *Recueil de Travaux,* tom. VI, p. 1 ff.

PART III.

Egyptian Texts untransliterated and untranslated* ... 275—289
Glossary ... ... 291—321

* These texts are taken from the Papyrus of Nebseni, the *Papyrus of Ani* (2nd edition), Lieblein, *Que mon nom fleurisse,* Birch, *Egyptian Antiquities at Alnwick Castle,* etc.

A LIST OF EGYPTIAN GRAMMARS.

Champollion (le Jeune), *Grammaire Égyptienne ou principes généraux de l'écriture sacrée Égyptienne appliquée à la représentation de la langue parlée, publiée sur le manuscrit autographe*, Paris, fol. MDCCCXXXVI.

Birch, S. *Hieroglyphic Grammar* (Published in Bunsen, *Egypt's Place in Universal History*, Vol. V, pp. 590—716, London, 1867).

Rougé, Emmanuel de, *Chrestomathie Égyptienne ou Choix de Textes Égyptiens transcrits, ... et précédés d'un abrégé grammatical.* Fasc. 1, Paris, 1867; fasc. 2, Paris, 1868; fasc. 3 and 4, Paris, 1875, 1876.

Brugsch, H. *Hieroglyphische Grammatik*, Leipzig, 1872.

Renouf, P. le Page, *An Elementary Grammar of the ancient Egyptian language in the hieroglyphic type*, London, 1875.

Rossi, Francesco, *Grammatica Copto-Geroglifica con un' appendice dei principali segni sillabici e del loro significato*, Roma-Torino-Firenze, 1877.

Erman, A. *Neuägyptische Grammatik*, Leipzig, 1880.

Coemans, E. M. *Manuel de la langue Égyptienne*, Gand et Paris, 1887.

Loret, V. *Manuel de la langue Égyptienne*, Paris, 1889.

Erman, E. *Egyptian Grammar with table of signs, bibliography, exercises for reading and glossary*, London, 1894. Published in German and in English. The English translation is by J. H. Breasted.

DICTIONARIES.

Birch, S. *Dictionary of Hieroglyphics* (Published in Bunsen's *Egypt's Place in Universal History*, vol. V, pp. 337—586, London, 1867.

Brugsch, H. *Hieroglyphisch-Demotisches Wörterbuch enthaltend in wissenschaftlicher Anordnung die gebräuchlichsten Wörter und Gruppen der heiligen und der Volkssprache und Schrift der alten Aegypter*, Bdd. I—IV, Leipzig, 1867, 68.

Do. Do. Do. Do., Bd. V—7, Leipzig, 1880.

Pierret, P. *Vocabulaire Hiéroglyphique*, Paris, 1875.

Levi, S. *Vocabolario geroglifico copto-ebraico*, tomm. I—VII. Torino, 1887—1889.

INTRODUCTION.

THE first decipherer who succeeded in assigning correct values to any of the Egyptian picture signs or hieroglyphics was Dr. Thomas Young, who already in 1818 had given to six[1] characters values which are accepted at the present time; the values of three others[2] were correctly stated as far as the consonants are concerned. Four years later M. Jean François Champollion published a complete system of decipherment, and was the first European in modern times who was able to translate Egyptian inscriptions and to understand them. He recovered the long lost alphabet, and deduced the values of many of the syllabic signs from a careful and exhaustive examination of all the names and titles of Greek and Roman kings of Egypt which are found written in hieroglyphic characters, and from the bilingual inscriptions in Greek and Egyptian which are found on an obelisk that stood originally[3] on the island of Philae, and on the famous Rosetta Stone now preserved in the British Museum.[4]

Egyptian decipherment.

[1] *Viz.*, 𓇌 *i*, 𓌳 *m*, 𓈖 *n*, 𓊪 *p*, 𓆑 *f*, 𓏏 *t*.

[2] *Viz.*, 𓃀, 𓃭 and 𓋴 which he read *bir*, *ole*, and *osh* or *os*, instead of *ba*, *r* or *l*, and *s*; if we accept the value of *qeb* for 𓅬 as some would do, we must not forget that Young assigned the value of *ke* to this sign.

[3] It was discovered by Mr. J. W. Bankes in 1815, and was removed at his expense by G. Belzoni to be set up at Kingston Hall in Dorsetshire. Both obelisk and pedestal are of red granite; the former is inscribed with one column of hieroglyphics on each side, and the latter with 24 lines of Greek.

[4] Southern Egyptian Gallery, No. 24.

Great antiquity of picture writing.

The inventors of the Egyptian system of picture writing are unknown and it is impossible either to assign a date to the period when it was introduced into Egypt, or to say what people first made use of it; that it belongs to a remote antiquity is certain. It is a remarkable fact that, whereas the ancient inhabitants of Mesopotamia, who wrote their inscriptions in cuneiform characters which were originally pictures like the Egyptian signs,[1] modified them in such a way that their original forms had disappeared some thousands of years before Christ, the Egyptians preserved the original forms of their picture signs from the time of the first historical king Menȧ to the period of the rule of the Roman Emperors, that is to say for a space of about five thousand years.

Permanence of hieroglyphic characters.

Various kinds of hieroglyphic writing.

Egyptian writing exists in three forms to which the names Hieroglyphic, Hieratic and Demotic have been given. **Hieroglyphic**[2] or picture writing is the earliest form known, and it remained in constant use in all periods of Egyptian history; it was employed chiefly for monumental purposes, *i. e.*, for inscriptions upon tombs of all kinds, temples, stelae, etc. The oldest hieroglyphic inscriptions are probably those which are found in the *maṣṭaba* tomb of Seker-khā-baiu, which MM. Mariette and Maspero believe to belong to the period of the first dynasty or

[1] This fact is proved by the fragment of a baked clay tablet, found on the site of the ancient Nineveh, whereon we have a number of cuneiform characters and the original pictures from which they have been developed arranged in parallel columns. The fragment is exhibited in the Nineveh Gallery, Table-case B. No. K. 8520; for the literature see Bezold, *Catalogue of the Cuneiform Tablets in the Kouyunjik Collection,* vol. II., p. 934.

[2] The first to describe the hieroglyphic characters systematically was the late Dr. Birch. In Bunsen's *Egypt's Place in Universal History*, Vol. 1. London, 1867, pp. 505—579 he quoted, with references, some 890 signs, and gave 201 determinatives. Lists of characters have also been given by de Rougé, *Chrestomathie Égyptienne,* Paris, 1867, p. 86 ff.; Brugsch, *Hieroglyphische Grammatik,* Leipzig, 1872, pp. 119—138; Loret, *Manuel de la Langue Égyptienne,* Paris, 1889, pp. 113—135; and Erman, *Aegyptische Grammatik,* Berlin, 1894, pp. 171—193.

earlier. **Hieratic** is a form of writing in which only the most salient features of the hieroglyphics or pictures are preserved.[1] It originated, no doubt, in the hastily written memoranda and drafts of inscriptions with which the scribes supplied the masons or sculptors who cut hieroglyphics in stone, and subsequently it was much used in making copies of literary compositions on papyrus, and for letters, etc. **Demotic**[2] is an abbreviated form of hieratic writing which was much used in legal documents from about B. C. 650 to the Roman period.

Egyptian palaeography:— Hieroglyphic inscriptions.

Hieroglyphics are written in columns or in horizontal lines which are sometimes to be read from left to right, and sometimes from right to left. In the former case the writing follows the direction in which Assyrian and Ethiopic texts are written, and in the latter that of inscriptions in Phoenician, Syriac and Arabic. This being so it is impossible to say which is the proper direction; there seems to be no example of a text written from left to right, and from right to left, alternately (*βουστροφηδόν*) as is found in Himyaritic. To ascertain the direction in which an inscription is to be read we observe in which way men, and birds, and animals face, and then read towards them. When hieroglyphics are written in columns this rule generally enables us to ascertain the correct order of the letters in the words. Allowance must, however, be made at times for the scribe's ideas of symmetry which made him misplace a letter that the balance of the arrangement of the hieroglyphics might be maintained. The following examples explain this paragraph.

[1] For lists of hieratic characters see Pleyte, *Catalogue raisonné de Types Égyptiens Hiératiques*, Leyden, 1865; Levi, *Raccolta dei Segni ieratici Egizi*, Turin, 1880.

[2] For the Demotic characters see Brugsch, *Grammaire Démotique*, Berlin, 1855, p. 18, and plates A. B. C. at the end of the book; Hess, *Der Demotische Roman von Stne Ḫa-m-us*, Leipzig, 1888, pp. 190—205.

Direction in which hieroglyphics are to be read.

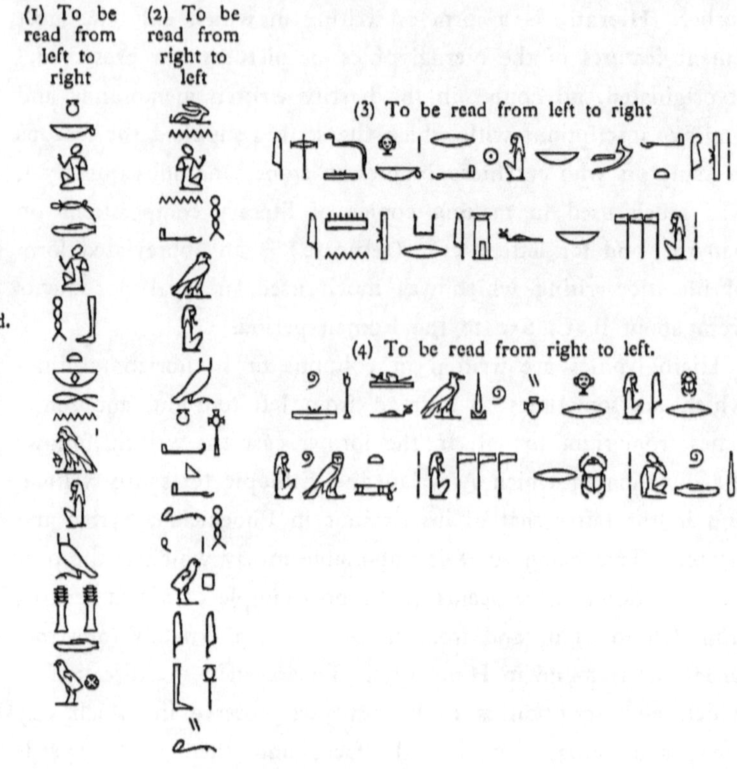
(1) To be read from left to right
(2) To be read from right to left
(3) To be read from left to right
(4) To be read from right to left.

(1) *nuk sešeṭ ḥebet en ba em Ṭeṭṭeṭu*

(2) *un-ȧ ḥenā Ḥeru em neť qāḥ pui ȧbi*

(3) *ȧneť ḥrȧ-k Rā neḅ maāt ȧmen karȧ-f neb neteru*

(4) *χeperȧ ḥeri-ȧb uťa-f ulu meṭu χeper neteru tememu.*

Hieratic and Demotic.

Hieratic is usually written in horizontal lines which are to be read from right to left, but in some papyri of the XIIth dynasty preserved at Berlin and in the British Museum the texts are arranged in short columns. Demotic texts are usually read from right to left.

Hieroglyphics as ideographs and phonetics.

Every hieroglyphic could be used either to express an idea, in which case it is called an ideograph, or as a character which represented a sound, in which case it is called a phonetic; phonetic characters may be either alphabetic or syllabic. Thus [hieroglyph], *reθ* (for *remθ*), represents a man, 𓁹 *maa*, an eye, 𓆈 *ḥentasu*, a lizard, 𓃬 *màu*, a lion, 𓍝 *māχait*, a pair of scales, 𓅬 *sa*, a goose, and so on; these are examples of ideographs. But 𓊪 is the letter *p*, 𓆑 is the letter *f*, 𓂋 is the letter *r*, 𓂧 is the letter *ṭ*, and so on. The signs 𓊪, 𓆑, 𓂋, and 𓂧 represent a door, a worm or snake of some kind, a mouth, and a hand, and, originally, when used as ideographs, would probably be pronounced *ptaḥ* (?), *fenṭ*, *re* and *ṭeṭ*; at a very early period, however, these, together with about twenty other ideographs, were set apart to represent alphabetic sounds. These sounds seem to have been obtained in the following way: the sound of the first letter in the name of an object was given to the picture or character which represented it, and henceforward the character bore that phonetic value. Thus 𓊪 is the picture of a door made up of a number of boards fastened together by three cross-pieces at the back, and there is no doubt that the word for door was connected with the root *ptḥ* "to open", and that it was pronounced something like *ptaḥ* (compare the Hebrew פְּתַח *pĕthaḥ*); the sound of the first letter of *ptaḥ* is *p*, and henceforward the phonetic value of 𓊪 was *p*. Similarly to the signs 𓆑, 𓂋 and 𓂧, the initial sounds of the words for which were *f*, *r*, and *ṭ*, were assigned the alphabetic values of *f*, *r*, and *ṭ*. Signs having alphabetic values are used to form words without any reference to their ideographic meanings. Thus the group of signs 𓋴𓆑𓈖𓂧𓌪 *sfnṭ* forms the word for "knife". The first 𓋴 is the picture of the back of a chair, 𓆑 as we have seen is the picture for a snake, 𓈖 is the picture of the wavy surface of water, and 𓂧 as we have seen, of a hand; the last two signs are *determinative* characters which will be discussed presently. Now in the word *sfnṭ* all these signs are used to express sounds only, and their original ideographic meanings of chair-back, snake, water, and hand are not considered. The Egyptians must have found at a very early date that when they needed to write the name of some foreign country or king, they

Origin of alphabetic signs.

Names of ideographs used as phonetics without reference to their meanings.

were obliged to use their ideographic signs to express alphabetic sounds only, or perhaps they found it necessary to preserve words by writing them alphabetically. Be this as it may, the use of alphabetic signs in Egypt is very ancient, for in the oldest inscriptions they appear side by side with signs used ideographically. Why the Egyptians did not go a step farther and abolish all signs which were not used alphabetically cannot be said; we owe them much, however, for our English alphabet is derived from the cursive hieratic forms of certain hieroglyphics through the Phoenician and Greek alphabets.[1] The Egyptian alphabetic characters are as follows:—

Egyptian alphabetic signs.

Sign	Value	Sign	Value
	a		*ḥ*
	á		*χ* (kh)
	ā		*s*
or	*i*		*s*
or	*u*		*ś* (sh)
	b		*k*
	p		*q*
	f		*ḳ*
or	*m*		*t*
or	*n*		*ṭ*
or	*r* and *l*	,	*θ* (th)
	h		*t'* (tch)

The values given above are those of one of the many systems of transliteration which have been proposed since the decipherment of the Egyptian hieroglyphics, and though it is probable

[1] For proofs of this statement see J. de Rougé, *Mémoire sur l'origine Égyptienne de l'Alphabet Phénicien*, Paris, 1874, 820; Dr. Maunde Thompson, *Handbook to Greek and Latin Palaeography*, London, 1893, plate facing p. 10;

that a few of them will eventually be modified, they are sufficiently simple and accurate to be retained for some time. It is evident from the above signs that we are dealing with an alphabet which resembles that of Phoenician or Hebrew, Syriac, Arabic, and the like, and it is equally clear that only the consonants which constitute the pith and substance of the language were set down as real letters, whilst, of the vowel-sounds, only the fuller ones, and even those not always, were represented by certain consonants. The pronunciation of Egyptian words was, of course, known to the educated in all periods, but curiously enough the Egyptians never invented a system of marks like the "points" in Arabic, Hebrew, and Syriac, whereby the correct vocalisation of every word was preserved. Speaking generally, the three primary vowel sounds A, I, U, were represented by , , and , and these are practically equivalent to the Hebrew letters א, י, and ו; for the other signs may be transcribed in Hebrew by ע *ayin*, by ב, by פ, by מ, by נ, by ר, by ה, by ח (has the sound of *ch* in the Scotch word *loch*, or the German *Rache*), by ס (?), by ש, by שׁ, by כ, by ק, by ג (*i. e.*, represents a sound similar to the hard *g* with which the people in Northern Africa pronounce the strongly articulated guttural ק), by ח, and by ת, by ט, and by צ.[1] From what has been said above it will be understood that the vowel sounds with which the Egyptian pronounced many of their words

Affinity of Egyptian and Semitic alphabets.

Consonants used for vowels.

Dr. Maunde Thompson in *Facsimiles of MSS. published by the Palaeographical Society*, Series II. plate 101; the article *Alphabetum* (Daremberg and Saglio, *Dictionnaire des Antiquités Grecques et Romaines*, Paris, 1873, p. 188 f.) by F. Lenormant; Isaac Taylor, *The Alphabet*, 2 vols. London, 1883; and Kirchoff, *Studien zur Geschichte des Griechischen Alphabets*, Berlin, 1877.

[1] Among recent contributions to Egyptian phonology the following should be consulted: Brugsch, *Die Aegyptologie*, Leipzig, 1891, p. 42; Erman, *Das Verhältniss des Aegyptischen zu den semitischen Sprachen* (*Zeitschrift d. Deutsch. Morgenl. Gesellsch.* Bd. XLVI. ss. 93—129); and Steindorff, *Das altägyptische Alphabet und seine Umschreibung* (*ibid.* ss. 709—730).

are unknown, and where this is the case a short *e* is usually inserted to make the transliteration pronounceable; thus *nfr* "good" is usually transcribed *nefer*, *ntr* "God" by *neter*, and so on.

Direct and symbolic meanings of ideographs.

Ideographic signs, *i. e.*, those which express an idea, are sometimes to be interpreted literally, and sometimes symbolically, thus *seš* "nest", *seχet* "field", *àneb* "wall", *teχen* "obelisk", are examples of ideographs which are to be understood literally; but the musical instrument is symbolic of "happiness", the seal of "treasure", the instrument of "God", the bier of "death", and so on.

Phonetic values of ideographs.

The phonetic values of ideographic signs were employed in the spelling of words without any reference to the original ideographic meaning. Thus , the picture of a digging tool, the phonetic value of which is *mer*, is found in the words *mer* "to love", *meri* "tree", *mer* "eye", simply because it has the syllabic value of *mer*. Again , the picture of a branch of a tree, is found in the words *em χet* "after", and *χet* "to engrave", etc., but only as a syllabic value. In theory every hieroglyphic could be used both as an ideograph and as a syllable. Some ideographs have more than one phonetic value, in which case they are called **polyphones**, and many different ideographs have similar values, in which case they are called **homophones**. The following signs and their values should be learnt by heart:—

Poly-phones and homophones.

List of signs with their phonetic values.

	ur		*ḥeḥ*		*uṫa*		*ka*
	ser		*šeps*		*ṫàt*		*χen*
	qa		*àmen*		*àn*		*àn, àl*
	qeṭ		*χer*		*àri*		*mā*
	àr		*ṭep*		*ḥu*		*neχt*
	fa		*ḥrà, ḥer*		*sept*		*ṭā*

List of signs with their phonetic values.

χu	*ḥā*	*qem*	*bener*
ṫeser	*at*	*ti*	*neṫem*
χen	*ṡef*	*pa*	*uaṫ*
ṫebā	*usr*	*ten*	*χa*
ka, met	*χen*	*reχit*	*meḥ*
sem	*χent*	*ṫa*	*ḥa*
seb	*fenṭ*	*senṭ*	*neḥeb*
ṡem	*mesṫer* *àten* *setem*	*meḥ* *ṭenḥ*	*enen*
àn		*maāt, ṡu*	*su*
ṡes (ṡems)	*àp*	*àr, sa*	*res*
θet	*àau*	*àn*	*qemā*
ret, uār	*āb*	*χa*	*renp*
āu	*χepeṡ*	*sebek*	*trà*
ser	*peḥ*	*ḥefen*	*ṡa*
sāb	*uḥem, nem*	*serq*	*seχet*
set	*ḥeru, bak*	*qem*	*mes*
nefer	*ba*	*net, bàt*	*ḥeṫ*
āu	*χu*	*χeper*	*sen*
ka	*āq*	*àm*	*ṡen*
àua	*ṡerà*	*χet*	*ḥen*
àb	*ur*	*ḥen*	*ut*
ba	*ba*	*un*	*às*
màu	*sa*	*uaḥ*	*ṫer*
peḥ	*neḥ*	*sek*	*pet*

List of signs with their phonetic values.

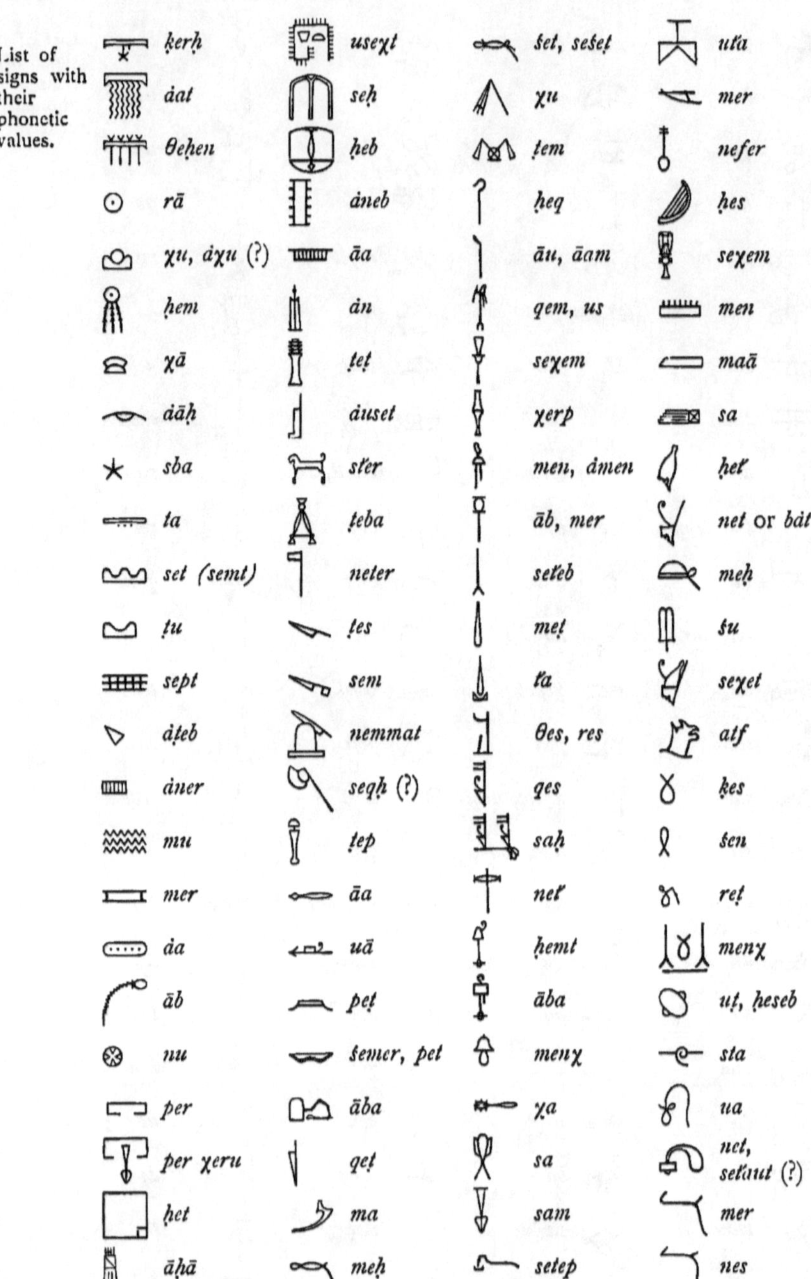

ḳerḥ	useχt	šet, šešeṭ	uťa
ȧat	seḥ	χu	mer
θeḥen	ḥeb	ṭem	nefer
rā	ȧneb	ḥeq	ḥes
χu, ȧχu (?)	āa	āu, āam	seχem
ḥem	ȧn	qem, us	men
χā	ṭeṭ	seχem	maā
ȧāḥ	ȧuset	χerp	sa
sba	sťer	men, ȧmen	ḥeť
ta	ṭeba	āb, mer	net or bȧt
set (semt)	neter	seťeb	meḥ
ṭu	ṭes	meṭ	šu
sept	sem	ťa	seχet
ȧṭeb	nemmat	θes, res	atf
ȧner	seqḥ (?)	qes	ḳes
mu	ṭep	saḥ	šen
mer	āa	neť	reṭ
ȧa	uā	ḥemt	menχ
āb	peṭ	āba	uṭ, ḥeseb
nu	šemer, pet	menχ	sta
per	āba	χa	ua
per χeru	qeṭ	sa	net, seťaut (?)
ḥet	ma	sam	mer
āḥā	meḥ	setep	nes

Determinatives.

As long as the Egyptians used picture writing pure and simple their meaning was easily understood, but when they began to spell their words with alphabetic signs and syllabic values of picture signs which had no reference whatever to the original meaning of the signs, it was at once found necessary to indicate in some way the meaning and even sounds of many of the words so written; this they did by adding to them signs which we call **determinatives.** It is impossible to say when the Egyptians first began to add determinatives to their words, but all hiero-

Great antiquity of the use of determinatives.

glyphic inscriptions known contain them, and it would seem that they originated in prehistoric times. It is, however, clear that they occur less frequently in the texts of the earlier than of the later dynasties. The following example will show how determinatives were added, and how ideographs were spelled out in alphabetic signs, and what alterations were made when ancient texts were copied by scribes.

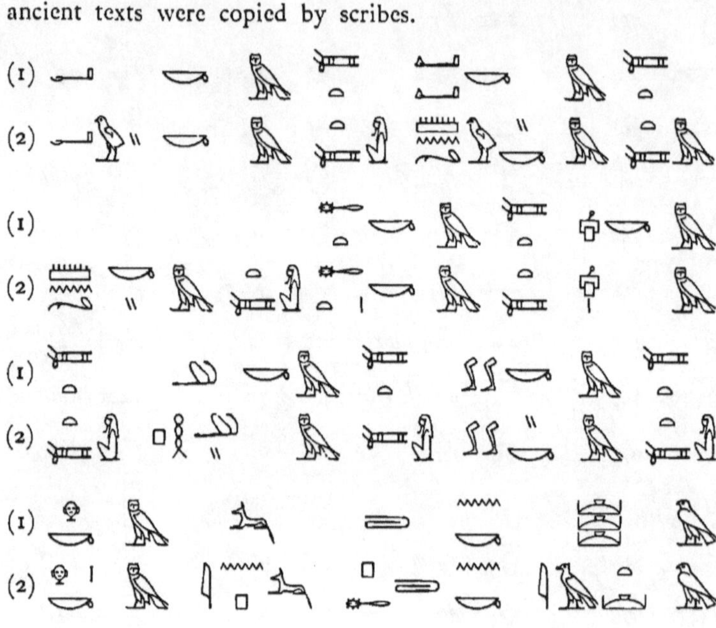

The version given in (1) is from the pyramid of Unás, the last king of the Vth dynasty, and that in (2) is from a coffin of the XIth or XIIth dynasty (see Maspero, *Rec. de Trav.*, t. III, p. 201).

Meanings of words indicated by determinatives.

It frequently happened that two or more words of different meanings had the same sound; in such cases the proper determinative is most useful in determining the exact sense of a word. Thus *āḥā* "to stand", and *āḥā* "boat", are two words having the same sound but different meanings; in the one case a pair of legs is the determinative, and in the other a boat. Similarly *men* "to abide", and *men* "to be ill", are distinguished in meaning by the determinative of abstract ideas, and by the determinative of evil or discomfort.

General and specific determinatives.

Determinatives may be divided into two groups: those which determine a single species, and those which determine a whole class. Examples of the first group are *teχen* "obelisk", *seś* "nest", *āa* "donkey", etc.; strictly speaking this group consists of pictures of objects preceded by the words for them written in alphabetic and syllabic characters. Of general determinatives the following are the most used:—

Common determinatives.

Character	Determinative of	Character	Determinative of
1.	to call	16.	to cut, slay
2.	man	17.	fire, to burn
3.	to eat, to think, to speak, and whatever is done with the mouth	18.	odour
		19.	to overthrow
		20.	strength
4.	inertness	21.	actions performed with the legs
5.	woman	22.	flesh
6. or	god, what is divine	23.	animal
7.	goddess	24.	bird
8.	tree	25.	evil, little
9.	plant, flower	26.	fish
10. ,	earth, land	27.	rain, storm-cloud, thunder
11.	road, to travel	28.	time
12.	foreign land	29.	town, city, village
13.	nome	30.	stone
14.	water	31. or	metal
15.	house		

Character	Determinative of	Character	Determinative of
32.	wood	35.	liquid, unguent
33.	wind, air	36.	abstract idea.
34.	foreigner		

The following words will show how the above are used.

Examples of words with common determinatives.

1.		*nȧs*	to call
2.		*āb*	a priest
3.		*ȧm*	to eat
		surȧ	to drink
		seχa	to remember
		ḳer	to be silent
		ṭept	to taste
4.		*ḳenen*	to be exhausted
5.		*sat*	daughter
6.		*χeperȧ*	the god Khepera
7.		*Mer-seḳer*	the goddess Merseker
8.		*āš*	cedar, persea tree
9.		*ānχ*	flower
10.		*seχet*	field
11.		*seuau*	to make to depart
12.		*Reθennu*	Northern Syria
13.		*Ḥerui*	the nome of two gods

14.	*qebḥ*	cold water
15.	*beχennu*	house
16.	*sma*	to slay
17.	*ta*	to burn
18.	*šefut*	putrid sore
19.	*seχer*	to throw down
20.	*āťau*	violence
21.	*āḥā*	to stand
	peḥ	to arrive
	hab	to send
	χenṭ	to step
	sper	to come
22.	*ḥāu*	members
23.	*pennu*	mouse
24.	*apṭ*	duck
25.	*àtu*	the destitute
26.	*nāru*	the nāru fish
27.	*šenrā*	tempest
28.	*rek*	time
	hru	day
29.	*Àbṭu*	Abydos
30.	*reṭ*	sandstone

31.	*ṭeḥt*	lead
32.	*ses*	bolt
33.	*meḥ*	air, wind
34.	*Āāmu*	Asiatics
35.	*merḥet*	unguent
36.	*χet*	thing.

Plurality of determinatives.

Many words have more than one determinative. Thus *beṭeš* "to be exhausted" is determined by "exhaustion", and "evil"; *qebḥ* "cold water" is determined by (the phonetic value of which is *qebḥ*) "water flowing from the top of a vase", and "water", and "a thing which contains water"; *šāṭ* "to slay" is determined by "something which is hacked to pieces", "a knife", and "strength"; *fa māhani* "carrier of milk" is determined by "liquid", "strength", and "man"; *reχit* "rational beings" is determined by , the phonetic value of which is *reχit*, "man", and , "woman", and , the sign of the plural.

Words having no determinative.

A large number of words are written without any determinative, *e. g.*, *ḥenā* "with", *ȧm* "in", *māk* "verily", etc.; these and similar common words were probably thought to need no determinative.

Many words are spelt wholly with alphabetic characters, *e. g.*, *sešeni* "lily", *ȧner* "stone", *semeḥi* "left side", *ḥeqt* "beer", etc.; but the greater number

Use of syllabic with alphabetic characters.

are written with a mixture of alphabetic and syllabic signs, which, though eventually helpful in showing the correct reading of the words, are at first confusing. Thus *ȧm* "to eat" is written and *i. e., ȧm + m*, which does not mean that we are to read the word *ȧmm*, but only *ȧm*, the was only added to help the reader to give the sound of the word readily; similarly *mesťem* "eye-paint" is written , *i. e., mesťem + m*; and *merer* "to love" is written *mer + r + r*, etc. For convenience' sake we may call such alphabetic helps to the reading of words "phonetic complements". Many examples occur of words which are practically written twice, once in alphabetic and once in syllabic signs, *e. g.*, … *neterit* "goddesses", wherein to *neter* are added the signs *ter* and the determinative of divinity; *āba* "courtyard of a temple" wherein we have the signs *āb* + *b* + *ba* + *a*; *Ṭem* "the god Tmu", where we have *t* + *tem* + *m*; *nefer* "good", where we have *nefer* + *f* + *r*; *neḥeḥ* "eternity", where we have *n* + *neḥ* + *ḥ* + *ḥ*; *sta* "to bring", where we have *s* + *t* + *ta* + *a* + *sta*; *χeper* "to come into being", where we have *χ* + *p* + *χeper* + *r*, etc.

Importance of variant readings.

The values of many characters have been ascertained by means of the variant readings which are found in different copies of the same text; compare the following:—

= *neferu*

= *ȧri*

= *reχit*

= *ua*

= *uṭat*

= *ermenui*

hru

āāabet

seba

χepeś

ba

χeperà

We have now seen how ideographs and alphabetic and syllabic phonetic signs, and determinatives may be used in writing words, let us now take a connected passage from a text and observe how the hieroglyphics are arranged therein.

Extract from a text analysed.

In the first place we must break the extract up into words, for whether written horizontally or perpendicularly the words of an inscription are never separated from each other by the Egyptians. Thus we have :—

The determinatives are marked by * and the syllabic values by †; the remaining signs are alphabetic. The passage may be transliterated :— *àu àri-nà ḥeseset reθ hereret neteru ḥer-s àu ṭā-nà tau en ḥeqer sesa-à àt àu šes-nà Ḥeru em per-f àn āā re-à em šenit àn peṭ em nemmat-à šem-à ḥer-sa χenṭ àri-nà em maāt mer en suten*, and read :—

"I have done (*àu àri-nà*) what is pleasing (*ḥeseset*) to men (*reθ*), and what is gratifying (*hereret*) unto the gods (*neteru*); because of it (*ḥer-s*) I have given (*àu ṭā-nà*) cakes (*tau*) to (*en*) the hungry (*ḥeqer*), I have satisfied (*sesa-à*) the poor and needy (*àt*), I have followed (*àu šes-nà*) Horus (*Ḥeru*) in (*em*) his house (*per-f*), not (*àn*) magnifying (*āā*) my mouth (*re-à*) against (*em*) nobles (*šenit*), not (*àn*) making long (*peṭ*) in (*em*) my stride (*nemmat-à*), I walked (*šem-à*) according (*ḥer-sa*) to the step of measure (*χenṭ*), I wrought (*àri-nà*) according to (*em*) what was right and true (*maāt*), which was beloved (*mer*) by (*en*) the king (*suten*)."

Difficulty of finding the meanings of words.

It has been shown on p. 17 how variant readings supply the correct values of many syllabic signs, and it is self-evident that the probable meaning of many words can be at once known by the determinatives which follow them, but there remains a large number of words the exact meaning of which cannot be exactly stated by the help of the hieroglyphics only. The early decipherers of the cuneiform inscriptions, when once they had obtained the alphabetic and syllabic values of the signs, relied largely on their knowledge of the languages cognate to that which they were studying for help in determining verbal forms, and for a supply of roots which, having made allowances for change in letters, etc., they believed would give them a clue to the meanings which they sought. Thus Sir Henry Rawlinson relied upon Zend and Sanskrit in his immortal work on the Behistun Inscription, and Norris and others succeeded in deciphering Babylonian and Assyrian inscriptions by the help of

Importance of cognate languages in decipherment of cuneiform and hieroglyphic inscriptions.

Hebrew and other Semitic dialects. Now although Egyptian is, in many particulars, similar to the great family of Semitic languages, yet among them all there is none which is as valuable in explaining its words and grammar as are Zend and Sanskrit to the Persian cuneiform inscriptions, and as are Hebrew, Syriac, and Chaldee to the cuneiform inscriptions which are written in the Semitic dialects of the ancient dwellers in the land which lay between the Tigris and Euphrates. We must, then, look elsewhere for help in determining the meaning of Egyptian words, and we find it in the language called Coptic, *i. e.*, the Egyptian language of the Graeco-Roman period which is written in Greek letters, and has been preserved for us chiefly by the ecclesiastical literature of the Egyptian Christians. Early in the first quarter of this century Champollion found it of the greatest value in deciphering the hieroglyphic inscriptions, indeed it is most probable that without the great knowledge of Coptic which he possessed his labours would never have been crowned with such brilliant success; the value of the study of this language remains undiminished for the purposes of Egyptian philology, and every student of hieroglyphics should make himself acquainted with as much of it as possible.[1]

Great value of Coptic.

It is not possible to say when the Egyptian language was first written in Greek letters; some believe the Bible to have been translated into Coptic in the second and others in the eighth century of our era. Be that as it may, it is a fact that Coptic has preserved a large number of the words which are found in ancient hieroglyphic inscriptions, and when an allowance has been made for phonetic decay and for the changes of letters which occur in all dialects of cognate languages, it is found that the meanings of words suggested by their determinatives are confirmed, that new ones are supplied, that many

Ancient Egyptian words preserved in Coptic.

[1] The beginner will find Steindorff's *Koptische Grammatik*, Berlin, 1894, a very useful book; it contains 64 pages of Coptic text and a vocabulary which will carry him on to larger works.

grammatical forms, etc., can be identified, and that the vowels which are added to the words in Coptic indicate the correct vocalization. Where there exists no Coptic equivalent of a word, the meaning of which cannot be decided by its determinative, the sense of that word can only be guessed at. The following examples show the close connection of Egyptian and Coptic words.

Egyptian and Coptic words compared.

Egyptian			Coptic
	ḥrà	face	ϩⲣⲁ[1]
	χat	body	ϧⲏⲧ
	ren	name	ⲣⲁⲛ
	pet	heaven	ⲫⲉ
	χatur	ichneumon	ϣⲁⲟⲟⲩⲗ
	nehet	sycamore	ⲛⲟⲩϩⲉ
	bàa en pet	iron	ⲃⲉⲛⲓⲡⲉ
	χeper	to be	ϣⲱⲡⲓ
	erṭeb	because of	ⲉⲑⲃⲉ
	fa	to carry	ϥⲁⲓ
	remθ	man	ⲣⲱⲙⲓ
	re	mouth	ⲣⲱ
	qenà	bosom	ⲕⲟⲩⲛ
	àtf	father	ⲉⲓⲱⲧ

[1] The Coptic alphabet is as follows:— ⲁ *a*, ⲃ *b*, ⲅ *g*, ⲇ *d*, ⲉ *e*, ⲍ *z*, ⲏ *ē*, ⲑ *th*, ⲓ *i*, ⲕ *k*, ⲗ *l*, ⲙ *m*, ⲛ *n*, ⲝ *x*, ⲟ *o*, ⲡ *p*, ⲣ *r*, ⲥ *s*, ⲧ *t*, ⲩ *y*, ⲫ *ph*, ⲭ *kh*, ⲯ *ps*, ⲱ *ō*, ϣ *sh*, ϥ *f*, ϧ *ḫ*, ϩ *h*, ϫ *dj*, ϭ *tch*, ϯ *ti*.

mȧu	lion	ⲙⲟⲩⲓ
bener	date palm	ⲃⲉⲛⲛⲉ
χemt	copper	ϩⲟⲙⲧ
at	back	ⲱⲧ
neḥem	to deliver	ⲛⲱϩⲉⲙ
ḥeqer	to hunger	ϩⲕⲟ
surȧ	to drink	ⲥⲱ
erper	temple	ⲉⲣⲫⲉⲓ

Pronouns.

The **personal** pronominal suffixes are:

Sing. 1.	*ȧ*		Plur. 1.	*n*	
" 2 m.	*k*		" 2.	*ten, θen*	
" 2 f.	*t, θ*				
" 3 m.	*f*		" 3.	*sen*	
" 3 f.	or	*s*			

The following examples illustrate their use:—

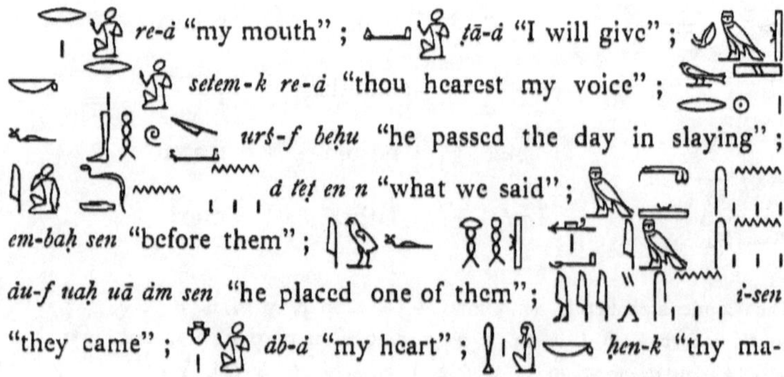

re-ȧ "my mouth"; *ṭā-ȧ* "I will give"; *setem-k re-ȧ* "thou hearest my voice"; *urš-f beḥu* "he passed the day in slaying"; *ȧ ṭeṭ en n* "what we said"; *em-baḥ sen* "before them"; *ȧu-f uaḥ uā ȧm sen* "he placed one of them"; *i-sen* "they came"; *ȧb-ȧ* "my heart"; *ḥen-k* "thy majesty"; *ṭet-k* "thy body"; *ṭes-á* "myself"; *ṭes-f* "himself".

The forms of the pronouns are:—

(A) Sing. 1.	*uá*	Plur. 1.	*n*
" 2 m.	*tu, θu*	" 2.	*ten, θen*
" 3 m.	*su*		
" 3 f.	*set*	" 3.	*sen*

(B) Sing. 1. *nuk, ánuk*

entek, entuk

entet, entut

entef, entuf

entes, entus

Plur. 1. (wanting)

" 2. *ent-ten, entu-ten*

" 3. *ent-sen, entu-sen*

The **demonstrative** pronouns are:

Sing. m.	*pen*	this
" f.	*ten*	this
" m.	*pef, pefa*	that
" f.	*tef, tefa*	that
" m.	*pa*	this
" f.	*ta*	this

Plur. m.	,	*àpen, pen*	these
" f.	,	*àpten, peten*	these
"		*nefa*	those
"		*na*	these
"		*pau*	these.

Other words for this are or *enen*, and *ennu*.

The **relative** pronouns are:— *à* and *ent*, or *enti*, or *entet*.

Nouns.

Nouns in the Singular.

Masculine nouns end in *u*, though this characteristic letter is usually omitted by the scribe: *e. g.*, *hru* "day", *ānu* "scribe", *uḥemu* "herald", *ta* "earth", *sen* "brother", etc. Feminine nouns end in *t*, *e. g.*, *reàat* "side", *ànt* "valley", *àuset* "place", *àmentet* "west", etc. Masc. nouns in the plural end in *u* or *iu*; *e. g.*, *seru* "princes", *utennu* "offerings", *māṭ'aiu* "police", *àpiu* "envoys", *tràiu* "seasons". Fem. nouns in the plural end in *ut*, but often the *t* only is written; *e. g.*, *àustut* "places", etc.

Nouns in the Plural.

The oldest way of expressing the plural is by writing the ideograph or picture sign three times:—

	qesu	bones
	àat	regions, zones
	seχet	fields

[hieroglyphs]	*ṭepu åbeṭ*	beginnings of months
[hieroglyphs]	*åbu*	hearts
[hieroglyphs]	*ånnu*	offerings
[hieroglyphs]	*useru*	powers
[hieroglyphs]	*seχemu*	forms.

These examples are taken from the pyramid texts of the Vth and VIth dynasties; in the same texts we find also [hieroglyphs] *χu* "intelligences", and [hieroglyphs] *uru* "chiefs", *i. e.*, an ideograph written once and also thrice followed by [hieroglyph] which afterwards, when modified into [hieroglyph] or III, became the common sign of the plural. Words spelt in full with alphabetic signs are also followed, at times, in these texts by [hieroglyph]; *e. g.*, [hieroglyphs] *åt* "fathers", [hieroglyphs] *reθ* "men", [hieroglyphs] *åt* "wheat", [hieroglyphs] *beṭet* "barley", [hieroglyphs] *ḥuaat* "humours", [hieroglyphs] *ḥunut* "young women", [hieroglyphs] *seχtet* "fields", [hieroglyphs] *urâu* "great ones", [hieroglyphs] *šerru* "little ones".

The plural is also expressed in the earliest times by writing the word in alphabetic or syllabic signs followed by the determinative written thrice: *e. g.*,

[hieroglyphs]	*neterut*	goddesses
[hieroglyphs]	*unnut*	hours
[hieroglyphs]	*meru*	lakes
[hieroglyphs]	*åru*	divine guardians
[hieroglyphs]	*åpt*	registers
[hieroglyphs]	*šesat*	darknesses

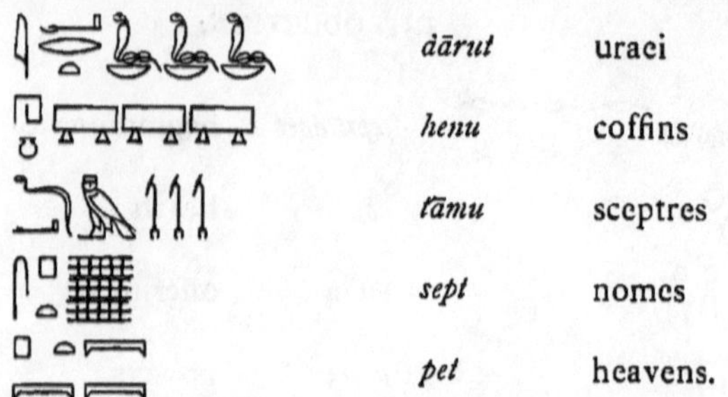

	ȧārut	uraei
	ḥenu	coffins
	ťāmu	sceptres
	sept	nomes
	pet	heavens.

Other examples of ways of writing the plural are :— *āat* "stones", *ťenut* "granaries", *šāt* "sand", *āḥu* "oxen", *neteru* "gods", *ḥenu* "priests", *ḥent* "priestesses". *ťuau* "praises", *θenre* "mighty deeds", *ȧaut em ḥefnu* "animals in hundreds of thousands", etc.

The dual. In the oldest inscriptions the dual is usually expressed by doubling the ideograph ; *e. g., mesťerui* "two ears", *χuti* "two horizons", *baui neterui* "two souls divine", etc. Frequently the word is spelt alphabetically or syllabically and is determined by the double ideograph ; *e. g., petti* "two heavens", *ḳesui* "two sides", *χui* "two lights", *θebut* "two soles of the feet", etc. Sometimes \\ is the mark of the dual in the early texts, *e. g., āāui-k* "thy two hands", and this sign, which strictly speaking should be written ||, indicated the dual to the latest times ; compare *āāui* "two hands", *reṭui* "two feet", *pa teχenui urui* "the two great obelisks" (also written in the same inscription), etc.

In Egyptian the noun is undeclined.

The article.

Definite article. The definite article masculine is or *pa*, feminine *ta* ; the plural is *na*.

EXAMPLES.

pa ser	the prince
pa ḥer	the terrifier
pa Rā	the Sun
pa sen	the brother
pa suten	the king
ta reȧat	the side
ta ḥurere	the flower
ta ȧuset	the place
na ābauti	the strivings
na reθ	the men
na šauabu	the persea tree
na ȧtʻau	the thieves
pa neter	the god
pa sep	the time
pa āā	the great one
pa ki	the other
pa χemti	the coppersmith
ta ȧnt	the valley
ta paut neteru	the company of the gods
ta ḥet	the temple
na ānu	the scribes

[hieroglyphs]	*na mu*	the water
[hieroglyphs]	*na neteru*	the gods.

Indefinite article.

The masc. indefinite article is expressed by [hieroglyphs] *uā en* literally "one of", and the fem. by [hieroglyphs] *uāt en.*

EXAMPLES.

[hieroglyphs]	*uā en ḥennu*	a jar
[hieroglyphs]	*uā en θebu*	a pot
[hieroglyphs]	*uā en šauabu*	a persea tree
[hieroglyphs]	*uā en bȧn*	a bad thing
[hieroglyphs]	*uā en sfenṭ*	a knife
[hieroglyphs]	*uā en beχennu*	a house
[hieroglyphs]	*uā en ka*	a bull
[hieroglyphs]	*uā en nefer*	a good thing.

Definite article and suffixes.

From the union of the definite article with the personal suffixes is formed the following series of words :—

SINGULAR.

[hieroglyphs]	*pai-ȧ* (masc.)	[hieroglyphs]	*tai-ȧ* (masc.)
[hieroglyphs]	*pai-ȧ* (fem.)	[hieroglyphs]	*tai-ȧ* (fem.)
[hieroglyphs]	*pai-k* (masc.)	[hieroglyphs]	*tai-k* (masc.)
[hieroglyphs] / [hieroglyphs]	*pai-t* (fem.)	[hieroglyphs] (or [hieroglyphs])	*tai-t* (fem.)
[hieroglyphs]	*pai-f* (masc.)	[hieroglyphs]	*tai-f* (masc.)

pai-s	(fem.)	*tai-s* (or ...)	(fem.)
pai-set		*tai-set*	
pai-n		*tai-n*	
pai-ten		*tai-ten*	
pai-sen		*tai-sen*	
pai-u		*tai-u*	

PLURAL.

nai-à	(masc.)	*nai-n*
nai-à	(fem.)	
nai-k	(masc.)	*nai-ten*
nai-θ	(fem.)	
nai-t		*nai-sen*
nai-f	(masc.)	
nai-s	(fem.)	*nai-u*

These are added to words in the following way:—

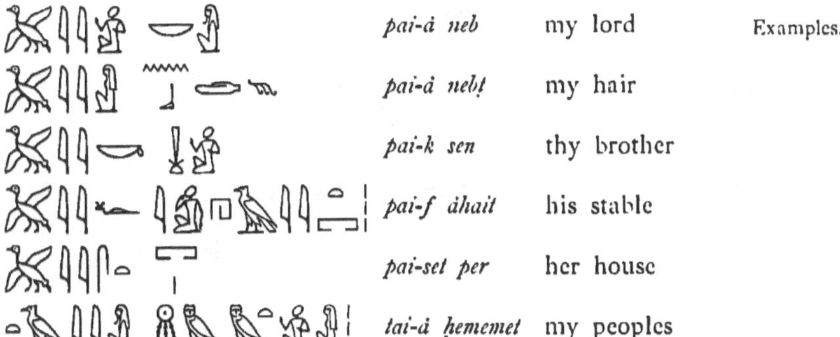

pai-à neb	my lord	Examples.
pai-à nebṭ	my hair	
pai-k sen	thy brother	
pai-f àhait	his stable	
pai-set per	her house	
tai-à ḥememet	my peoples	

tai-ȧ māȧu	my hair
tai-k mut	thy mother
tai-f ḥemt	his wife
tai-f suten ḥemt	his queen
tai-set ȧuset	her place
pai-ten ȧhai	your sentences of death
pai-sen ḥetrȧ	their tribute
pai-u peḥ	their arrival
nai-ȧ seru	my princes
nai-k ȧaut	thy cattle
nai-sen uti	their coffins
nai-u nebu	their lords.

Adjectives.

The adjective is, in form, often similar to the noun, with which it agrees in gender and number ; with a few exceptions it comes after its noun, *e. g.*,

hru nefer	a good day
sa ȧqer	a wise man
betau āa	great wickedness
meṭeṭ nefert	fine speech
bȧnt nebt	every evil
beṭet nebt	every abominable thing.

χet	*nebt*	*nefert*	*ābet*	*χet*	*nebt*	*neṭemet*	*beneret*
thing	every	good,	pure ;	thing	every	pleasant,	sweet.

ḥebsu neferu	beautiful clothes
seru āāaiu	great chiefs
nefer neferui	a good thing doubly good
sti neṭem	a sweet smell
àusetut āāaiut	great abodes.

The adjectives "royal" and "divine" are usually written before the noun : *e. g.*,

suten ān "royal scribe", *suten mesu* "royal children", *suten ḥemt* "royal women" (*i. e.*, queens), *suten mut* "royal mothers", *suten per* "royal house" (*i. e.*, palace), *neter ḥet* "divine house" (*i. e.*, temple), *neter ḥen* "divine servant", *neter àtf* "divine father".

Adjectives are without degrees of comparison in Egyptian, but the comparative and superlative may be expressed in the following manner :— Methods of comparing adjectives.

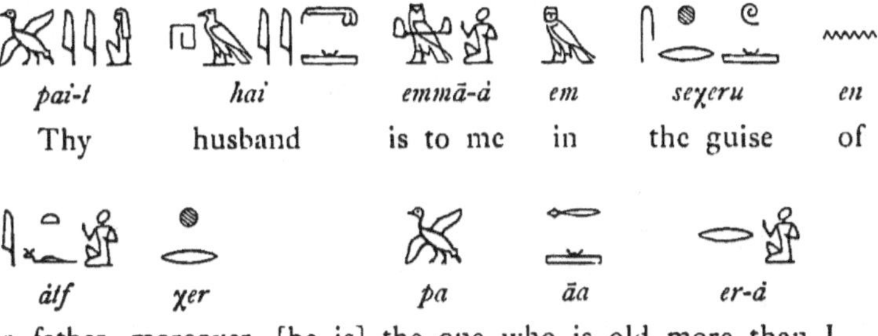

pai-t *hai* *emmā-à* *em* *seχeru* *en*
Thy husband is to me in the guise of

àtf *χer* *pa* *āa* *er-à*
a father, moreover, [he is] the one who is old more than I.

χeper *àqer - k* *er-f* *em* *ḳer*

Thou wilt be wise more than he in keeping silence.

nefer *setem* *er* *entet* *neb*

[It is] good to hearken more than anything, *i. e.*, to listen, or to obey, is better than anything, or best of all.

àu - set *nefer* *em* *ḥāt - set* *er* *set* *ḥemt* *nebt*

Was she beautiful in her person more than woman any.

Numbers.

I	=		*uā*	=	1
II	=		*sen*	=	2
III	=		*χemet*	=	3
IIII	=		*fțu*	=	4
III or ★	=	★	*ṭuau*	=	5
IIIIII	=		*sàs*	=	6
IIIIIII	=		*sefeχ*	=	7
IIIIIIII	=	or	*χemennu*	=	8
IIIIIIIII	=		*paut* / *pesț*	=	9
∩	=		*met*	=	10
∩∩	=		*ṭaut*	=	20

	=		*māb*	=	30
	=		*ḥement*	=	40
				=	50
				=	60
	=		*sefeχ*	=	70
	=		*χemennui*	=	80
				=	90
	=		*śaā*	=	100
	=		*śetau*	=	200
	=		*χa*	=	1,000
	=		*ṭāb*	=	10,000
	=		*ḥefennu*	=	100,000
	=		*ḥeḥ*	=	1,000,000
	=		*śennu*	=	10,000,000

Fractions.

(1) = $^1/_3$, = $^1/_2$, = $^2/_3$, = $^1/_{10}$, = $^1/_{100}$, = $^1/_{1000}$, = $^1/_{45}$, = $17^1/_2$, = $^1/_{18}$, = $^1/_{60}$, = $^1/_{2090}$.

(2) , that is, $^1/_2 \times 400 = 200$.

(3) , that is, $^1/_3 \times 400 = 133^1/_3$.

Numbers are expressed in the following manner:—

āqu *āa*

loaves large, 900,000 + 90,000 + 2000 + 700 + 50, *i. e.*, "992,750 large loaves of bread".

Ordinal numbers are indicated either by *meḥ* placed before the figure, or by following it; *e. g.*, *meḥ sås* "sixth", "fifteenth", *meḥ met ṭuau*, *sefeχ* "seventh", etc.

Measures.

(1) Of length:— *meḥ* "cubit"; *suten meḥ* "royal cubit" of 7 palms or 20 fingers; *meḥ neṭes* "little cubit" of 6 palms or 24 fingers; *ermen* "arm" of 20 fingers; *ṭeser*, of 16 fingers; *śa āa* "the great *śa*" of 14 fingers; *śa neṭes* "the little *śa*" of 12 fingers; *śepui*, the "double palm" of 8 fingers; *χefā*, the "fist" of 6 fingers; *ṭeṭ*, the "hand" of 5 fingers; or *śep*, the "palm" of 4 fingers; *ṭebā*, the "finger".

(2) Of superficies:— *sa ta*, the *arura*, *i. e.*, 100 cubits; *ermen*, one half of an *arura*; *ḥesp*, one quarter of an *arura*; *sa*, one eighth of an *arura*; *su*, one sixteenth of an *arura*; *erma*, one thirty-second part of an *arura*.

(3) Dry measure:— = 1/4 *hin*; *hin* = 9/20 of a *litre*; *ṭenāt* = 20 *hin*; *āpt* = 40 *hin*: *ḥetep* = 160 *hin*.

(4) Of weight:— *θen*; *qeṭ* = one tenth of a *θen*; *pek* = 1/128 of a *θen*.

TIME.

The principal divisions of time are :—

ḥat	second	*at*	minute
unnut	hour	*hru*	day
àbeṭ	month	*renpit*	year
seṭ	period of 30 years	*ḥen*	period of 60 years
ḥenti	period of 120 years	*ḥeḥ*	a long period of time
ṭetta	eternity	*ḥeḥ*	a million of years.

In an interesting inscription quoted by Brugsch (*Thesaurus*, Abth. II., p. 195) the god Thoth, addressing one of the Ptolemies says that he has ordained the sovereignty of the royal house for a period of time equal to:— that is, "an eternity of periods of 120 years, "and an indefinite number of periods of 30 years, and millions "of years, and ten millions of months, and hundreds of thousands "of days, and tens of thousands of hours, and thousands of mi-"nutes, and hundreds of seconds, and tens of third parts of "seconds."

The year, *renpit*, consisted of twelve months of thirty days each (or thirty-six weeks of ten days each), to which were added five additional days to make up 365 days. Each month was dedicated to a god. The twelve months were divided into three seasons of four months each; *šat* = time of inundation and period of sowing, *pert* = time of "coming forth" or growing, and *šemut* = time of harvest and beginning of inundation. The Copts, or

Egyptian Christians, have preserved, in a corrupt form, the old Egyptian names of the months, which read :—

	=	ⲑⲱⲟⲩⲧ	Thoth
	=	ⲡⲁⲟⲡⲓ	Paopi
	=	ⲁⲑⲱⲣ	Hathor
	=	ⲭⲟⲓⲁⲕ	Khoiak
	=	ⲧⲱⲃⲓ	Tobi
	=	ⲙⲉⲭⲓⲣ	Mekhir
	=	ⲫⲁⲙⲉⲛⲱⲑ	Phamenoth
	=	ⲫⲁⲣⲙⲟⲩⲑⲓ	Pharmuthi
	=	ⲡⲁⲭⲱⲛ	Pakhon
	=	ⲡⲁⲱⲛⲓ	Paoni
	=	ⲉⲡⲏⲡ	Epep
	=	ⲙⲉⲥⲱⲣⲏ	Mesore

hru ṭuau ḥeru renpit "the five days over the year".

Thoth, the first month of the Egyptian year, began on the 29th of August.

The verb.

The consideration of the Egyptian verb, or stem-word, is a difficult subject which can only be properly illustrated by a large number of extracts from texts of all periods. Egyptologists have, moreover, agreed neither as to the manner in which it should be treated, nor as to the classification of the forms which have been distinguished. The older generation of scholars were undecided as to the class of languages under which the Egyptian language should be placed, and contented themselves with pointing out grammatical forms analogous to those in Coptic, and perhaps in some of the Semitic dialects; but the modern German Egyptologists boldly affirm the relationship of Egyptian to the Semitic family of languages, and the most recent exponent of this view applies the nomenclature of the Semitic verb or stem-word to that of Egyptian.

The stem-word.

The Egyptian stem-word may be indifferently a verb or a noun; thus *χeper* means both "to be", and the "thing which hath come into being"; so likewise *nefer* may mean "to be good", and a "thing which is good", and placed after a noun it becomes the adjective "good", as we see from the following:— *nefer set ḥer āb-sen* "good is it for their hearts"; *ren-k nefer em reχ en seru* "thy name is good in the opinion of princes"; *hru nefer* "a good day"; with the addition of the prefix *bu, nefer* means "prosperity", "goodness", "happiness", *e. g.*,

bu - nefer χeper em bu - bån
prosperity turneth into adversity.

The stem-word with additions.

Returning to the word *χeper*: by the addition of *å* we have "I am", or "I was"; by the addition of the stem-word has a participial meaning like "being" or "becoming"; by the addition of in the masc. and in the fem. *χeper* becomes a noun in the plural meaning "things which exist", "created things", and the like; by the addition of *å* we have *χeperå* "the god to whom it belongeth to make things come into being", etc.

Stem-words in Egyptian, like those in Hebrew and other Semitic dialects, consist of two, three, four and five consonants, as examples of which may be cited *qem* "to find",

Biliteral roots.

χesef "to drive back", *seχseχ* "to flee", *nememes* "to heap up". The stem-words with three consonants, which are ordinarily regarded as triliteral roots, may be reduced to two consonants, which were pronounced by the help of some vowel between; these we may call primary or biliteral roots. Originally all roots consisted of one syllable. By the addition of feeble consonants in the middle or at the end of the monosyllabic root, or by repeating the second consonant roots of three letters were formed. Roots of four consonants are formed by adding a fourth consonant or by combining two roots of two letters; and so on. Speaking generally, the Egyptian verb has no conjugations or species, like Hebrew and the other Semitic dialects, and no Perfect (Preterite) or Imperfect (Future) tenses, but Dr. Erman believes in the existence of the Infinitive and Imperative Moods and of a Participle. The exact pronunciation of a great many verbs must always remain unknown, because the Egyptians never invented a system of vocalisation like the Massorah of the sages of Tiberias, or like the additions and the modifications in the forms of the letters to express the vowels adopted by the Ethiopians, or even any means of indicating the chief vowel sounds like the Syrians and Arabs; but very good guesses may sometimes be made by the help of the Coptic forms of words which are common to the two languages.

Formation of other roots.

Uncertainty of pronunciation.

The Causative.

There is in Egyptian a derivative formation of the word-stem or verb, which is made by the addition of or to the simple form of the verb, and which has a causative signification; *e. g.*, *ānχ* "to live", *se-ānχ* "to vivify"; *āb* "to wash", *se-āb* "to purify"; *men* "to abide", *se-men* "to perpetuate"; *ḥetep* "to rest, be at peace", *se-ḥetep* "to pacify"; *χeper* "to be", *se-χeper* "to bring into being", etc. In Coptic the causative is expressed both by a prefixed *s* and *t* (see Stern, *Koptische*

Gram., § 328, p. 157; Steindorff, *Koptische Grammatik*, § 230, p. 103 f.).

The verb is usually inflected by the addition of the pronominal personal suffixes; *e. g.*, Inflection.

Sing. 1 com.			*reχ-ȧ*
„ 2 m.			*neḥem-k*
„ 2 f.		(or)	*ṭeṭ-t*
„ 3 m.			*šāṭ-f*
„ 3 f.			*qem-s*
Plur. 1			*ȧri-n*
„ 2 com.			*mit-ten*
„ 3 com.			*χeper-sen*

The commonest auxiliary verbs are *āḥā* "to stand", *un* "to be", *ȧu* "to be", *ȧri* "to do", *ṭā* "to give"; examples of their use are:—

(1)

āḥā	*en*	*se-āḥā*	*ḥen*	*en*	*suten net*	*Seneferu*
Stood up	made	to arise	the majesty	of	the king of the North and South	Seneferu,

i. e., when king Huni was dead Seneferu set himself up as king of all Egypt.

(2)

un	*pa*	*ta*	*en*	*Qemt*	*χaā*	*em*
Was	the	land	of	Egypt	left	in

ruti
a state of ruin.

(3)

àu - sen ḥer reṭ em šauabu sen

Were they growing into persea trees two.

(4)

em àri meḥ àb - k aχetu kai

Do not make to fill thy heart [with] the wealth of another.

(5) 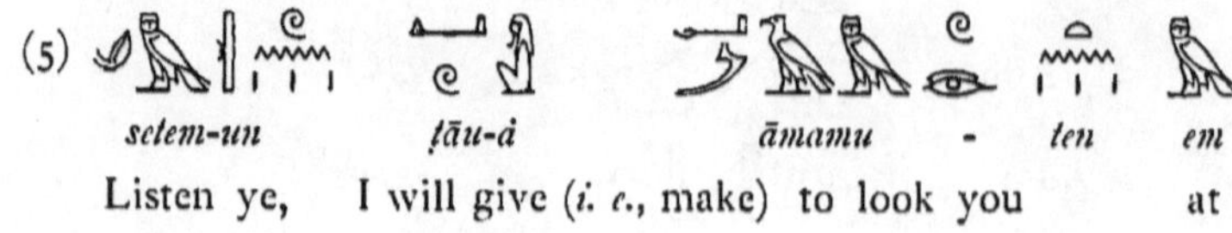

setem-un ṭāu-à āmamu - ten em

Listen ye, I will give (*i. e.*, make) to look you at

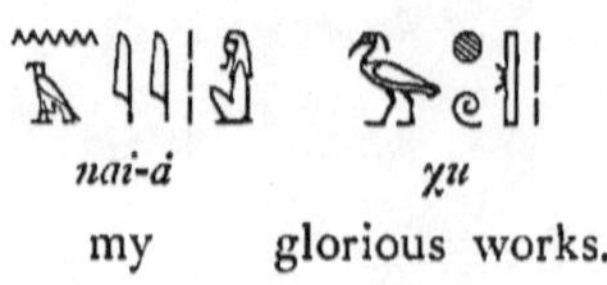

nai-à χu

my glorious works.

As so many examples occur in the texts at the end of the book the following limited number of extracts must suffice to illustrate the simplest use of the verb :—

1.

nuk neter āā χeper t'esef 2. *Rā pu em*

I am the god great the creator of himself. Rā it is when

uben - f 3. *nuk sef reχ - kuà ṭuau*

he riseth. I am yesterday, I know to-morrow.

4. *iu en tu er t'eṭ en ḥen-f* 5. *ḳer - nek*

Came one to speak to his majesty. Be thou silent.

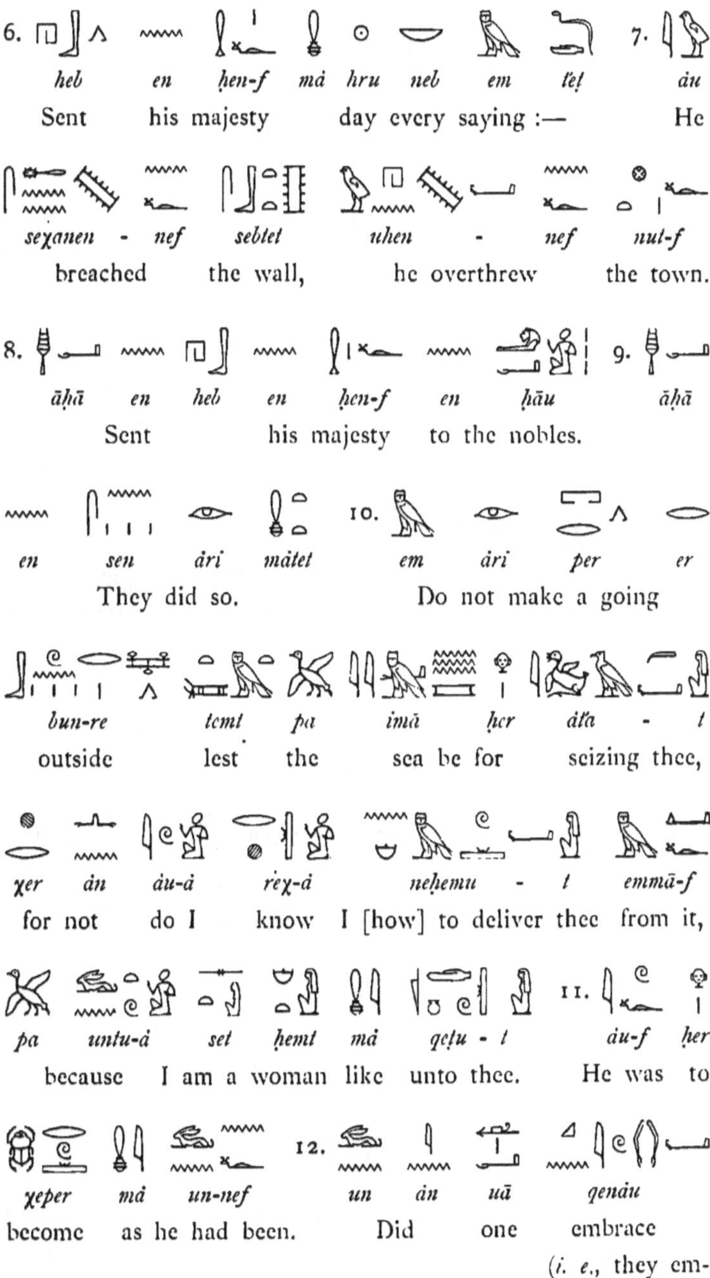

6. *heb en ḥen-f mȧ hru neb em ṭeṭ* 7. *ȧu*
Sent his majesty day every saying :— He

seχanen - nef sebtet uhen - nef nut-f
breached the wall, he overthrew the town.

8. *āḥā en heb en ḥen-f en ḥāu* 9. *āḥā*
Sent his majesty to the nobles.

en sen ȧri mȧtet 10. *em ȧri per er*
They did so. Do not make a going

bun-re temt pa imā ḥer ȧṭa - t
outside lest the sea be for seizing thee,

χer ȧn ȧu-ȧ reχ-ȧ neḥemu - t emmā-f
for not do I know I [how] to deliver thee from it,

pa untu-ȧ set ḥemt mȧ qeṭu - t 11. *ȧu-f ḥer*
because I am a woman like unto thee. He was to

χeper mȧ un-nef 12. *un ȧn uā qenȧu*
become as he had been. Did one embrace
(*i. e.*, they em-

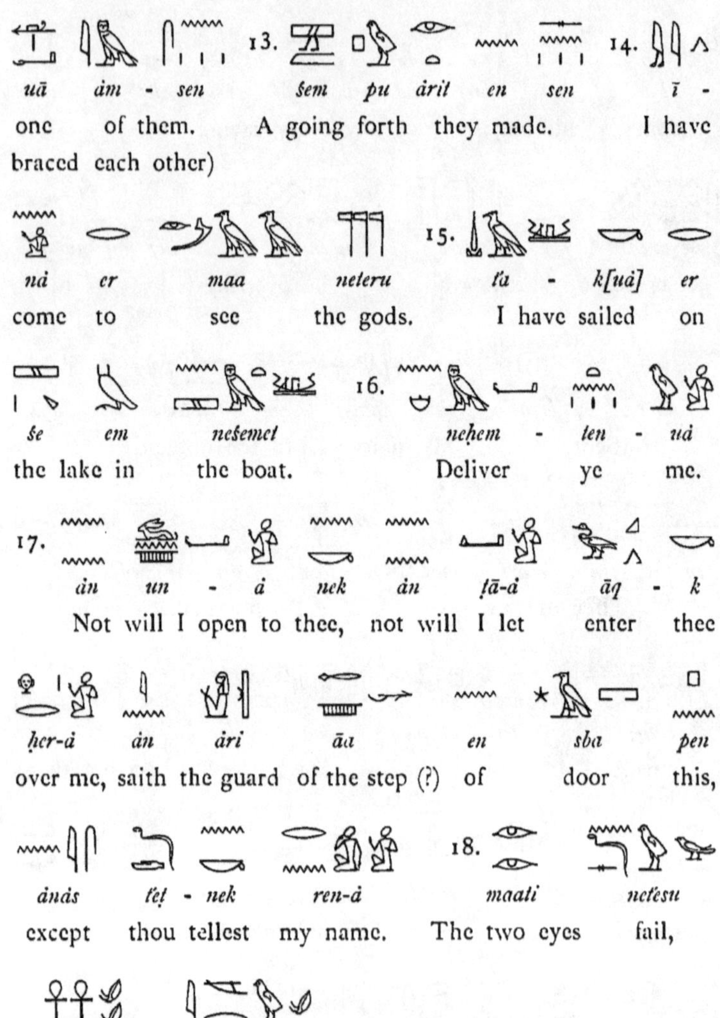

13. 14.

uā àm - sen šem pu àrit en sen ī -

one of them. A going forth they made. I have

braced each other)

15.

nà er maa neteru t'a - k[uà] er

come to see the gods. I have sailed on

16.

še em nešemet neḥem - ten - uà

the lake in the boat. Deliver ye me.

17.

àn un - à nek àn ṭā-à āq - k

Not will I open to thee, not will I let enter thee

ḥer-à àn àri āa en sba pen

over me, saith the guard of the step (?) of door this,

18.

ànàs t'eṭ - nek ren-à maati net'esu

except thou tellest my name. The two eyes fail,

mest'erui àmeru

the two ears become stopped.

Adverbs.

In Egyptian the prepositions and certain substantives and adjectives to which ⊂⊃ *er* is prefixed take the place of adverbs;

e. g., the preposition *àm* "in" becomes the adverb "there". Other examples of adverbs are :— *er bunre* "outside" ; *er àqer* "very much", "exceedingly", *er āa ur* "very much indeed", "exceedingly".

Prepositions.

Prepositions, which may also be used adverbially, are simple and compound. The simple prepositions are :— *en* for, to, in, because ; *em* from, out of, in, into, on, of, among, as, conformably to, as, with, in the state of, if, when, and *em* sometimes introduces a quotation ; *er* to, into, against, by, at, from, every, each, until ; or *ḥer* upon, in, besides, from, for, at, by reason of ; *ṭep* upon ; *χer* under, with ; *χer* from, with, under, during ; *mā* of, from, by ; *ḥenā* with ; *χeft* in the face of, before, at the time of ; *χent* in front of ; *ḥa* behind ; *mà* like ; *àmi* among ; *ṭer* since ; *àn* a particle placed between the verb and the subject.

Some compound prepositions are :—

	em àsu	in recompense for, in consequence of
	em āqa	in the midst, opposite (?)
	em āb	opposite, against
	em uāu	alone
	em uaḥ ḥer	in addition to
	em baḥ	before, in the presence of (also written)
	emem	in, with, among, together with

emmā	in, with, among, together with
em mātet	likewise
em-rā	in the condition of
em rer	about, around
em ḥau	moreover, besides
em ḥāt	in front, before
em ḥer	opposite, in front of
em ḥer āb	in the middle of
em χem	without
em χennu	within
em χer	with
em χet	after, with
em sa	behind, after, at the back of
em qeb	among, amidst
em qeṭ	around, in the circuit of
em ṭep	upon
em ṭebu	in return for
em ṭer	since
er āmtu	between
er āq	in the middle
er āuṭ	between

er ḳes	at the side of
ȧire māu	with
er enti	because
er ḥāt	before
er ḥenā	with
er ḥer	in addition to
er ḥer	in the presence of
er χet	after
er tem	so that not
er śaā	as far as, until
er t'er	to the limit of
ḥeru	besides
ḥer ṭep	upon
ḥer ȧb	in the middle
ḥer ā	at once
ḥer baḥ	before
ḥer χeru	beneath
ḥer sa	behind, at the back
ḥer qeṭ	conformably
χer ā	subordinate to
χer ḥāt	before
χer peḥ	behind

	t'er ā	at once
	t'er baḥ	before, originally
	t'er embaḥ	
	t'er enti	because
	neferit er	up to, as far as
	ȧp ḥer	except

Conjunctions.

Conjunctions are :— *en* because of, *er* until, *ḥer* because, *χeft* when, *mā* as, *re pu* or, *ȧs*, *ȧst*, *ȧsk* when, *χer* now, and the particles *ȧr*, *ȧref*, *ref*, now, therefore, etc.

Particles.

Interrogative particles are :— *ȧn*, which is placed at the beginning of a sentence and is to be rendered by "?" *ȧχ* "what?", *nimā* "who?", *ȧšeset* or *ȧqes* "who?", "what?", *tennu* "where", *petrȧ* or *peti* (?) "what?", etc. The following passages show their use :—

1. *hau ka en ta paut neteru ȧn*
O bull of the company of the gods,

ȧu-k t'i uā - θȧ
dost thou remain by thyself?

2. *su* *mȧ* *ȧχ*

It is like what?

Ȧuθu *mȧ* *ȧχ*

Authu is like what? *I. e.*, "What sort of a place is Authu?"

3. *nimā* *meṭet* *emmā - t*

Who hath had word with thee?

4. *ȧ* *Tem* *ȧšeset* *pu* *šas* - *ȧ* *er* *set*

Hail Tmu, what is it which I have come into it? *I. e.*, "What manner of place is this into which I have come?"

ȧšeset *pu* *āḥā* *em* *ānχ*

What is [my] duration of life? *I. e.*, "How long shall I live?"

5. *su* *tennu* - *nef*

He, where is he?

6. *petrȧ* *ren - k* *petrȧ* *maa* - *nek*

What is thy name? What didst thou see?

Negative particles are :— or *ȧn* "not", *ȧn sep* "at no time", *bu* "not", *ben* "not", *tem* "not", or "so that not", [hieroglyphs] *àm* "not". The following examples show their use :—

1. [hieroglyphs]

àn	*qem*	-	*f*	*àn*	*reχ-tu*	*paif*	*seχeru*
Not	found	he	[it].	Not	is known	his	pattern.

2. [hieroglyphs]

àu	*bu*	*i*	*na*	*šemi*	*er*	*ta*	*ànt*
Not	came		the	travellers	to	the	valley.

3. [hieroglyphs]

ben	*àu-à*	*er*	*ṭāt*	*per*	-	*f*	*em*	*re-à*
Not	am I	for	letting	come	forth	it	from	my mouth.

4. [hieroglyphs]

tem	-	*k*	*ṭeṭ*	*tem*	-	*k*	*qenṭet*
Not	do	thou	speak.	Not	do	thou	rage.

5. [hieroglyphs]

àm	-	*k*	*ḥems*	*àu*	*kai*	*āḥā*
Not	do	thou	sit	being	another	standing up.

List of Words.

The following common words should be learnt by heart; this can best be done by writing out a few of them daily.

[hieroglyphs]	*ṭep*	head
[hieroglyphs]	*àn*	hair
[hieroglyphs]	*ḥenkset*	hair
[hieroglyphs]	*šenti*	hair

fenṭ	nose
re	mouth
åbeḥ	tooth
nes	tongue
ānχui	the two ears
ťeru	skull
neḥebet	neck
χeχ	neck
θes	vertebrae
erment	arm, shoulder
ā	fore-arm
χefā	fist
ṡenbet	body
at	back
menṭ	breast
åb	heart
maāset	liver
χat	belly
mast	thigh
uārt	thigh
reṭ	foot and leg
ånem	skin

t'et	body
ḥāu	flesh, members
āt	limbs
ba	soul
χaibit	shade, shadow
sāḥu	the spiritual body
ka	double, genius
χu	intelligence
seχem	form, image
qes	bone
ren	name
ḥrà	face
ṭehen	forehead
ȧnḥu	eyebrow
maat	eye
šeràti	the two nostrils
septi	the two lips
ārti	the two jaws
ȧnä	chin
mest'er	ear
ḥenḳeḳ	throat
mākḥa	back of the head

 *qāḥu*	shoulder
 *qeb*	elbow
 *ṭet*	hand
 *t'ebā*	finger
 *χat*	corpse
 *pesṭ*	backbone
 *ḥāt*	heart
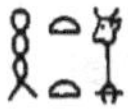 *ḥetet*	lungs
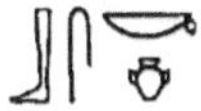 *besek*	intestines
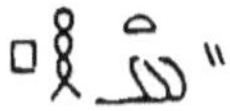 *peḥti*	back
sa	back
 *χepeš*	thigh
 *ment*	leg
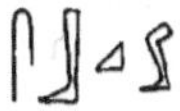 *sebeq*	foot and ankle
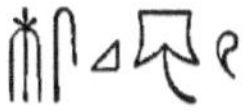 *mesq*	skin
 *åf*	flesh
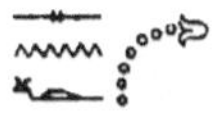 *snef*	blood
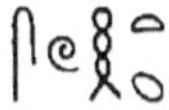 *suḥt*	egg
 *χer*	voice
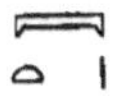 *pet*	heaven, sky
 *ta*	earth
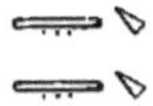 *taui*	the two lands (*i. e.*, north and south)

taiu world, universe

ṭuat underworld

Rā sun

Āāḥ moon

χut horizon

seb star

χabes star, luminary

sepṭet Sothis (Sirius)

saḥ Orion

χepeš Great Bear

hru day

ḳerḥ night

ṭuat daybreak

māšer evening

ḥeṭ' ta dawn

ḥeṭet light

satut rays of light

ḥeṭut light, sunshine

maāu rays of light

sešep brilliance

kekiu darkness

ḥai rain

ḳep	rain flood
šenār	tempest
mu	water
nebȧt	fire
rekḥu	fire, heat
χet	fire
ṭu	mountain
ȧntet	valley
imā	sea
ȧtur	river
ȧaṭet	dew
šā	sand
ȧner	stone
mat	granite
reṭ	sandstone
šes	alabaster
beχan	porphyry
mafek	turquoise
χesbeṭ	lapis-lazuli
uaṭet	mother-of-emerald
sehert	cornelian
nub	gold

ḥeṭ	silver
uasm, smu	electrum (?)
χemt	copper
baa	iron
ṭeḥt	lead
χet	wood, stick
χet	tree
šennu	hard wood tree
nehat	sycamore
āš	cedar
baq	olive tree
ṭebaȧa	fig tree
ȧarer	vine
aḥet	field
benrȧ	date palm
beti	barley
peru	wheat, grain
neprȧ	grain
s[ti]mu	vegetables, herbs
ȧrp	wine
ȧarer	grapes
benrȧ	dates

ṭeb	figs
ȧrt	milk
net (*bȧt*)	honey
renp	young plant, flower
ḥeqt	beer
beq	oil
urḥu	unguent
merḥu	unguent
ānta	perfume
ta	bread
pesen	cake
sennu	cake
per āa	Pharaoh
suten	king
sutenit	queen
suteni	royalty
suten ḥemt	royal wife
suten mut	royal mother
suten sa	royal son (prince)
suten sat	royal daughter (princess)
suten mesu	royal child
suten an	royal scribe

àθi	prince
suten net (*bàt*)	King of the South and North
. . . .	lord of crowns
ur	prefect, nobleman
erpā	hereditary prince
ḥā	a title of very high rank
ṭat	general
smer uāti	a title of high rank
suten reχ	royal kinsman
suten reχ maā	real royal kinsman
ḥer ṭep	chief
ḥer ṭep āa	great chief
mer	governor
šennu	royal attendant
sāḥ	noble
ḥen	majesty
χerp	prefect
ḥen	servant
ḥent	servant (female)
neter ḥen	minister, prophet
neter àtf	divine father
āb	libationer

χer ḥeb	he that hath the book (*i. e.*, the reader)
χer ḥeb ṭep	the chief reader
sem	name of a priest
setem	name of a priest
ur χerp ḥem	title of the high priest of Memphis
ān	scribe
ān neter ḥet	scribe of the temple
ān neter šāt	scribe of holy books
ḥer	chief, president
menfit (*māša*)	soldiers (rank and file)
qen	soldiers picked for bravery
rem[θ]	men and women
re[m]θ	men and women
ṭememu	mortals
reχit	men and women
pāt	ancestor, noble
ḥememu	mankind
ḥrâu nebu	all faces (*i. e.*, mankind)
sa	person
sat	person (fem.)
sat ḥemt	woman
ḥemt	woman

	mut	mother
	menāt	nurse
	sa	son
	sat	daughter
	sen	brother
	sent	sister
	semsu	firstborn
	āu	heir
	mesu	child
	neb	lord
	nebt	lady
	θesemu	greyhound
	maau	cat
	uher	dog, jackal
	ȧu	dog
	unš	wolf
	sȧbi	jackal
	pennu	mouse *or* rat
	ka	bull
	ȧua	ox
	ȧḥ	cow, ox
	beḥes	calf

rerȧ	pig
ser	ram, sheep
āa	ass
ḥetrȧ	horse
sesemut	horses
maḥet'	antelope
maḥes	lion
ȧbi	panther
ṭebt	hippopotamus
ābu	elephant
bāḥes	wild animals
āut	quadrupeds
emsuḥ	crocodile
ḥentasu	lizard
t'art	scorpion
χeper	beetle
ārȧ	uraeus
fenṭ	worm
ḥeft	snake
t'etfet	creeping things
pi	flea
aāani	ape

habu	ibis
bȧk	hawk
šent	heron
šeta	vulture
apṭ	duck, goose
ment	pigeon
bennu	phoenix (?)
smen	goose
pai	birds
remu	fish
χepanen	fish
še	pool
mer	lake, pool
sešet	nest
babat	hole of an animal
ur	great, exceedingly
neṭʿset	little
neb	all, every
ȧšt	many
ȧȧa	great
trȧ	season
rek	period, time

unnut	hour, season
ḥat	second
at	minute
àbeṭ	month
renpit	year
seṭ	period of 30 years
ḥen	period of 60 years
ḥeḥ	millions of years
ṭetta	everlastingness
hru ṭuau ḥeru renpit	the 5 epagomenal days
šat	period of sowing
pert	period of growing (*i. e.*, winter)
šemut	period of inundation (*i. e.*, summer)
χer	cemetery
mer	pyramid tomb
àsit	tomb
māḥāit	sepulchre
useχt	hall, part of a tomb
uti	coffin
ṭebu	sarcophagus
perχeru	funeral offerings

statet passage in the tomb

àmḥet hall of the tomb

tut statue, image

uṭḥu altar, table

ḥesmen natron

χet things, furniture, wealth

urś pillow

ḥetepu funeral offerings

utu tablet, stele

sāḥ mummy

ḥes singer, mourner

maāχeru triumphant, victorious

bent harp

seśeś sistrum

ureret name of a crown

śuti plumes

ḥeťet white crown

ṭeśert red crown

atfu the *atef* crown

seχti the double crown

nemmes the *nemmes* crown

neχeχu whip

θes	a captain
qem	black
ḥeṭeṭ	white
ṭešer	red
χesbeṭ	blue (of lapis-lazuli)
unemi	right hand
semeḥi	left hand
šeps	venerable, sacred
ȧmaχ	revered
mert	beloved, friend
nefer	good, happy
neṭem	pleasant, happy
benrȧ	sweet
maa	what is right and true
menu	monuments
peru ḥeṭ	treasury
šenti	granary
ḥet	temple
per	house
ḥet aat	palace, great house
ȧuset	place, seat
sba	door, doorway

äāui	folding door
sebχet	large doors, pylons
nemmat	block of punishment
χet	staircase
teχennu	obelisk
nest	throne
karā	shrine
ṭemāt	village
nut	city
t'erāu	bounds, limits
enti	things which do exist
unenet	things which shall exist
uā	one, only
uāu	alone
uat	way
māṭennu	road, way
mest'emut	eye paint
maa-ḥrā	seer of the face (*i. e.*, mirror)
sešen	lily
šeta	secret, hidden
šāt	book
t'amā	roll of papyrus

mesθȧ	writing palette
pes	ink-jar
qeš	writing reed
ānχ	life
mit	death
χeft	enemy
χakȧb	rebel, coward
ȧm	camp
pet	bow
šemert	bow
ābau	arrow, bolt
urer	chariot
sebȧu	fiend
senb	health
ut'a	strength
uȧa	boat
sektet	morning boat of the sun
āṭeṭ	evening boat of the sun
ḥemi	rudder
ḥeqer	hunger
ȧb	thirst
sam ta	union with the earth, *i.e.*, funeral

ȧnet' ḥrȧ-k	hail to thee!
ȧau	adoration
peḥti	strength
šefit	might, terror
āu	joy, gladness
sen ta	adoration
ȧn	not
ben	not
ȧt	destitute
sebtet	wall
feqa	reward, wages
seqer	prisoner
ḥeb	festival
uṭen	offering
ȧp	messenger, envoy
ȧnnu	offerings, tribute
ses	bolt of a door
meṭu	a word, thing
betau	bad, wickedness
ȧsfet	faults, sins
ṭenḥ	wing
uteb	furrow, water-course

neχṭ	might, victory
usr	to be strong
sfenṭ	knife
nemmat	footsteps
χāu	crowns
χeru	terrestrial beings
ḥeru	celestial beings
seχeru	plans, schemes
ťefau	funeral meals
χert	things, provisions
ṭemṭ	all
χai	defeat
neh	few
χesef	to meet, to repulse
utu	to command
sa	to know
ṭer	to destroy
χāā	to rise, be crowned
senṭ	to fear
uaš	to adore
ḥeḥi	to seek
χaā	to leave

seb	to pass
ṭep	to taste
àmen	to hide, be hidden
qet	to build
seš	to open
ānχ	to live
mit	to die
maa	to see
setem	to hear
rerem	to weep
t'eṭ	to say, speak
mer	to love
mest'eṭ	to hate
āḥā	to stand
ḥems	to sit
st'er	to lie down
χeper	to become
àru	to make
qemam	to create
àm	to eat
surà	to drink
θetet	to carry off

	āq	to go in
	per	to come out
	sper	to set out
	i	to come
	atep	to load oneself
	fa	to bear, to carry
	urš	to pass the day
	seχem	to gain the mastery
	ābau	to fight
	sma	to slay, kill
	χeṭbu	to slay
	uben	to rise (of the sun)
	ḥetep	to set
	pesṭ	to shine
	seḥeť	to illumine
	bāḥ	to overflow, to flood
	θes	to lift up
	qa	to be high
	χeṭ	to float down stream
	χent	to sail up stream
	ušebt	to answer
	beṭeš	to be weak, feeble

ḥāā	to rejoice
ṭuau	to praise
smȧ	to announce
ṭā	to give
ṭebḥ	to pray, entreat
ȧpt	to announce
men	to stablish, to abide
sam	to unite
sepṭ	to provide, prepare
āper	to be provided with
peṭ	to stretch
pai	to fly
peḥrer	to run
šes	to follow
seχseχ	to flee
hab	to send
šem (*māšem*)	to walk, to travel
t'a	to set out
sen	to pass
seš	to go, to pass by, to go in
peḥ	to attain, to arrive
sau	to watch, to guard

	χnemu	to join to
	χent	to sail up stream
	mās	to bring
	tut	to engender
	mes	to bear children
	qem	to find
	meḥ	to fill
	uaḥ	to place
	āā	to wash
	neḥem	to save, to carry off
	un	to open
	seχer	to overthrow

Gods and Goddesses.

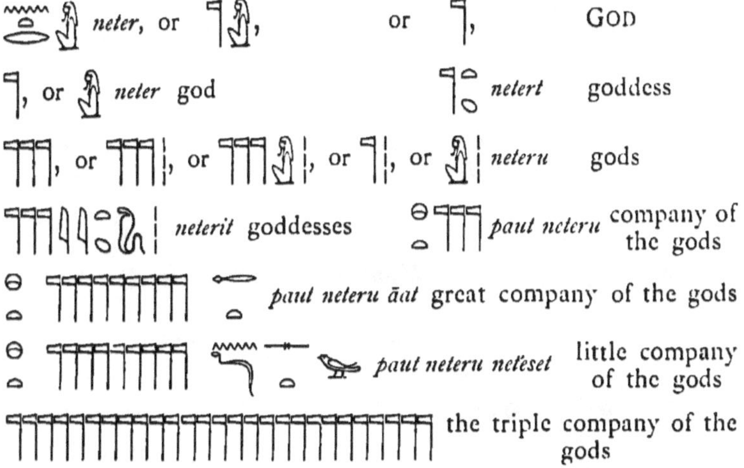

neter, or , or , God

, or *neter* god — *netert* goddess

, or , or , or , or *neteru* gods

neterit goddesses — *paut neteru* company of the gods

paut neteru āat great company of the gods

paut neteru neťeset little company of the gods

the triple company of the gods

Ȧusȧr	Osiris
Ȧuset	Isis
Ȧp-uat	Ȧp-uat
Ȧmen	Ȧmen (Ammon)
Ȧmen-Rā	Ȧmen-Rā
Ȧmsu or *Min*	Ȧmsu, Min, Khem
Ȧmsu-Ȧmen	Ȧmsu-Ȧmen
Ȧmset	Ȧmset
Ȧni	Ȧni
Ānθȧt	Anata
Ȧnpu	Anubis
Ȧn-ḥeru	Ȧn-ḥeru
Ānqet	Ānqet
Ȧtmu	Ȧtmu (Tmu)
Ȧsṭes	Ȧsṭes
Iusāaset	Iusāaset
I-em-ḥetep	Imouthis
Un-nefer	Un-nefer
Uaťet	Uatchet
Baba	Baba
Bār	Bār (Baal)

Bes	Bes
Ptaḥ	Ptaḥ
Ptaḥ-Seker-Ȧusȧr	Ptah-Socharis-Osiris
Maāt	Maāt
Menθu	Menthu
Meḥ-urt	Meḥurt
Mesχenet	Meskhenet
Mut	Mut
Nu	Nu
Nut	Nut
Neb-er-ṭer	Neb-er-tcher
Nebt-ḥet	Nephthys
Nefer-Tmu	Nefer-Tmu
Nit	Neith
Rā	Rā
Renenet	Renenet
Reśpu	Reshpu
Ḥu	Ḥu
Ḥāpi	The Nile
Ḥāpi	Ḥāpi
Ḥāpi	Apis

Ḥeruur	Horus the elder (Aroeris)
Ḥeru-sa-Àuset	Horus, son of Isis (Harsiesi)
Ḥeru-pa-χarṭ	Horus the child (Harpocrates)
Ḥeru-maati	Horus of the two eyes
Ḥeru-χenti-àn-maa	Horus dwelling in darkness
Ḥeru-χenti-Seχem	Horus of Sekhem
Ḥet-ḥert	Hathor
Χnemu	Khnemu
Χensu	Khensu
Χensu-nefer-ḥetep	Khensu-nefer-ḥetep
Sa	Sa
Seb	Seb
Sebek	Sebek
Sept	Sept
Sefeχet	Sefekhet
Serqet	Serqet
Seχetet	Sekhet
Seker	Socharis
Set	Set or Sut
Sati	Sati
Suteχ	Sutekh
Śu	Shu

Śai	Shai
Qebḥ-sennu-f	Qebḥ-sennu-f
Ta-urt	Thoueris
Tanen	Tanen
Ta-tenen	Tatenen
Ṭua-māut-f	Ṭuamāutef
Tmu	Tmu
Teḥuti	Thoth
Tefnet	Tefnet

TEXTS

WITH INTERLINEAR TRANSLITERATION AND WORD FOR WORD TRANSLATION

EXTRACTS FROM THE PRISSE PAPYRUS.

Maxims of Kaqemna and Ptaḥ-ḥetep.

[IIIrd and Vth dynasties.]

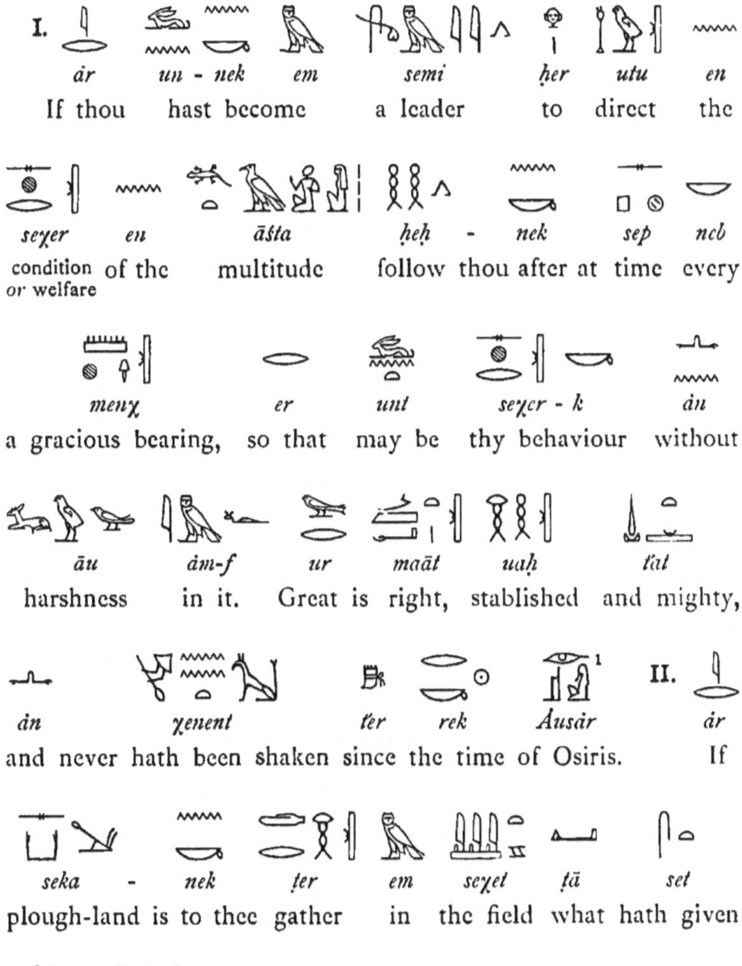

I. *ȧr un - nek em semi ḥer utu en*
If thou hast become a leader to direct the

seχer en ā́šta ḥeḥ - nek sep neb
condition or welfare of the multitude follow thou after at time every

menχ er unt seχer - k ȧn
a gracious bearing, so that may be thy behaviour without

āu ȧm-f ur maāt uaḥ ťat
harshness in it. Great is right, stablished and mighty,

ȧn χenent ťer rek Ȧusȧr[1] II. *ȧr*
and never hath been shaken since the time of Osiris. If

seka - nek ťer em seχet ťā set
plough-land is to thee gather in the field what hath given

[1] Plate VI., ll. 3—5.

[1] **III.**

neter *àr* *un - nek* *em* *sa* *àqer* *àri - k*
God. If thou wouldst be a man perfect make thou

sa *en* *semam* *neter* *àr* *met - f*
[thy] son to please God. If he directeth straight

peχar-f *en* *qeṭ - k* *ennu - f* *χet-*
his course according to thy example, and he dealeth in thy

k *er* *àuset* *àri* *àri - nef* *bu* *neb*
affairs in the place *or* way belonging thereto, do unto him thing every

nefer *sa - k* *pu* *nesu* *set*
good, for thy son is he belonging unto the seed

ka - k *àm-k* *āuṭ* *àb-k* *er - f*
of thy person. Do not thou remove thy heart from him,

àu *metu* *àri* *senθi*[2] **IV.** *àr*
[for it] is [thy] seed [which] maketh appeal [to thee]. If thou

àqer - k *ḳer - k* *per - k* *mer - k* *ḥemt-*
wouldst be perfect possess thou thy house, love thou thy

[1] Plate VII., l. 5. [2] Plate VII., ll. 10—13.

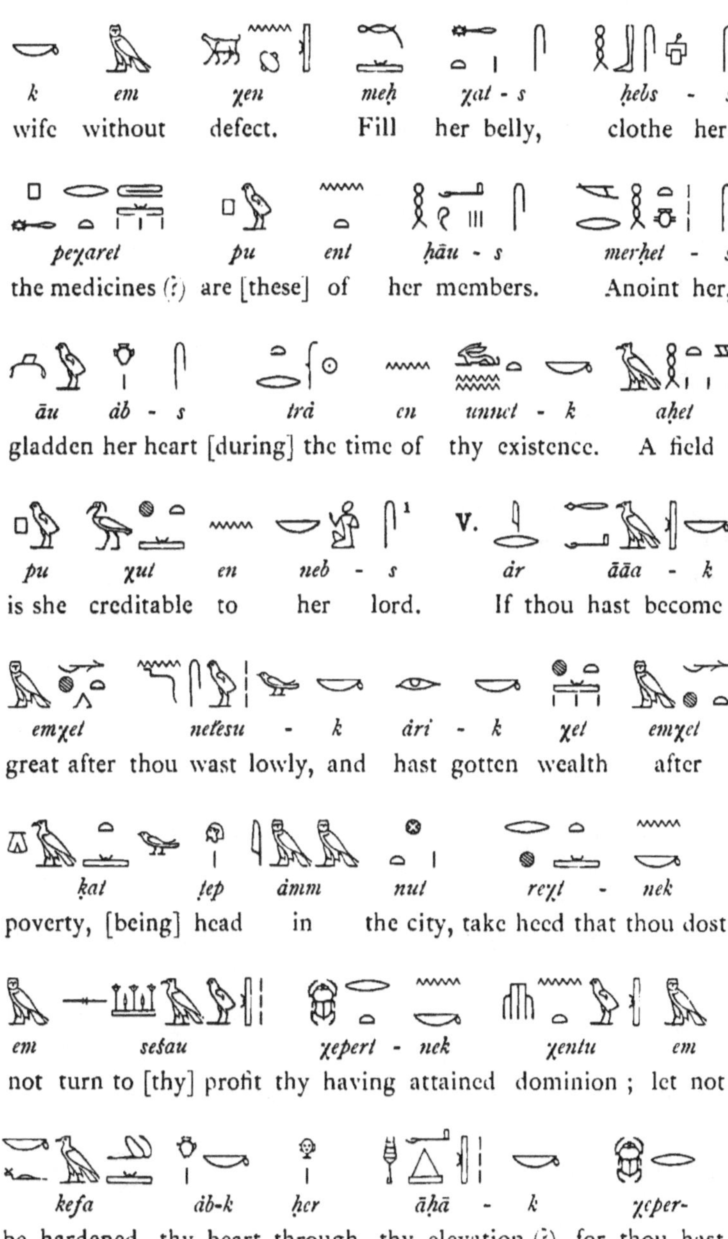

k em χen meḥ χat - s ḥebs - s
wife without defect. Fill her belly, clothe her,

peχaret pu ent ḥāu - s merḥet - s
the medicines (?) are [these] of her members. Anoint her,

āu àb - s trà en unnut - k aḥet
gladden her heart [during] the time of thy existence. A field

pu χut en neb - s
is she creditable to her lord.[1]

V. *àr āāa - k*
If thou hast become

emχet neṭesu - k àri - k χet emχet
great after thou wast lowly, and hast gotten wealth after

ḳat ṭep àmm nut reχt - nek
poverty, [being] head in the city, take heed that thou dost

em sešau χepert - nek χentu em
not turn to [thy] profit thy having attained dominion ; let not

kefa àb-k ḥer āḥā - k χeper-
be hardened thy heart through thy elevation (?), for thou hast

[1] Plate X., ll. 8—10.

6

nek mer sepṭ neter[1] **VI.** *ȧri ṭeṭet*

become [only] the steward of the goods of God. Perform the command

neb - k er-ek nefer-ui sba en

of thy lord to thee. Doubly good is the instruction of

ȧtf - f per - nef ȧm - f χent

his (*i. e.*, a man's) father [for] he hath come forth from him from

ḥāu - f ṭeṭ - nef nef ȧu - f em χat er

his body. [What] he saith to him let it be within [him] to

āu ur ȧrit - nef er ṭeṭet - nef

its fulness greatest, let him do more than his words.

māk sa nefer en ṭāṭā neter rā

Verily a son good [is] of the gifts of God, [he] doeth

ḥau ṭeṭet - nef χer neb - f ȧri - f

over and above [what] he hath said. Before his lord he doeth right

maā ȧri en ȧb - f er nemtet - f

and truth, and worketh his heart in his steps.

[1] Plate XIII., ll. 6—8.

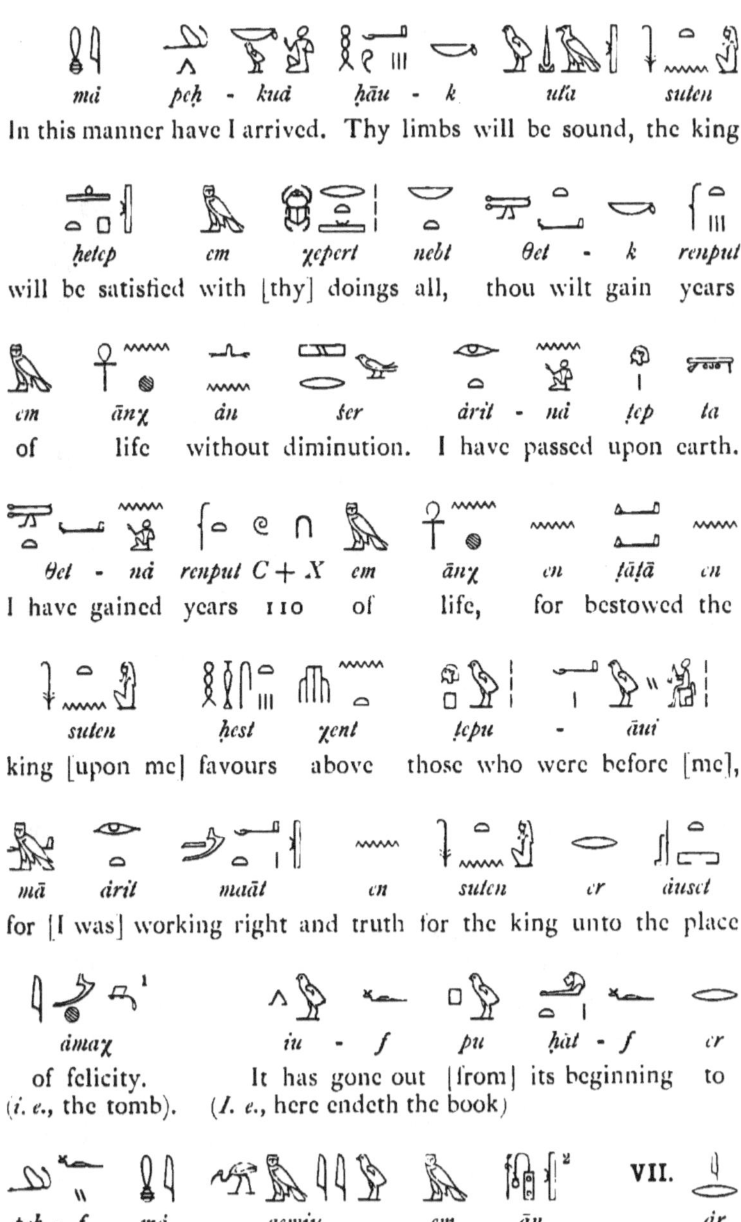

mā peḥ - kuȧ ḥāu - k uťa suten
In this manner have I arrived. Thy limbs will be sound, the king

ḥetep em χepert nebt θet - k renput
will be satisfied with [thy] doings all, thou wilt gain years

em ānχ ȧn šer ȧrit - nȧ ṭep ta
of life without diminution. I have passed upon earth.

θet - nȧ renput C + X em ānχ en ṭāṭā en
I have gained years 110 of life, for bestowed the

suten ḥest χent ṭepu - āui
king [upon me] favours above those who were before [me],

mā ȧrit maāt en suten er ȧuset
for [I was] working right and truth for the king unto the place

ȧmaχ[1] *iu - f pu ḥȧt - f er*
of felicity. It has gone out [from] its beginning to
(*i. e.*, the tomb). (*I. e.*, here endeth the book)

peḥ - f mā qemiu em ān[2] **VII.** *ȧr*
its end, even as it is found in writing.[3] If

[1] Plate XIX., ll. 3—8. [2] Plate XIX., l. 9. [3] This is a colo-

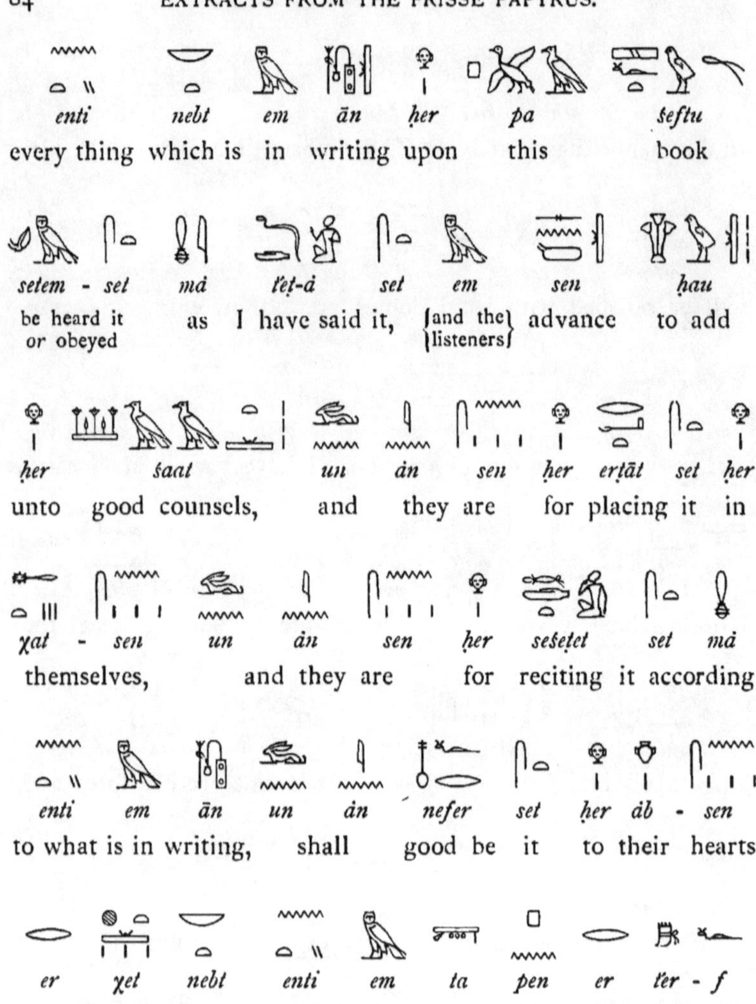

enti nebt em ān ḥer pa šeftu
every thing which is in writing upon this book

setem - set mȧ ṭeṭ-ȧ set em sen ḥau
be heard it or obeyed as I have said it, {and the listeners} advance to add

ḥer šaat un ȧn sen ḥer erṭāt set ḥer
unto good counsels, and they are for placing it in

χat - sen un ȧn sen ḥer sešeṭet set mȧ
themselves, and they are for reciting it according

enti em ān un ȧn nefer set ḥer ȧb - sen
to what is in writing, shall good be it to their hearts

er χet nebt enti em ta pen er ṭer - f
more than thing any which is in earth this to the whole of it,

phon. Another reads :—

iu - f pu em ḥetep mȧ pa
It hath gone out in peace according to what

qemu
was found, *i. e.*, here happily endeth an exact copy.

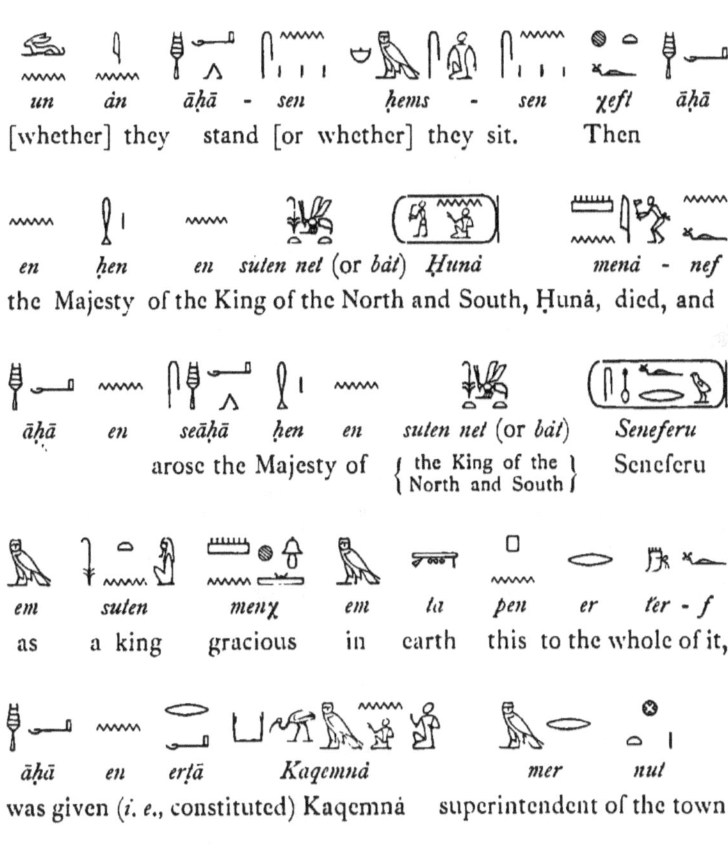

un ȧn āḥā - sen ḥems - sen χeft āḥā

[whether] they stand [or whether] they sit. Then

en ḥen en suten net (or *bȧt*) *Ḥunȧ menȧ - nef*

the Majesty of the King of the North and South, Ḥunȧ, died, and

āḥā en seāḥā ḥen en suten net (or *bȧt*) *Seneferu*

arose the Majesty of {the King of the North and South} Seneferu

em suten menχ em ta pen er ṭer - f

as a king gracious in earth this to the whole of it,

āḥā en erṭā Kaqemnȧ mer nut

was given (*i. e.*, constituted) Kaqemnȧ superintendent of the town

ṭat

and governor.[1]

[1] Plate II., ll. 4—9.

EXTRACTS FROM THE PYRAMID TEXTS.

Pyramid of Unȧs.

[Vth dynasty.]

I. … **II.**

ṭ nek su em ṭert - k … *seb*

Line 3. Place thou it in thy palm. 4. Goeth

III.

Ḥeru ḥenā ka - f … *ā ka - k*

Horus with his *ka* (*i. e.*, double *or* genius). 7. The hand of thy *ka* [is]

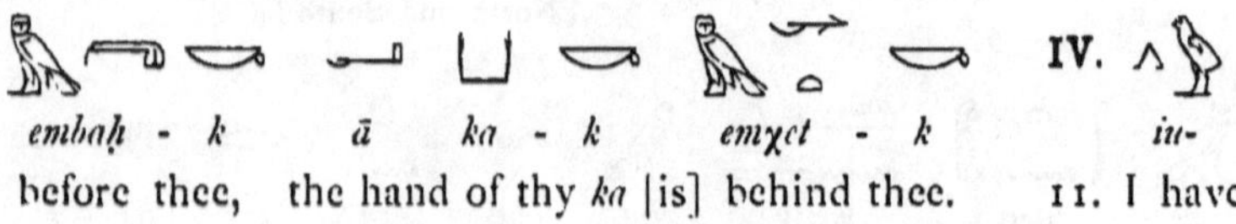

IV.

embaḥ - k ā ka - k emχet - k in-

before thee, the hand of thy *ka* [is] behind thee. 11. I have

nȧ ȧn - nȧ nek maat Ḥeru qeb ȧb - k

come, I have brought to thee the eye of Horus, refresh thy heart

χer - s ȧn - nȧ nek s χer ṭebti - k

with it; I have brought to thee it beneath thy sandals.

V. … **VI.**

ȧṭep - k ṭept - f χent neter ḥet … *re - k*

14. Taste thou its taste in the divine dwellings. 20. Thy mouth

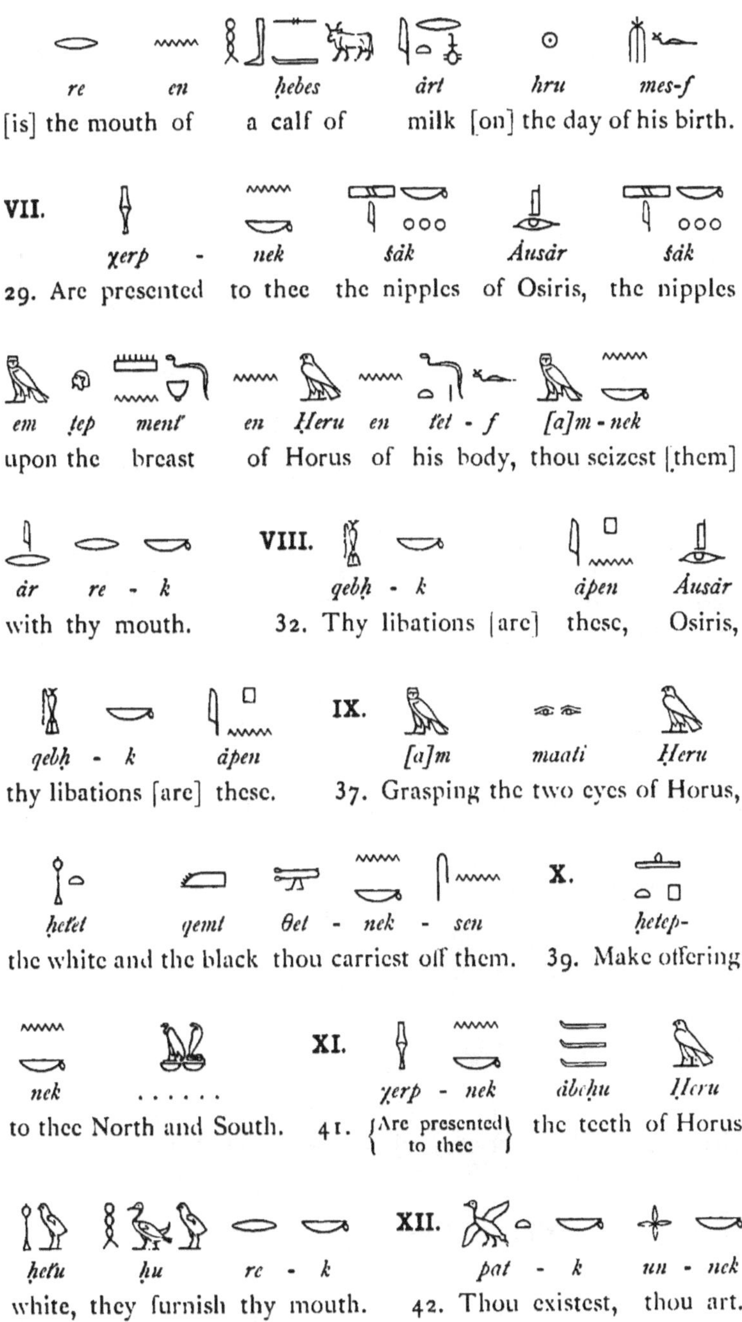

re en ḥebes ȧrt hru mes-f
[is] the mouth of a calf of milk [on] the day of his birth.

VII. *χerp - nek šȧk Ȧusȧr šȧk*
29. Are presented to thee the nipples of Osiris, the nipples

em ṭep menť en Ḥeru en ṭ'et - f [a]m - nek
upon the breast of Horus of his body, thou seizest [them]

ȧr re - k
with thy mouth.

VIII. *qebḥ - k ȧpen Ȧusȧr*
32. Thy libations [are] these, Osiris,

qebḥ - k ȧpen
thy libations [are] these.

IX. *[a]m maati Ḥeru*
37. Grasping the two eyes of Horus,

ḥeṭ'et qemt θet - nek - sen
the white and the black thou carriest off them.

X. *ḥetep-*
39. Make offering

nek . . . . . .
to thee North and South.

XI. *χerp - nek ȧbeḥu Ḥeru*
41. {Are presented to thee} the teeth of Horus

ḥeṭ'u ḥu re - k
white, they furnish thy mouth.

XII. *pat - k un - nek*
42. Thou existest, thou art.

XIII. *pat ent uṭen* **XIV.** *seχu - θ su*

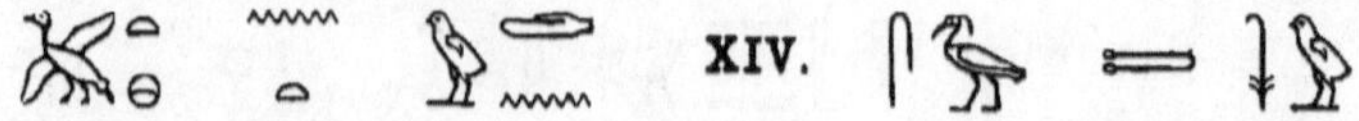

42. A cake of offering. 62. Make strong thou him

χer - θ ṭā - θ seχem - f em t'et - f

with thyself, grant thou that he may gain power over his body.

ṭā - θ šāšet - f em maati **XV.** *baqet*

Grant thou that he may be open in his two eyes. 170. The olive tree

àmt Ànnu **XVI.** *àn àb àn ḥeqer - f*

in Heliopolis. 172. Not let thirst, not let him hunger,

àn sàr àb en Unàs **XVII.** *χefā - sen*

not let be sad the heart of Unàs. 176. They shall grasp

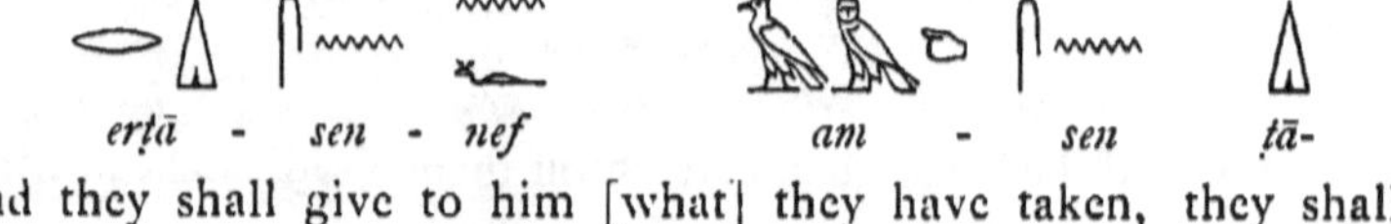

erṭā - sen - nef am - sen ṭā-

and they shall give to him [what] they have taken, they shall

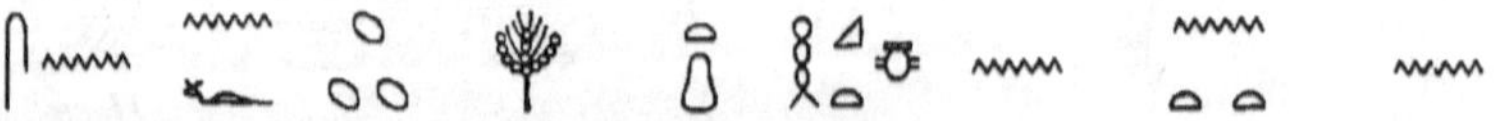

sen nef peru beti ta ḥeqt en entet en

give to him wheat, barley, cakes, ale of that which [is] of

Unàs **XVIII.** *seṭaa ur per em*

Unàs. 187. Trembler mighty coming out of

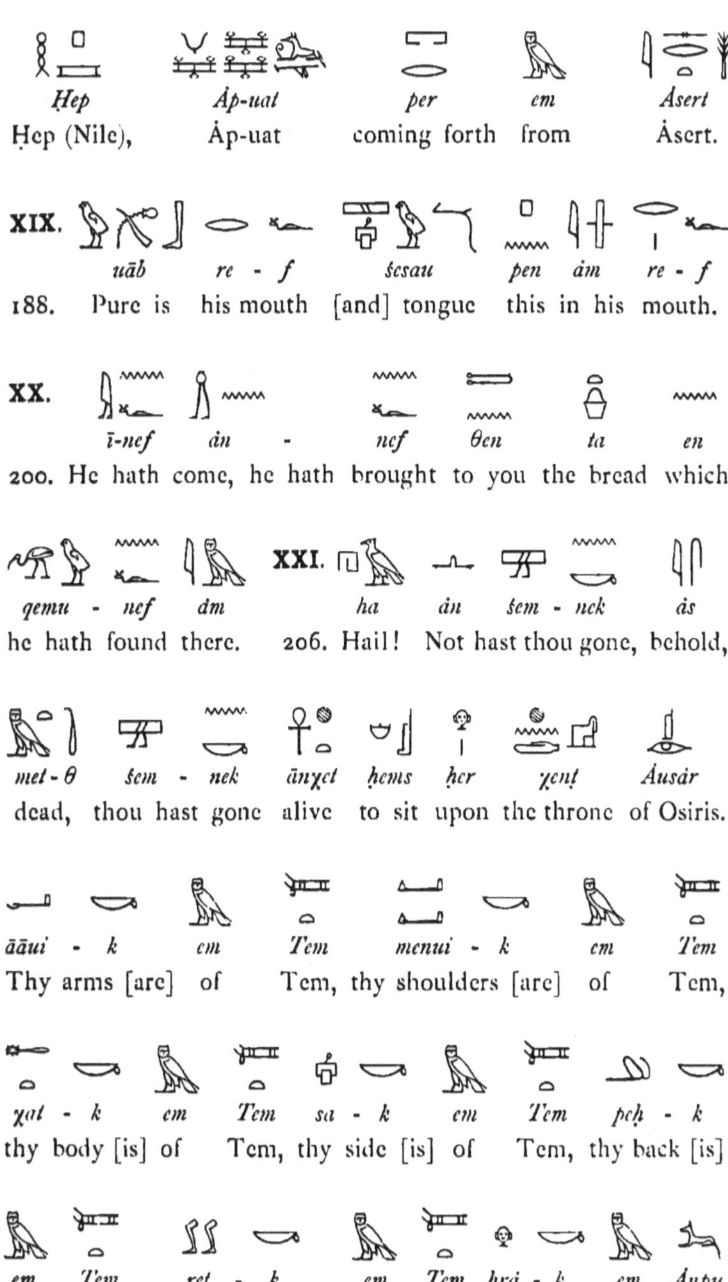

Ḥep *Ȧp-uat* *per* *em* *Ȧsert*

Ḥep (Nile), Ȧp-uat coming forth from Ȧsert.

XIX. *uāb re - f šesau pen ȧm re - f*

188. Pure is his mouth [and] tongue this in his mouth.

XX. *ī-nef ȧn - nef θen ta en*

200. He hath come, he hath brought to you the bread which

qemu - nef ȧm XXI. *ha ȧn šem - nek ȧs*

he hath found there. 206. Hail! Not hast thou gone, behold,

met - θ šem - nek ānχet ḥems ḥer χenṭ Ȧusȧr

dead, thou hast gone alive to sit upon the throne of Osiris.

āāui - k em Tem menui - k em Tem

Thy arms [are] of Tem, thy shoulders [are] of Tem,

χat - k em Tem sa - k em Tem peḥ - k

thy body [is] of Tem, thy side [is] of Tem, thy back [is]

em Tem reṭ - k em Tem ḥrȧ - k em Ȧnpu

of Tem, thy feet and legs [are] of Tem, thy face [is] of Anpu.

XXII. *uāb - k ārek em qebḥ sbau*

210. Thou art pure therefore with the cool water of the stars.

XXIII. *kāu - nek ḥenmemet uθes - neku*

211. Cry to thee the heavenly ones, lift thee up the

āχem - seku āaq ārek ār bu χer

never-setting stars, enter then into the place containing

āt - k bu χer Seb **XXIV.** *i - nek*

thy father, the place containing Seb. 232. Hath come to thee

sa - k sāā - nek su šen - nek su

thy son, thou hast received him, thou hast grasped him

em χennu ā - k sa - k pu en tet - k en

in thy hand, thy son is he of thy body for

tetta **XXV.** *āp - f ābu neḥem - f kau neḥeb - f*

ever. 233. He judgeth hearts, he punisheth *ka*'s, he subdueth

kau **XXVI.** *ta - f re - f ṭeṭ en Seb*

ka's. 234. His bread of his mouth [is] the word of Seb

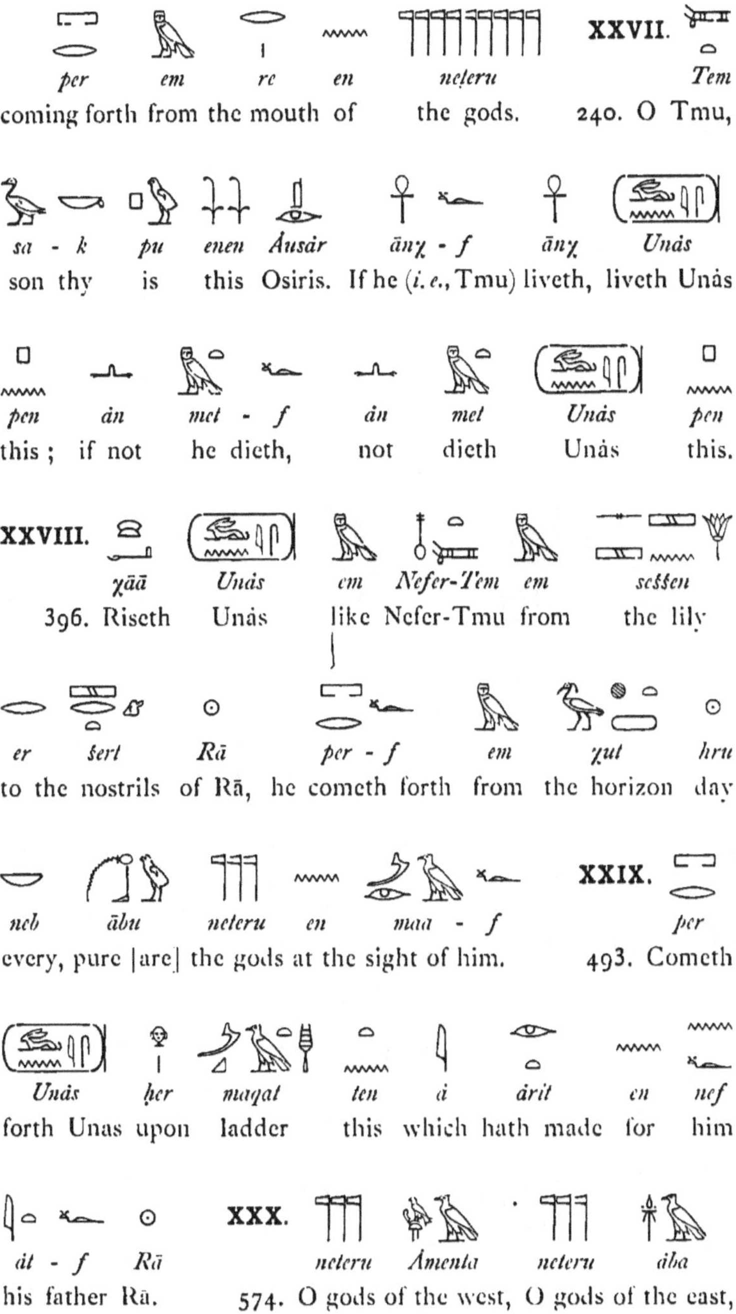

per em re en neṭeru **XXVII.** *Tem*
coming forth from the mouth of the gods. 240. O Tmu,

sa - k pu enen Ȧusȧr ānχ - f ānχ Unȧs
son thy is this Osiris. If he (*i.e.*, Tmu) liveth, liveth Unȧs

pen ȧn met - f ȧn met Unȧs pen
this; if not he dieth, not dieth Unȧs this.

XXVIII. *χāā Unȧs em Nefer-Tem em seššen*
396. Riseth Unȧs like Nefer-Tmu from the lily

er šert Rā per - f em χut hru
to the nostrils of Rā, he cometh forth from the horizon day

neb ābu neteru en maa - f **XXIX.** *per*
every, pure [are] the gods at the sight of him. 493. Cometh

Unȧs ḥer maqat ten ȧ ȧrit en nef
forth Unas upon ladder this which hath made for him

ȧt - f Rā **XXX.** *neteru Ȧmenta neteru ȧba*
his father Rā. 574. O gods of the west, O gods of the east,

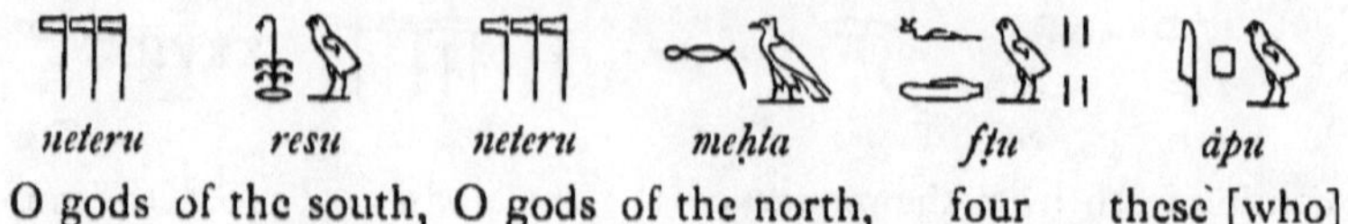

neteru *resu* *neteru* *meḥta* *fṭu* *àpu*

O gods of the south, O gods of the north, four these [who]

seχen *taiu* *uāb*

embrace the four quarters of earth holy.

Pyramid of Tetà.

[VIth dynasty.]

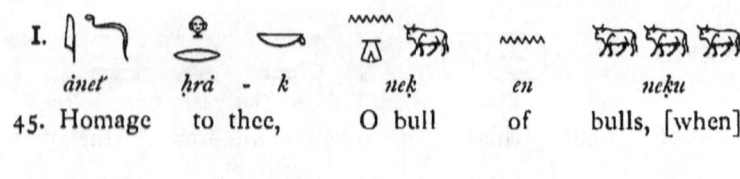

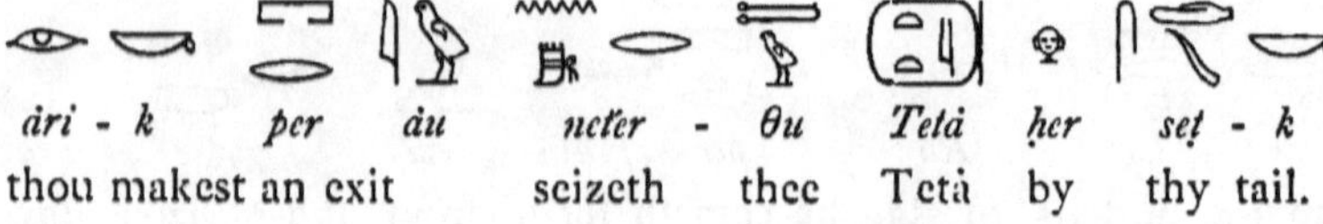

I. *àneṭ* *ḥrà - k* *neḳ* *en* *neḳu*

45. Homage to thee, O bull of bulls, [when]

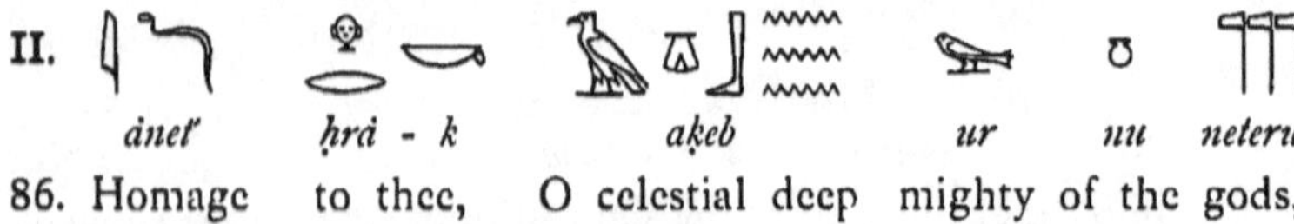

àri - k *per* *àu* *neṭer - θu* *Tetà* *ḥer* *seṭ - k*

thou makest an exit seizeth thee Tetà by thy tail.

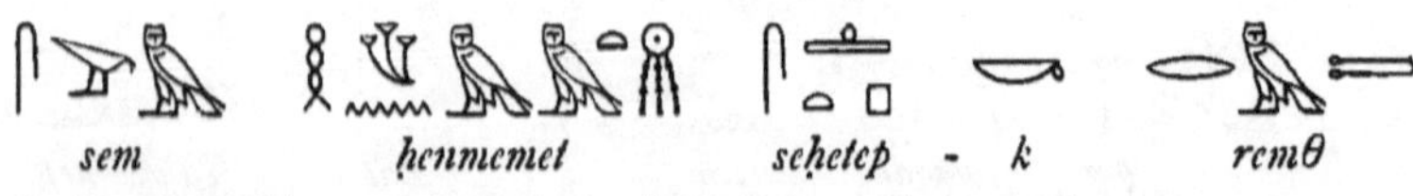

II. *àneṭ* *ḥrà - k* *aḳeb* *ur* *nu* *neteru*

86. Homage to thee, O celestial deep mighty of the gods,

sem *ḥenmemet* *seḥetep - k* *remθ*

fashioned of heavenly beings (?), thou makest to be at peace men

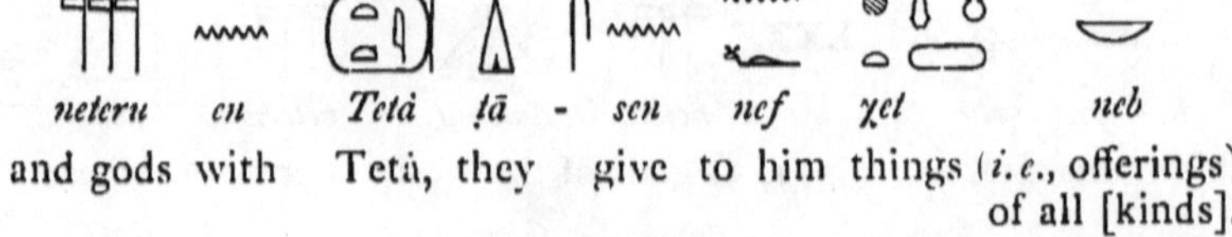

neteru *en* *Tetà* *ṭā - sen* *nef* *χet* *neb*

and gods with Tetà, they give to him things (*i.e.*, offerings) of all [kinds].

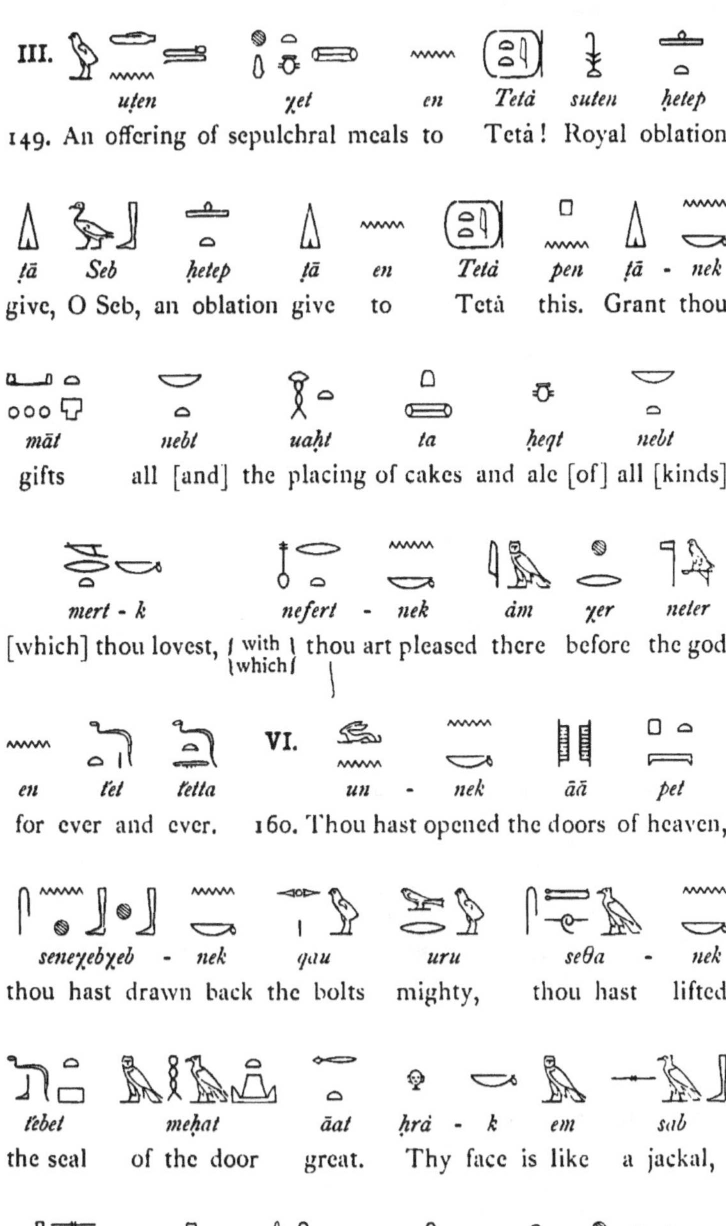

III. *uṭen* *χet* *en* *Tetȧ* *suten* *ḥetep*
149. An offering of sepulchral meals to Tetȧ! Royal oblation

ṭā *Seb* *ḥetep* *ṭā* *en* *Tetȧ* *pen* *ṭā* - *nek*
give, O Seb, an oblation give to Tetȧ this. Grant thou

māt *nebt* *uaḥt* *ta* *ḥeqt* *nebt*
gifts all [and] the placing of cakes and ale [of] all [kinds]

mert - *k* *nefert* - *nek* *ȧm* *χer* *neter*
[which] thou lovest, {with which} thou art pleased there before the god

en *t'et* *t'etta* VI. *un* - *nek* *āā* *pet*
for ever and ever. 160. Thou hast opened the doors of heaven,

seneχebχeb - *nek* *qau* *uru* *seθa* - *nek*
thou hast drawn back the bolts mighty, thou hast lifted

t'ebet *meḥat* *āat* *ḥrȧ* - *k* *em* *sab*
the seal of the door great. Thy face is like a jackal,

χebset - *k* *em* *maḥes* *ḥems* - *k* *her* *χenṭ* - *k*
thy hind part is like a lion, thou sittest upon thy throne

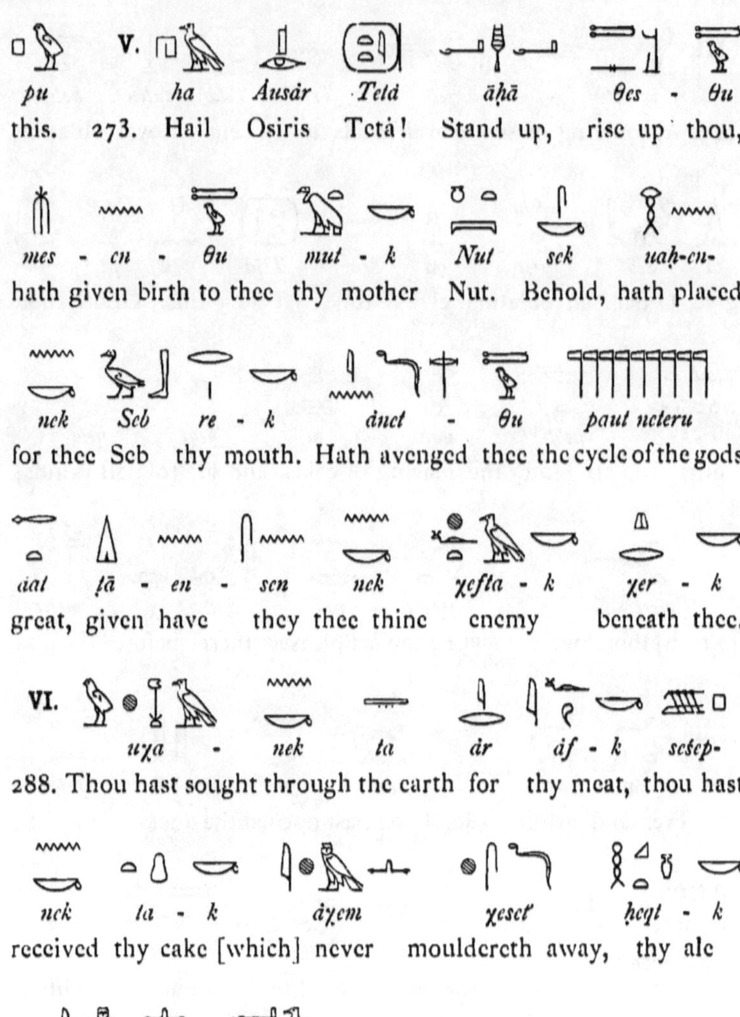

pu V. *ha* *Ȧusȧr* *Tetȧ* *āḥā* *θes* - *θu*
this. 273. Hail Osiris Tetȧ! Stand up, rise up thou,

mes - *en* - *θu* *mut* - *k* *Nut* *sek* *uaḥ-en-*
hath given birth to thee thy mother Nut. Behold, hath placed

nek *Seb* *re* - *k* *ȧnet* - *θu* *paut neteru*
for thee Seb thy mouth. Hath avenged thee the cycle of the gods

ȧat *ṭā* - *en* - *sen* *nek* *χefta* - *k* *χer* - *k*
great, given have they thee thine enemy beneath thee.

VI. *uχa* - *nek* *ta* *ȧr* *ȧf* - *k* *sešep-*
288. Thou hast sought through the earth for thy meat, thou hast

nek *ta* - *k* *ȧχem* *χeset'* *ḥeqt* - *k*
received thy cake [which] never mouldereth away, thy ale

ȧχemet *āua*
[which] never stinketh.

FROM THE TOMB OF ḤER-KHUF AT ASWÂN.

[VIth dynasty.]

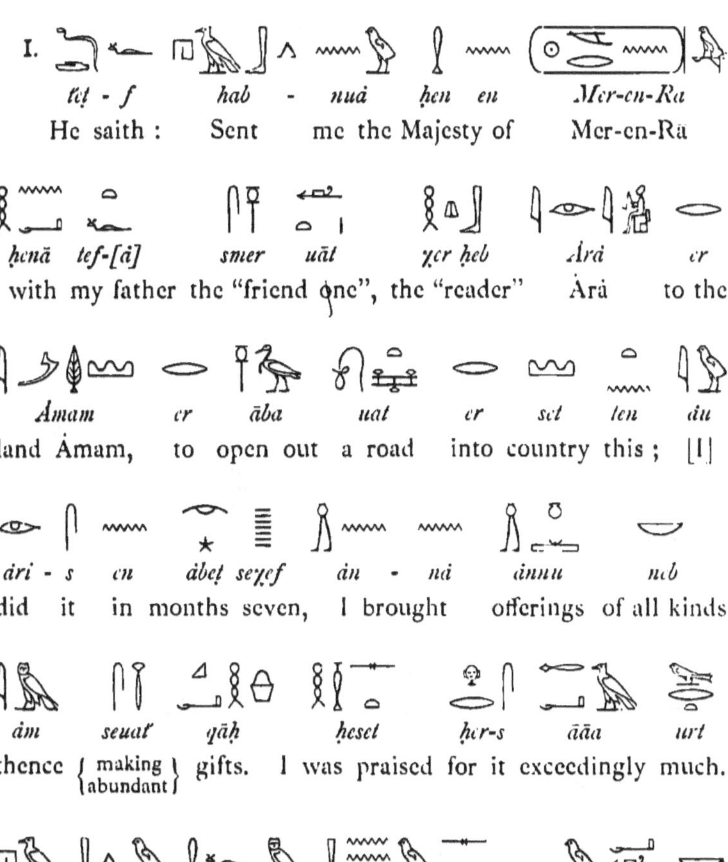

I. *ṭeṭ - f hab - nuȧ ḥen en Mer-en-Ra*
He saith: Sent me the Majesty of Mer-en-Rā

ḥenā tef-[ȧ] smer uāt χer ḥeb Ȧrȧ er
with my father the "friend one", the "reader" Ȧrȧ to the

Ȧmam er āba uat er set ten ȧu
land Ȧmam, to open out a road into country this; [I]

ȧri - s en ȧbeṭ seχef ȧn - nȧ ȧnnu neb
did it in months seven, I brought offerings of all kinds

ȧm seuaṭ qāḥ ḥeset ḥer-s āāa urt
thence {making abundant} gifts. I was praised for it exceedingly much.

hab - uȧ ḥen-f em sennu sep uā - k
Sent me his majesty a second time and I was by myself.

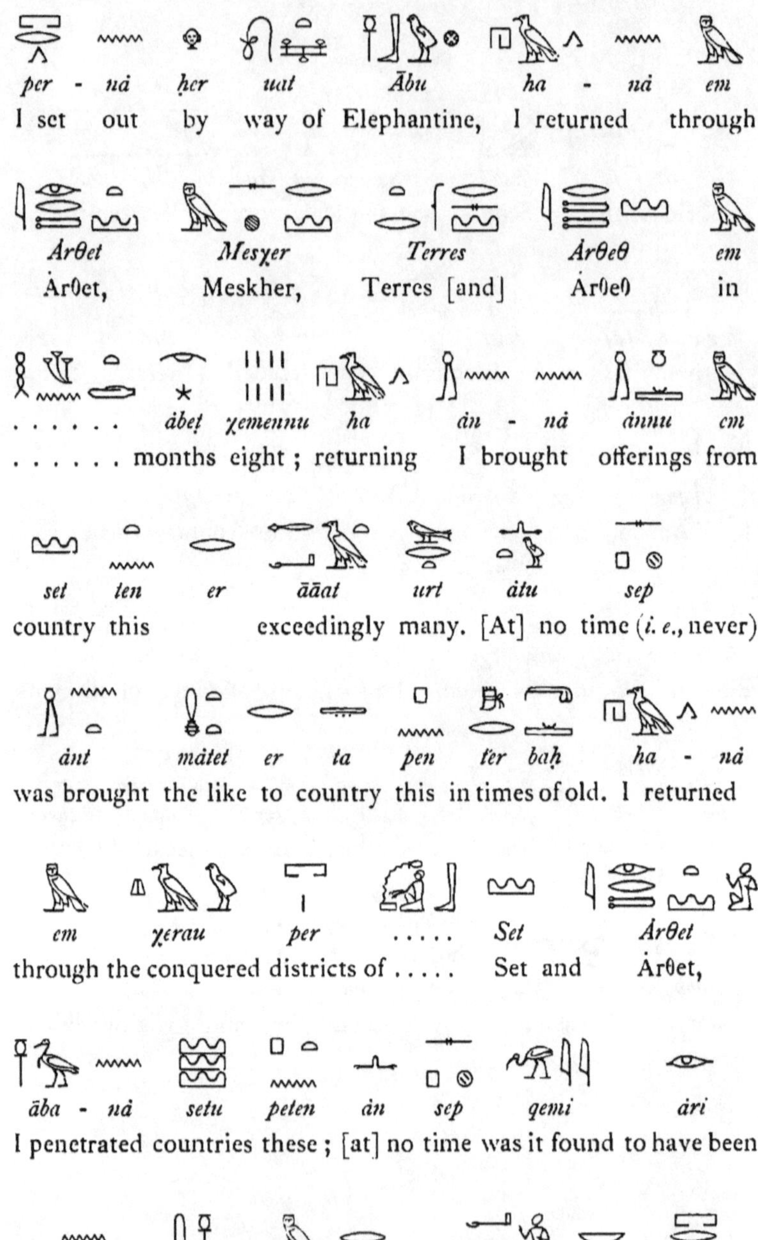

per - nȧ ḥer uat Ābu ha - nȧ em
I set out by way of Elephantine, I returned through

Ȧrθet Mesχer Terres Ȧrθeθ em
Ȧrθet, Meskher, Terres [and] Ȧrθeθ in

. . . . . . ȧbeṭ χemennu ha ȧn - nȧ ȧnnu em
. . . . . . months eight ; returning I brought offerings from

set ten er āāat urt ȧtu sep
country this exceedingly many. [At] no time (*i. e.,* never)

ȧnt mȧtet er ta pen ṭer baḥ ha - nȧ
was brought the like to country this in times of old. I returned

em χerau per . . . . . Set Ȧrθet
through the conquered districts of . . . . . Set and Ȧrθet,

āba - nȧ setu peten ȧn sep qemi ȧri
I penetrated countries these ; [at] no time was it found to have been

en smer mer . . . . . neb per
made by a "friend" and superintendent of . . . . . any an advance

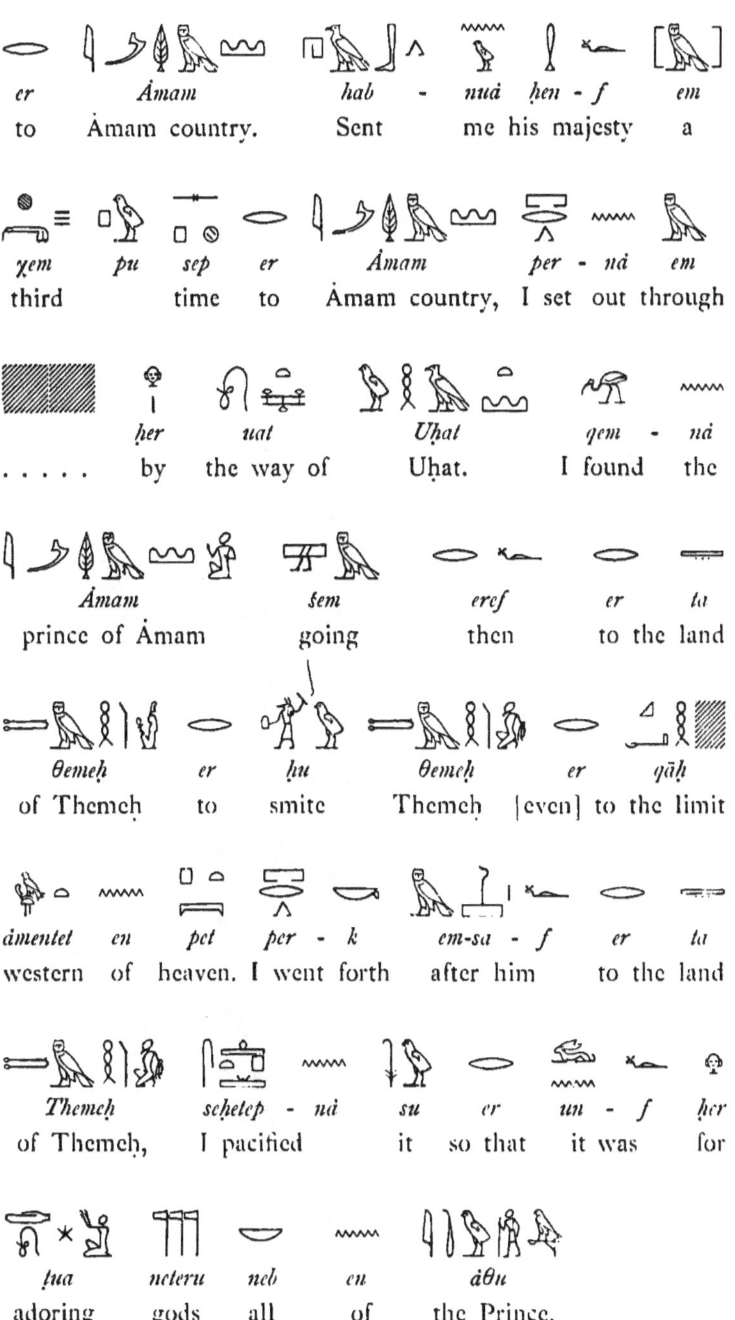

er Åmam hab - nuå ḥen - f em
to Åmam country. Sent me his majesty a

χem pu sep er Åmam per - nå em
third time to Åmam country, I set out through

ḥer uat Uḥat qem - nå
. . . . . by the way of Uḥat. I found the

Åmam šem eref er ta
prince of Åmam going then to the land

θemeḥ er ḥu θemeḥ er qāḥ
of Themeḥ to smite Themeḥ [even] to the limit

åmentet en pet per - k em-sa - f er ta
western of heaven. I went forth after him to the land

Themeḥ seḥetep - nå su er un - f ḥer
of Themeḥ, I pacified it so that it was for

ṭua neteru neb en åθu
adoring gods all of the Prince.

II.

mer ḥen maa ṭenk pu er
Desireth the Majesty to see pigmy this from

ȧnnu en (?) Bata Punt ȧr sper er
the offerings of Bata country and Punt. If thou arrivest at

ta - k er χennu . . . . - k ṭenk pu
thy country [and] at the palace and bringest pigmy this

mā-k ānχ ȧu senb ȧu ḥen er
with thee living being in good condition, is the Majesty for

ȧrit - k en āāat er ȧrit en neter net
making thee greater than was made the treasurer

Ba-ur-Ṭeṭṭeṭ em rek Ȧssȧ χeft ȧuset ȧb
Ba-ur-Tattu in the time of Ȧssa conformably to the desire

ent er maa ṭenk pu
of [the Majesty] to see pigmy this.

FROM THE STELE OF ABU.

[XIth dynasty.]

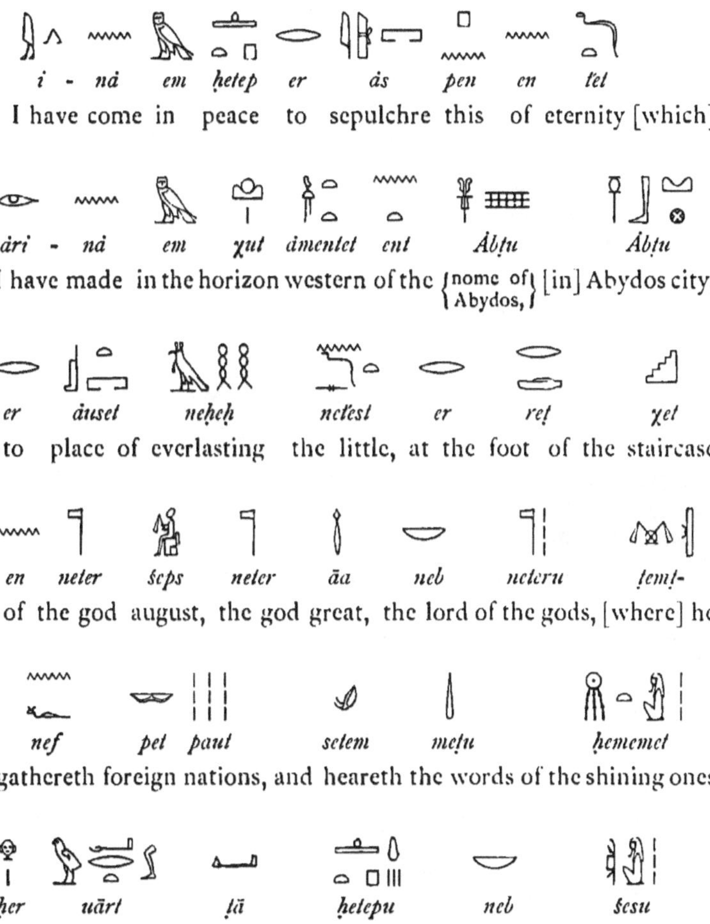

i - nȧ em ḥetep er ȧs pen en t'et
I have come in peace to sepulchre this of eternity [which]

ȧri - nȧ em χut ȧmentet ent Ȧbṭu Ȧbṭu
I have made in the horizon western of the {nome of Abydos,} [in] Abydos city,

er ȧuset neḥeḥ net'est er reṭ χet
to place of everlasting the little, at the foot of the staircase

en neter šeps neter āa neb neteru ṭemṭ-
of the god august, the god great, the lord of the gods, [where] he

nef pet paut setem meṭu ḥememet
gathereth foreign nations, and heareth the words of the shining ones

ḥer uārt ṭā ḥetepu neb šesu
at the passage, the giver of offerings, the lord of divine followers

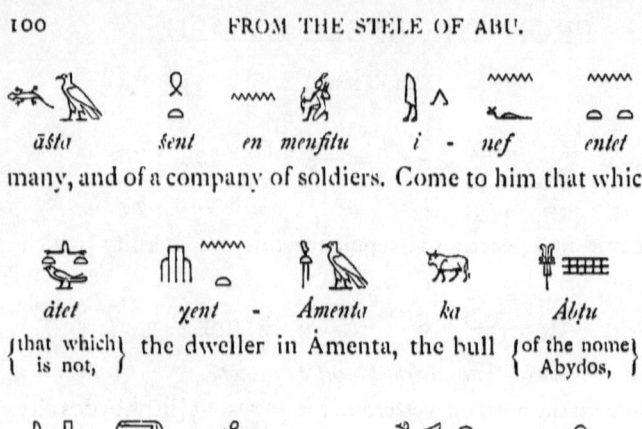

āšta šent en menfitu i - nef entet

many, and of a company of soldiers. Come to him that which is [and]

ȧtet χent - Ȧmenta ka Ȧbṭu neb

{that which is not,} the dweller in Ȧmenta, the bull {of the nome Abydos,} the lord

ȧm baḥ ser pat ḥer ṭep neteru

{of those who are in the presence,} prince of those who have been, ruler of the gods

ṫerti āu neḥeḥ Ḥenti neteru χerp āa

of old, heir everlasting, O Ḥenti of the gods, prince great

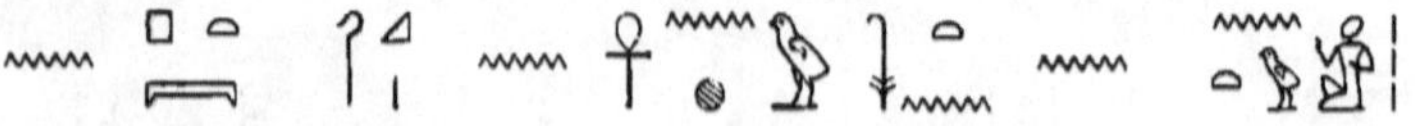

en pet ḥeq en ānχu suten en entu

of heaven, governor of the living, king of those who exist.

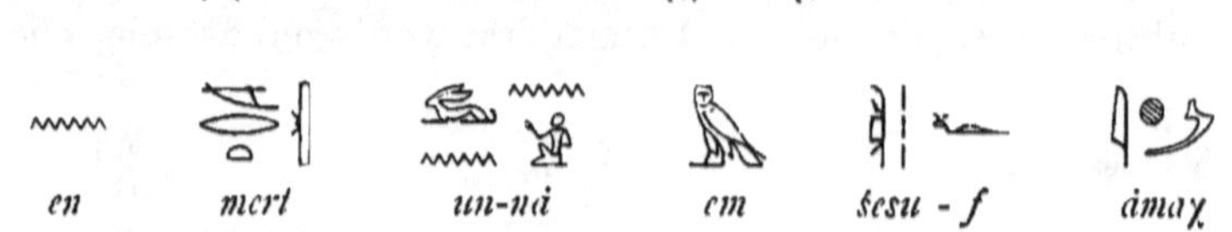

en mert un-nȧ em šesu - f ȧmaχ

Through love of my being among his followers revered,

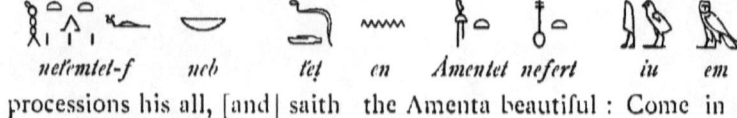

ȧri - ȧ ḥer sešeta em ḥebu - f neb em

I made myself chief of the mysteries at his festivals all, and at

neṫemtet-f neb ṭeṭ en Ȧmentet nefert iu em

processions his all, [and] saith the Amenta beautiful : Come in

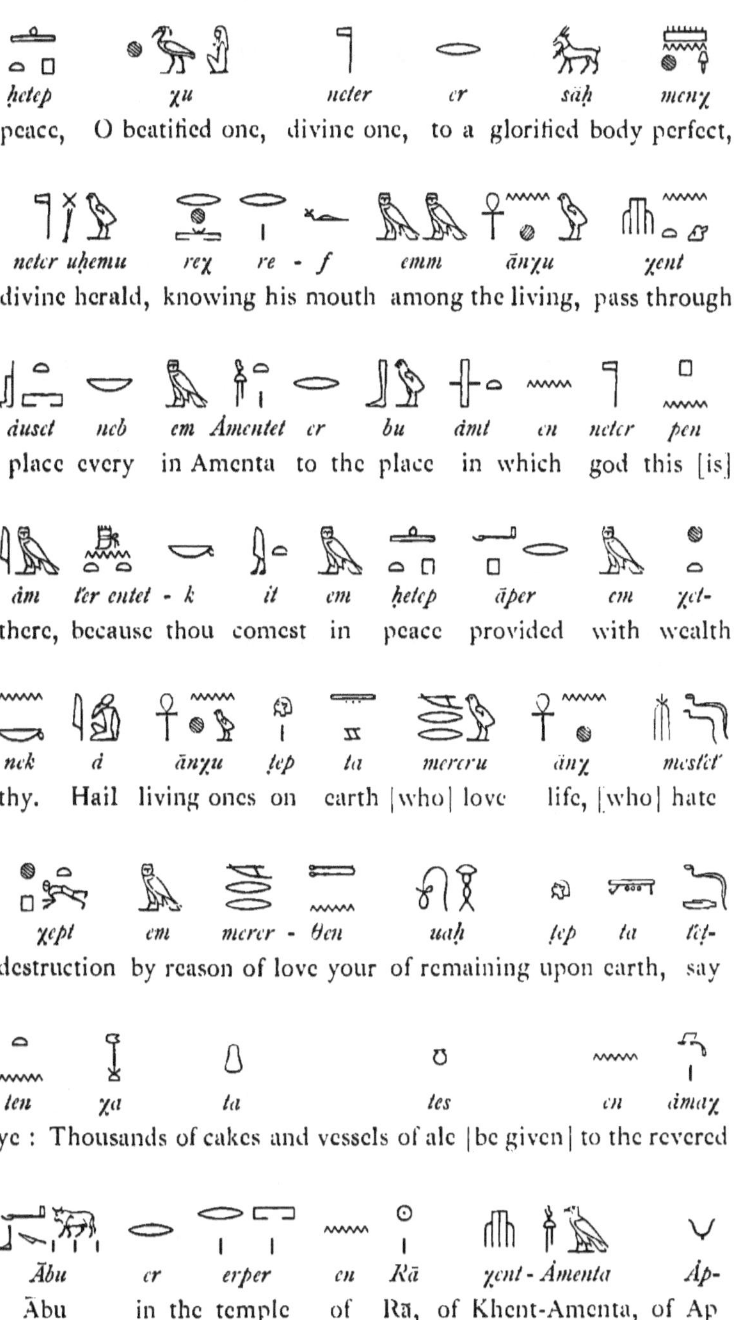

ḥetep *χu* *neter* *er* *sāḥ* *menχ*
peace, O beatified one, divine one, to a glorified body perfect,

neter uḥemu *reχ* *re - f* *emm* *ānχu* *χent*
divine herald, knowing his mouth among the living, pass through

åuset *neb* *em Åmentet* *er* *bu* *åmt* *en* *neter* *pen*
place every in Amenta to the place in which god this [is]

åm *t'er entet - k* *it* *em* *ḥetep* *āper* *em* *χet-*
there, because thou comest in peace provided with wealth

nek *å* *ānχu* *ṭep* *ta* *mereru* *ānχ* *mest'et'*
thy. Hail living ones on earth [who] love life, [who] hate

χept *em* *merer - θen* *uaḥ* *ṭep* *ta* *t'et-*
destruction by reason of love your of remaining upon earth, say

ten *χa* *ta* *tes* *en* *åmaχ*
ye : Thousands of cakes and vessels of ale [be given] to the revered

Ābu *er* *erper* *en* *Rā* *χent - Åmenta* *Åp-*
Ābu in the temple of Rā, of Khent-Amenta, of Ap

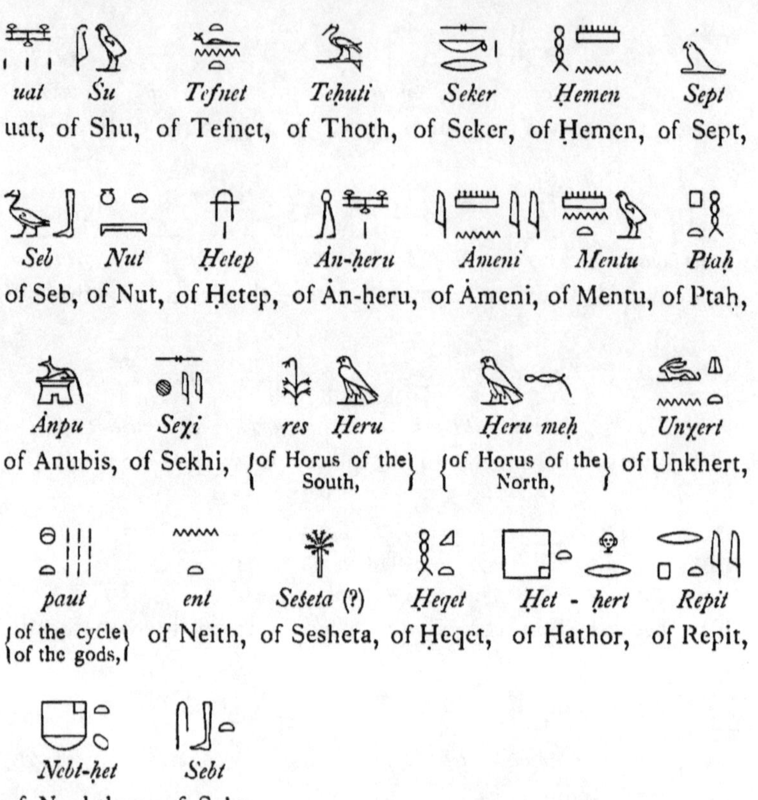

uat *Śu* *Tefnet* *Teḥuti* *Seker* *Ḥemen* *Sept*
uat, of Shu, of Tefnet, of Thoth, of Seker, of Ḥemen, of Sept,

Seb *Nut* *Ḥetep* *Ȧn-ḥeru* *Ȧmeni* *Mentu* *Ptaḥ*
of Seb, of Nut, of Ḥetep, of Ȧn-ḥeru, of Ȧmeni, of Mentu, of Ptaḥ,

Ȧnpu *Seχi* *res Ḥeru* *Ḥeru meḥ* *Unχert*
of Anubis, of Sekhi, {of Horus of the South,} {of Horus of the North,} of Unkhert,

paut *ent* *Seśeta* (?) *Ḥeqet* *Ḥet - ḥert* *Repit*
{of the cycle of the gods,} of Neith, of Sesheta, of Ḥeqet, of Hathor, of Repit,

Nebt-ḥet *Sebt*
of Nephthys, of Sebt.

INSCRIPTION OF ĀṬA.

[XIIth dynasty.]

renpit ābeṭ χemt Śemu hru χemt iut smer uāt

Year .... month three of summer, day three, came the "friend one",

mer āḥ Āṭā er sehat āner en

the overseer of cattle Ata to bring down a stone for

neter meri erpā ḥā χer-ḥeb smer

the god-beloved, {the hereditary prince,} the duke, {the chief reader,} the "friend

uāt mer res mer neter ḥen

one", the governor of the south, the overseer of the priests

Āmsu ṭatu - āqer āu seha - ni nef āner

of Amsu (or Min), Tchaut - àqer. I brought down to him a stone

meḥ XII em sa CC āu ān - nā

of cubits twelve with men two hundred, I brought

āḥ sen maḥeṭ L ār ṭua

oxen two, gazelles fifty, stags five.

ADDRESS TO THE LIVING BY KHNEMU-ḤETEP.

From his tomb at Beni-hasan.

[XIIth dynasty.]

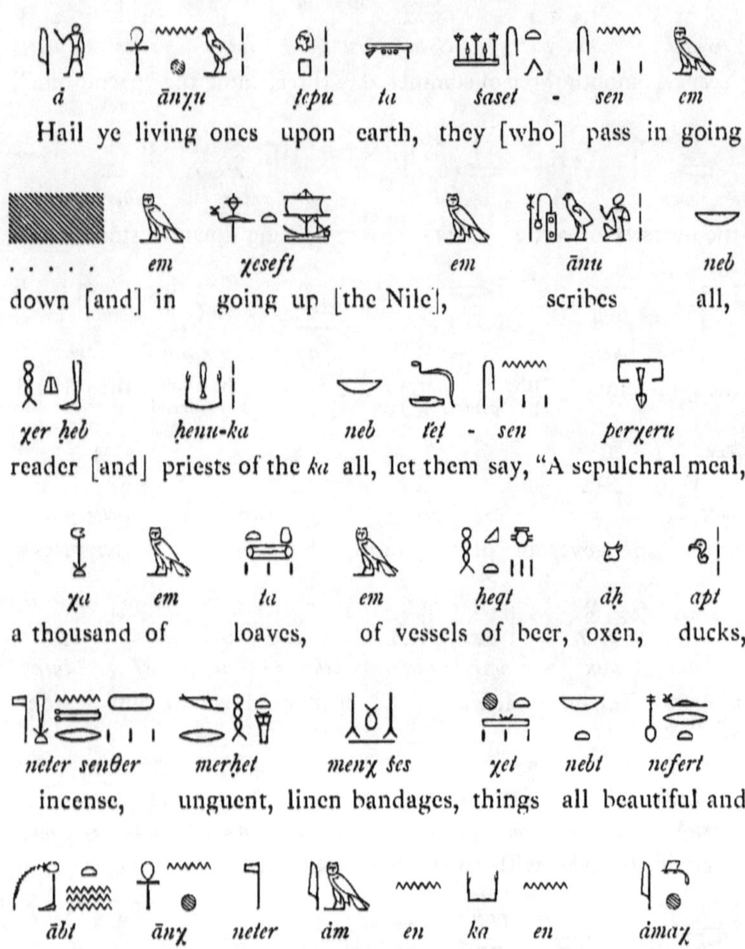

ȧ ānχu ṭepu ta šaset - sen em

Hail ye living ones upon earth, they [who] pass in going

. . . . . em χeseft em ānu neb

down [and] in going up [the Nile], scribes all,

χer ḥeb ḥenu-ka neb ṫeṭ - sen perχeru

reader [and] priests of the *ka* all, let them say, "A sepulchral meal,

χa em ta em ḥeqt ȧḥ apt

a thousand of loaves, of vessels of beer, oxen, ducks,

neter senθer merḥet menχ šes χet nebt nefert

incense, unguent, linen bandages, things all beautiful and

ābt ānχ neter ȧm en ka en ȧmaχ

pure liveth god on them to the *ka* of the revered one,

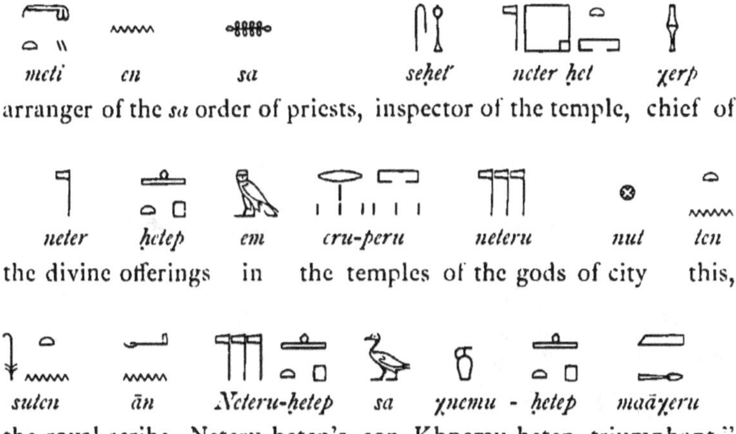

meti en sa sehet' neter ḥet χerp

arranger of the *sa* order of priests, inspector of the temple, chief of

neter ḥetep em eru-peru neteru nut ten

the divine offerings in the temples of the gods of city this,

suten ān Neteru-ḥetep sa χnemu - ḥetep maāχeru

the royal scribe, Neteru-ḥetep's son Khnemu-ḥetep, triumphant."

FROM THE TOMB OF ÀMENI-EM-ḤĀT AT BENI-HASAN.

[XIIth dynasty.]

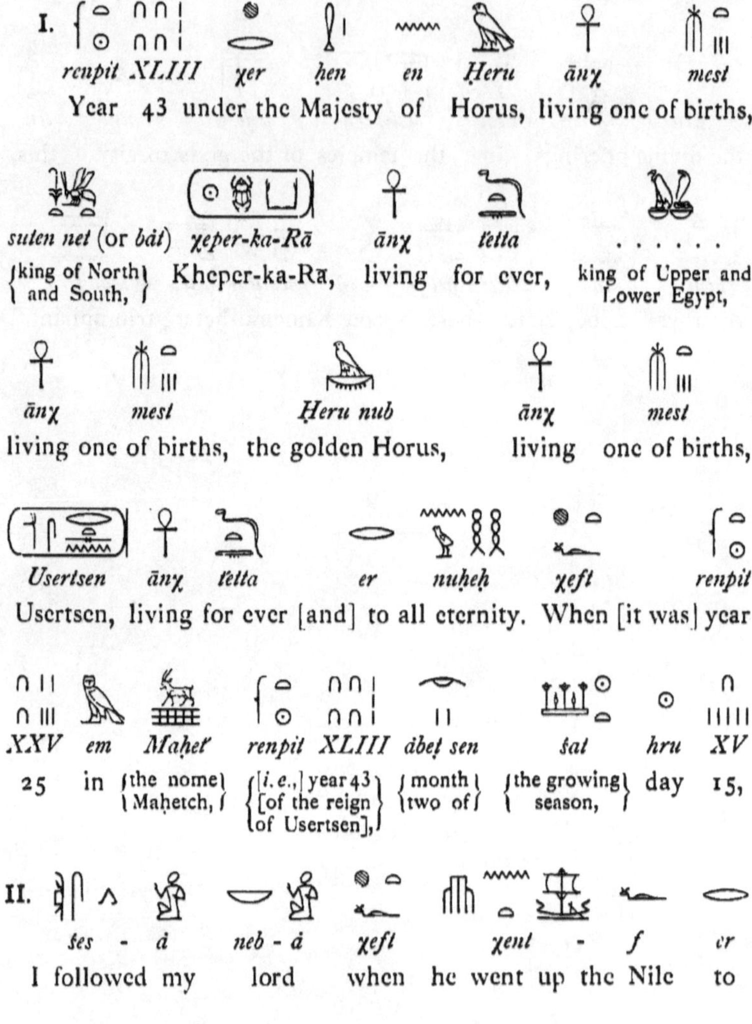

I. *renpit XLIII χer ḥen en Ḥeru ānχ mest*
Year 43 under the Majesty of Horus, living one of births,

suten net (or *bàt*) *χeper-ka-Rā ānχ t'etta . . . . . .*
{king of North and South,} Kheper-ka-Rā, living for ever, king of Upper and Lower Egypt,

ānχ mest Ḥeru nub ānχ mest
living one of births, the golden Horus, living one of births,

Usertsen ānχ t'etta er nuḥeḥ χeft renpit
Usertsen, living for ever [and] to all eternity. When [it was] year

XXV em Maḥet' renpit XLIII àbeṭ sen šat hru XV
25 in {the nome Maḥetch,} {[*i.e.*,] year 43 [of the reign of Usertsen],} {month two of} {the growing season,} day 15,

II. *šes - à neb - à χeft χent - f er*
I followed my lord when he went up the Nile to

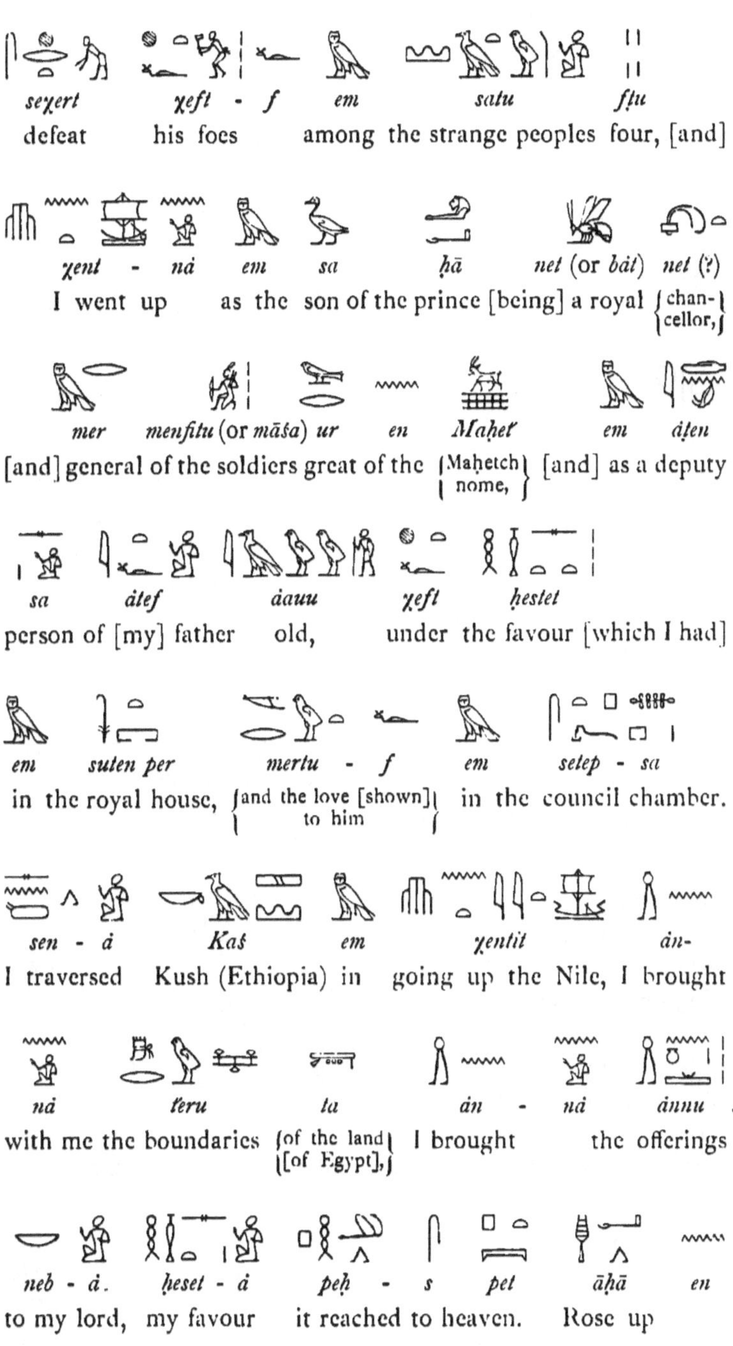

seχert *χeft* - *f* *em* *satu* *fṭu*
defeat his foes among the strange peoples four, [and]

χent - *nà* *em* *sa* *ḥā* *net* (or *bàt*) *net* (?)
I went up as the son of the prince [being] a royal {chan-cellor,}

mer *menfitu* (or *māša*) *ur* *en* *Maḥet* *em* *àṭen*
[and] general of the soldiers great of the {Maḥetch nome,} [and] as a deputy

sa *àtef* *àauu* *χeft* *ḥestet*
person of [my] father old, under the favour [which I had]

em *suten per* *mertu* - *f* *em* *setep* - *sa*
in the royal house, {and the love [shown] to him} in the council chamber.

sen - *à* *Kaš* *em* *χentit* *àn*-
I traversed Kush (Ethiopia) in going up the Nile, I brought

nà *ṭeru* *ta* *àn* - *nà* *ànnu*.
with me the boundaries {of the land [of Egypt],} I brought the offerings

neb - *à*. *ḥeset* - *à* *peḥ* - *s* *pet* *āḥā* *en*
to my lord, my favour it reached to heaven. Rose up

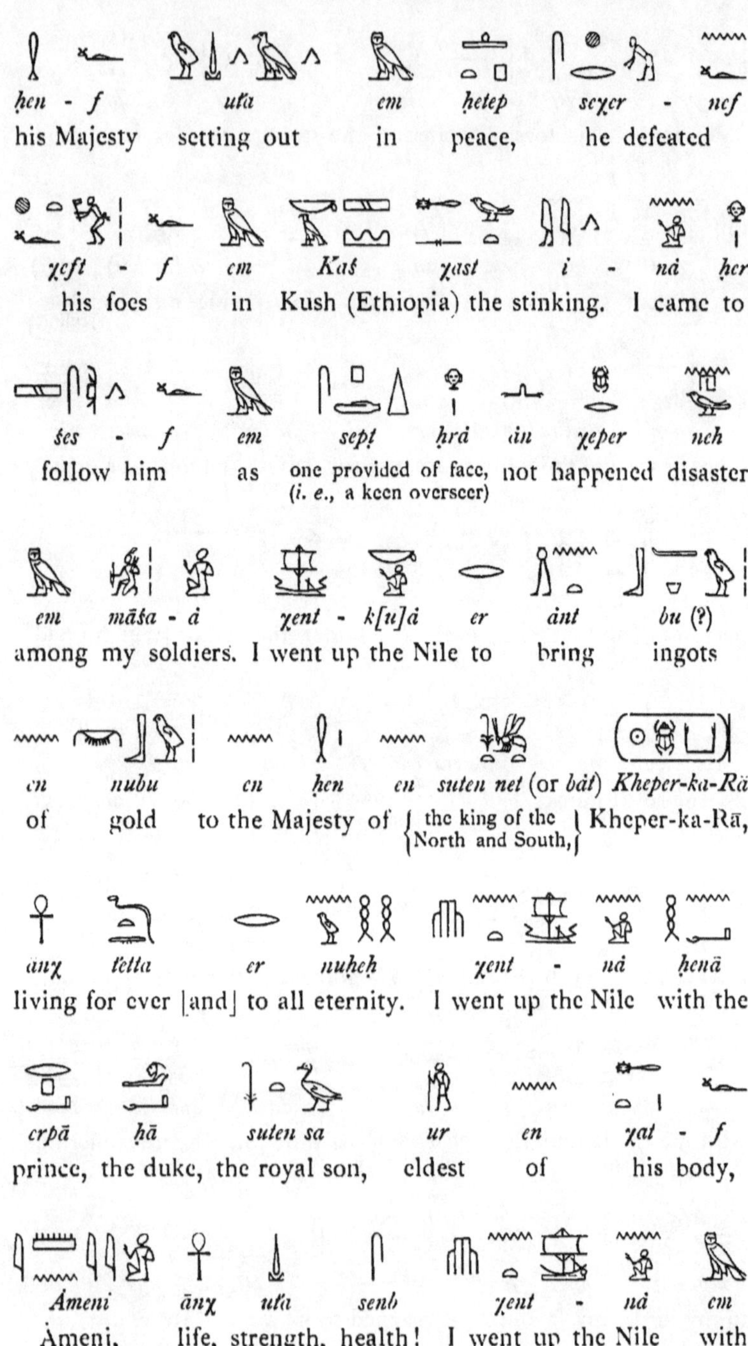

ḥen - f uṫa em ḥetep seχer - nef

his Majesty setting out in peace, he defeated

χeft - f em Kaš χast i - nȧ ḥer

his foes in Kush (Ethiopia) the stinking. I came to

šes - f em sepṭ ḥrȧ ȧn χeper neh

follow him as one provided of face, (*i. e.*, a keen overseer) not happened disaster

em māša - ȧ χent - k[u]ȧ er ȧnt bu (?)

among my soldiers. I went up the Nile to bring ingots

en nubu en ḥen en suten net (or *bȧt*) *Kheper-ka-Rā*

of gold to the Majesty of {the king of the North and South,} Kheper-ka-Rā,

ȧnχ ṫetta er nuḥeḥ χent - nȧ ḥenā

living for ever [and] to all eternity. I went up the Nile with the

erpā ḥā suten sa ur en χat - f

prince, the duke, the royal son, eldest of his body,

Àmeni ānχ uṫa senb χent - nȧ em

Àmeni, life, strength, health! I went up the Nile with

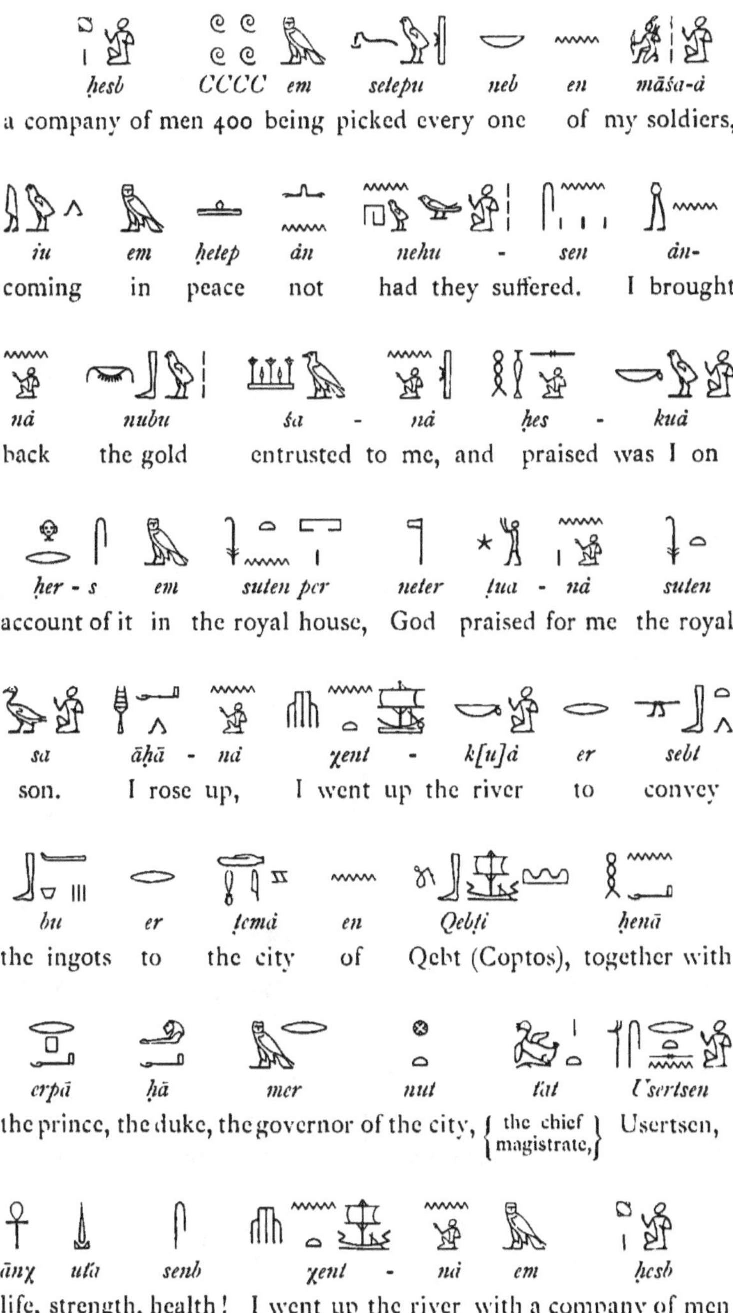

ḥesb CCCC em setepu neb en māša-à
a company of men 400 being picked every one of my soldiers,

iu em ḥetep àn nehu - sen àn-
coming in peace not had they suffered. I brought

nà nubu ša - nà ḥes - kuà
back the gold entrusted to me, and praised was I on

ḥer - s em suten per neter ṭua - nà suten
account of it in the royal house, God praised for me the royal

sa āḥā - nà χent - k[u]à er sebt
son. I rose up, I went up the river to convey

bu er ṭemà en Qebṭi ḥenā
the ingots to the city of Qebt (Coptos), together with

erpā ḥā mer nut ṭat Usertsen
the prince, the duke, the governor of the city, {the chief magistrate,} Usertsen,

ānχ uṭa senb χent - nà em ḥesb
life, strength, health! I went up the river with a company of men

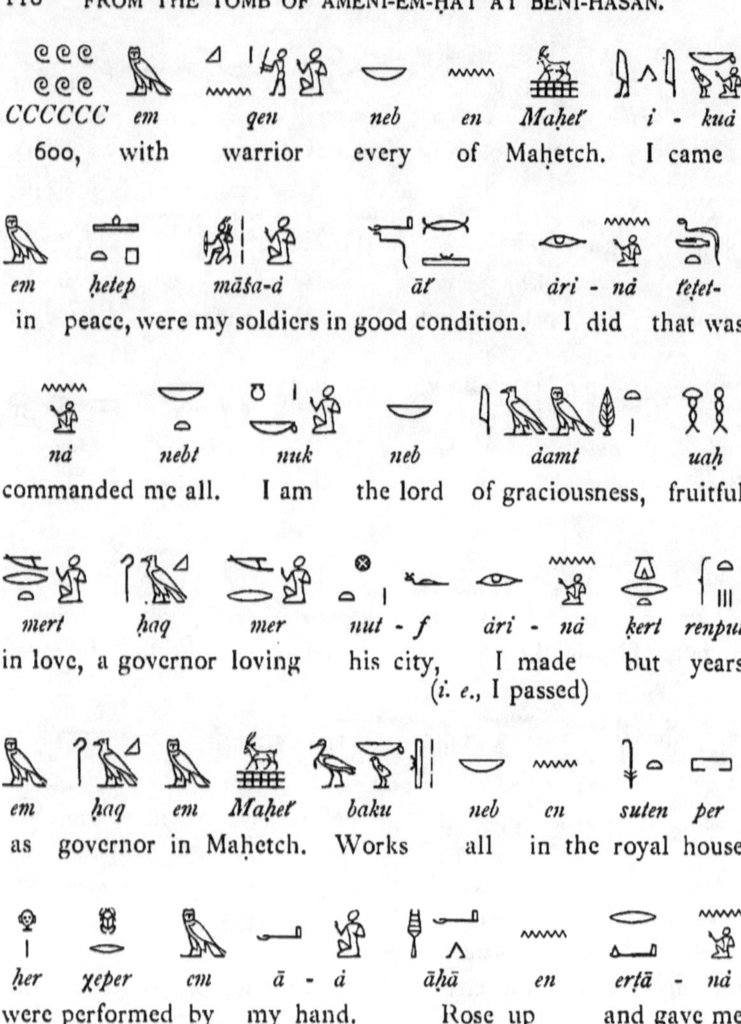

CCCCCC em qen neb en Maheť i - kuȧ
600, with warrior every of Maḥetch. I came

em ḥetep māša-ȧ āť ȧri - nȧ ťeṭet-
in peace, were my soldiers in good condition. I did that was

nȧ nebt nuk neb ȧamt uaḥ
commanded me all. I am the lord of graciousness, fruitful

mert ḥaq mer nut - f ȧri - nȧ ḳert renput
in love, a governor loving his city, I made but years
(*i. e.*, I passed)

em ḥaq em Maḥeť baku neb en suten per
as governor in Maḥetch. Works all in the royal house

ḥer χeper em ā - ȧ āḥā en erṭā - nȧ
were performed by my hand. Rose up and gave me

mer θest en ḳesu (?) per nu sau
the governor of the companies of the pasture houses of the shepherds

nu Maḥeť ka MMM em nuḥbu - sen
of Maḥetch bulls three thousand of their yoke animals,

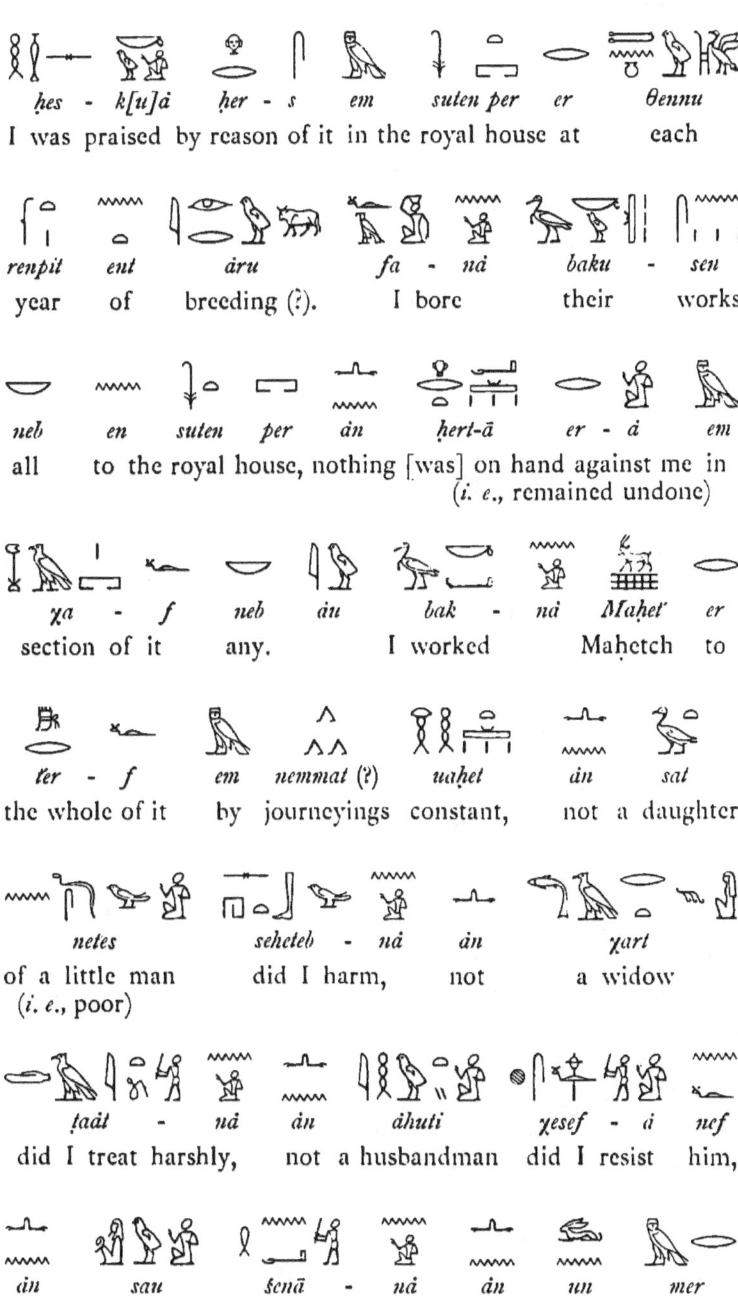

ḥes - k[u]à ḥer - s em suten per er θennu
I was praised by reason of it in the royal house at each

renpit ent àru fa - nà baku - sen
year of breeding (?). I bore their works

neb en suten per àn ḥert-ā er - à em
all to the royal house, nothing [was] on hand against me in
(*i. e.*, remained undone)

χa - f neb àn bak - nà Maḥet' er
section of it any. I worked Maḥetch to

t'er - f em nemmat (?) uaḥet àn sat
the whole of it by journeyings constant, not a daughter

netes seheteb - nà àn χart
of a little man did I harm, not a widow
(*i. e.*, poor)

ṭaàt - nà àn àhuti χesef - à nef
did I treat harshly, not a husbandman did I resist him,

àn sau šenā - nà àn un mer
not a shepherd did I turn back, not existed overseer

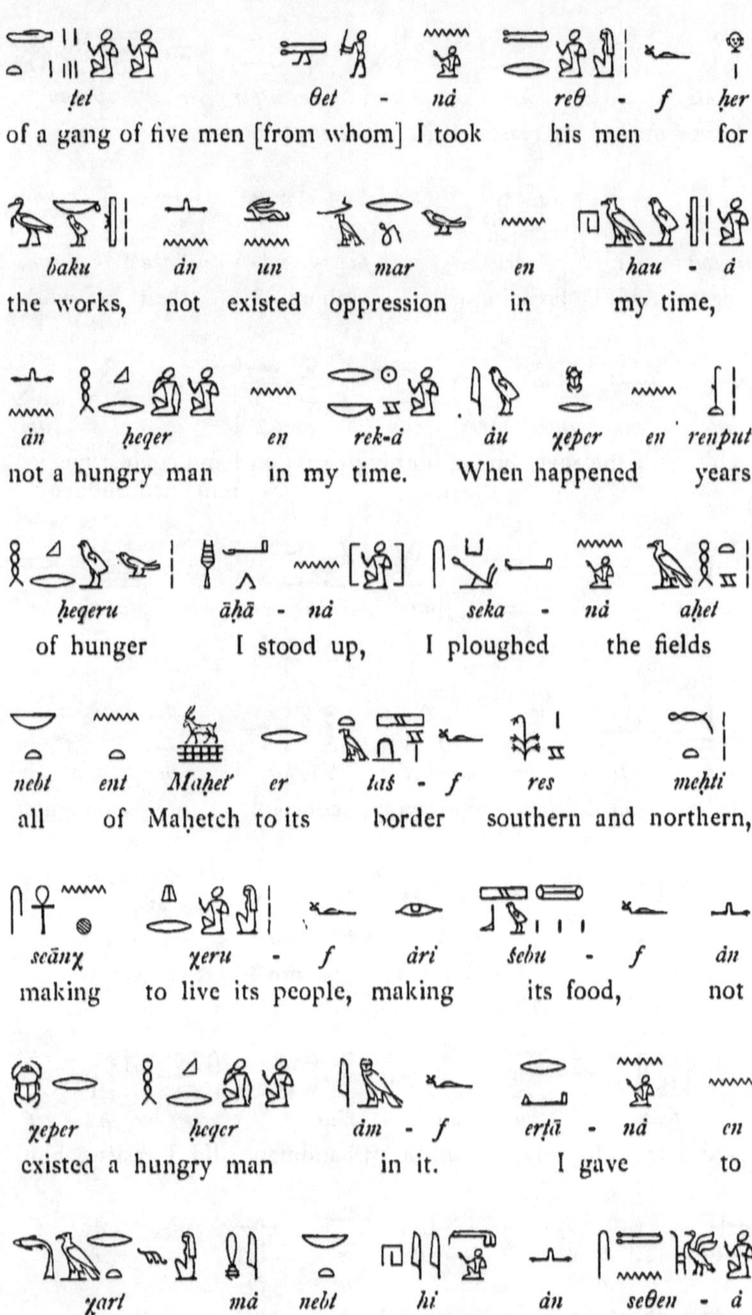

ṭet θet - nȧ reθ - f ḥer

of a gang of five men [from whom] I took his men for

baku ȧn un mar en hau - ȧ

the works, not existed oppression in my time,

ȧn ḥeqer en rek-ȧ ȧu χeper en renput

not a hungry man in my time. When happened years

ḥeqeru āḥā - nȧ seka - nȧ aḥet

of hunger I stood up, I ploughed the fields

nebt ent Maḥet' er taš - f res meḥti

all of Maḥetch to its border southern and northern,

seānχ χeru - f ȧri šebu - f ȧn

making to live its people, making its food, not

χeper ḥeqer ȧm - f erṭā - nȧ en

existed a hungry man in it. I gave to

χart mȧ nebt hi ȧn seθen - ȧ

the widow as to the possessor of a husband, not did I magnify

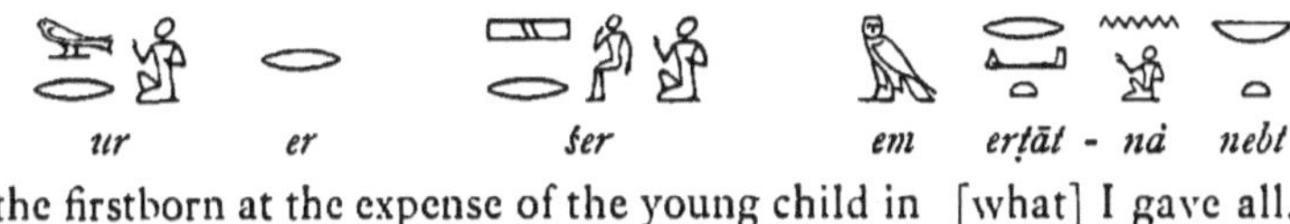

ur *er* *šer* *em* *erṭāt - nȧ* *nebt*

the firstborn at the expense of the young child in [what] I gave all.

āḥā *en* *Ḥāp* *er* *mu* *uru* *χeper*

[When] rose Ḥāpi with waters great happened,
(*i. e.*, when an abundant inundation took place)

nebu *pertu* *beti* *nebu* *χet* *neb* *ȧn*

the lords of wheat and barley, the lords of things all, not

sešeṭ - ȧ *ḥer-ā* *ent* *ȧḥet*

did I cut off the surplus growth of the field.
(*i. e.*, deduct for myself)

STORIES OF THE REIGNS OF SENEFERU AND KHUFU (CHEOPS).

[Early XVIIIth dynasty.]

āḥā en ṭeṭ en χer ḥeb ḥeri
Rose up spake the reader chief,

Ṭaṭa - em - ānχ ṭeṭet - nef em ḥekau
Tchatcha-em-ānkh, his words of magical power,

āḥā en erṭā - nef ermen en mu en pa
[and] he placed [one] side of the water of the

še ḥer uāu - sen qem - nef pa
pool upon each other, he found the

neχau uaḥ ḥer pa qit āḥā en
ornament lying upon the stone; rose up

àn - nef su erṭā en ḥent - f àst eref
he brought up it [and] gave [it] to his mistress. Behold now

àr pa mu àu-f em meḥ XII ḥer
the water was it of cubits twelve at

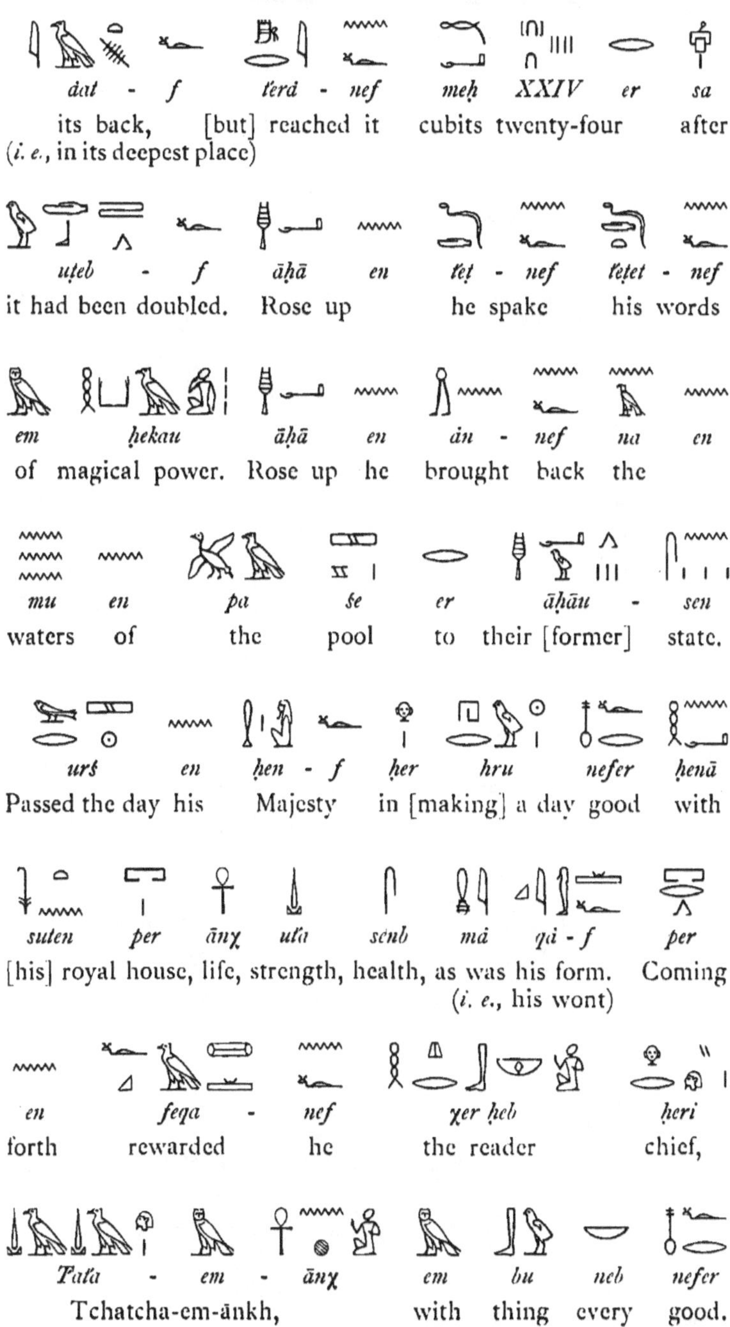

ȧat - f ṭerȧ - nef meḥ XXIV er sa
its back, [but] reached it cubits twenty-four after
(*i. e.*, in its deepest place)

uṭeb - f āḥā en ṭeṭ - nef ṭeṭet - nef
it had been doubled. Rose up he spake his words

em ḥekau āḥā en ȧn - nef na en
of magical power. Rose up he brought back the

mu en pa śe er āḥāu - sen
waters of the pool to their [former] state.

urś en ḥen - f ḥer hru nefer ḥenā
Passed the day his Majesty in [making] a day good with

suten per ānχ uṭa senb mȧ qi - f per
[his] royal house, life, strength, health, as was his form. Coming
(*i. e.*, his wont)

en feqa - nef χer ḥeb ḥeri
forth rewarded he the reader chief,

Ṭaṭa - em - ānχ em bu neb nefer
Tchatcha-em-ānkh, with thing every good.

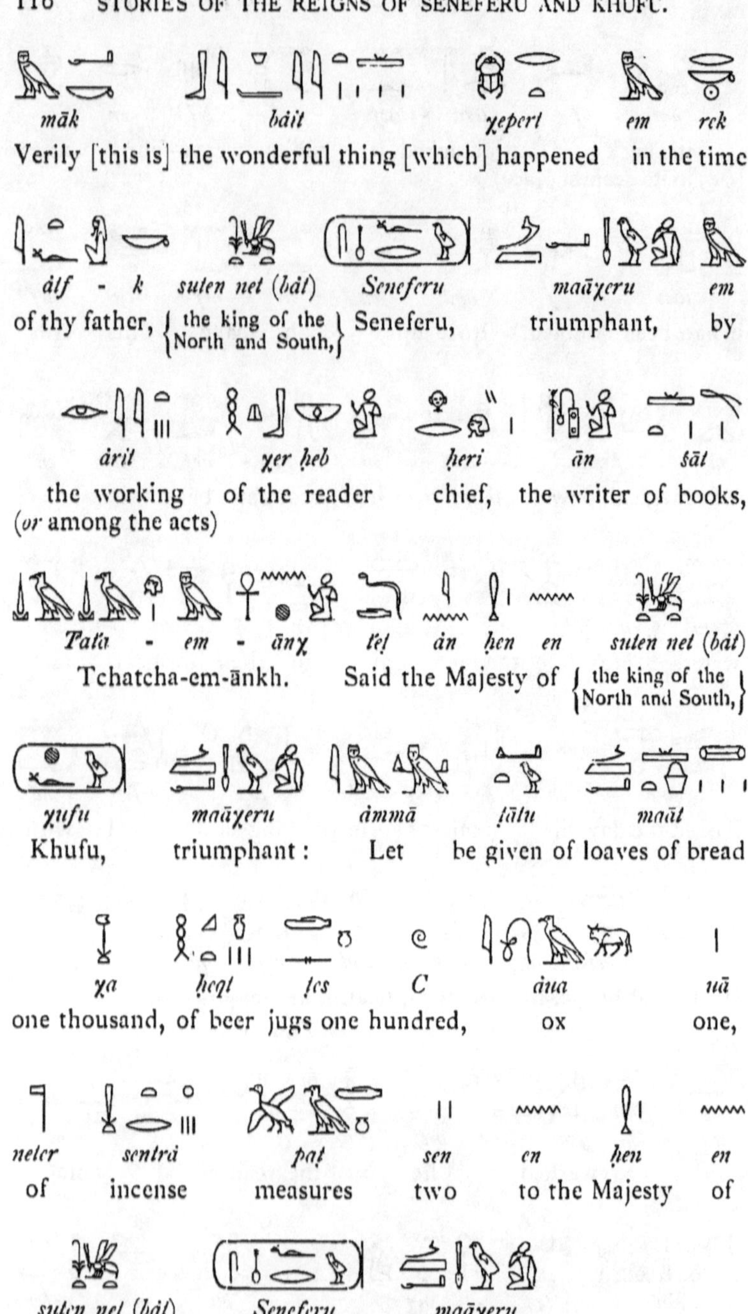
māk bāit χepert em rek
Verily [this is] the wonderful thing [which] happened in the time
àtf - k suten net (bàt) Seneferu maāχeru em
of thy father, {the king of the North and South,} Seneferu, triumphant, by
àrit χer ḥeb ḥeri ān šāt
the working of the reader chief, the writer of books,
(or among the acts)
Tata - em - ānχ t'et àn ḥen en suten net (bàt)
Tchatcha-em-ānkh. Said the Majesty of {the king of the North and South,}
χufu maāχeru àmmā ṭātu maāt
Khufu, triumphant: Let be given of loaves of bread
χa ḥeqt ṭes C àua uā
one thousand, of beer jugs one hundred, ox one,
neter sentrà paṭ sen en ḥen en
of incense measures two to the Majesty of
suten net (bàt) Seneferu maāχeru
{the king of the North and South,} Seneferu, triumphant.

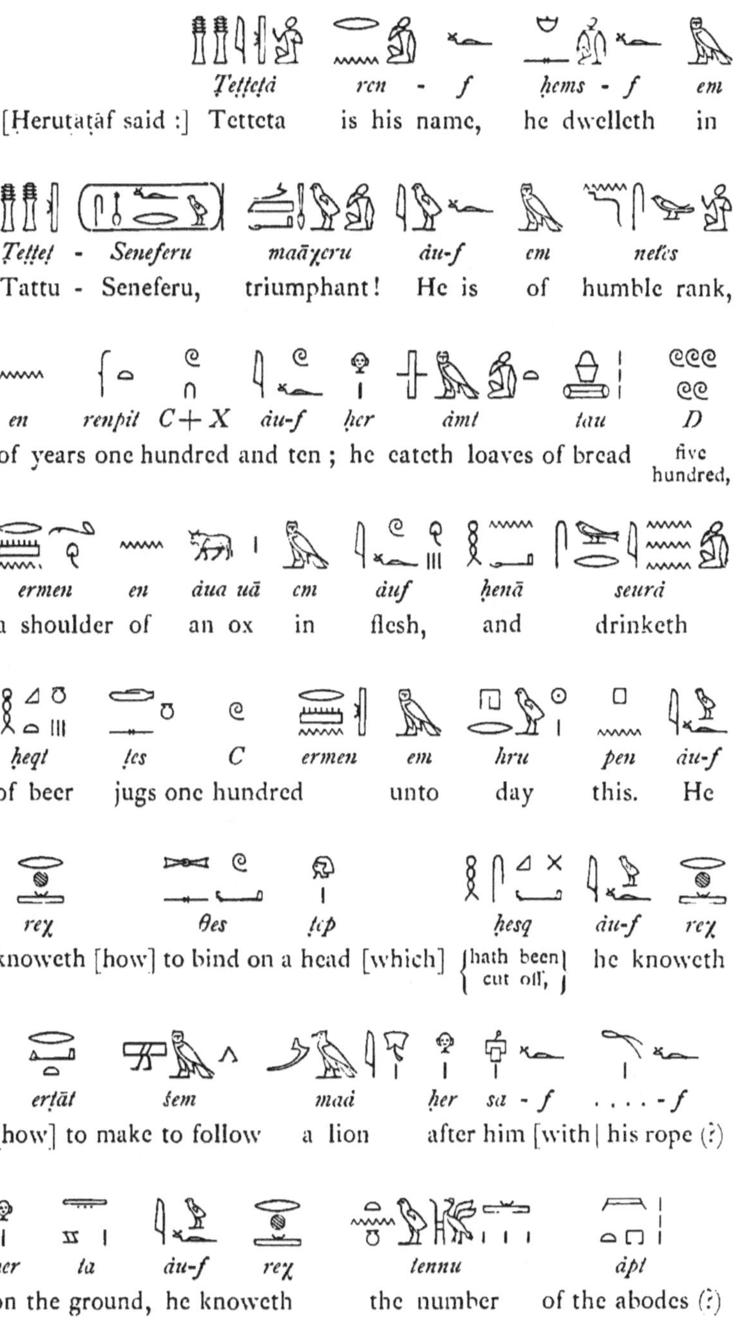

Ṭeṭṭetȧ *ren - f* *ḥems - f* *em*

[Ḥeruṭaṭāf said :] Tetteta is his name, he dwelleth in

Ṭeṭṭeṭ - Seneferu *maāχeru* *ȧu-f* *em* *neṭes*

Tattu - Seneferu, triumphant! He is of humble rank,

en *renpit* *C + X* *ȧu-f* *ḥer* *ȧmt* *tau* *D*

of years one hundred and ten ; he eateth loaves of bread five hundred,

ermen *en* *ȧua uā* *em* *ȧuf* *ḥenā* *seurȧ*

a shoulder of an ox in flesh, and drinketh

ḥeqt *ṭes* *C* *ermen* *em* *hru* *pen* *ȧu-f*

of beer jugs one hundred unto day this. He

reχ *θes* *ṭep* *ḥesq* *ȧu-f* *reχ*

knoweth [how] to bind on a head [which] {hath been cut off,} he knoweth

erṭāt *šem* *maȧ* *ḥer* *sa - f* *. . . . - f*

[how] to make to follow a lion after him [with] his rope (?)

ḥer *ta* *ȧu-f* *reχ* *tennu* *ȧpt*

on the ground, he knoweth the number of the abodes (?)

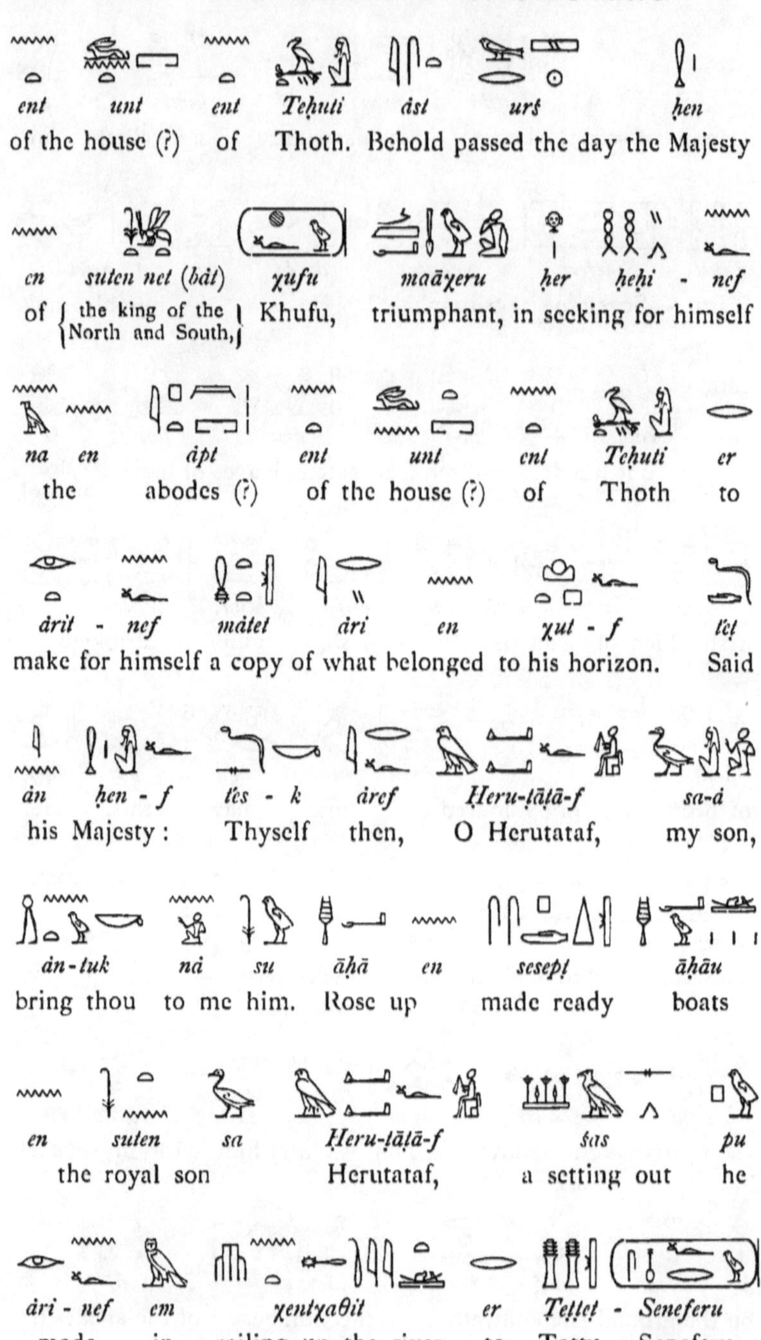

ent unt ent Teḥuti ȧst urš ḥen
of the house (?) of Thoth. Behold passed the day the Majesty

en suten net (bȧt) χufu maāχeru ḥer ḥeḥi - nef
of {the king of the North and South,} Khufu, triumphant, in seeking for himself

na en ȧpt ent unt ent Teḥuti er
the abodes (?) of the house (?) of Thoth to

ȧrit - nef mȧtet ȧri en χut - f t'eṭ
make for himself a copy of what belonged to his horizon. Said

ȧn ḥen - f t'es - k ȧref Ḥeru-ṭāṭā-f sa-ȧ
his Majesty: Thyself then, O Herutataf, my son,

ȧn - tuk nȧ su āḥā en sesepṭ āḥāu
bring thou to me him. Rose up made ready boats

en suten sa Ḥeru-ṭāṭā-f šas pu
the royal son Herutataf, a setting out he

ȧri - nef em χentχaθit er Ṭeṭṭeṭ - Seneferu
made in sailing up the river to Tattu - Seneferu,

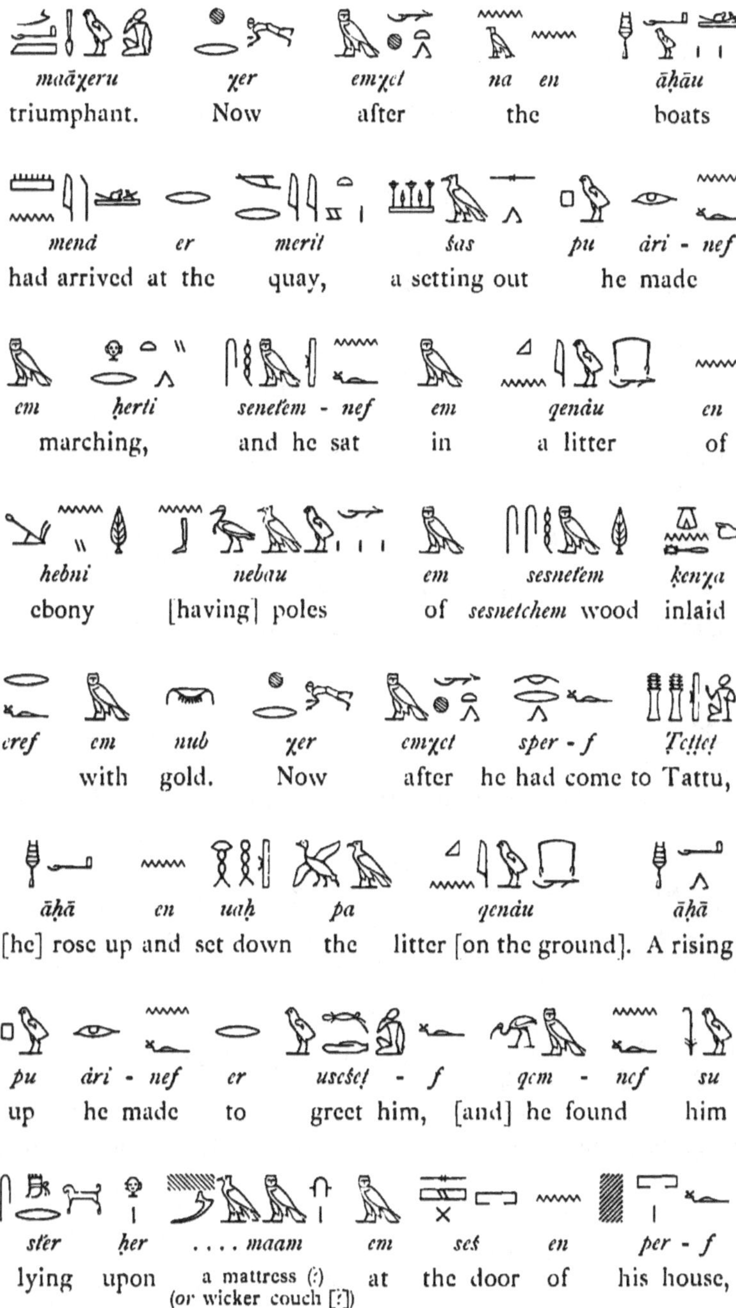

maāχeru *χer* *emχet* *na en* *āḥāu*
triumphant. Now after the boats

mend *er* *merit* *ṡas* *pu* *ȧri - nef*
had arrived at the quay, a setting out he made

em *ḥerti* *seneṭem - nef* *em* *qenȧu* *en*
marching, and he sat in a litter of

hebni *nebau* *em* *sesneṭem* *ḳenχa*
ebony [having] poles of *sesnetchem* wood inlaid

eref *em* *nub* *χer* *emχet* *sper - f* *Ṭeṭṭeṭ*
with gold. Now after he had come to Tattu,

āḥā *en* *uaḥ* *pa* *qenȧu* *āḥā*
[he] rose up and set down the litter [on the ground]. A rising

pu *ȧri - nef* *er* *useśeṭ - f* *qem - nef* *su*
up he made to greet him, [and] he found him

sṭer *ḥer* *. . . . maam* *em* *seś* *en* *per - f*
lying upon a mattress (?) (or wicker couch [?]) at the door of his house,

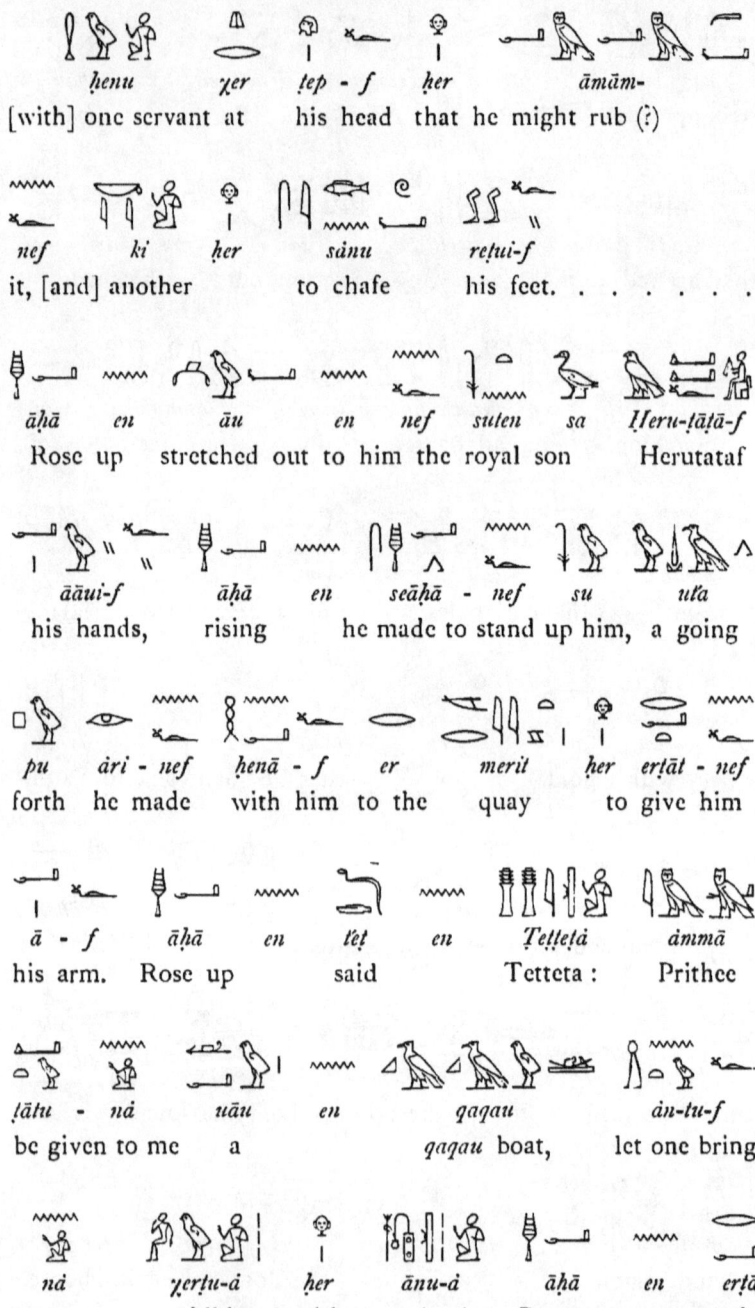

ḥenu χer ṭep - f ḥer āmām-
[with] one servant at his head that he might rub (?)

nef ki ḥer sȧnu reṭui-f
it, [and] another to chafe his feet. . . . . . .

āḥā en āu en nef suten sa Ḥeru-ṭāṭā-f
Rose up stretched out to him the royal son Herutataf

āāui-f āḥā en seāḥā - nef su uťa
his hands, rising he made to stand up him, a going

pu ȧri - nef ḥenā - f er merit ḥer erṭāt - nef
forth he made with him to the quay to give him

ā - f āḥā en ťeṭ en Ṭeṭṭeṭȧ ȧmmā
his arm. Rose up said Tetteta: Prithee

ṭātu - nȧ uāu en qaqau ȧn-tu-f
be given to me a *qaqau* boat, let one bring

nȧ χerṭu-ȧ ḥer ānu-ȧ āḥā en erṭā
to me my children with my books. Rose up was made

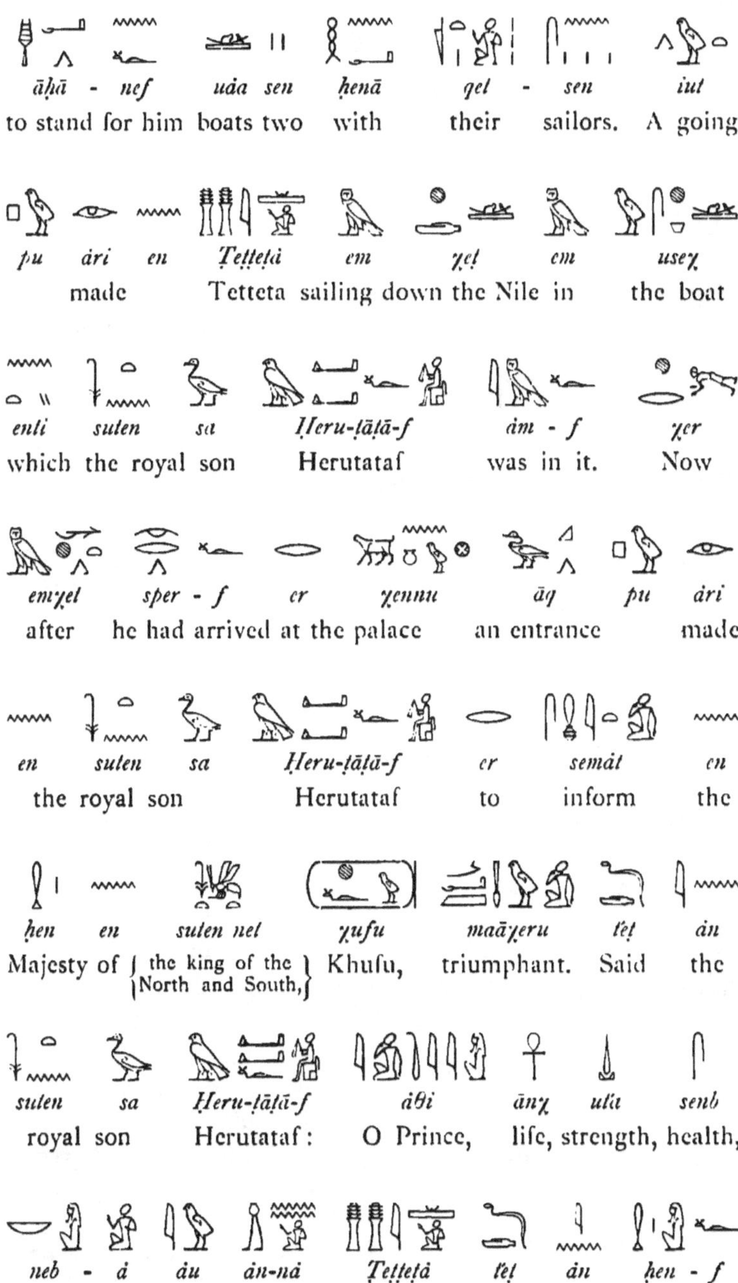
āḥā - nef uȧa sen ḥenā qet - sen iut
to stand for him boats two with their sailors. A going
pu ȧri en Ṭeṭṭeṭȧ em χet em useχ
made Tetteta sailing down the Nile in the boat
enti suten sa Ḥeru-ṭāṭā-f ȧm - f χer
which the royal son Herutataf was in it. Now
emχet sper - f er χennu āq pu ȧri
after he had arrived at the palace an entrance made
en suten sa Ḥeru-ṭāṭā-f er semȧt en
the royal son Herutataf to inform the
ḥen en suten net χufu maāχeru ṭeṭ ȧn
Majesty of {the king of the North and South,} Khufu, triumphant. Said the
suten sa Ḥeru-ṭāṭā-f ȧθi ānχ uṭa senb
royal son Herutataf: O Prince, life, strength, health,
neb - ȧ ȧu ȧn-nȧ Ṭeṭṭeṭȧ ṭeṭ ȧn ḥen - f
my lord, I have brought Tetteta. Said his Majesty:

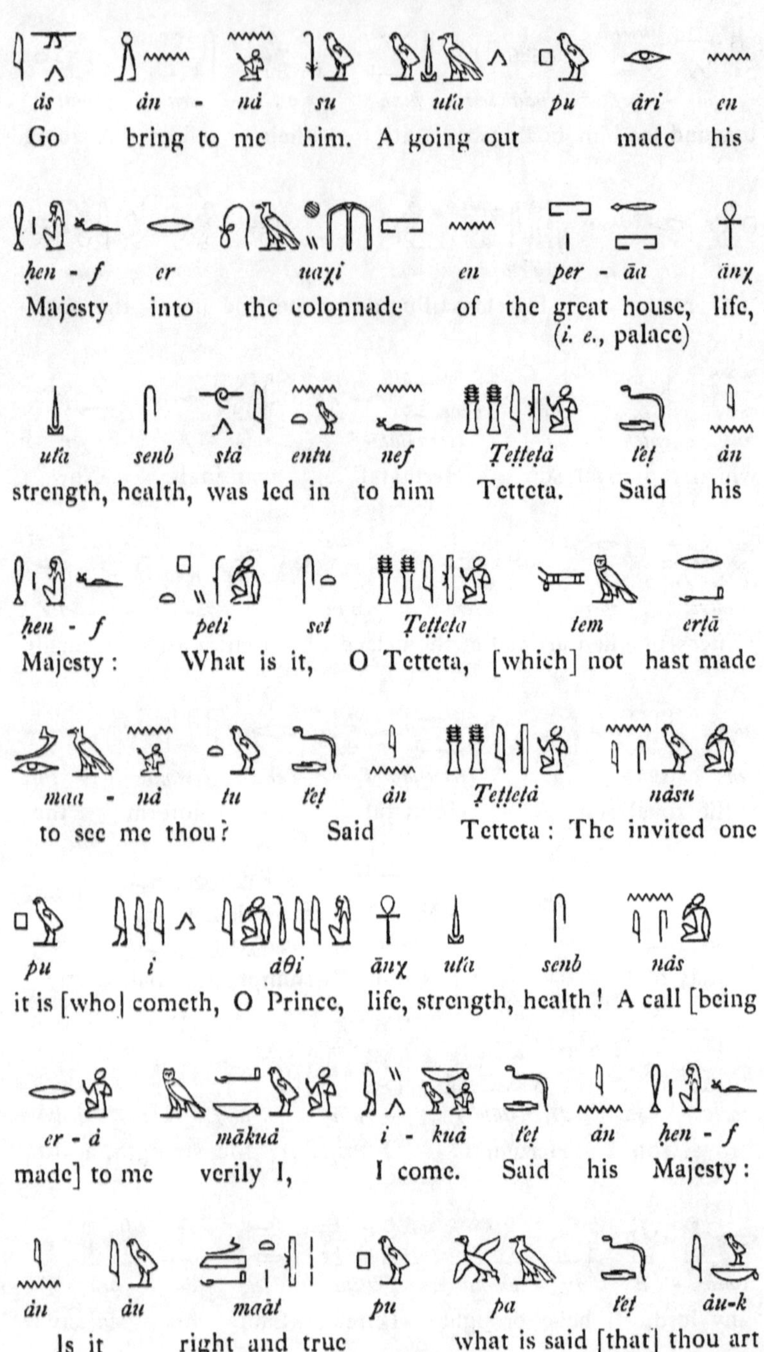

ȧs ȧn - nȧ su uṭa pu ȧri en

Go bring to me him. A going out made his

ḥen - f er uaχi en per - āa ānχ

Majesty into the colonnade of the great house, life,
(*i. e.*, palace)

uṭa senb stȧ entu nef Ṭeṭṭeṭȧ ṭeṭ ȧn

strength, health, was led in to him Tetteta. Said his

ḥen - f peti set Ṭeṭṭeṭa tem erṭā

Majesty: What is it, O Tetteta, [which] not hast made

maa - nȧ tu ṭeṭ ȧn Ṭeṭṭeṭȧ nȧsu

to see me thou? Said Tetteta: The invited one

pu i ȧθi ānχ uṭa senb nȧs

it is [who] cometh, O Prince, life, strength, health! A call [being

er - ȧ mākuȧ i - kuȧ ṭeṭ ȧn ḥen - f

made] to me verily I, I come. Said his Majesty:

ȧn ȧu maāt pu pa ṭeṭ ȧu-k

Is it right and true what is said [that] thou art

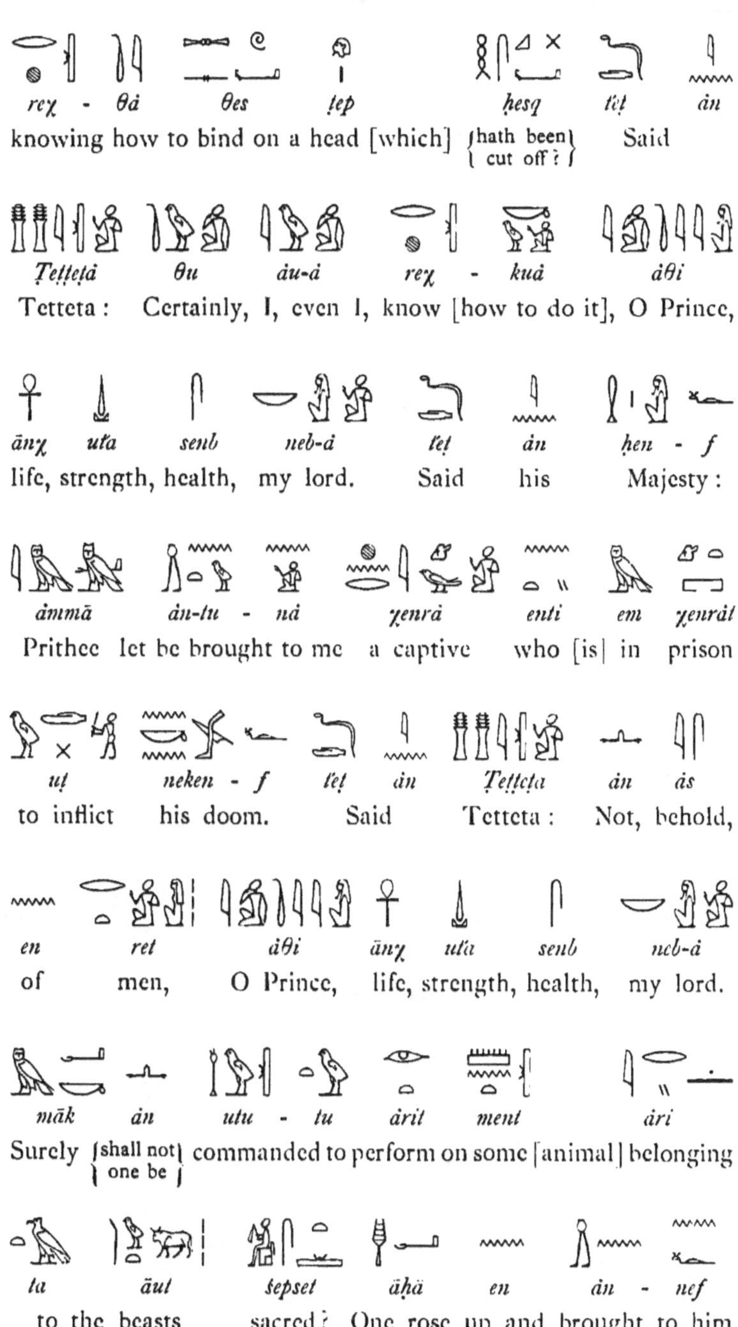

reχ - θà θes ṭep ḥesq ṭeṭ àn
knowing how to bind on a head [which] {hath been cut off?} Said

Ṭeṭṭeṭà θu àu-à reχ - kuà àθi
Tetteta: Certainly, I, even I, know [how to do it], O Prince,

ānχ uṭa senb neb-à ṭeṭ àn ḥen - f
life, strength, health, my lord. Said his Majesty:

àmmā àn-tu - nà χenrà enti em χenràt
Prithee let be brought to me a captive who [is] in prison

uṭ neken - f ṭeṭ àn Ṭeṭṭeṭa àn às
to inflict his doom. Said Tetteta: Not, behold,

en ret àθi ānχ uṭa senb neb-à
of men, O Prince, life, strength, health, my lord.

māk àn utu - tu àrit ment àri
Surely {shall not one be} commanded to perform on some [animal] belonging

ta āut šepset āḥā en àn - nef
to the beasts sacred? One rose up and brought to him

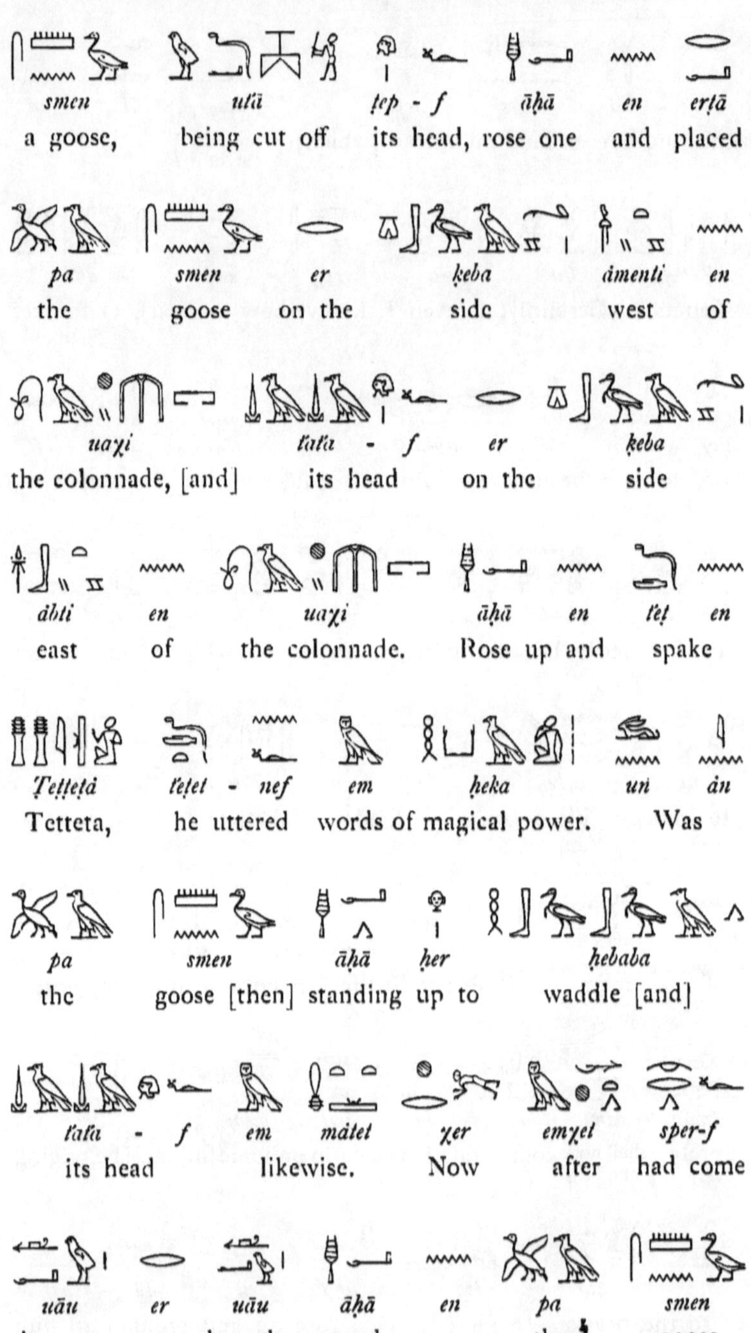

smen uťā ṭep - f āḥā en erṭā
a goose, being cut off its head, rose one and placed

pa smen er ḳeba ȧmenti en
the goose on the side west of

uaχi ťaťa - f er ḳeba
the colonnade, [and] its head on the side

ȧbti en uaχi āḥā en ťeṭ en
east of the colonnade. Rose up and spake

Ṭeṭṭeṭȧ ťeṭet - nef em ḥeka un ȧn
Tetteta, he uttered words of magical power. Was

pa smen āḥā ḥer ḥebaba
the goose [then] standing up to waddle [and]

ťaťa - f em mātet χer emχet sper-f
its head likewise. Now after had come

uāu er uāu āḥā en pa smen
the one upon the other, stood up the goose

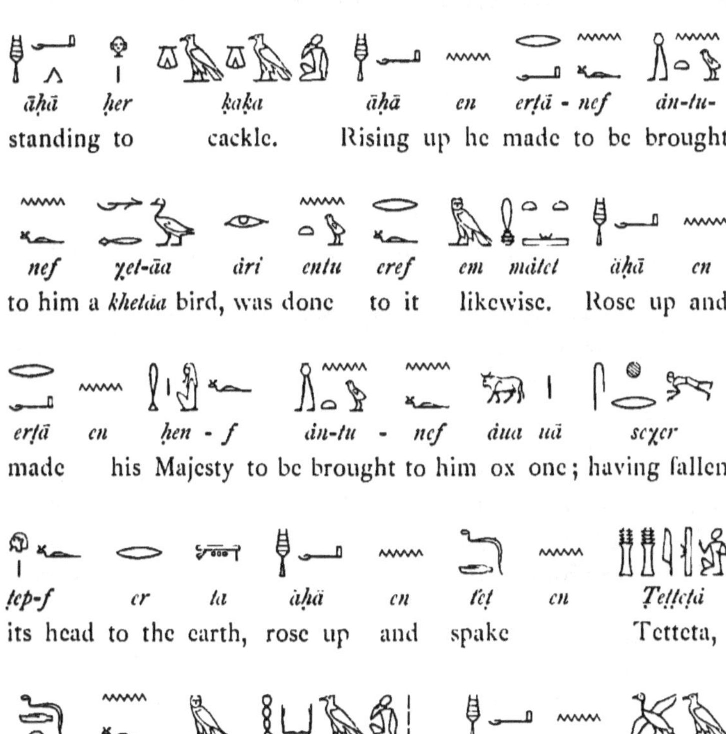

āḥā ḥer ḳaḳa āḥā en erṭā - nef ȧn-tu-
standing to cackle. Rising up he made to be brought

nef χet-āa ȧri entu eref em mȧtet ȧḥā en
to him a *khetāa* bird, was done to it likewise. Rose up and

erṭā en ḥen - f ȧn-tu - nef ȧua uā seχer
made his Majesty to be brought to him ox one; having fallen

ṭep-f er ta ȧḥā en ṭeṭ en Ṭeṭṭeṭȧ
its head to the earth, rose up and spake Tetteta,

ṭeṭet - nef em ḥeka āḥā en pa
he uttered words of magical power, and stood up the

ȧua uā
ox.

THE LIFE OF ÅĀḤMES, THE NAVAL OFFICER, AS TOLD BY HIMSELF.

[XVIIIth dynasty.]

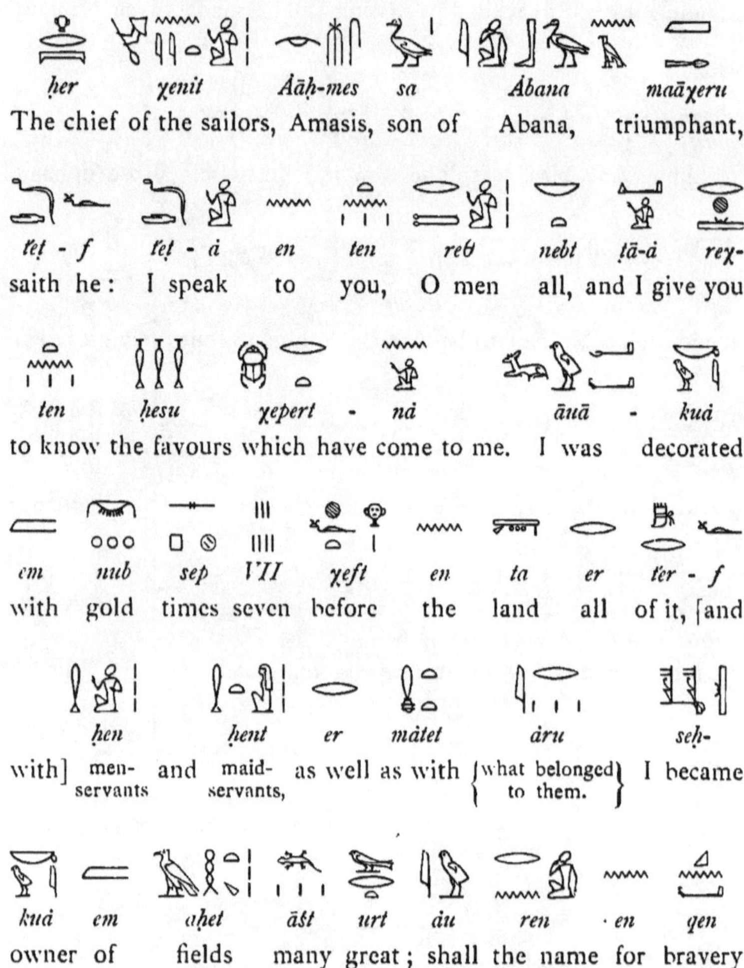

ḥer χenit Åāḥ-mes sa Åbana maāχeru
The chief of the sailors, Amasis, son of Abana, triumphant,

t'eṭ - f t'eṭ - å en ten reθ nebt ṭā-å reχ-
saith he: I speak to you, O men all, and I give you

ten ḥesu χepert - nå āuā - kuå
to know the favours which have come to me. I was decorated

em nub sep VII χeft en ta er t'er - f
with gold times seven before the land all of it, [and

ḥen ḥent er måtet åru seḥ-
with] men-servants and maid-servants, as well as with {what belonged to them.} I became

kuå em aḥet āšt urt åu ren · en qen
owner of fields many great; shall the name for bravery

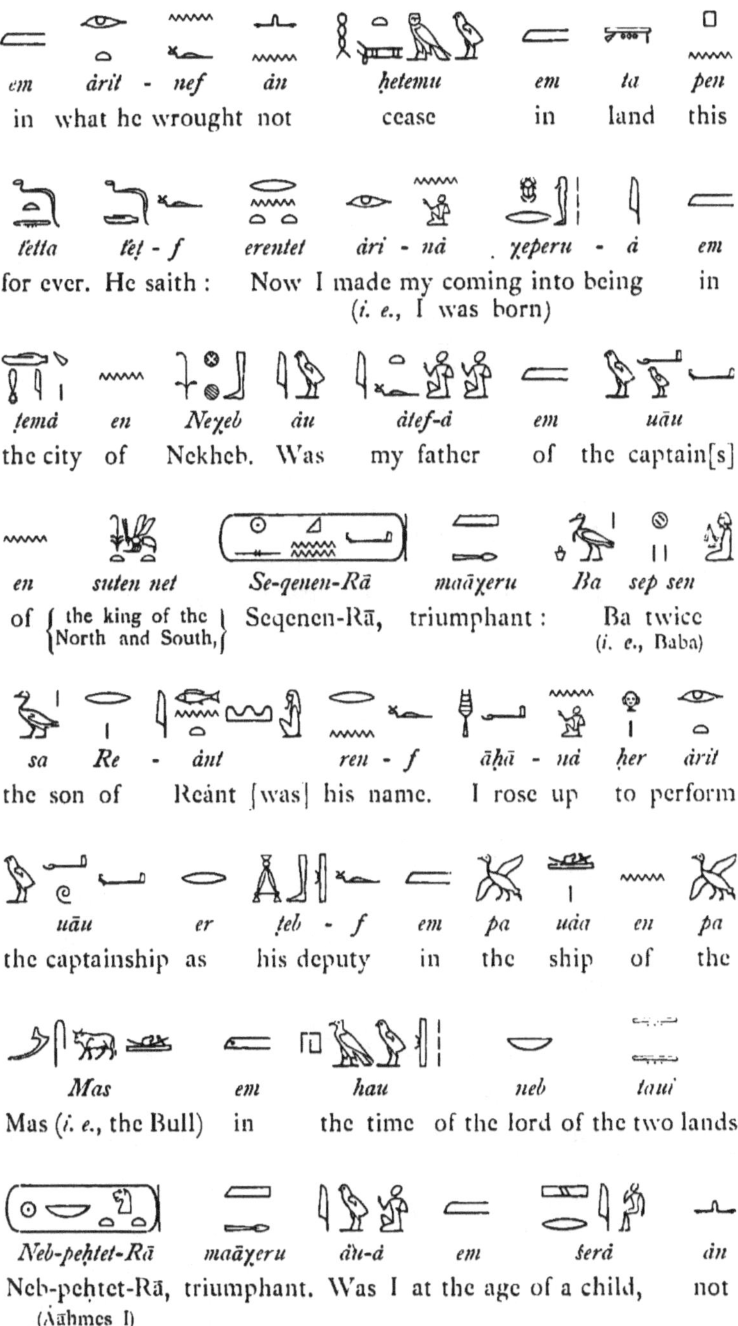

em àrit - nef àn ḥetemu em ta pen

in what he wrought not cease in land this

t'etta t'eṭ - f erentet àri - nà χeperu - à em

for ever. He saith: Now I made my coming into being in
(*i. e.*, I was born)

ṭemà en Neχeb àu àtef-à em uāu

the city of Nekheb. Was my father of the captain[s]

en suten net Se-qenen-Rā maāχeru Ba sep sen

of {the king of the North and South,} Seqenen-Rā, triumphant: Ba twice
(*i. e.*, Baba)

sa Re - ànt ren - f āḥā - nà ḥer àrit

the son of Reànt [was] his name. I rose up to perform

uāu er ṭeb - f em pa uàa en pa

the captainship as his deputy in the ship of the

Mas em hau neb taui

Mas (*i. e.*, the Bull) in the time of the lord of the two lands

Neb-peḥtet-Rā maāχeru àu-à em šerà àn

Neb-peḥtet-Rā, triumphant. Was I at the age of a child, not
(Àāḥmes I)

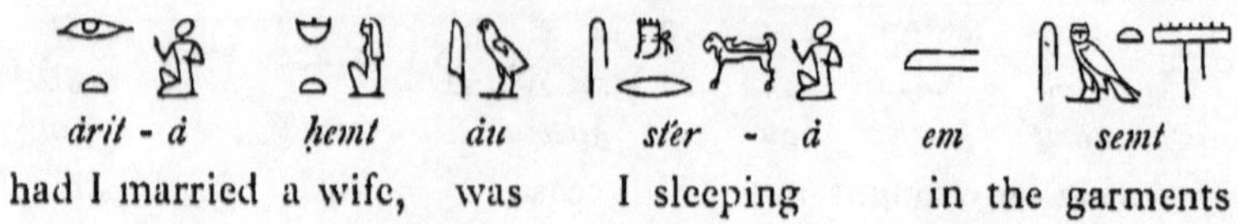

ȧrit - ȧ ḥemt ȧu sṫer - ȧ em semt

had I married a wife, was I sleeping in the garments

šennu χer emχet ḳer - nȧ per āḥā - nȧ

of netted work. But afterwards I possessed a house, I rose up,

θetet - kuȧ er pa uȧa Meḥti ḥer qenen - ȧ

I betook myself to the ship Meḥti that I might fight,
(*i. e.*, the North)

un χer-ȧ ḥer šes ȧθi ānχ uṫa senb

[it] being upon me to follow the Prince, life, strength, health,

ḥer reṭ-ȧ emχet sutut - f ḥer ureret - f

upon my feet after his journeyings in his chariot.

ȧu ḥems - tu ḥer ṭemȧ en Ḥet - Uārt

Being encamped One against the city of Avaris
(*i. e.*, the king)

un χer-ȧ ḥer qent ḥer reṭ - ȧ embaḥ ḥen - f

was [it] upon me to fight upon my feet before his Majesty.

āḥä - nȧ ṭehen - kuȧ er χāā-em-Men-nefer

I rose up, I was advanced to Khāā-em-Men-nefer.
(*i. e.*, to a ship of this name)

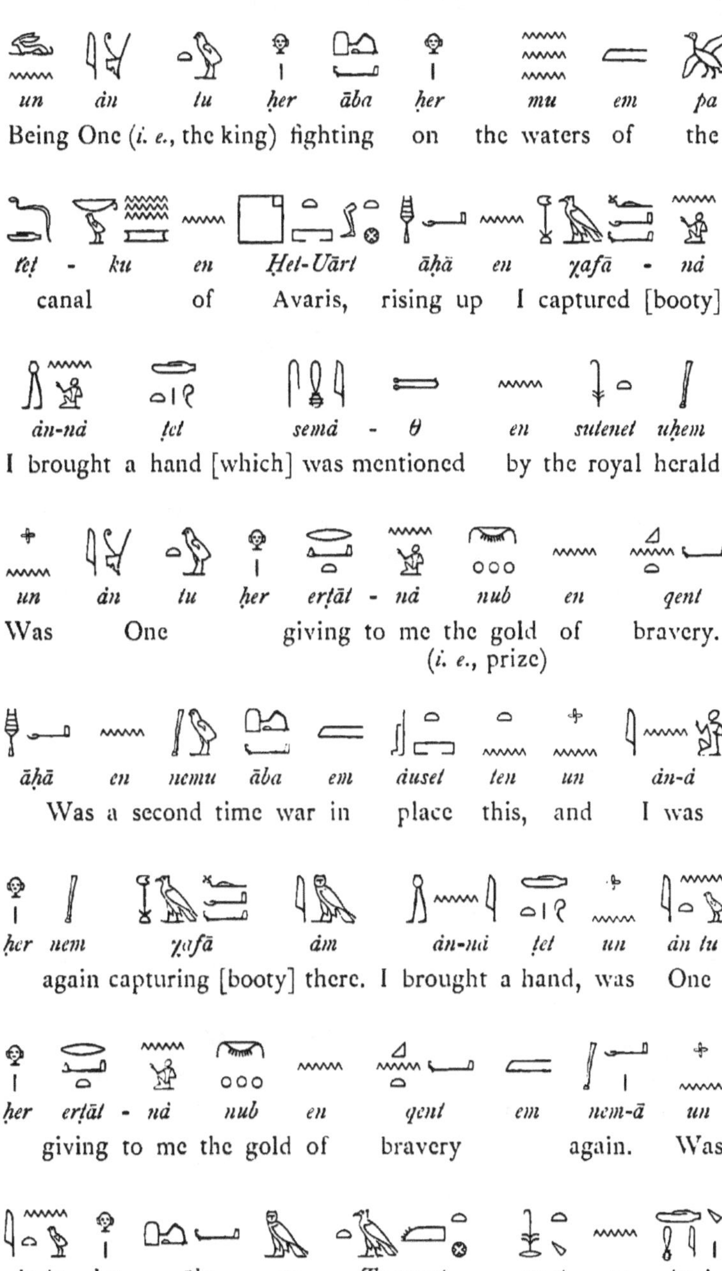

un ȧn tu ḥer āba ḥer mu em pa
Being One (*i. e.*, the king) fighting on the waters of the

ṭeṭ - ku en Ḥet-Uārt āḥā en χafā - nȧ
canal of Avaris, rising up I captured [booty].

ȧn-nȧ ṭet semȧ - θ en sutenet uḥem
I brought a hand [which] was mentioned by the royal herald.

un ȧn tu ḥer erṭāt - nȧ nub en qent
Was One giving to me the gold of bravery.
(*i. e.*, prize)

āḥā en nemu āba em ȧuset ten un ȧn-ȧ
Was a second time war in place this, and I was

ḥer nem χafā ȧm ȧn-nȧ ṭet un ȧn tu
again capturing [booty] there. I brought a hand, was One

ḥer erṭāt - nȧ nub en qent em nem-ā un
giving to me the gold of bravery again. Was

ȧn tu ḥer āba em Ta-qemet reset en ṭemȧ
One fighting in Ta-qemet to the south of city

pen āḥā en ȧn - nȧ seqerȧ ānχ sa
this, rising up brought I captive a living person.

ha - nȧ er pa mu māk ȧn - tu - f
I went down into the water verily bringing him

em seśeṭ ḥer ta uat pa ṭemȧ ṭa-
by force along the road of the town, I set out

nȧ χer - f ḥer mu semȧu en sutenet uḥem
with him on the water. Reported it the royal herald,

āḥā en tu māk āuā - ȧ em nub ḥer - s sen
rose up One, verily I was rewarded with gold for it a second time.

un ȧn tu ḥer ḥaq Ḥet-uārt un ȧn-ȧ
Was One capturing Avaris, was I

ḥer ȧnt ḥaqet ȧm sa uā set ḥemt χemt ṭemṭ
bringing in captives there, man one, women three, in all

ṭepu fṭu un ȧn ḥen-f ḥer erṭāt - set nȧ er
heads four, was his Majesty giving them to me for

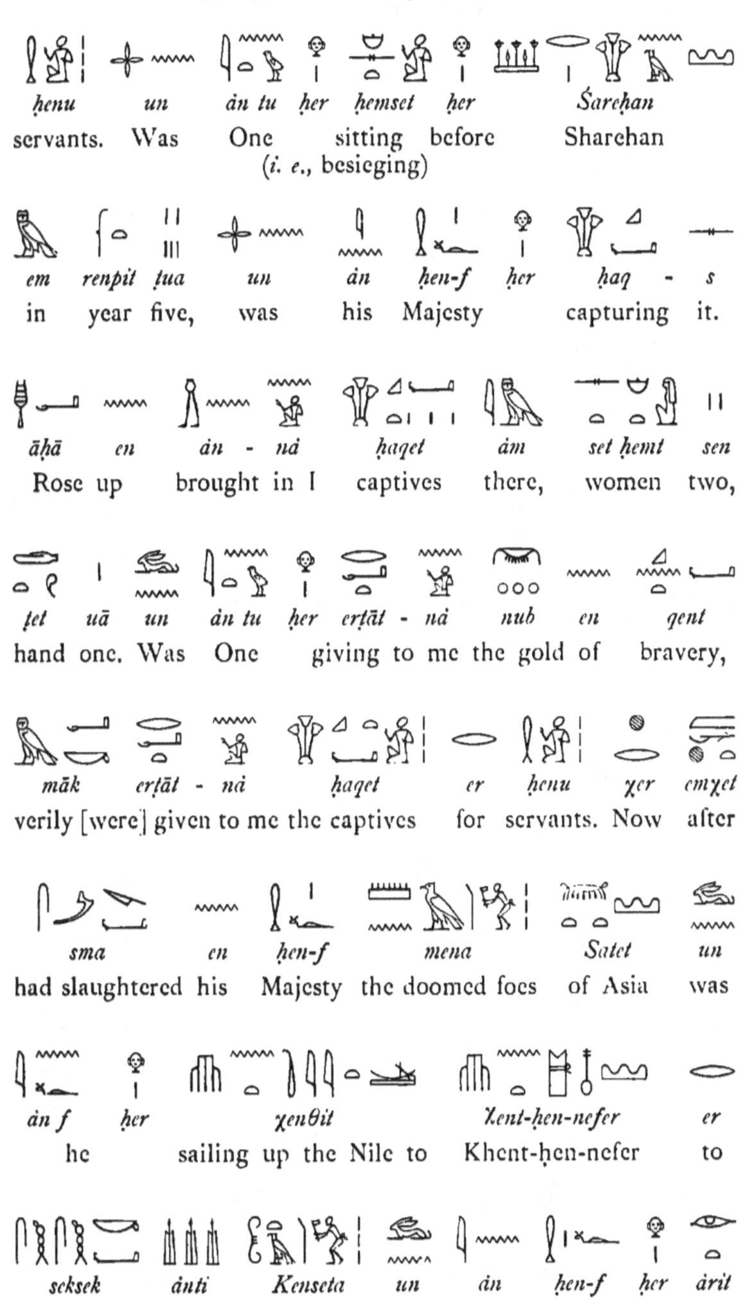

ḥenu un àn tu ḥer ḥemset ḥer Śareḥan
servants. Was One sitting before Sharehan
(*i. e.*, besieging)

em renpit ṭua un àn ḥen-f ḥer ḥaq - s
in year five, was his Majesty capturing it.

āḥā en àn - nà ḥaqet àm set ḥemt sen
Rose up brought in I captives there, women two,

ṭet uā un àn tu ḥer erṭāt - nà nub en qent
hand one. Was One giving to me the gold of bravery,

māk erṭāt - nà ḥaqet er ḥenu χer emχet
verily [were] given to me the captives for servants. Now after

sma en ḥen-f mena Satet un
had slaughtered his Majesty the doomed foes of Asia was

àn f ḥer χenθit Χent-ḥen-nefer er
he sailing up the Nile to Khent-ḥen-nefer to

seksek ànti Kenseta un àn ḥen-f ḥer àrit
chastise the Anti of Nubia. Was his Majesty making

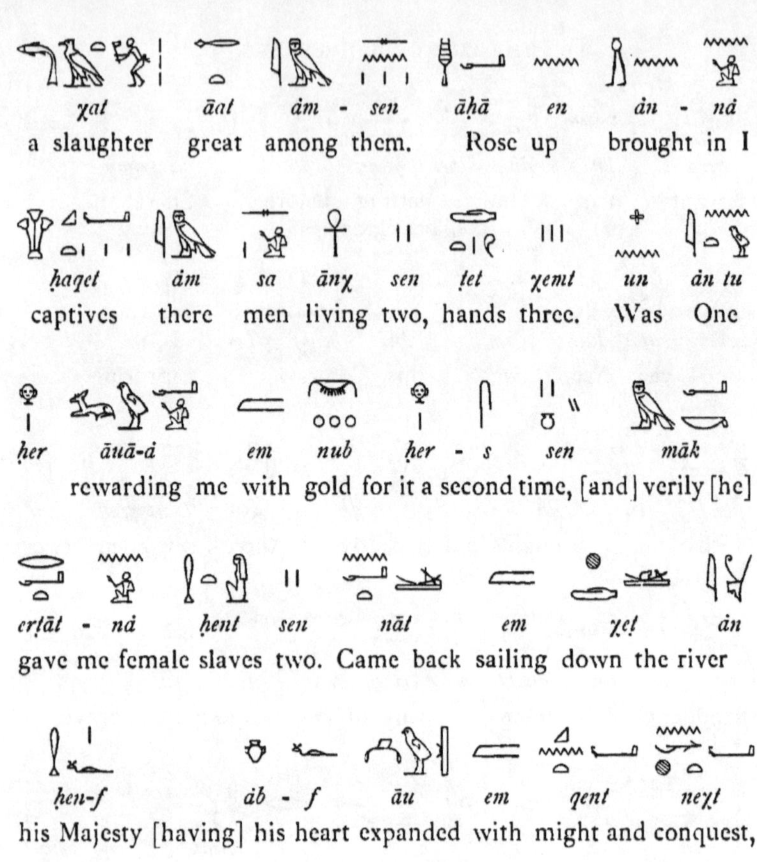

χat āat àm - sen āḥā en àn - nà

a slaughter great among them. Rose up brought in I

ḥaqet àm sa ānχ sen ṭet χemt un àn tu

captives there men living two, hands three. Was One

ḥer āuā-à em nub ḥer - s sen māk

rewarding me with gold for it a second time, [and] verily [he]

erṭāt - nà ḥent sen nāt em χeṭ àn

gave me female slaves two. Came back sailing down the river

ḥen-f àb - f āu em qent neχt

his Majesty [having] his heart expanded with might and conquest,

θetet - nef resu meḥta

[for] he had vanquished those of the south and those of the north.

āḥā en aata iu en res

Rose up the "Scourge" coming to the south,

seteken śau - f utu - f neteru qemāu

making to enter his disease (?), defiled he the gods of the south

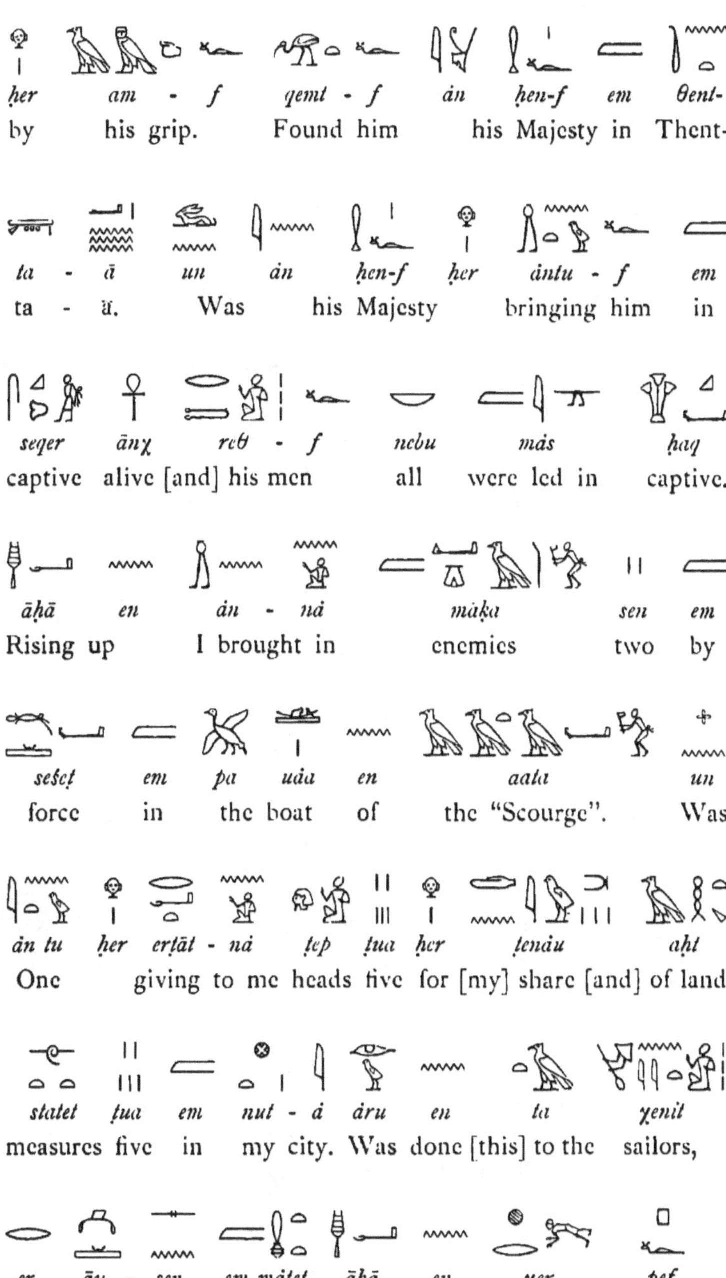

ḥer am - f qemt - f àn ḥen-f em θent-
by his grip. Found him his Majesty in Thent-

ta - ā un àn ḥen-f ḥer àntu - f em
ta - ā. Was his Majesty bringing him in

seqer ānχ reθ - f nebu màs ḥaq
captive alive [and] his men all were led in captive.

āḥā en àn - nà màḳa sen em
Rising up I brought in enemies two by

sešeṭ em pa uàa en aata un
force in the boat of the "Scourge". Was

àn tu ḥer erṭāt - nà ṭep ṭua ḥer ṭenàu aḥt
One giving to me heads five for [my] share [and] of land

statet ṭua em nut - à àru en ta χenit
measures five in my city. Was done [this] to the sailors,

er āu - sen em màtet āḥā en χer pef
all of them, likewise. Rose up degraded one that and

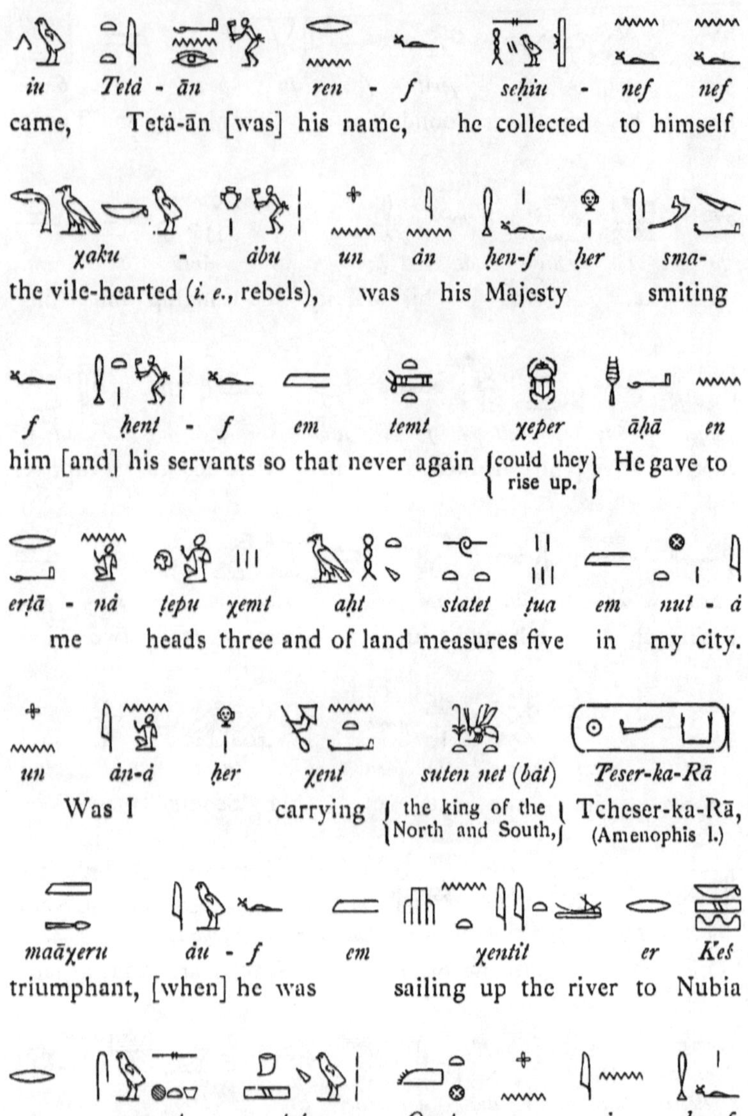

iu *Tetȧ* - *ān* *ren* - *f* *seḥiu* - *nef* *nef*
came, Tetȧ-ān [was] his name, he collected to himself

χaku - *ȧbu* *un* *ȧn* *ḥen-f* *ḥer* *sma-*
the vile-hearted (*i. e.*, rebels), was his Majesty smiting

f *ḥent* - *f* *em* *temt* *χeper* *āḥā* *en*
him [and] his servants so that never again {could they rise up.} He gave to

erṭā - *nȧ* *ṭepu* *χemt* *aḥt* *statet* *ṭua* *em* *nut* - *ȧ*
me heads three and of land measures five in my city.

un *ȧn-ȧ* *ḥer* *χent* *suten net* (*bȧt*) *Ṭeser-ka-Rā*
Was I carrying {the king of the North and South,} Tcheser-ka-Rā, (Amenophis I.)

maāχeru *ȧu* - *f* *em* *χentit* *er* *Keš*
triumphant, [when] he was sailing up the river to Nubia

er *seuseχt* *tašu* *Qemt* *un* *ȧn* *ḥen-f*
to widen the boundaries of Egypt. Was his Majesty

ḥer *seqer* *Ȧnti Kenset* *pef* *em* *ḥer ȧb* *menfitu* - *f*
taking captive Ȧnti of Nubia that among his soldiers,

àntu em ḳua àn nehup - sen
being led into an ambush not could escape they,

utexu em ṭāi ḥer ḳes mà entu àn
being scattered and yielding on [their] ground so that never again

xeper àst - uà em ṭep en menfitu - n àu
{could they rise up.} Behold I was at the head of our soldiers,

āba - nà er un maā maa en ḥen-f qent - à
I fought in very truth, saw his Majesty my valour.
(*i. e.*, to the utmost of my power)

àn-nà ṭet sen mās en ḥen-f un
I brought in hands two, carrying [them] to his Majesty. Was

àn tu ḥer ḥeḥi reθ - f menment - f
One seeking out his people and his cattle,

āḥā en àn-nà seqer ānx mās en
rose up brought in I a captive living bringing [him] to

ḥen-f àn-nà ḥen-f hru sen er Qemt
his Majesty. I brought his Majesty in days two to Egypt

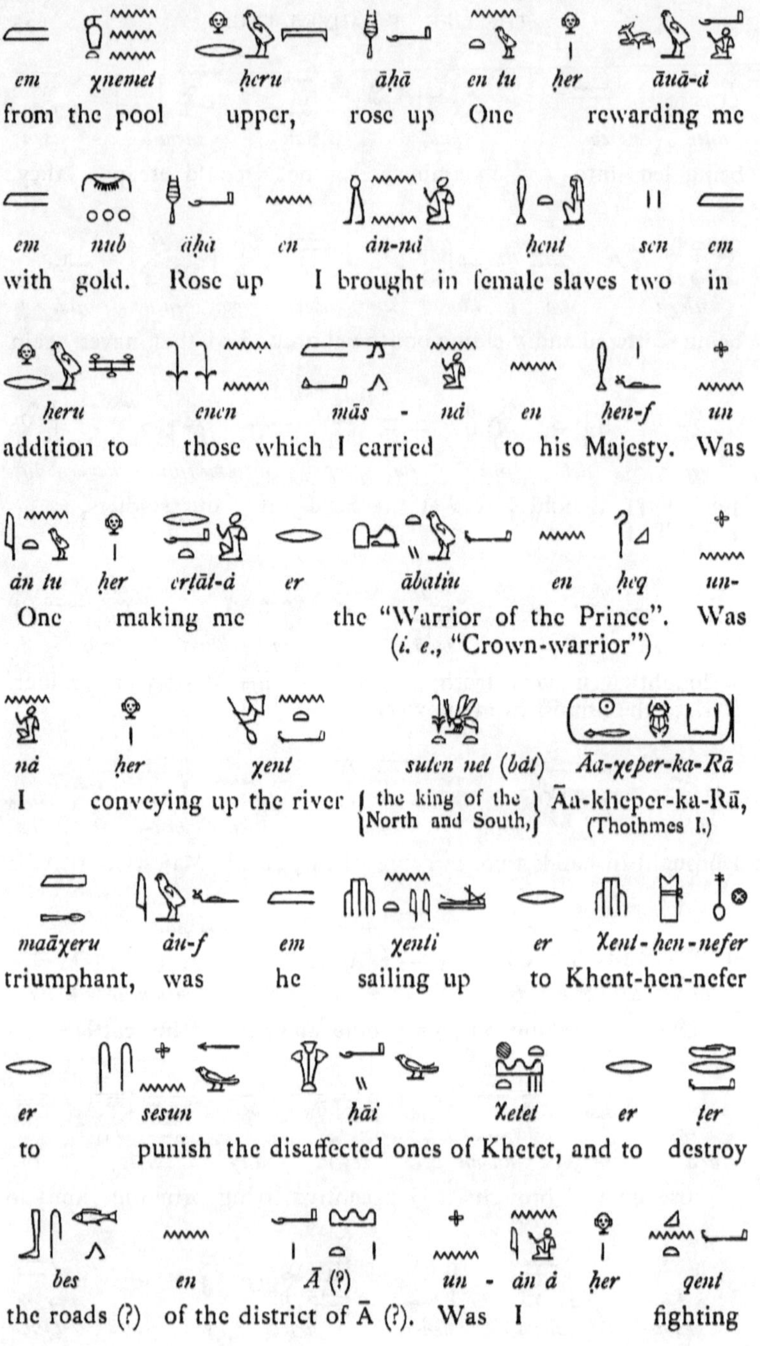

em χnemet ḥeru āḥā en tu ḥer āuā-à
from the pool upper, rose up One rewarding me

em nub āḥā en àn-nà ḥent sen em
with gold. Rose up I brought in female slaves two in

ḥeru enen mās - nà en ḥen-f un
addition to those which I carried to his Majesty. Was

àn tu ḥer erṭāt-à er ābatiu en ḥeq un-
One making me the "Warrior of the Prince". Was
(*i. e.*, "Crown-warrior")

nà ḥer χent suten net (bàt) Āa-χeper-ka-Rā
I conveying up the river {the king of the North and South,} Āa-kheper-ka-Rā, (Thothmes I.)

maāχeru àu-f em χenti er Χent-ḥen-nefer
triumphant, was he sailing up to Khent-ḥen-nefer

er sesun ḥāi Χetet er ṭer
to punish the disaffected ones of Khetet, and to destroy

bes en Ā (?) un - àn à ḥer qent
the roads (?) of the district of Ā (?). Was I fighting

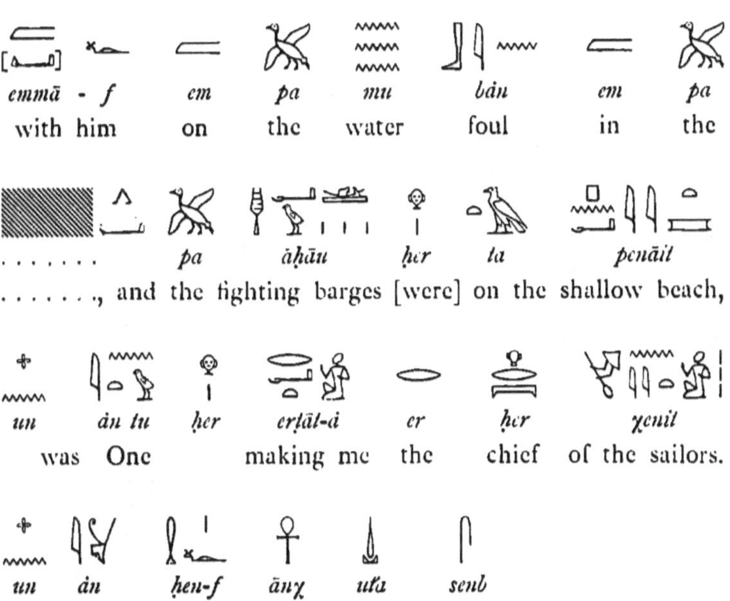
emmā - f em pa mu bån em pa
with him on the water foul in the
. . . . pa åḥāu ḥer ta penāit
. . . ., and the fighting barges [were] on the shallow beach,
un ån tu ḥer ertāt-å er ḥer χenit
was One making me the chief of the sailors.
un ån ḥen-f ānχ uta senb
Was his Majesty, life, strength, health . . .

THE HARPER'S LAMENT.

From the tomb of Nefer-ḥetep.

[XVIIIth dynasty.]

ťeṭ en pa ḥes em bent enti em

Saith the singer to the harp who is in

ta māḥāt en Ȧusȧr neter ȧtf en Ȧmen

the tomb of Osiris, the divine father of Amen,

Nefer-ḥetep maāχeru ťeṭ - f urṭ uru pu

Nefer-ḥetep, triumphant. Saith he: Resteth mighty one this,

maā pa śau nefer χeper χat

right and true [is] the decree good. {What hath come into being [from]} bodies (*i. e.*, women)

ḥer sebt χer - k Rā ťamā ḥer

must pass away before thee, O Rā, the young men and women

it er ȧuset - sen Rā ṭā - f su ṭep ṭuait

go to their places. Ra giveth (*i. e.*, sheweth) himself at dawn,

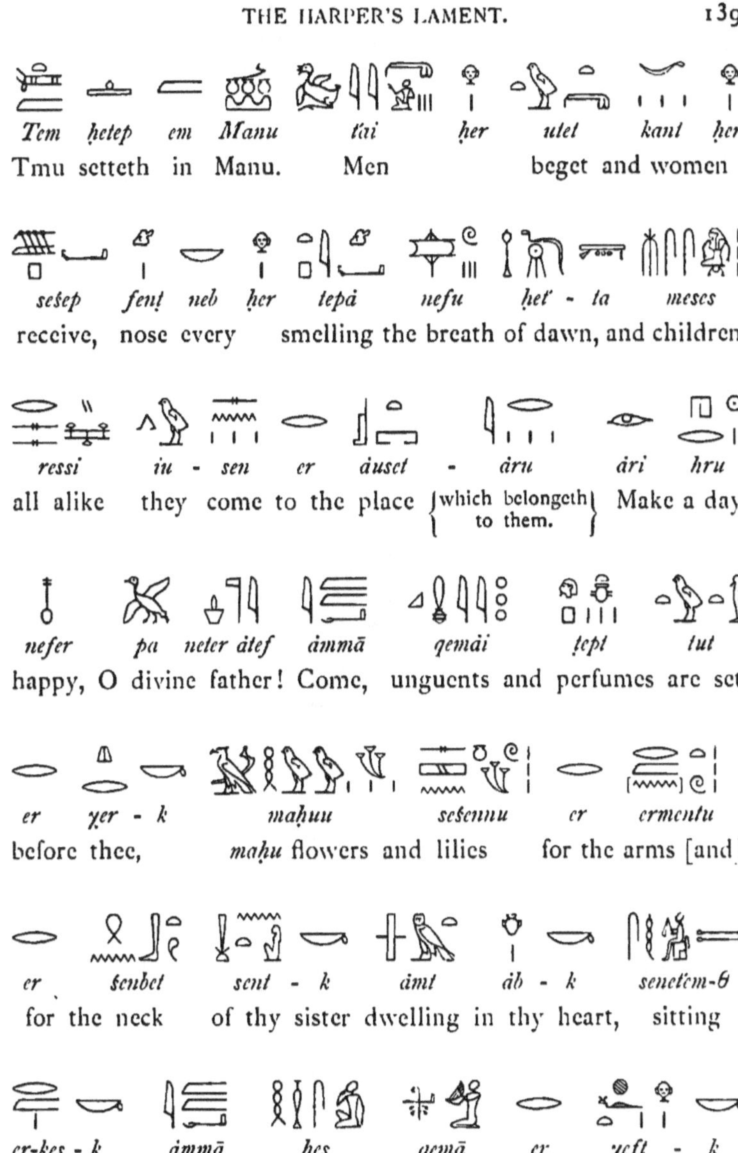

Tem ḥetep em Manu t'ai ḥer utet kant ḥer
Tmu setteth in Manu. Men beget and women

sešep fent neb ḥer tepȧ nefu ḥet' - ta meses
receive, nose every smelling the breath of dawn, and children

ressi iu - sen er ȧuset - ȧru ȧri hru
all alike they come to the place {which belongeth to them.} Make a day

nefer pa neter ȧtef ȧmmā qemȧi tept tut
happy, O divine father! Come, unguents and perfumes are set

er χer - k maḥuu sešennu er ermentu
before thee, *maḥu* flowers and lilies for the arms [and]

er šenbet sent - k ȧmt ȧb - k senet'em-θ
for the neck of thy sister dwelling in thy heart, sitting

er-ḳes - k ȧmmā ḥes qemā er χeft - k
near thee. Come then, song [and] music are before thee.

mā ḥa tutu nebt seχa - nek reštu
Set behind [thee] evil things all, think thou upon gladness [only]

er *it* *hru* *pefi* *en* *menå* *åm-f* *er*
until cometh day that arriveth [a man] in it at

pa *ta* *mer - s* *ḳer*
the land [which] loveth it silence.

THE BATTLE OF MEGIDDO.

From the Annals of Thothmes III.

[XVIIIth dynasty.]

renpit XXIII ṭep šemu hru XVI er ṭemȧ
Year twenty-three, first month of summer, day sixteen, at the town

en Iḥem utu en ḥen-f neťu - re ḥenā
of Ihem. Ordered his Majesty a council of war with

menfitu-f en neχt er ťeṭ erenti χeru
his soldiers of valour, saying: Inasmuch as wretch

pef en Qeṭešu iu āq er
that of Kadesh hath come [and] gone into

Mākθȧ su ȧm em ta at seḥui-
Megiddo, [and] he is there at this moment, and hath

nef nef seru nu set nebt enti ḥer
gathered to him the princes of countries all who are on

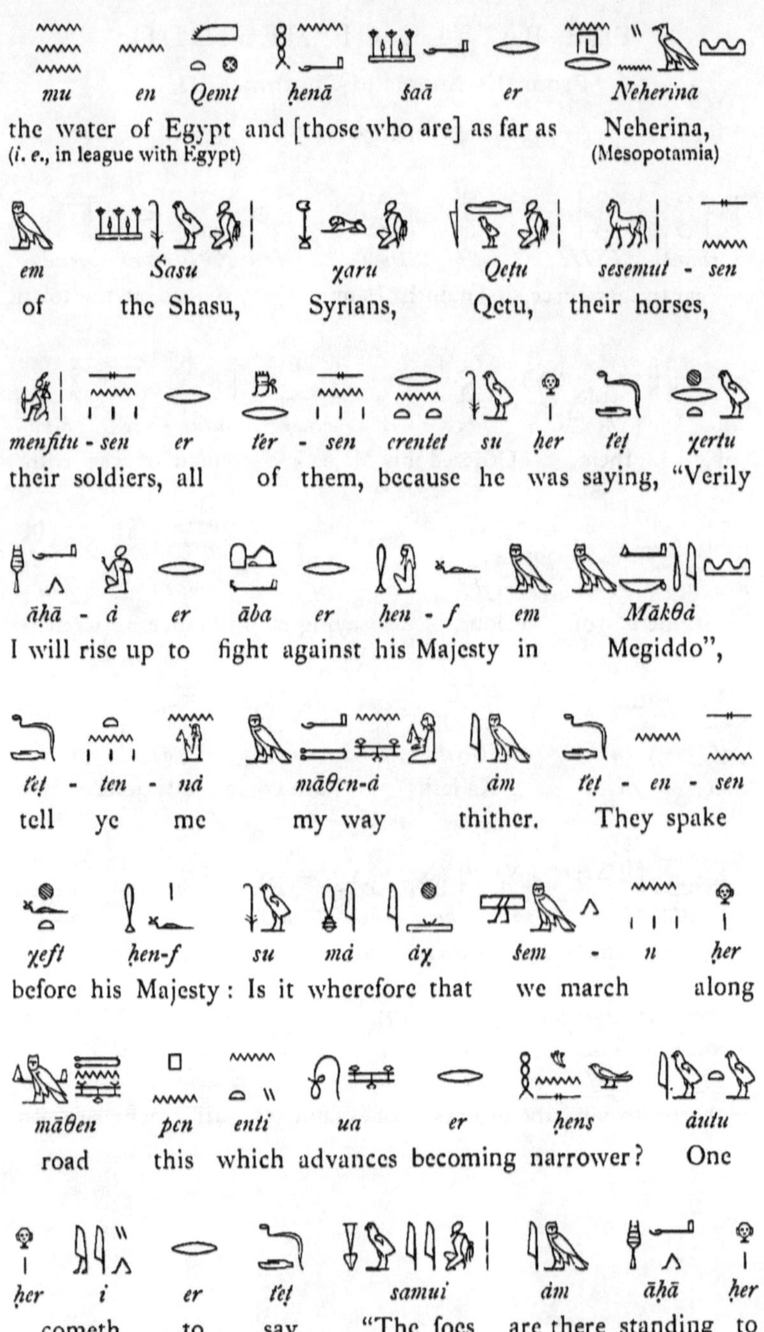

mu en Qemt ḥenā śaā er Neherina

the water of Egypt and [those who are] as far as Neherina,
(*i. e.*, in league with Egypt) (Mesopotamia)

em Śasu χaru Qeṭu sesemut - sen

of the Shasu, Syrians, Qetu, their horses,

menfitu - sen er ter - sen crentet su ḥer ṭeṭ χertu

their soldiers, all of them, because he was saying, "Verily

āḥā - ȧ er āba er ḥen - f em Mākθȧ

I will rise up to fight against his Majesty in Megiddo",

ṭeṭ - ten - nȧ māθen-ȧ ȧm ṭeṭ - en - sen

tell ye me my way thither. They spake

χeft ḥen-f su mȧ ȧχ śem - n ḥer

before his Majesty: Is it wherefore that we march along

māθen pen enti ua er ḥens ȧutu

road this which advances becoming narrower? One

ḥer i er ṭeṭ samui ȧm āḥā ḥer

cometh to say, "The foes are there standing to

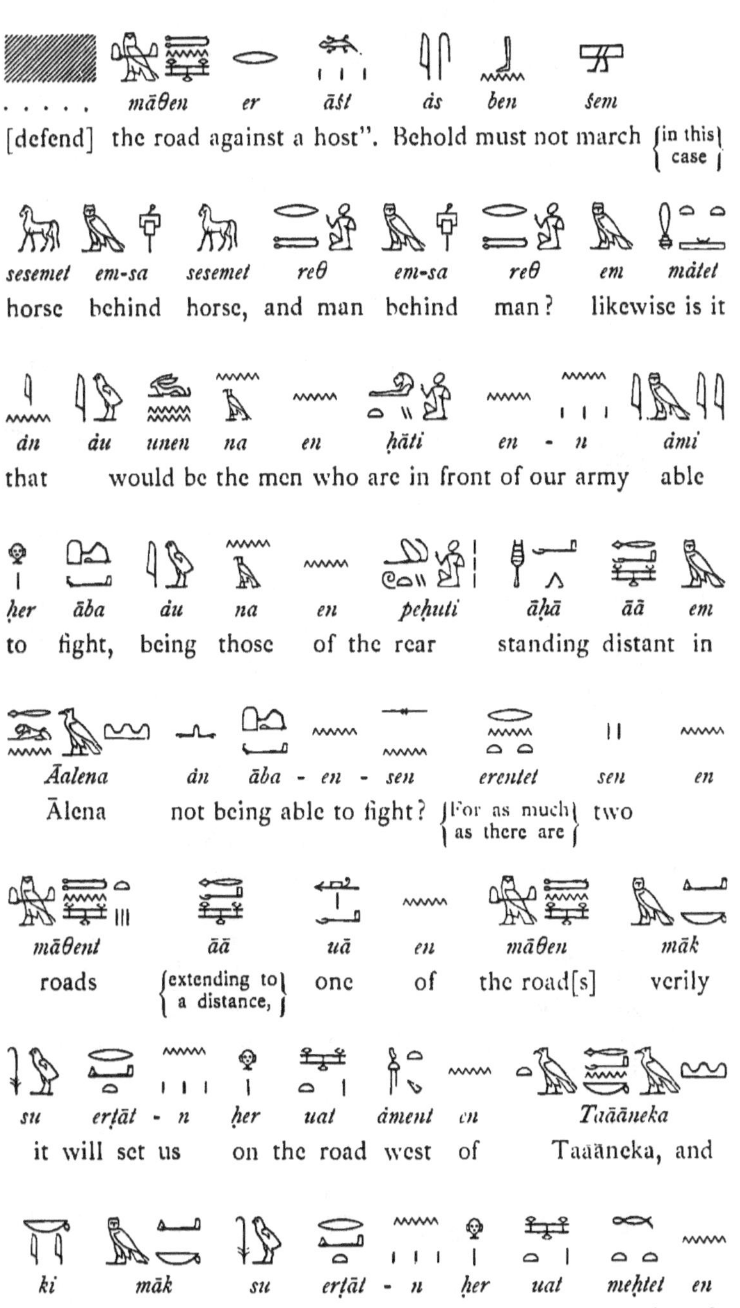
. . . . . māθen er āšt ȧs ben šem
[defend] the road against a host". Behold must not march {in this case}
sesemet em-sa sesemet reθ em-sa reθ em mātet
horse behind horse, and man behind man? likewise is it
ȧn ȧu unen na en ḥāti en - n ȧmi
that would be the men who are in front of our army able
ḥer āba ȧu na en peḥuti āḥā āā em
to fight, being those of the rear standing distant in
Āalena ȧn āba - en - sen erentet sen en
Ālena not being able to fight? {For as much as there are} two
māθent āā uā en māθen māk
roads {extending to a distance,} one of the road[s] verily
su erṭāt - n ḥer uat ȧment en Taāāneka
it will set us on the road west of Taāāneka, and
ki māk su erṭāt - n ḥer uat meḥtet en
the other verily it will set us on the road north of

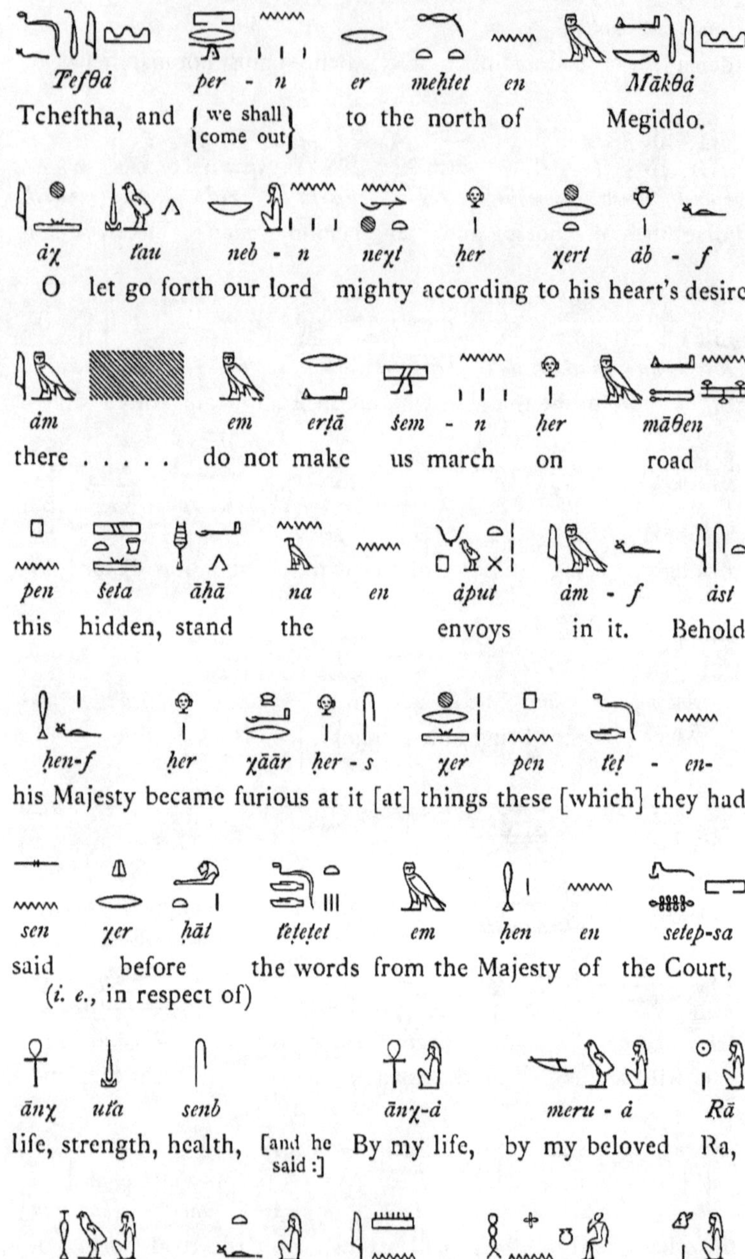

Teſθȧ per - n er meḥtet en Māktθȧ
Tcheſtha, and {we shall come out} to the north of Megiddo.

ȧχ ťau neb - n neχt ḥer χert ȧb - f
O let go forth our lord mighty according to his heart's desire

ȧm em erťā šem - n ḥer māθen
there . . . . . do not make us march on road

pen šeta āḥā na en ȧput ȧm - f ȧst
this hidden, stand the envoys in it. Behold

ḥen-f ḥer χāār ḥer - s χer pen ťeṭ - en-
his Majesty became furious at it [at] things these [which] they had

sen χer ḥāt ťeṭeṭet em ḥen en setep-sa
said before the words from the Majesty of the Court,
(*i. e.*, in respect of)

ānχ uťa senb ānχ-ȧ meru - ȧ Rā
life, strength, health, [and he said :] By my life, by my beloved Ra,

ḥesu-ȧ tef - ȧ Ȧmen ḥunnu fenṭ-ȧ
by my ſavour with my father Amen, who maketh young my nose

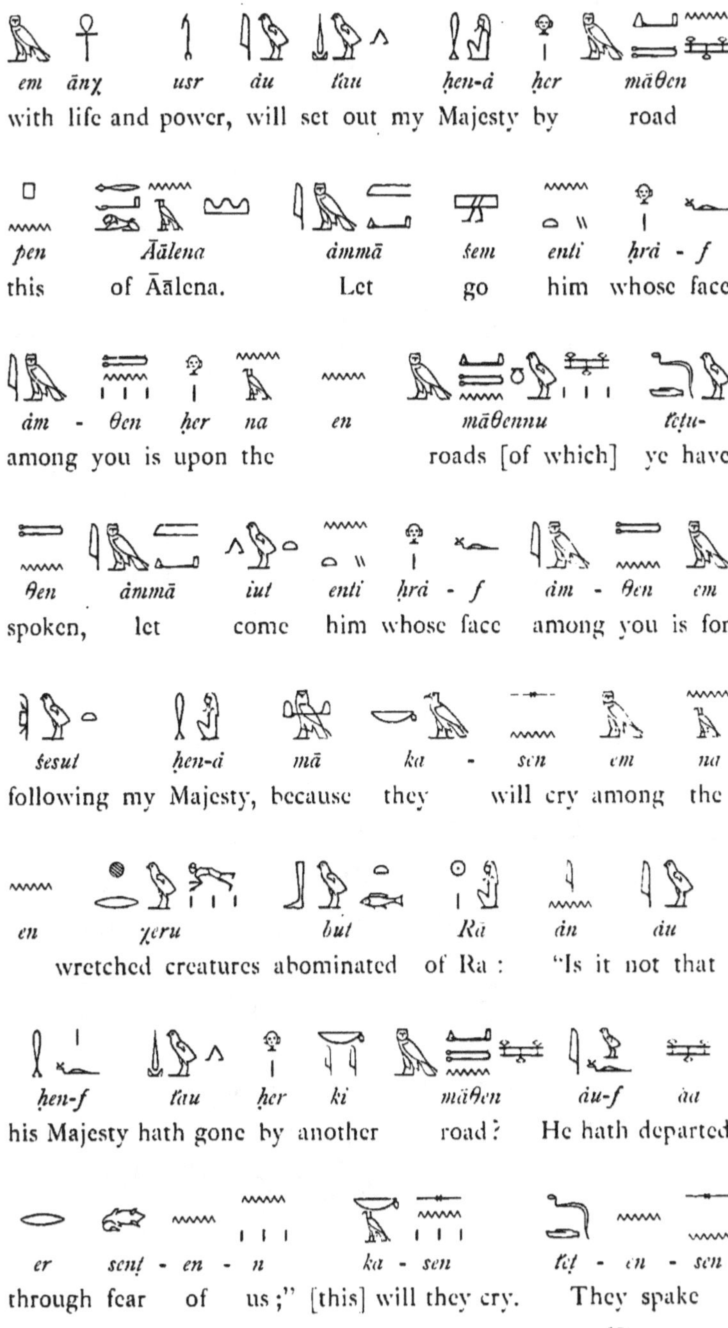

em ānχ usr ȧu ťau ḥen-ȧ ḥer māθen
with life and power, will set out my Majesty by road

pen Āālena ȧmmā šem enti ḥrȧ - f
this of Āālena. Let go him whose face

ȧm - θen ḥer na en māθennu ṭeṭu-
among you is upon the roads [of which] ye have

θen ȧmmā iut enti ḥrȧ - f ȧm - θen em
spoken, let come him whose face among you is for

šesut ḥen-ȧ mā ka - sen em na
following my Majesty, because they will cry among the

en χeru but Rā ȧn ȧu
wretched creatures abominated of Ra : "Is it not that

ḥen-f ťau ḥer ki māθen ȧu-f ȧa
his Majesty hath gone by another road? He hath departed

er senṭ - en - n ka - sen ṭeṭ - en - sen
through fear of us;" [this] will they cry. They spake

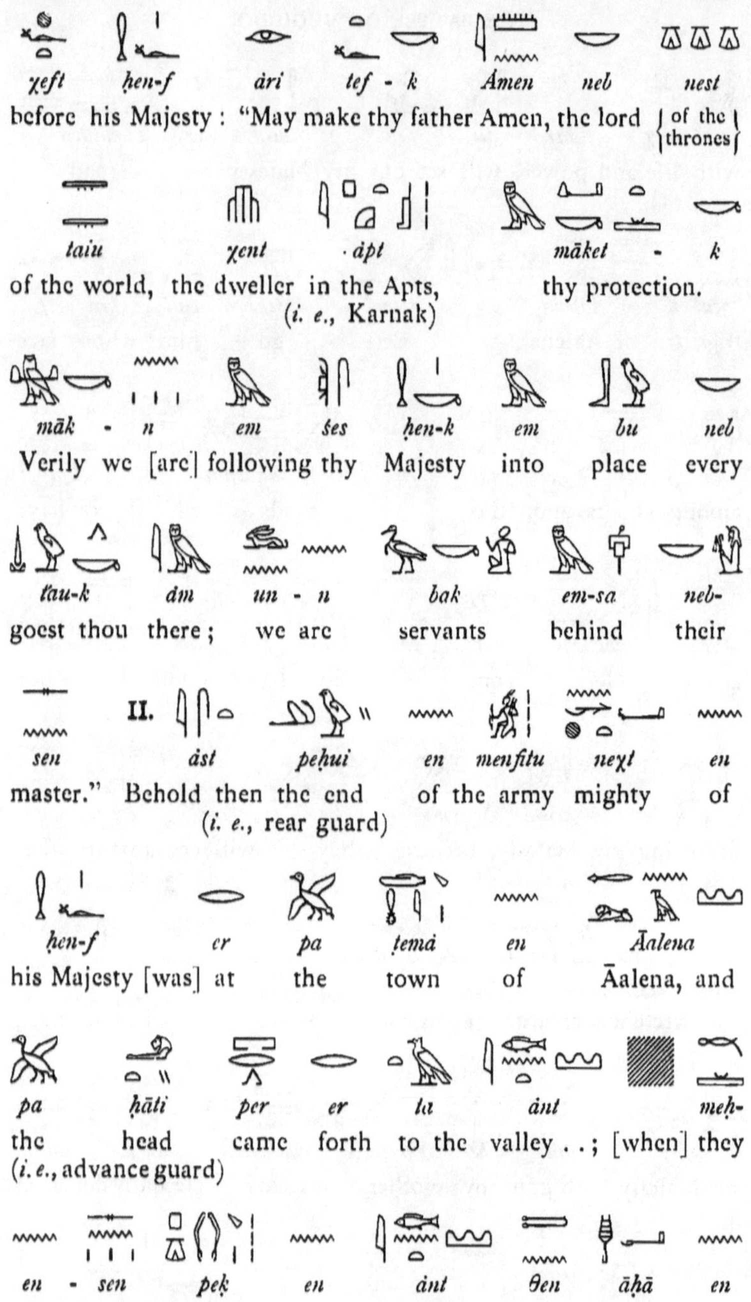

χeft ḥen-f àri tef - k Àmen neb nest
before his Majesty: "May make thy father Amen, the lord {of the thrones}

taiu χent · àpt māket - k
of the world, the dweller in the Apts, (*i. e.*, Karnak) thy protection.

māk - n em šes ḥen-k em bu neb
Verily we [are] following thy Majesty into place every

ṭau-k àm un - n bak em-sa neb-
goest thou there; we are servants behind their

sen II. *àst peḥui en menfitu neχt en*
master." Behold then the end (*i. e.*, rear guard) of the army mighty of

ḥen-f er pa ṭemà en Āalena
his Majesty [was] at the town of Āalena, and

pa ḥāti per er ta ànt meḥ-
the head (*i. e.*, advance guard) came forth to the valley . . ; [when] they

en - sen peḳ en ànt θen āḥā en
had filled the ravines of valley this, rose and

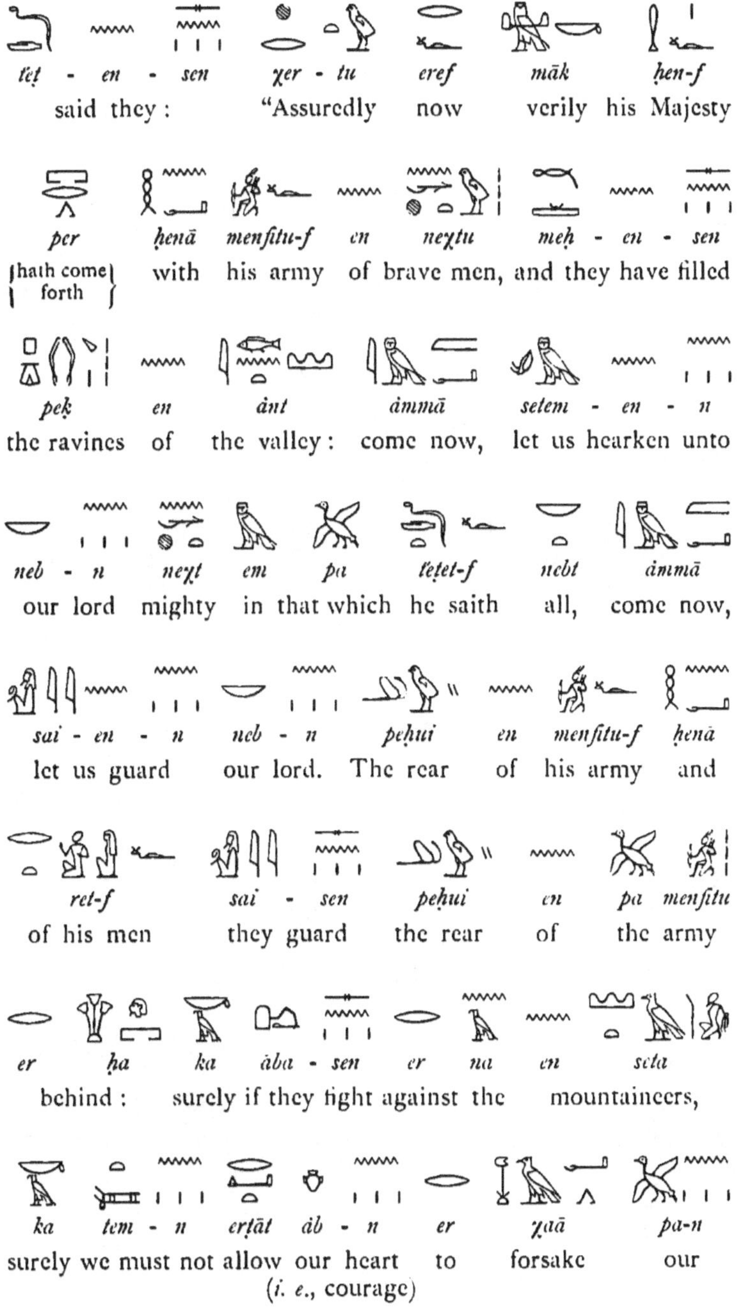

ṭeṭ - en - sen χer - tu eref māk ḥen-f
said they: "Assuredly now verily his Majesty

per ḥenā menfitu-f en neχtu meḥ - en - sen
{hath come forth} with his army of brave men, and they have filled

peḳ en ȧnt ȧmmā setem - en - n
the ravines of the valley: come now, let us hearken unto

neb - n neχt em pa ṭeṭet-f nebt ȧmmā
our lord mighty in that which he saith all, come now,

sai - en - n neb - n peḥui en menfitu-f ḥenā
let us guard our lord. The rear of his army and

ret-f sai - sen peḥui en pa menfitu
of his men they guard the rear of the army

er ḥa ka ȧba - sen er na en seta
behind: surely if they fight against the mountaineers,

ka tem - n erṭāt ȧb - n er χaā pa-n
surely we must not allow our heart (*i. e.*, courage) to forsake our

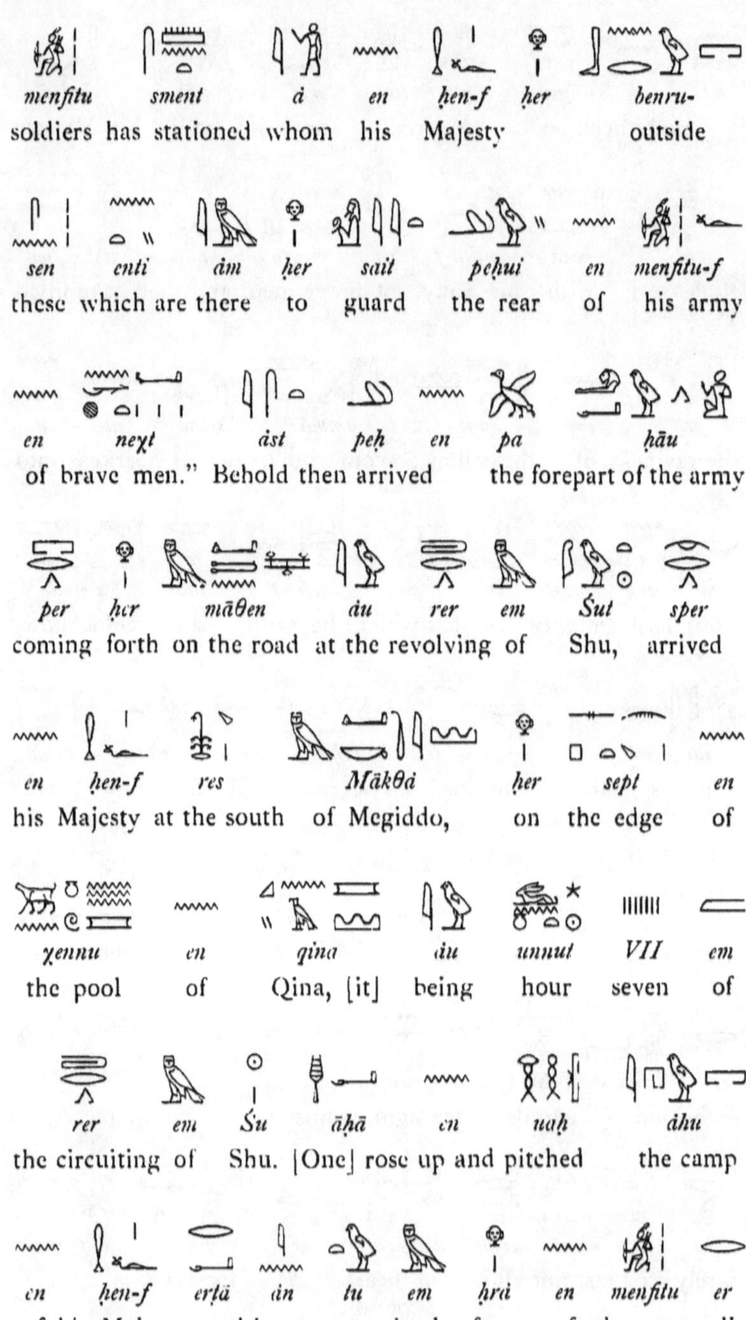

menfitu sment ȧ en ḥen-f ḥer benru-
soldiers has stationed whom his Majesty outside

sen enti ȧm ḥer sait peḥui en menfitu-f
these which are there to guard the rear of his army

en neχt ȧst peḥ en pa ḥāu
of brave men." Behold then arrived the forepart of the army

per ḥer māθen ȧu rer em Śut sper
coming forth on the road at the revolving of Shu, arrived

en ḥen-f res Mākθȧ ḥer sept en
his Majesty at the south of Megiddo, on the edge of

χennu en qina ȧu unnut VII em
the pool of Qina, [it] being hour seven of

rer em Śu āḥā en uaḥ ȧhu
the circuiting of Shu. [One] rose up and pitched the camp

en ḥen-f erṭā ȧn tu em ḥrȧ en menfitu er
of his Majesty, and it gave in the face of the army all

ṭer - f er ṭeṭ ḳer - θen sesepṭ χāān-
of it, saying: "Lay ye hold upon [and] prepare your

θen erentet àu - tu er θeḥen er āba
arms inasmuch as it will be to advance to do battle

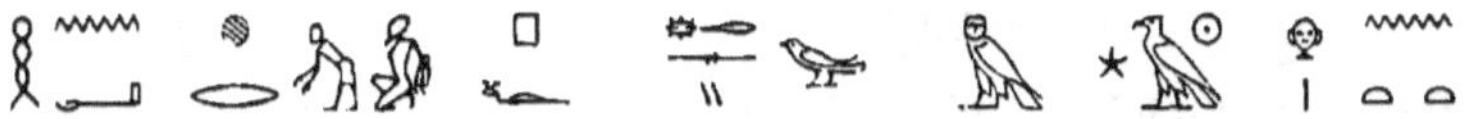

ḥenā χer pef χasi em ṭua ḥer entet
with wretched one this and abominable at daybreak, because

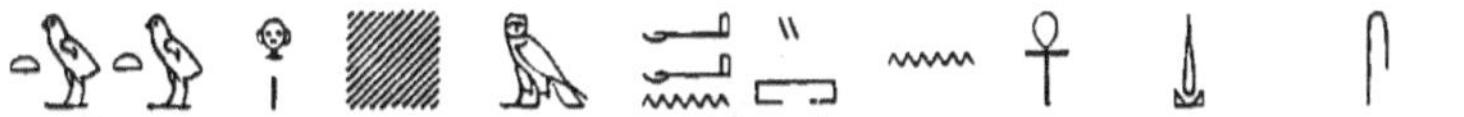

tutu ḥer . . . . . em āāni en ānχ uṭa senb
it will be to . . . . . in the camp of life, strength, health".

àrit meχer (?) urn uā en šesu
Made preparations (?) the overseers {of the provisions} of the foot-soldiers,

seš resu en menfitu ṭeṭ - en - sen
passed along the watchmen of the soldiers, they said:

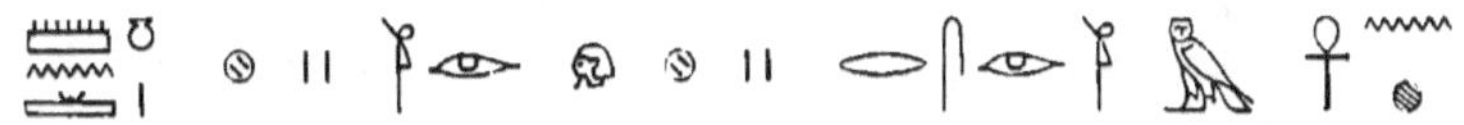

men sep sen res ṭep sep sen res em ānχ
"Be firm, twice; watch well, twice; watch for life

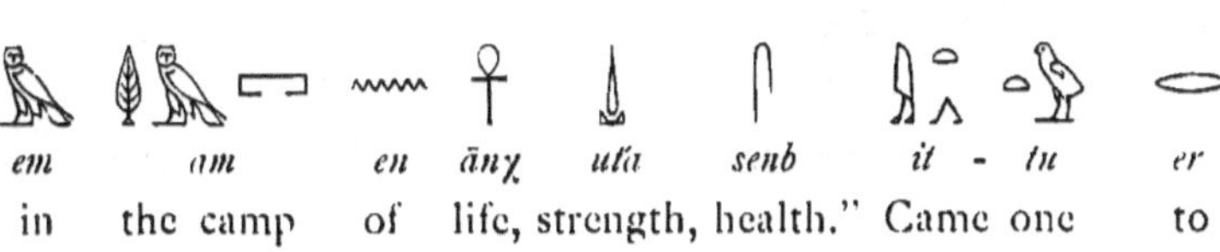

em am en ānχ uṭa senb ìt - tu er
in the camp of life, strength, health." Came one to

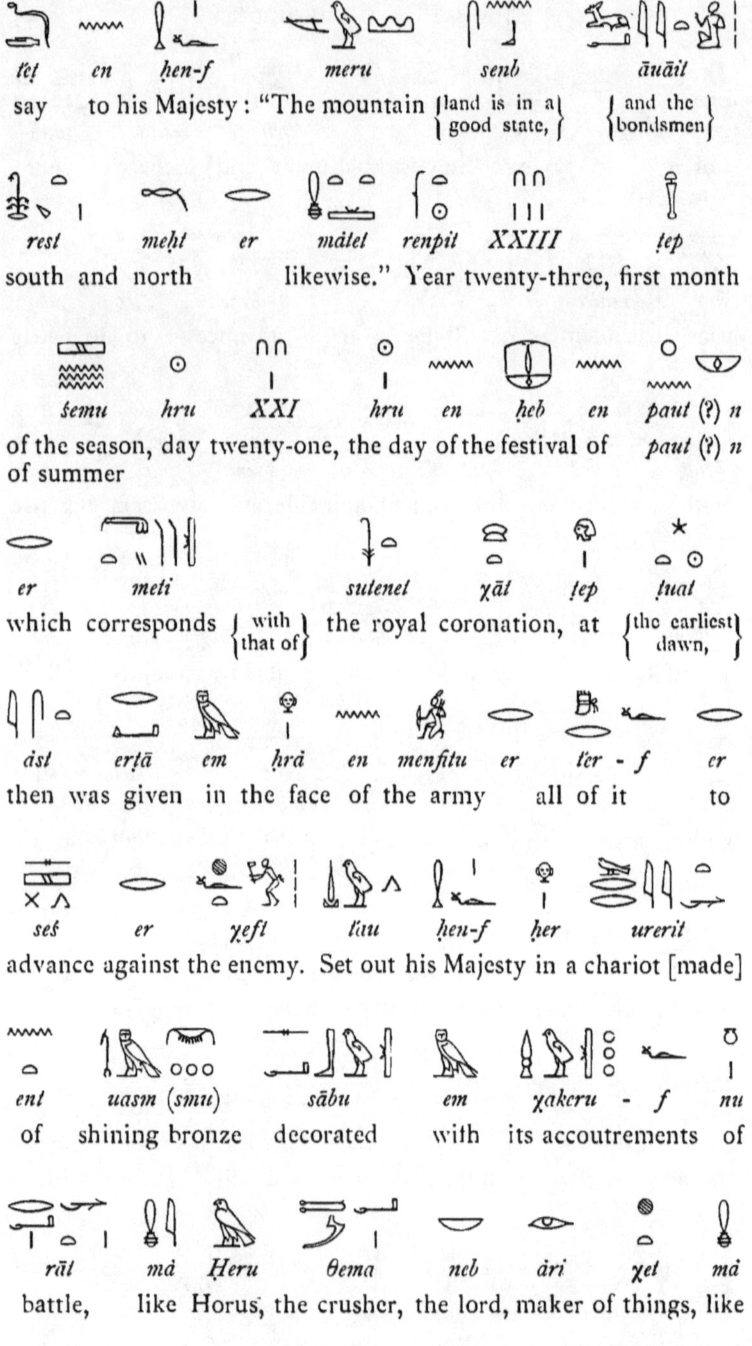

t'et *en* *ḥen-f* *meru* *senb* *āuāit*
say to his Majesty: "The mountain {land is in a good state,} {and the bondsmen}

rest *meḥt* *er* *mātet* *renpit* *XXIII* *tep*
south and north likewise." Year twenty-three, first month

šemu *hru* *XXI* *hru* *en* *ḥeb* *en* *paut* (?) *n*
of the season, day twenty-one, the day of the festival of *paut* (?) *n*
of summer

er *meti* *sutenet* *χāt* *tep* *tuat*
which corresponds {with that of} the royal coronation, at {the earliest dawn,}

àst *ertā* *em* *ḥrā* *en* *menfitu* *er* *t'er - f* *er*
then was given in the face of the army all of it to

seš *er* *χeft* *t'au* *ḥen-f* *ḥer* *urerit*
advance against the enemy. Set out his Majesty in a chariot [made]

ent *uasm* (*smu*) *sābu* *em* *χakeru* - *f* *nu*
of shining bronze decorated with its accoutrements of

rāt *mà* *Ḥeru* *θema* *neb* *àri* *χet* *mà*
battle, like Horus, the crusher, the lord, maker of things, like

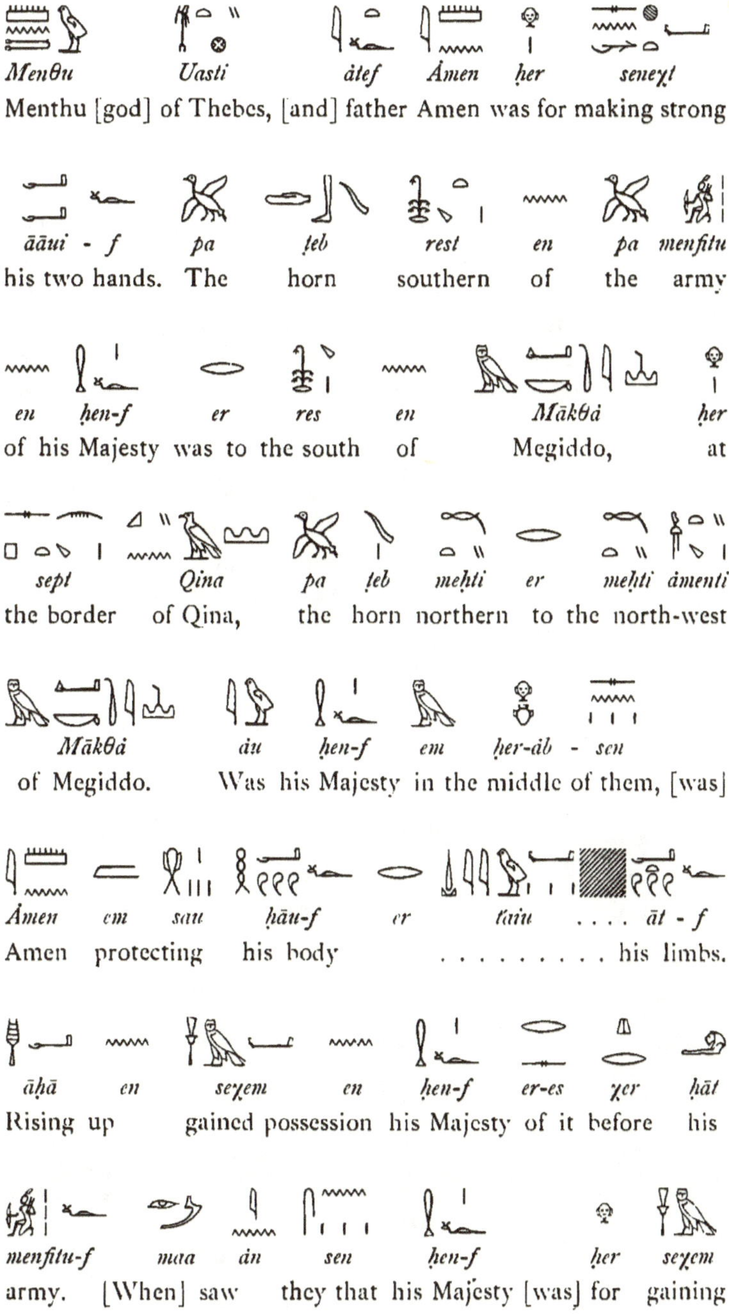

Menθu *Uasti* *àtef* *Àmen* *ḥer* *seneχt*
Menthu [god] of Thebes, [and] father Amen was for making strong

āāui - f *pa* *ṭeb* *rest* *en* *pa* *menfitu*
his two hands. The horn southern of the army

en *ḥen-f* *er* *res* *en* *Mākθà* *ḥer*
of his Majesty was to the south of Megiddo, at

sept *Qina* *pa* *ṭeb* *meḥti* *er* *meḥti* *àmenti*
the border of Qina, the horn northern to the north-west

Mākθà *àu* *ḥen-f* *em* *ḥer-àb - sen*
of Megiddo. Was his Majesty in the middle of them, [was]

Àmen *em* *sau* *ḥāu-f* *er* *ṭaiu* . . . . *āt - f*
Amen protecting his body . . . . his limbs.

āḥā *en* *seχem* *en* *ḥen-f* *er-es* *χer* *ḥāt*
Rising up gained possession his Majesty of it before his

menfitu-f *maa* *àn* *sen* *ḥen-f* *ḥer* *seχem*
army. [When] saw they that his Majesty [was] for gaining

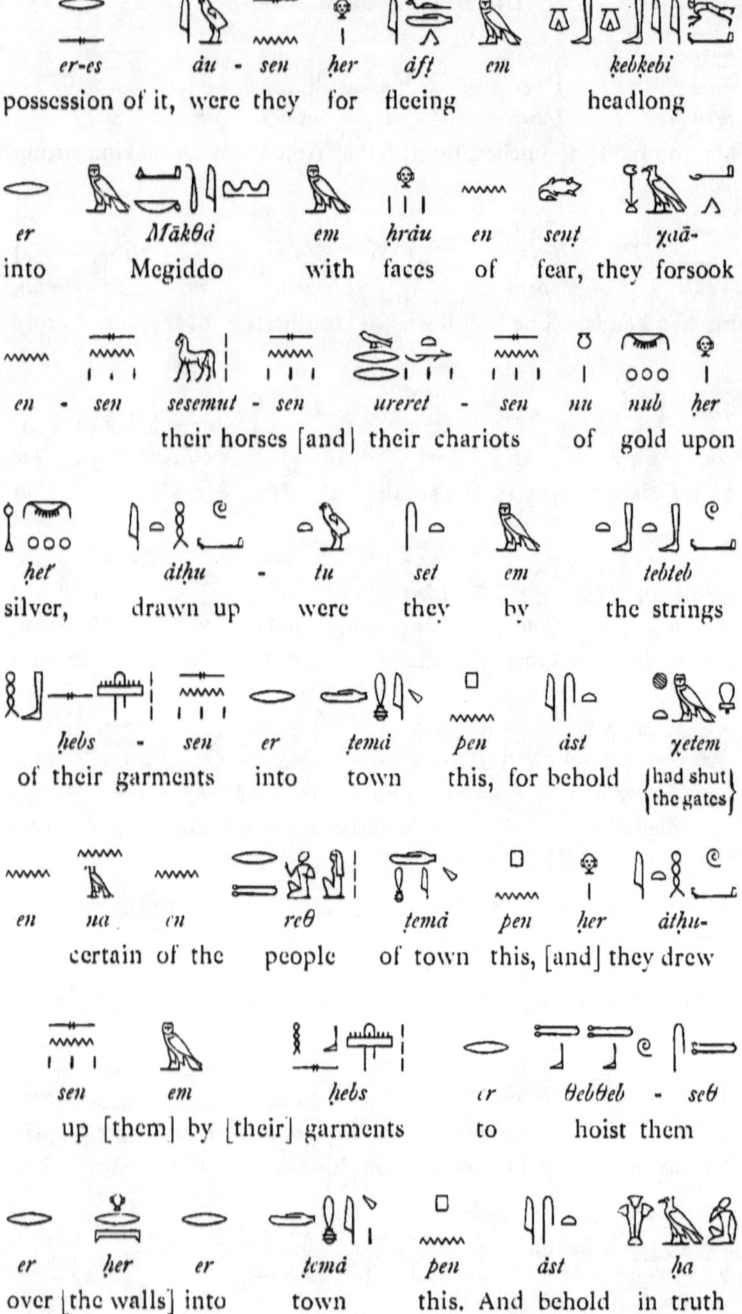

er-es àu - sen ḥer àfṭ em ḳebḳebi
possession of it, were they for fleeing headlong

er Māk θ à em ḥràu en senṭ χaā-
into Megiddo with faces of fear, they forsook

en - sen sesemut - sen ureret - sen nu nub ḥer
their horses [and] their chariots of gold upon

ḥet àtḥu - tu set em tebteb
silver, drawn up were they by the strings

ḥebs - sen er ṭemà pen àst χetem
of their garments into town this, for behold {had shut the gates}

en na en reθ ṭemà pen ḥer àtḥu-
certain of the people of town this, [and] they drew

sen em ḥebs er θebθeb - seθ
up [them] by [their] garments to hoist them

er ḥer er ṭemà pen àst ḥa
over [the walls] into town this. And behold in truth

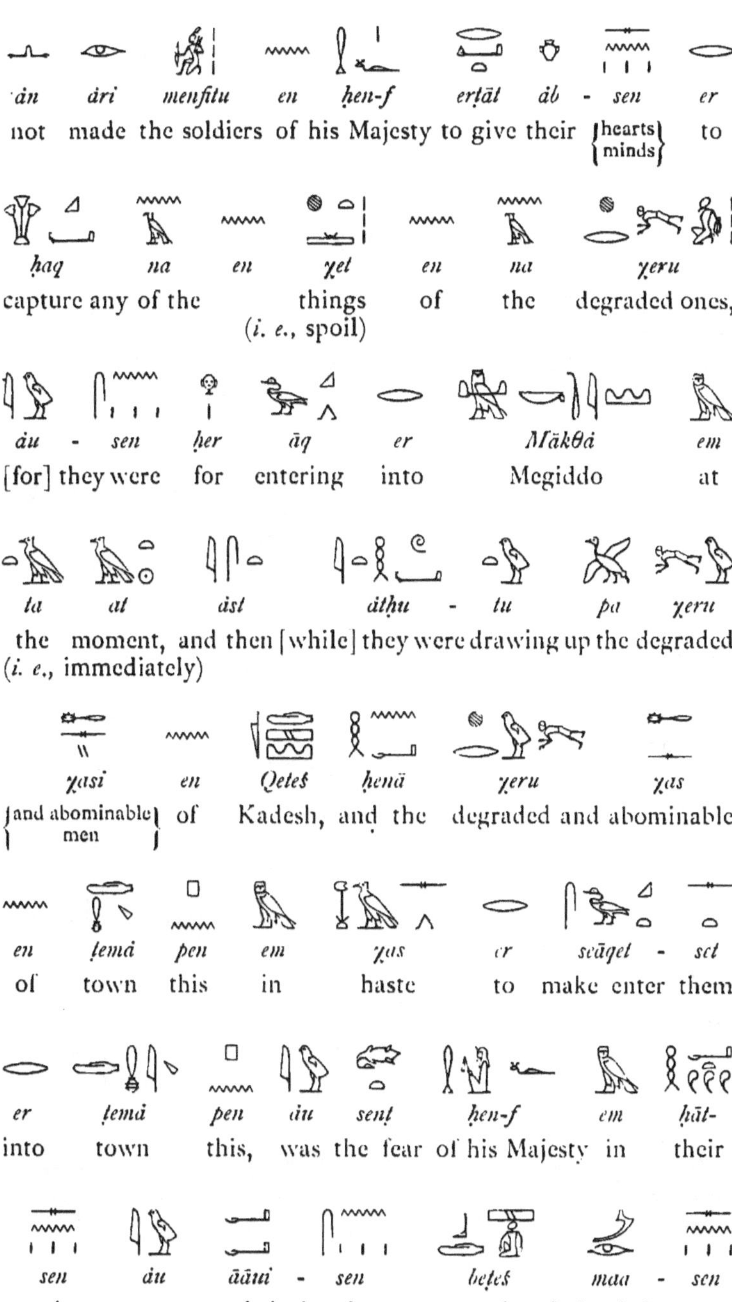

àn àri menfitu en ḥen-f erṭāt àb - sen er
not made the soldiers of his Majesty to give their {hearts / minds} to

ḥaq na en χet en na χeru
capture any of the things (*i. e.*, spoil) of the degraded ones,

àu - sen her āq er Mākθà em
[for] they were for entering into Megiddo at

ta at àst àthu - tu pa χeru
the moment, (*i. e.*, immediately) and then [while] they were drawing up the degraded

χasi en Qeteš henā χeru χas
{and abominable men} of Kadesh, and the degraded and abominable

en temà pen em χas er seāqet - set
of town this in haste to make enter them

er temà pen àu sent ḥen-f em ḥāt-
into town this, was the fear of his Majesty in their

sen àu āāui - sen beteš maa - sen
members, were their hands powerless [when] they saw

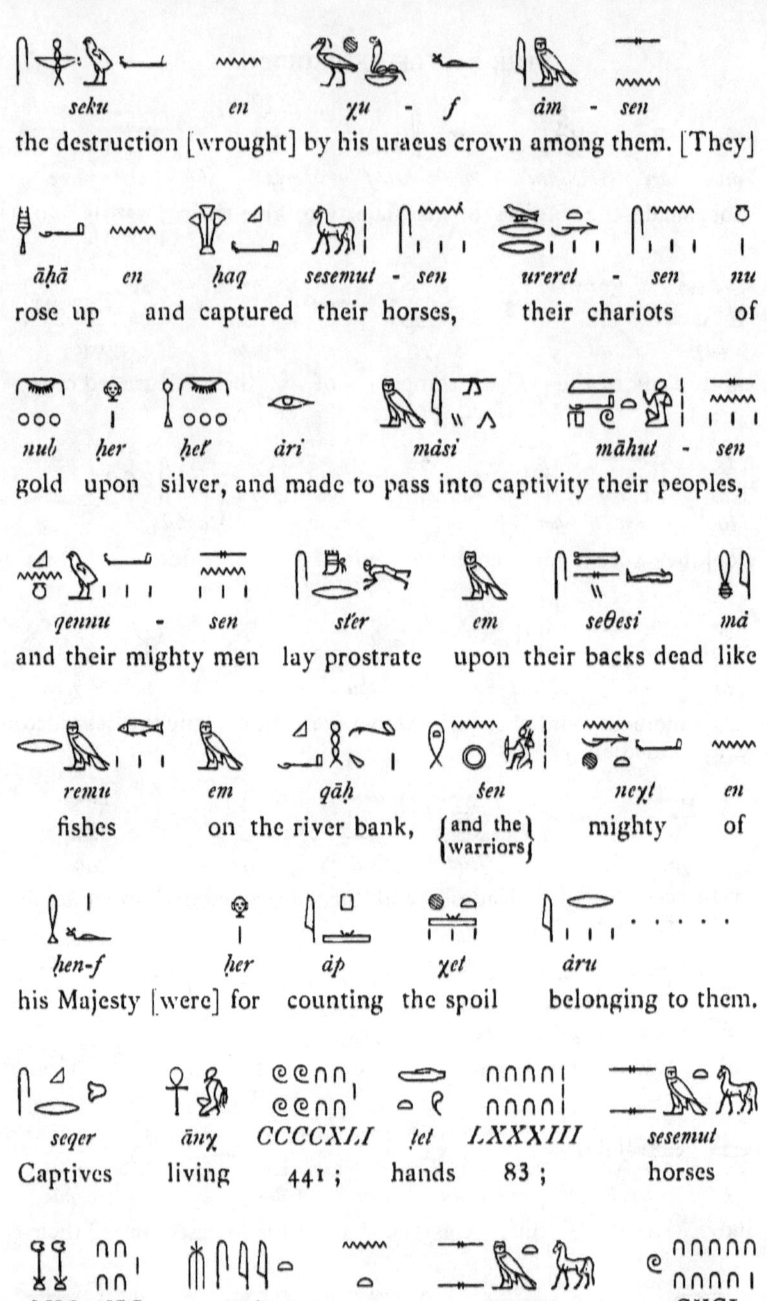

seku en χu - f àm - sen

the destruction [wrought] by his uraeus crown among them. [They]

āḥā en ḥaq sesemut - sen urerет - sen nu

rose up and captured their horses, their chariots of

nub ḥer ḥet' àri màsi māhut - sen

gold upon silver, and made to pass into captivity their peoples,

qennu - sen st'er em seθesi mà

and their mighty men lay prostrate upon their backs dead like

remu em qāḥ šen neχt en

fishes on the river bank, {and the warriors} mighty of

ḥen-f ḥer àp χet àru . . . . . .

his Majesty [were] for counting the spoil belonging to them.

seqer ānχ CCCCXLI ṭet LXXXIII sesemut

Captives living 441; hands 83; horses

MM XLI mesit ent sesemut CXCI

2041; the young of horses 191;

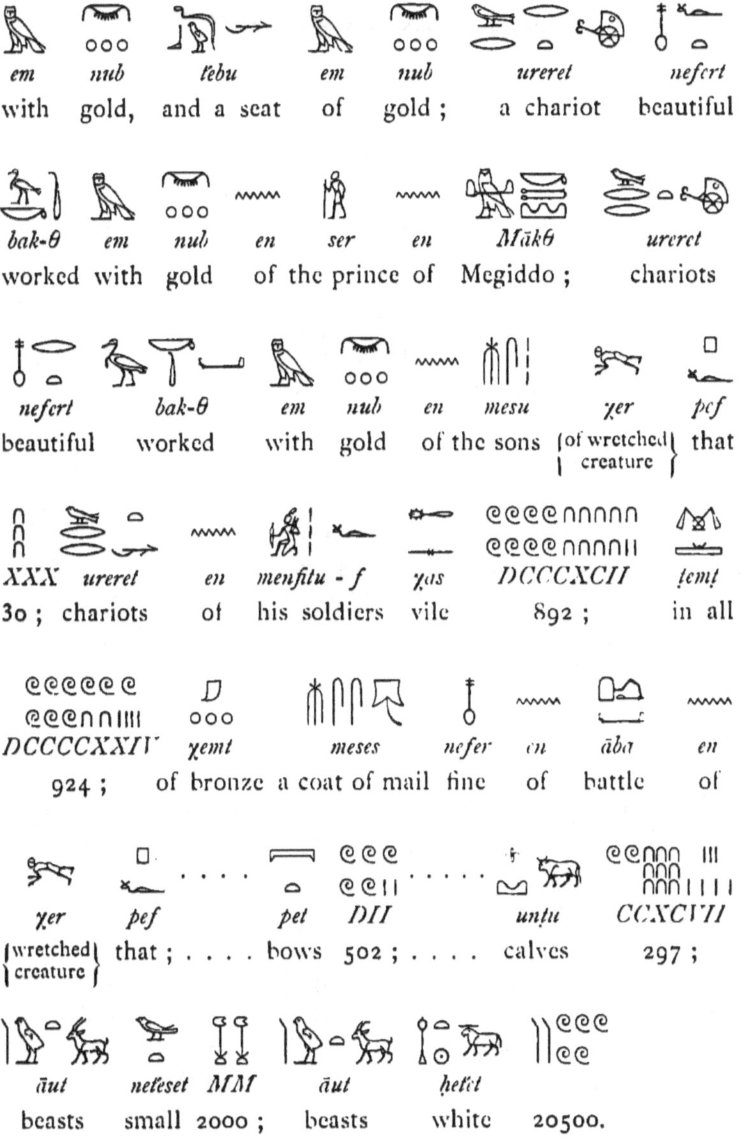
em nub ťebu em nub ureret nefert
with gold, and a seat of gold; a chariot beautiful
bak-θ em nub en ser en Mākθureret
worked with gold of the prince of Megiddo; chariots
nefert bak-θ em nub en mesu χer pef
beautiful worked with gold of the sons {of wretched creature} that
XXX ureret en menfitu-f χas DCCCXCII ṭemṭ
30; chariots of his soldiers vile 892; in all
DCCCCXXIV χemt meses nefer en āba en
924; of bronze a coat of mail fine of battle of
χer pef . . . . pet DII . . . . unṭu CCXCVII
{wretched creature} that; . . . . bows 502; . . . . calves 297;
āut neťeset MM āut heťet
beasts small 2000; beasts white 20500.

SPEECH OF ÀMEN-RĀ TO THOTHMES III.

[XVIIIth dynasty.]

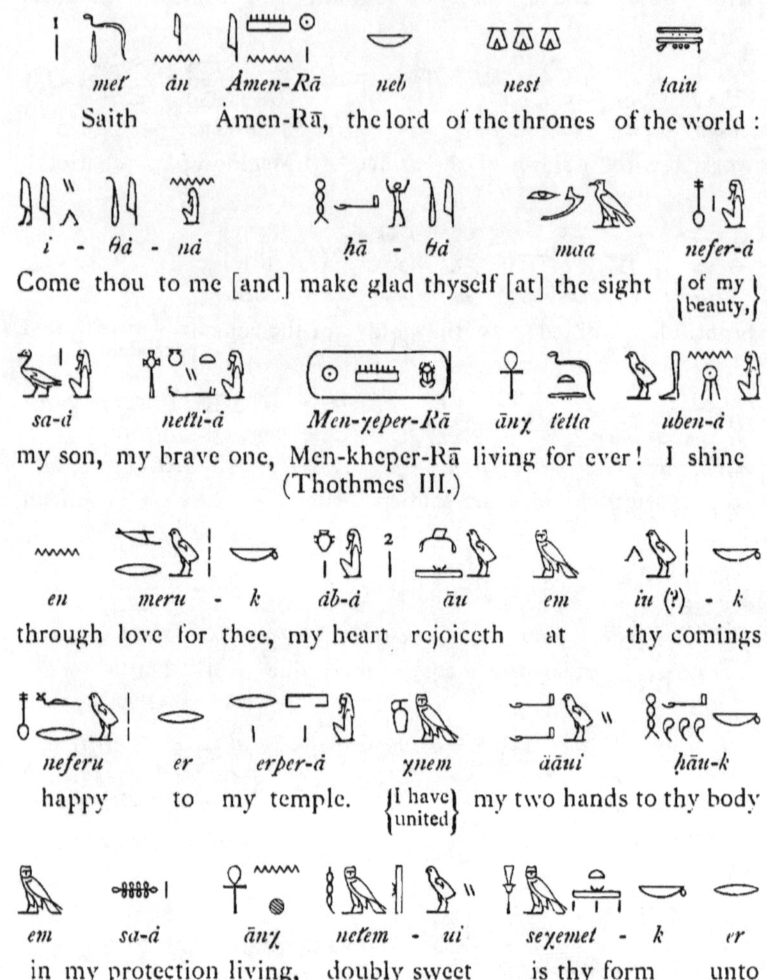

meť *àn* *Àmen-Rā* *neb* *nest* *taiu*

Saith Àmen-Rā, the lord of the thrones of the world:

i - *θà* - *nà* *ḥā* - *θà* *maa* *nefer-à*

Come thou to me [and] make glad thyself [at] the sight {of my beauty,}

sa-à *neťťi-à* *Men-χeper-Rā* *ānχ* *ťetta* *uben-à*

my son, my brave one, Men-kheper-Rā (Thothmes III.) living for ever! I shine

en *meru* - *k* *àb-à* *āu* *em* *iu* (?) - *k*

through love for thee, my heart rejoiceth at thy comings

neferu *er* *erper-à* *χnem* *äāui* *ḥāu-k*

happy to my temple. {I have united} my two hands to thy body

em *sa-à* *ānχ* *neťem* - *ui* *seχemet* - *k* *er*

in my protection living, doubly sweet is thy form unto

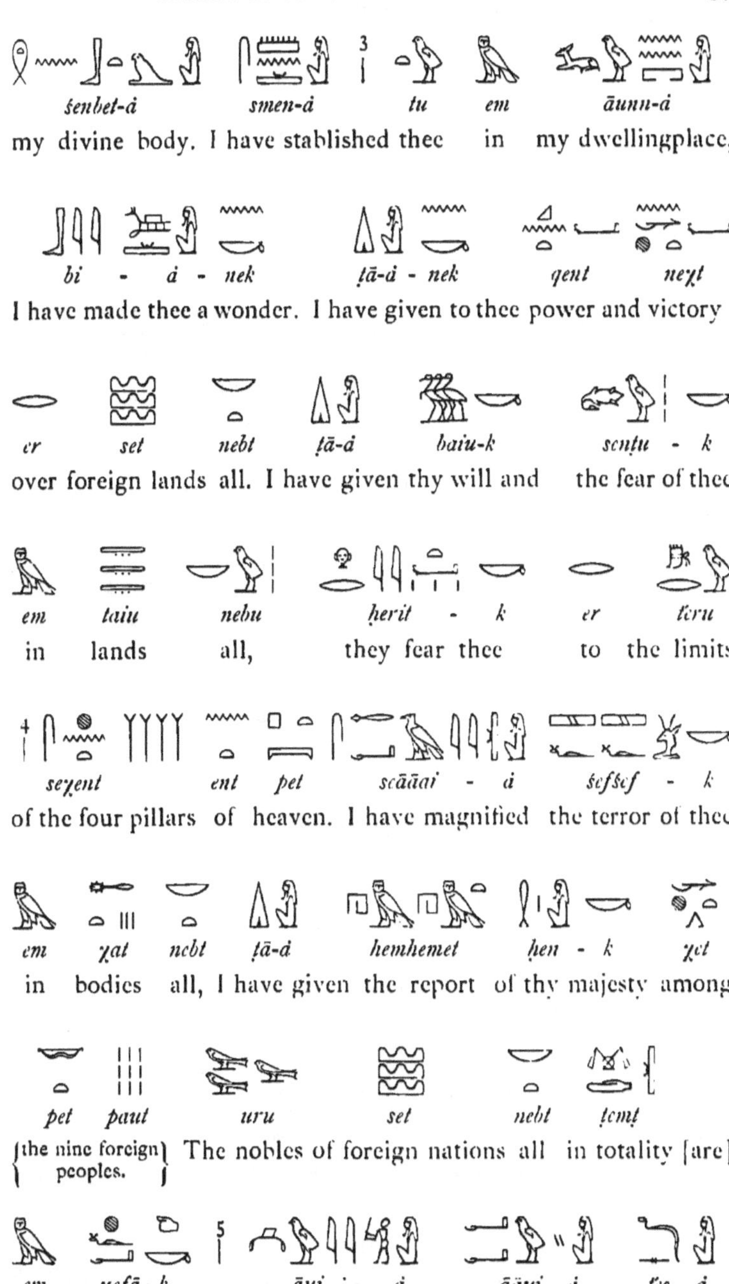

śenbet-å smen-å tu em āunn-å
my divine body. I have stablished thee in my dwellingplace,

bi - å - nek ṭā-å - nek qent nexṭ
I have made thee a wonder. I have given to thee power and victory

er set nebt ṭā-å baiu-k sentu - k
over foreign lands all. I have given thy will and the fear of thee

em taiu nebu ḥerit - k er ṭeru
in lands all, they fear thee to the limits

seχent ent pet seāāai - å śefśef - k
of the four pillars of heaven. I have magnified the terror of thee

em χat nebt ṭā-å hemhemet ḥen - k χet
in bodies all, I have given the report of thy majesty among

pet paut uru set nebt ṭemṭ
{the nine foreign peoples.} The nobles of foreign nations all in totality [are]

em χefā - k āui - å āāui - å ṭes - å
in thy fist. I have stretched out my hands, mine own,

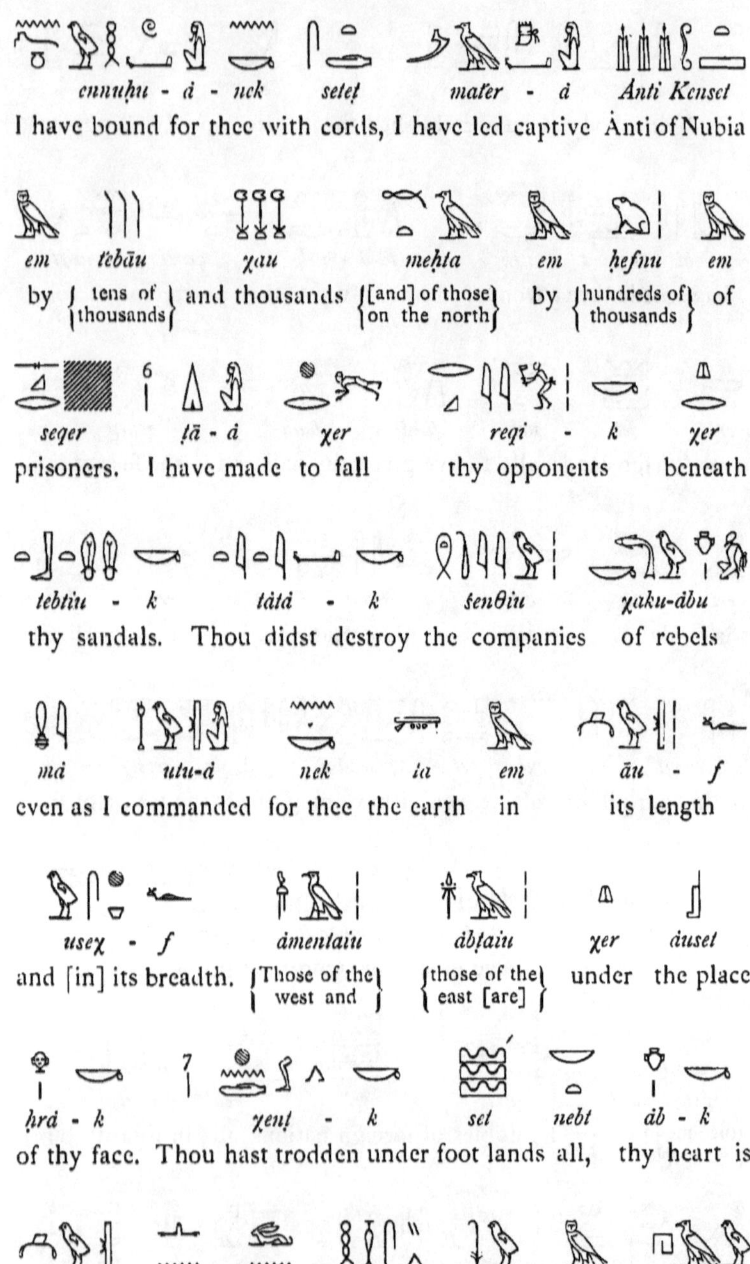

ennuḥu - à - nek seteṭ maṭer - à Ànti Kenset

I have bound for thee with cords, I have led captive Ànti of Nubia

em ṭebāu χau meḥta em ḥefnu em

by {tens of thousands} and thousands {[and] of those on the north} by {hundreds of thousands} of

seqer 6 *ṭā - à χer reqi - k χer*

prisoners. I have made to fall thy opponents beneath

tebtiu - k tàtà - k šenθiu χaku-àbu

thy sandals. Thou didst destroy the companies of rebels

mà utu-à nek ta em āu - f

even as I commanded for thee the earth in its length

useχ - f àmentaiu àbṭaiu χer àuset

and [in] its breadth. {Those of the west and} {those of the east [are]} under the place

ḥrà - k 7 *χenṭ - k set nebt àb - k*

of thy face. Thou hast trodden under foot lands all, thy heart is

āu àn un ḥesi su em hau

glad, not were penetrated they [until] in the time

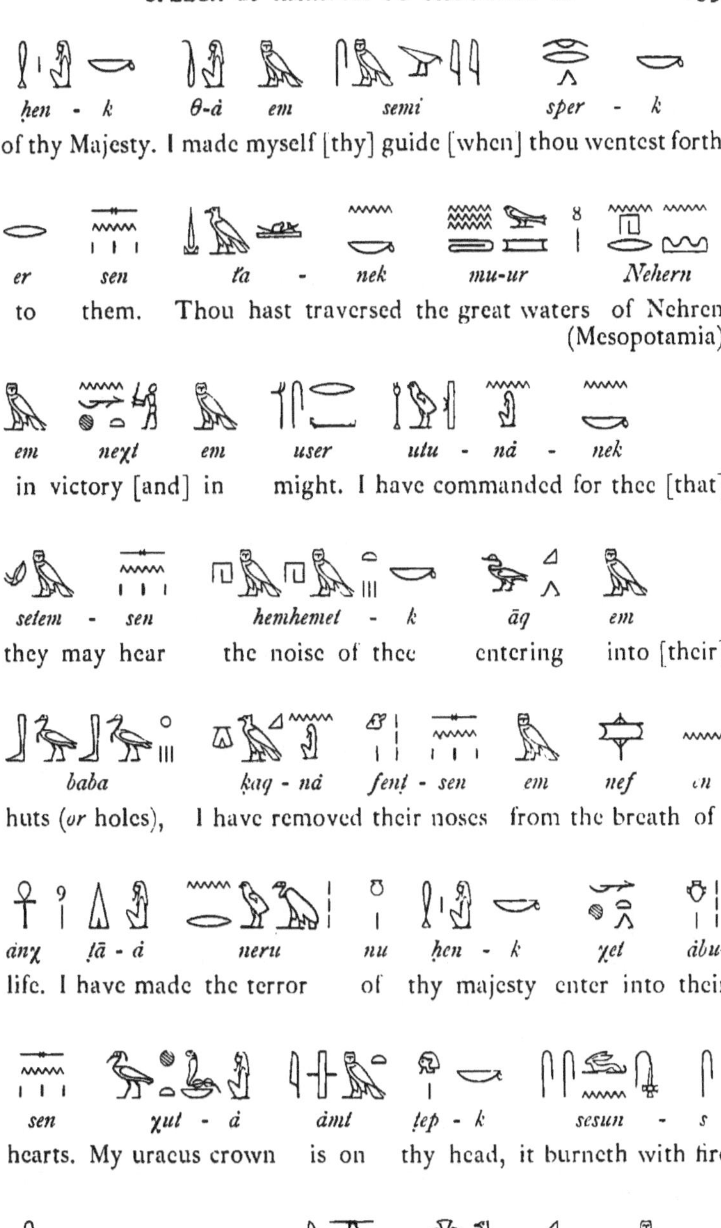

ḥen - k θ-à em semi sper - k

of thy Majesty. I made myself [thy] guide [when] thou wentest forth

er sen t'a - nek mu-ur Nehern

to them. Thou hast traversed the great waters of Nehren (Mesopotamia)

em neχt em user utu - nà - nek

in victory [and] in might. I have commanded for thee [that]

setem - sen hemhemet - k āq em

they may hear the noise of thee entering into [their]

baba ḳaq - nà fenṭ - sen em nef en

huts (*or* holes), I have removed their noses from the breath of

ànχ ṭā - à neru nu ḥen - k χet àbu-

life. I have made the terror of thy majesty enter into their

sen χut - à àmt ṭep - k sesun - s

hearts. My uraeus crown is on thy head, it burneth with fire

set àri - s àseb ḥaq em

them, it maketh [thee] to lead away captives from among

nebṭu *Qeṭ* 10 *amem* - *s* *ȧmu*

the wicked of the peoples of Qeṭ, it burns up those who are among

nebu - *sen* *em* *nesut* *seṭen-s* *ṭepu* *Āmu*

their lords with fire, it cutteth off the heads of the Āmu,

ȧn *nehu* - *sen* *χer* *meses* *en*

not can they escape, [it] overthroweth {him that cometh within the compass} of

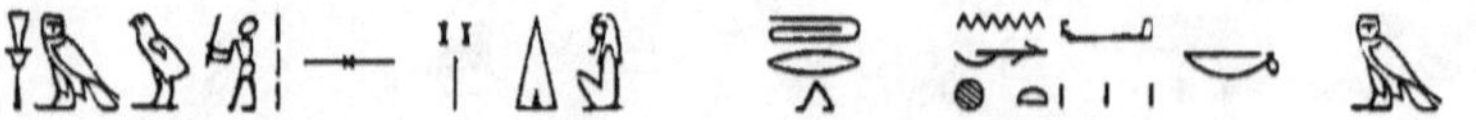

seχemu - *s* 11 *ṭā-ȧ* *rer* *neχt* - *k* *em*

its power. I have made {to go round about} thy victories among

taiu *nebu* *seḥeṭet* *ṭept* - *ȧ* *em* *en* *ṭet* - *k*

lands all, shining with my crown upon thy body.

ȧn *χeper* *bešta* - *k* *er* *šenentu* *pet*

Not shall arise an enemy of thine as far as the circuit of heaven.

iu - *sen* *χer* *ȧnnu* *ḥer* *pesṭu* - *sen* *em*

They come having offerings upon their backs with
(*i. e.*, peoples)

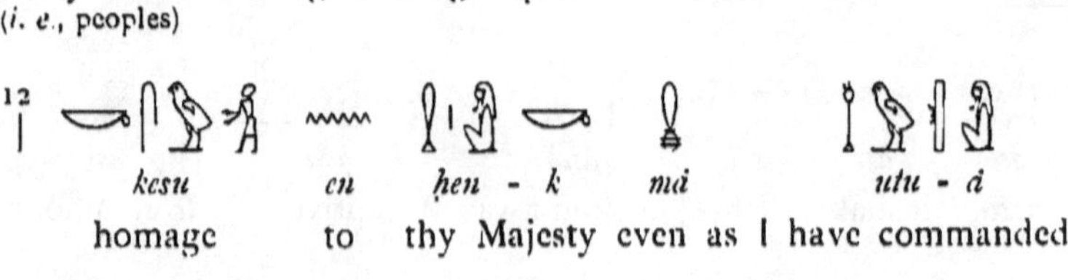

12 *kesu* *en* *ḥen* - *k* *mȧ* *utu* - *ȧ*

homage to thy Majesty even as I have commanded

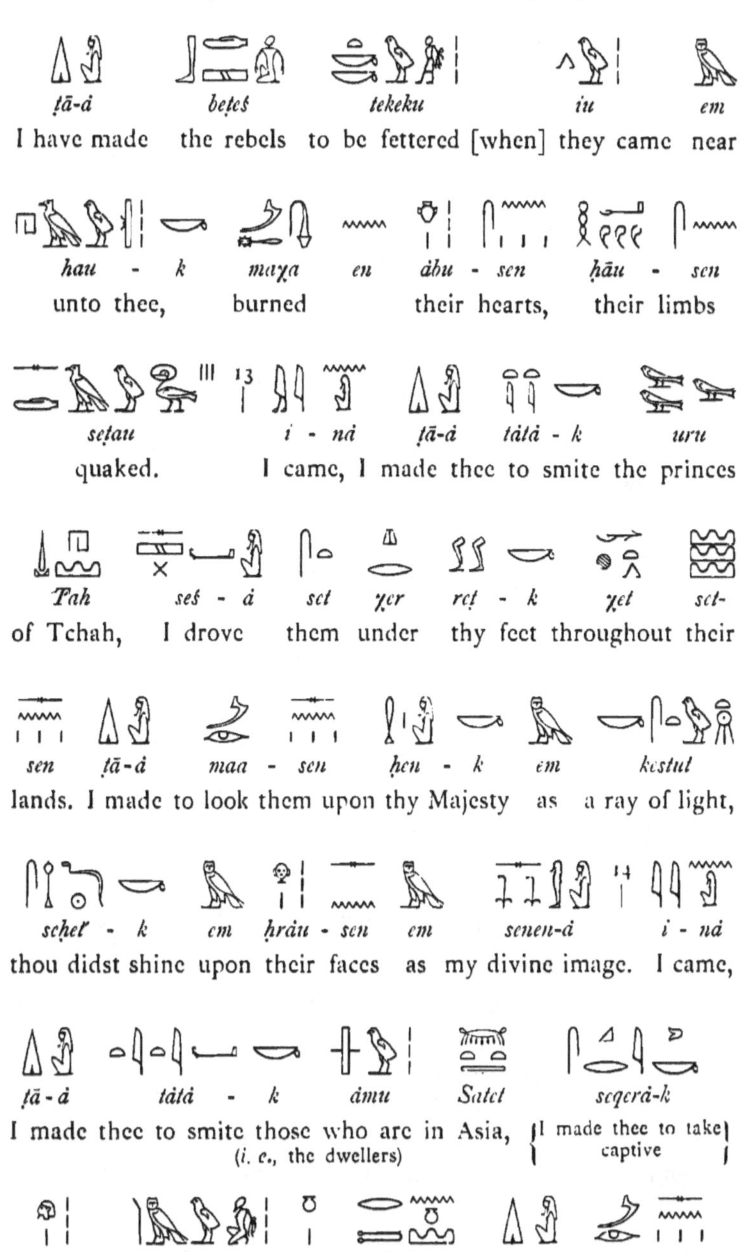

ṭā-à *beṭeš* *tekeku* *iu* *em*
I have made the rebels to be fettered [when] they came near

hau - k *maχa* *en* *àbu - sen* *ḥāu - sen*
unto thee, burned their hearts, their limbs

seṭau *i - nà* *ṭā-à* *tàtà - k* *uru*
quaked. I came, I made thee to smite the princes

Tah *seš - à* *set* *χer* *reṭ - k* *χet* *set-*
of Tchah, I drove them under thy feet throughout their

sen *ṭā-à* *maa - sen* *ḥen - k* *em* *kestut*
lands. I made to look them upon thy Majesty as a ray of light,

scheṭ - k *em* *ḥràu - sen* *em* *senen-à* *i - nà*
thou didst shine upon their faces as my divine image. I came,

ṭā - à *tàtà - k* *àmu* *Satet* *seqerà-k*
I made thee to smite those who are in Asia, (i. e., the dwellers) {I made thee to take captive}

ṭepu *Āmu* *nu* *Reθen* *ṭā - à* *maa - sen*
the chiefs {of the conquered nomads} of Syria, I have made them to see

ḥen - k āper em χaχer - k seśep-k χāā

thy Majesty provided with thy panoply, {thou didst grasp} [thy] weapons

āba ḥer urerit 15 *i - nȧ ṭā-ȧ tàtȧ - k*

[and] fight upon [thy] chariot. I came, I made thee to smite

ta ȧbtet χenṭ - k entau em uu

the land of the east, thou didst trample down those in the regions

nu Ta-neter ṭā - ȧ maa - sen ḥen - k mȧ

of Ta-neter. I made them to look upon thy Majesty as one

seśeṭ sba set bes - f em seśet

circling [like] a star and pouring out his radiance in fire,

ṭā - f ȧṭet - f 16 *i - nȧ ṭā-ȧ tàtȧ - k*

he giveth forth his dew. I came, I made thee to smite

ta Ȧmentet Kefa Ȧsebi χer

the land of the west, Phoenicia and Cyprus hold [thee]

śefśef ṭā - ȧ maa - sen ḥen - k em ka

in fear. I made them to look upon thy Majesty like a bull

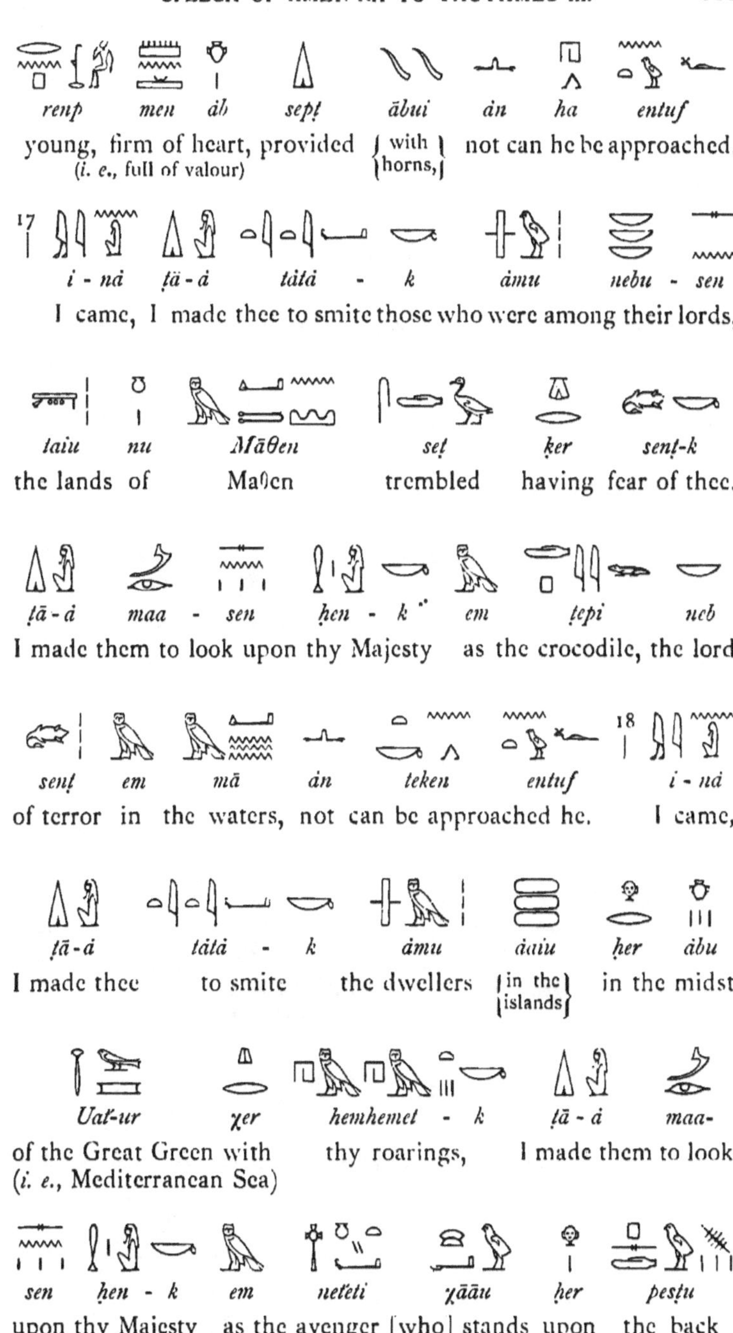

renp men åb sept ābui ån ha entuf

young, firm of heart, (i. e., full of valour) provided {with horns,} not can he be approached.

17 *i - nå tā - å tåtå - k åmu nebu - sen*

I came, I made thee to smite those who were among their lords,

taiu nu Māθen set ḳer sent-k

the lands of Maθen trembled having fear of thee.

tā - å maa - sen ḥen - k em tepi neb

I made them to look upon thy Majesty as the crocodile, the lord

sent em mā ån teken entuf i - nå

of terror in the waters, not can be approached he. 18 I came,

tā - å tåtå - k åmu åaiu ḥer åbu

I made thee to smite the dwellers {in the islands} in the midst

Uat'-ur χer hemhemet - k tā - å maa-

of the Great Green (i. e., Mediterranean Sea) with thy roarings, I made them to look

sen ḥen - k em net'eti χāāu ḥer pestu

upon thy Majesty as the avenger [who] stands upon the back

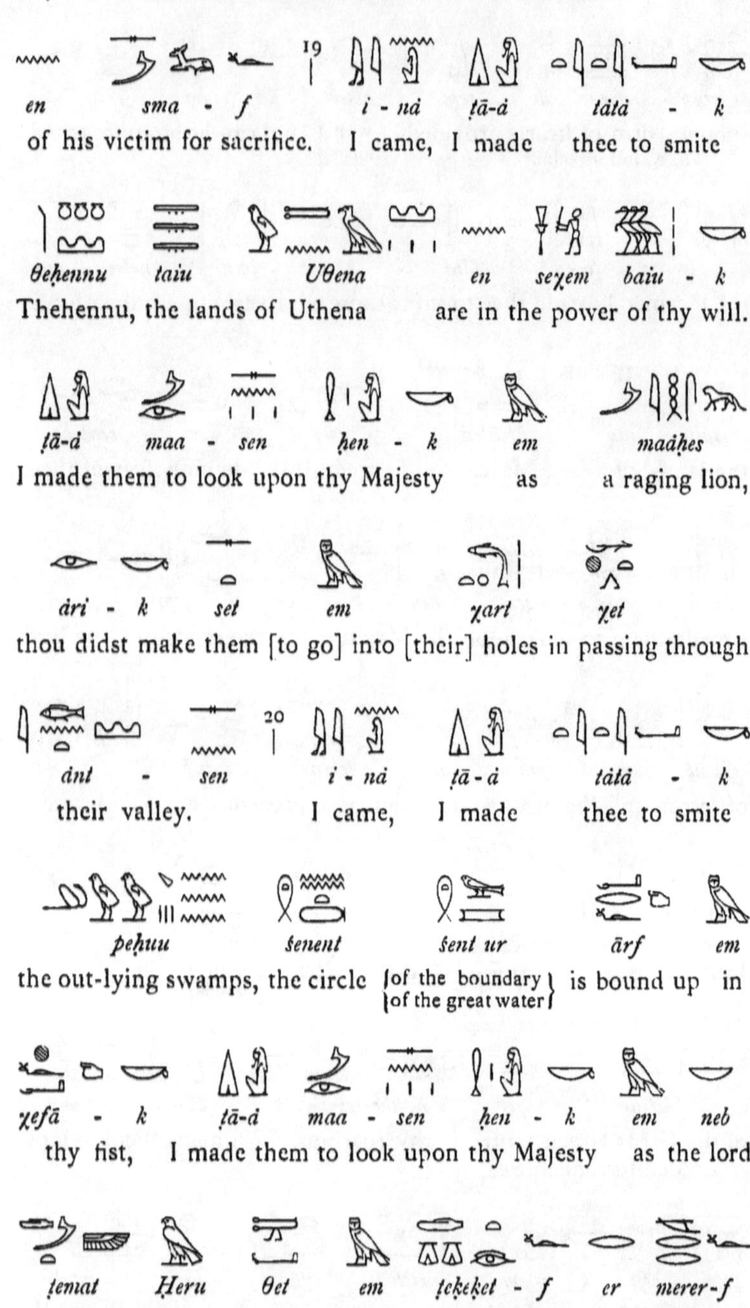

en sma - f 19 *i - nà ṭā-à tàtà - k*

of his victim for sacrifice. I came, I made thee to smite

θeḥennu taiu Uθena en seχem baiu - k

Thehennu, the lands of Uthena are in the power of thy will.

ṭā-à maa - sen ḥen - k em maàḥes

I made them to look upon thy Majesty as a raging lion,

àri - k set em χart χet

thou didst make them [to go] into [their] holes in passing through

ànt - sen 20 *i - nà ṭā - à tàtà - k*

their valley. I came, I made thee to smite

peḥuu šenent šent ur ārf em

the out-lying swamps, the circle {of the boundary / of the great water} is bound up in

χefā - k ṭā-à maa - sen ḥen - k em neb

thy fist, I made them to look upon thy Majesty as the lord

ṭemat Ḥeru θet em ṭeḳeḳet - f er merer-f

of pinions, Horus carrying off with his glance {what he / pleaseth.}

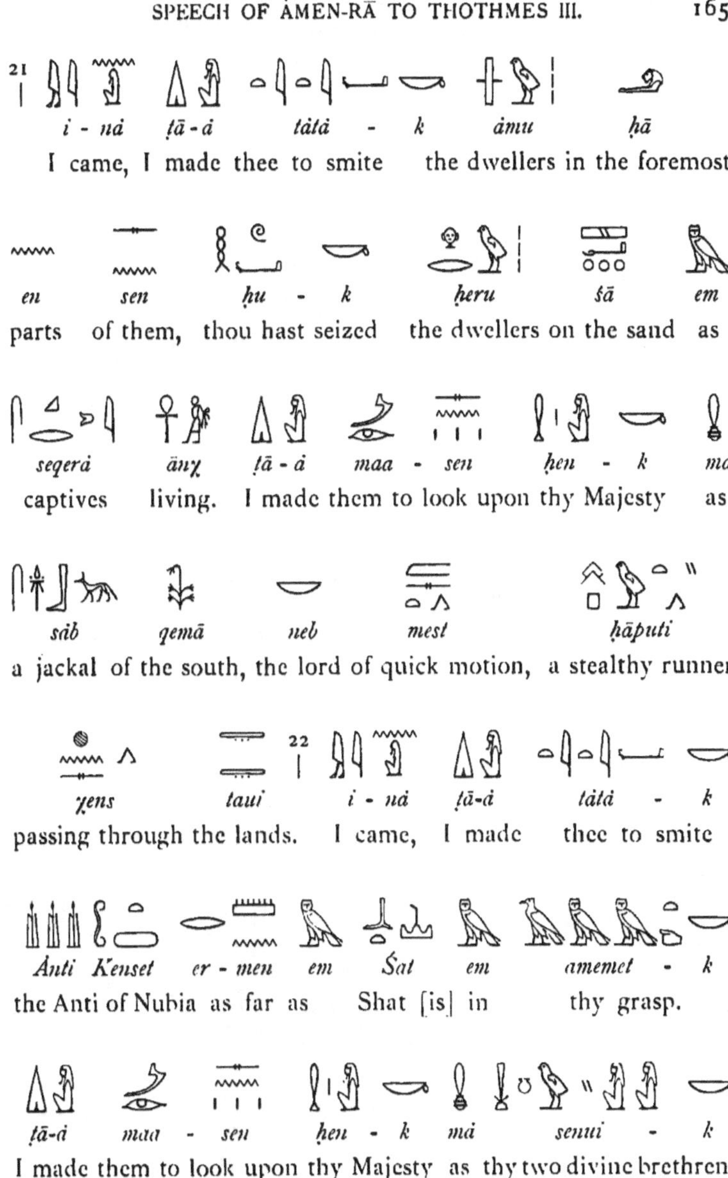

21 *i - nà ṭā - à tàtà - k àmu ḥā*
I came, I made thee to smite the dwellers in the foremost

en sen ḥu - k ḥeru šā em
parts of them, thou hast seized the dwellers on the sand as

seqerà ānχ ṭā - à maa - sen ḥen - k mà
captives living. I made them to look upon thy Majesty as

sàb qemā neb mest ḥāputi
a jackal of the south, the lord of quick motion, a stealthy runner

χens taui 22 *i - nà ṭā-à tàtà - k*
passing through the lands. I came, I made thee to smite

Ànti Kenset er - men em Šat em amemet - k
the Anti of Nubia as far as Shat [is] in thy grasp.

ṭā-à maa - sen ḥen - k mà senui - k
I made them to look upon thy Majesty as thy two divine brethren,

ṭemṭ - nà āāui - sen nek em n . . . 23 *sent - k*
I have united their two hands unto thee in . . . . . ., {thy two divine sisters}

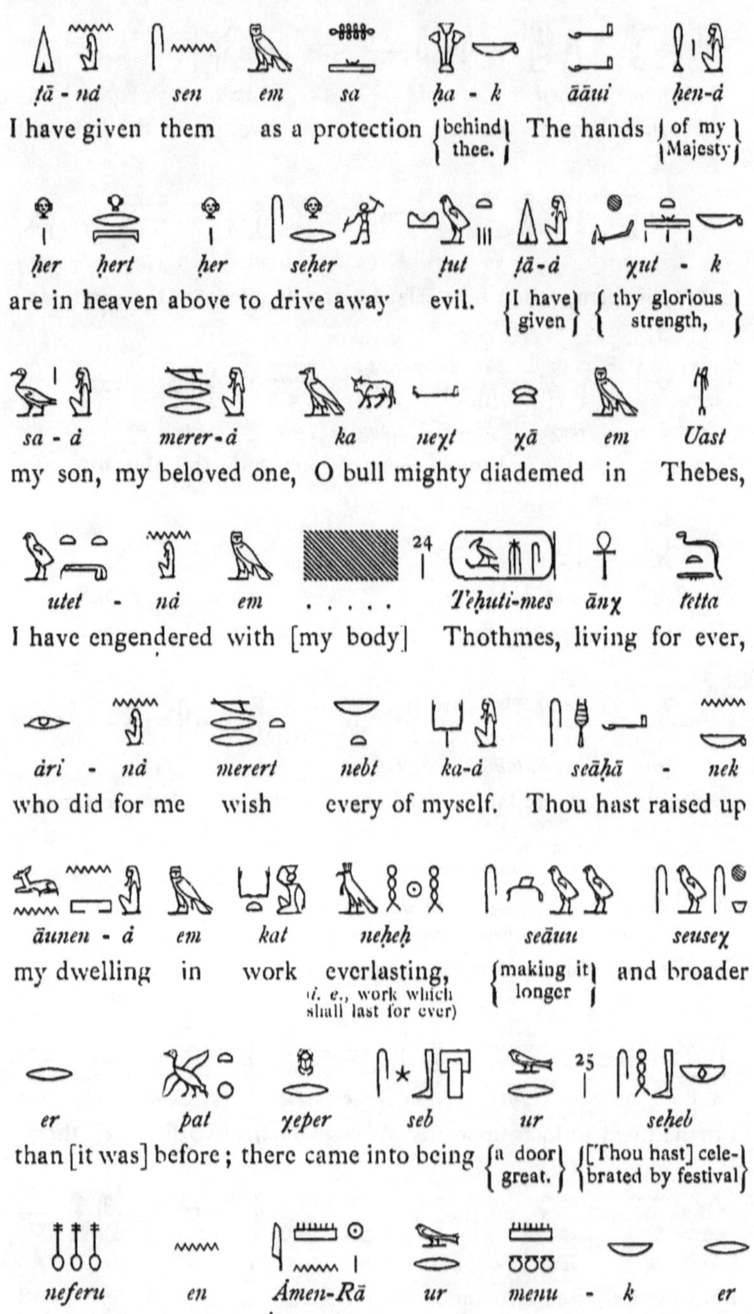

ṭā - nȧ sen em sa ḥa - k āāui ḥen-ȧ

I have given them as a protection {behind thee.} The hands {of my Majesty}

ḥer ḥert ḥer seḥer ṭut ṭā - ȧ χut - k

are in heaven above to drive away evil. {I have given} {thy glorious strength,}

sa - ȧ merer - ȧ ka neχt χā em Uast

my son, my beloved one, O bull mighty diademed in Thebes,

utet - nȧ em . . . . . 24 Teḥuti-mes ānχ tetta

I have engendered with [my body] Thothmes, living for ever,

ȧri - nȧ merert nebt ka-ȧ seāḥā - nek

who did for me wish every of myself. Thou hast raised up

āunen - ȧ em kat neḥeḥ seāuu seuseχ

my dwelling in work everlasting, (*i. e.*, work which shall last for ever) {making it longer} and broader

er pat χeper seb ur 25 seḥeb

than [it was] before; there came into being {a door great.} {[Thou hast] celebrated by festival}

neferu en Åmen-Rā ur menu - k er

the beauties of Åmen-Rā, great are thy monuments more

suten - k neb χeper utu - nȧ - nek

than [those of] king any that hath existed. I commanded thee

ȧrit - set ḥetep - ku ḥer - s smen-ȧ

to make them, and thou hast been content thereat. I have established

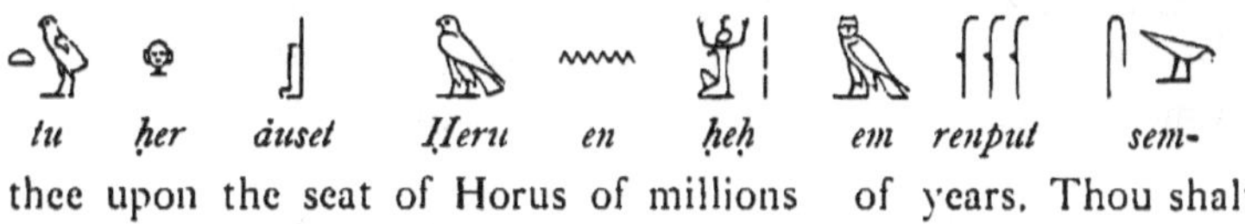

tu ḥer ȧuset Ḥeru en ḥeḥ em renput sem-

thee upon the seat of Horus of millions of years. Thou shalt

k ānχ

guide living . . . . . .

EXTRACT FROM THE 154TH CHAPTER OF THE BOOK OF THE DEAD.

[XVIIIth dynasty.]

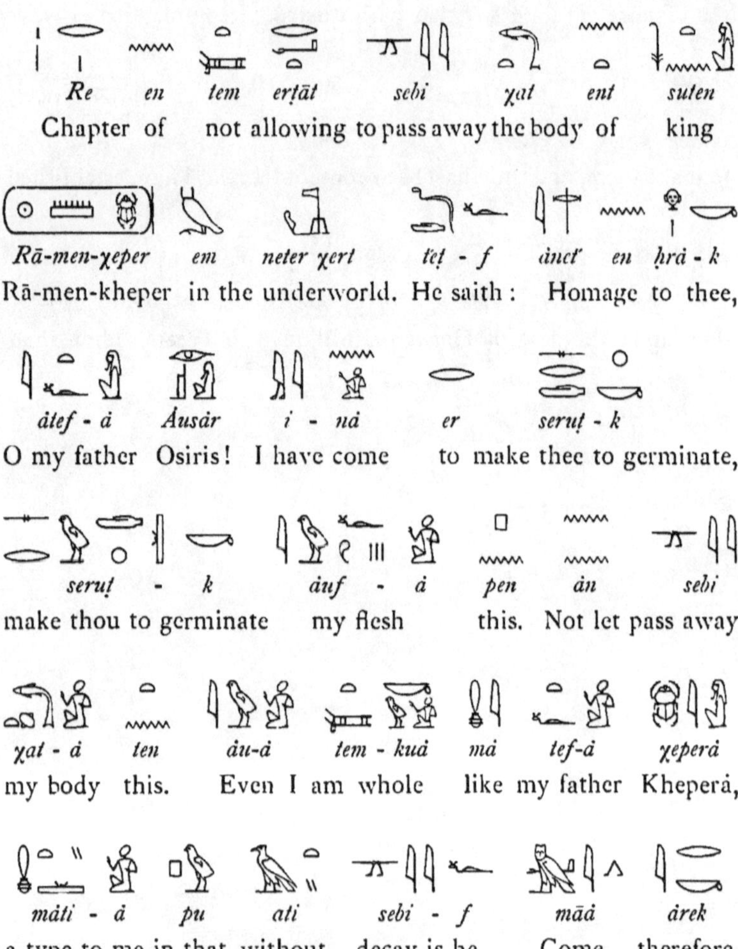

Re en tem erṭāt sebi χat ent suten
Chapter of not allowing to pass away the body of king
Rā-men-χeper em neter χert ṫeṭ - f ȧnet' en ḥrȧ - k
Rā-men-kheper in the underworld. He saith: Homage to thee,
ȧtef - ȧ Ȧusȧr i - nȧ er seruṭ - k
O my father Osiris! I have come to make thee to germinate,
seruṭ - k ȧuf - ȧ pen ȧn sebi
make thou to germinate my flesh this. Not let pass away
χat - ȧ ten ȧu-ȧ tem - kuȧ mȧ tef-ȧ χeperȧ
my body this. Even I am whole like my father Kheperȧ,
mȧti - ȧ pu ati sebi - f māȧ ȧrek
a type to me in that without decay is he. Come, therefore,

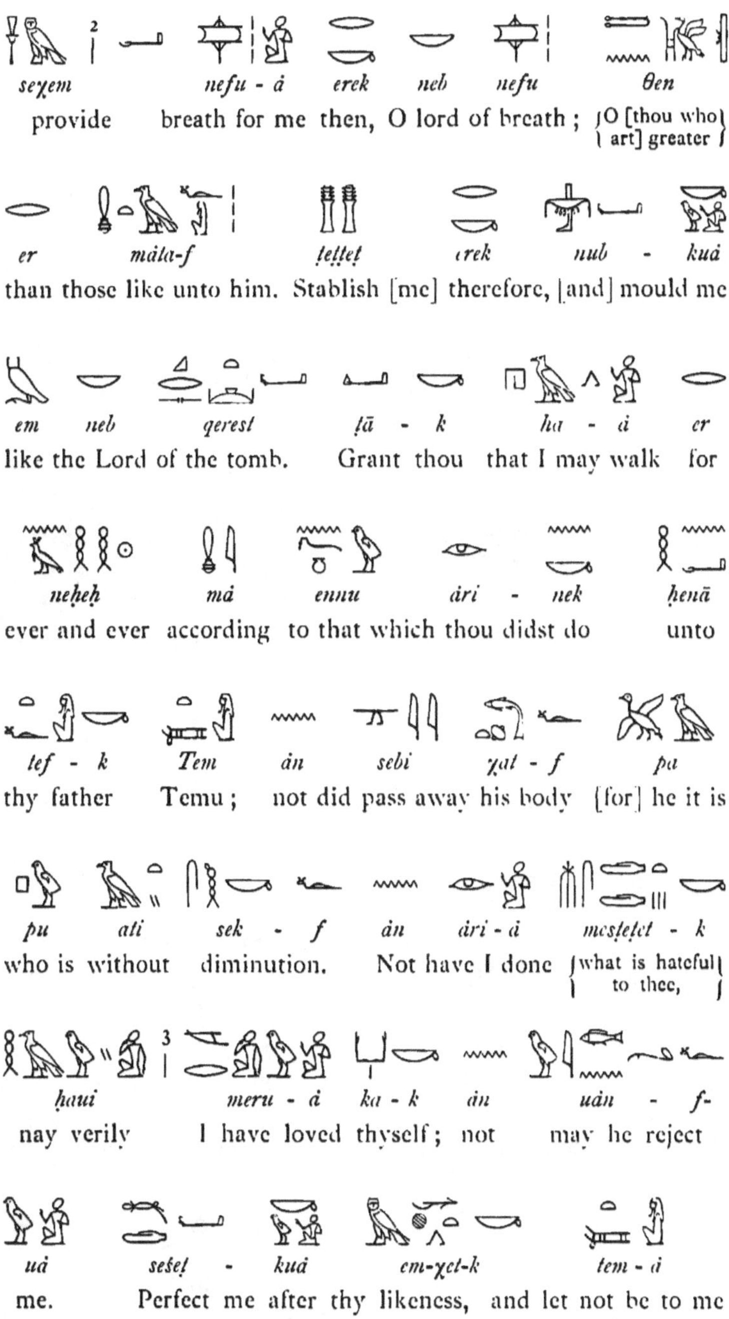

2 seχem nefu - à erek neb nefu θen

provide breath for me then, O lord of breath; {O [thou who art] greater}

er màla-f ṭeṭṭeṭ erek nub - kuà

than those like unto him. Stablish [me] therefore, [and] mould me

em neb qerest ṭā - k ha - à er

like the Lord of the tomb. Grant thou that I may walk for

neḥeḥ mà ennu àri - nek ḥenā

ever and ever according to that which thou didst do unto

tef - k Tem àn sebi χat - f pa

thy father Temu; not did pass away his body [for] he it is

pu ati sek - f àn àri - à mesṭeṭet - k

who is without diminution. Not have I done {what is hateful to thee,}

ḥaui 3 meru - à ka - k àn uàn - f-

nay verily I have loved thyself; not may he reject

uà seśeṭ - kuà em-χet-k tem - à

me. Perfect me after thy likeness, and let not be to me

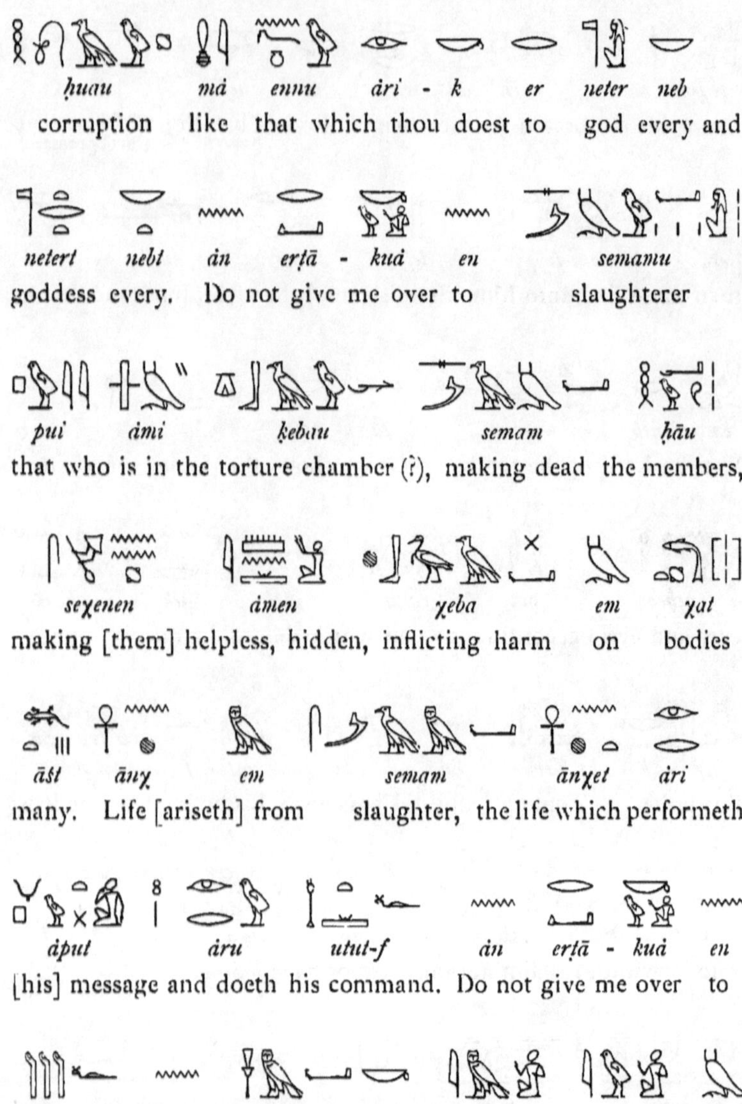

ḥuau mȧ ennu ȧri - k er neter neb

corruption like that which thou doest to god every and

netert nebt ȧn erṭā - kuȧ en semamu

goddess every. Do not give me over to slaughterer

pui ȧmi ḳebau semam ḥāu

that who is in the torture chamber (?), making dead the members,

seχenen ȧmen χeba em χat

making [them] helpless, hidden, inflicting harm on bodies

āšt ānχ em semam ānχet ȧri

many. Life [ariseth] from slaughter, the life which performeth

ȧput ȧru utut-f ȧn erṭā - kuȧ en

[his] message and doeth his command. Do not give me over to

ṭebā - f ȧn seχem - k ȧm - ȧ ȧu-ȧ em

his fingers. Do not gain the mastery over me. I am under

utu - k neb neteru ȧnet' ḥrȧ - k ȧtef - ȧ

thy command, O lord of the gods. Homage to thee, O my father

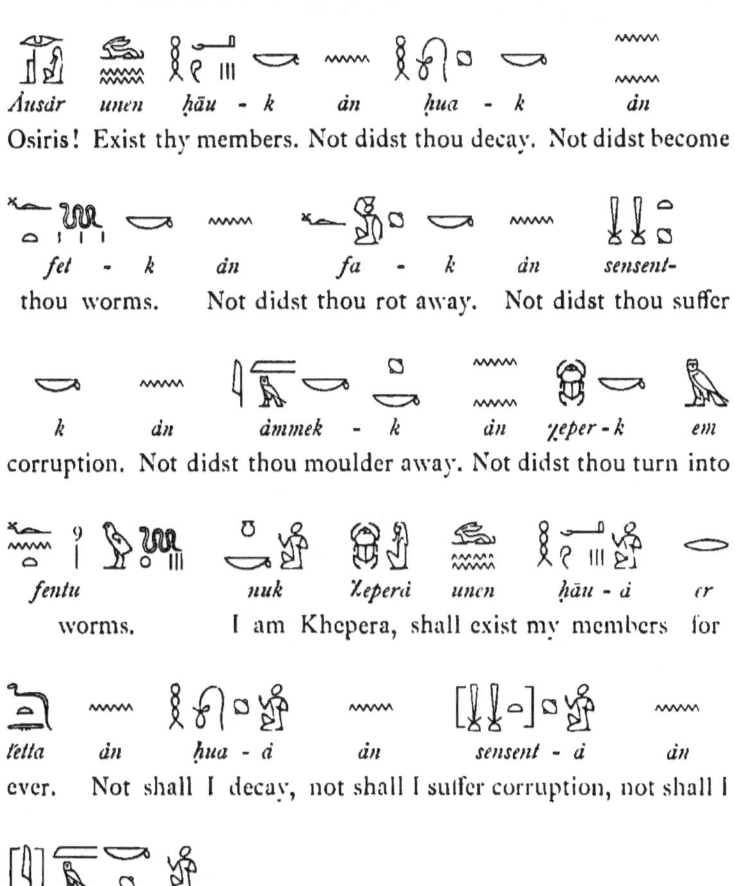

Ȧusȧr unen ḥāu - k ȧn ḥua - k ȧn

Osiris! Exist thy members. Not didst thou decay. Not didst become

fet - k ȧn fa - k ȧn sensent-

thou worms. Not didst thou rot away. Not didst thou suffer

k ȧn ȧmmek - k ȧn χeper - k em

corruption. Not didst thou moulder away. Not didst thou turn into

fentu nuk Χeperȧ unen ḥāu - ȧ er

worms. I am Khepera, shall exist my members for

t'etta ȧn ḥua - ȧ ȧn sensent - ȧ ȧn

ever. Not shall I decay, not shall I suffer corruption, not shall I

ȧmmek - ȧ

moulder away.

SPECIMENS OF THE MAXIMS OF ANI.

[XVIIIth dynasty.]

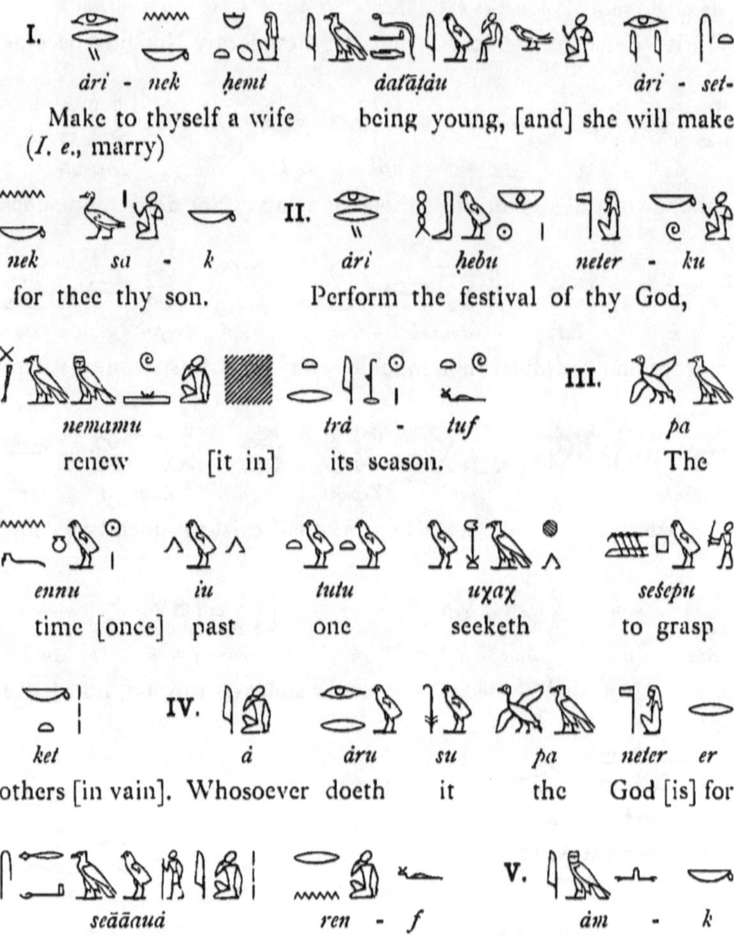

I. *àri - nek ḥemt daťāṭàu àri - set-*

Make to thyself a wife being young, [and] she will make
(*I. e.*, marry)

nek sa - k II. *àri ḥebu neter - ku*

for thee thy son. Perform the festival of thy God,

nemamu trà - tuf III. *pa*

renew [it in] its season. The

ennu iu tutu uχaχ seśepu

time [once] past one seeketh to grasp

ket IV. *à àru su pa neter er*

others [in vain]. Whosoever doeth it the God [is] for

seāāauà ren - f V. *àm - k*

magnifying his name. Not do thou

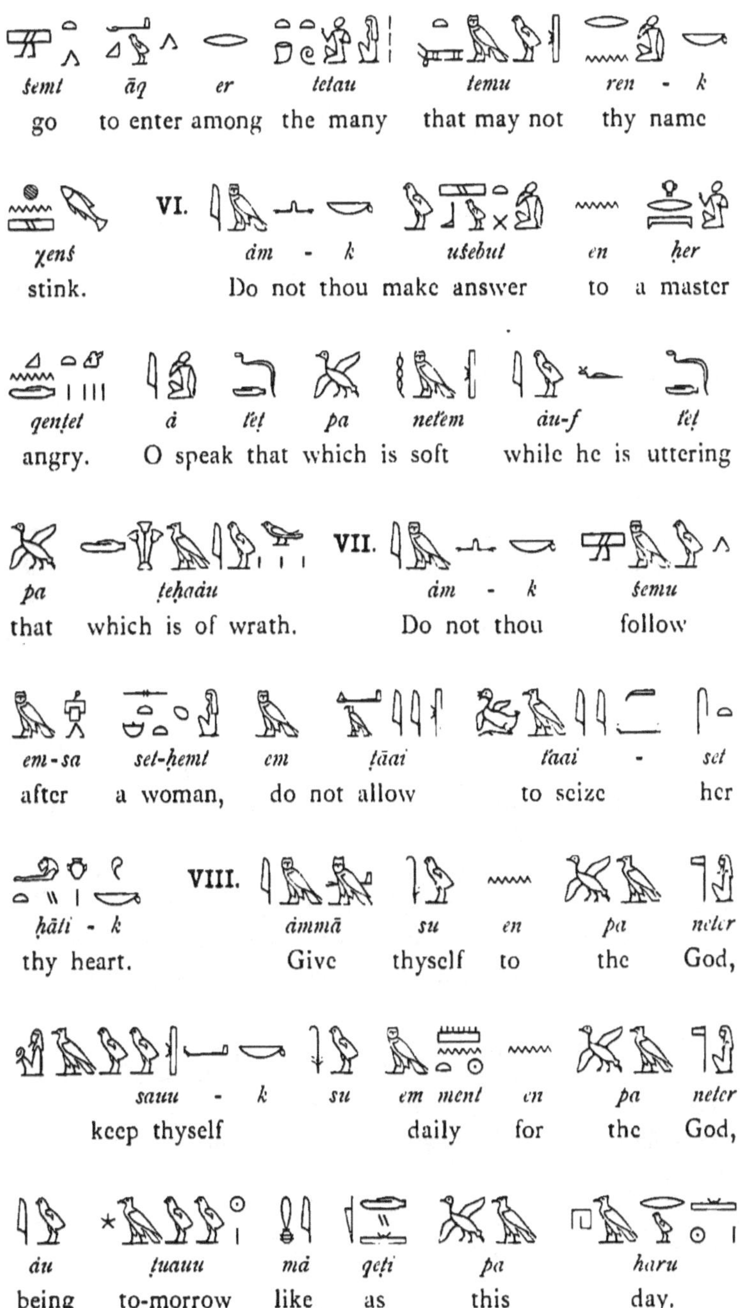

šemt āq er tetau temu ren - k
go to enter among the many that may not thy name

χenš VI. *ȧm - k ušebut en ḥer*
stink. Do not thou make answer to a master

qenṭet ȧ ṫeṭ pa neṫem ȧu-f ṫeṭ
angry. O speak that which is soft while he is uttering

pa ṭeḥaȧu VII. *ȧm - k šemu*
that which is of wrath. Do not thou follow

em-sa set-ḥemt em ṭāai ṫaai - set
after a woman, do not allow to seize her

ḥāti - k VIII. *ȧmmā su en pa neter*
thy heart. Give thyself to the God,

sauu - k su em ment en pa neter
keep thyself daily for the God,

ȧu ṭuauu mā qeṭi pa haru
being to-morrow like as this day.

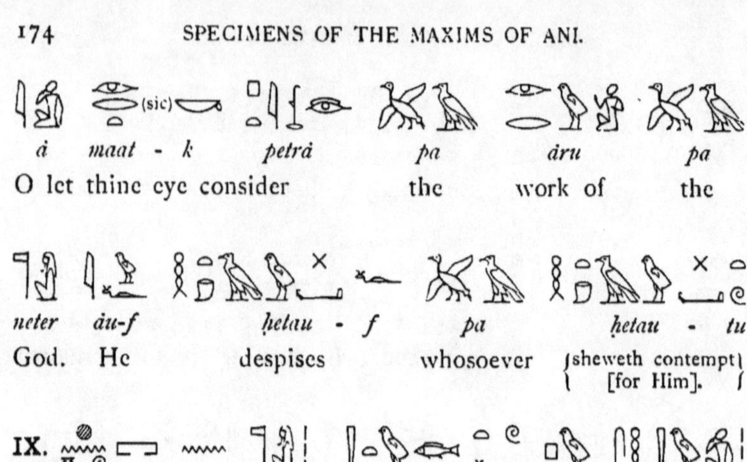

à maat - k petrà pa àru pa

O let thine eye consider the work of the

neter àu-f ḥetau - f pa ḥetau - tu

God. He despises whosoever {sheweth contempt [for Him].}

IX. 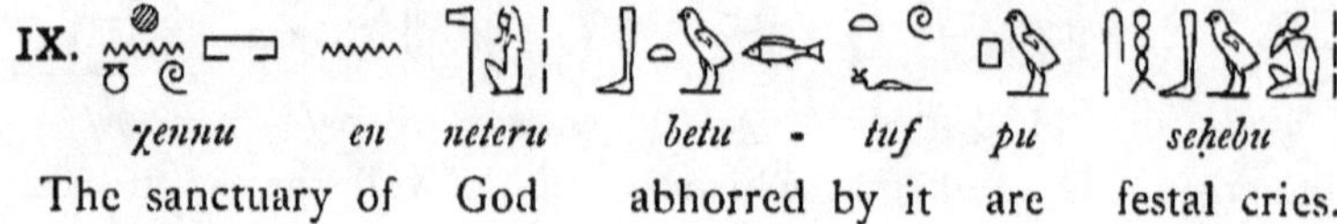

χennu en neteru betu - tuf pu seḥebu

The sanctuary of God abhorred by it are festal cries.

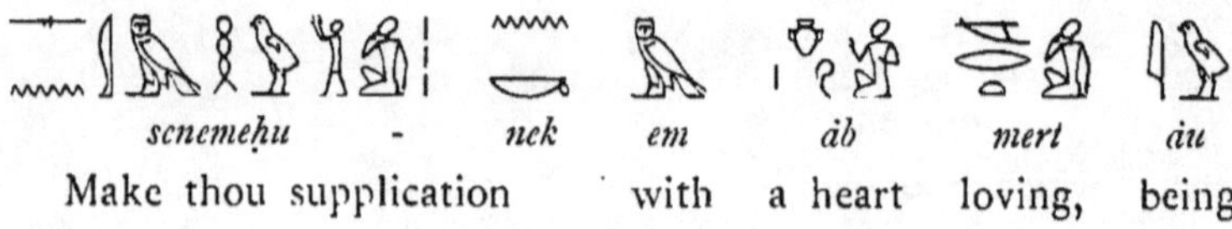

senemeḥu - nek em àb mert àu

Make thou supplication with a heart loving, being

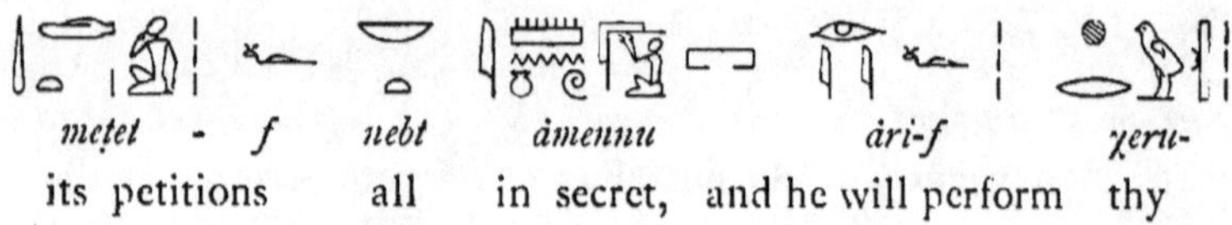

meṭet - f nebt àmennu àri-f χeru-

its petitions all in secret, and he will perform thy

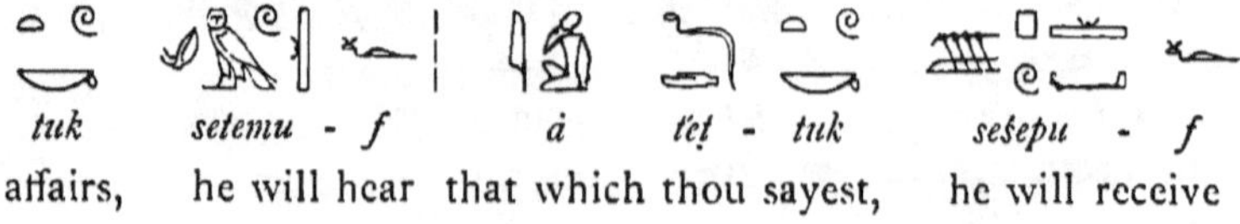

tuk setemu - f à t'eṭ - tuk sešepu - f

affairs, he will hear that which thou sayest, he will receive

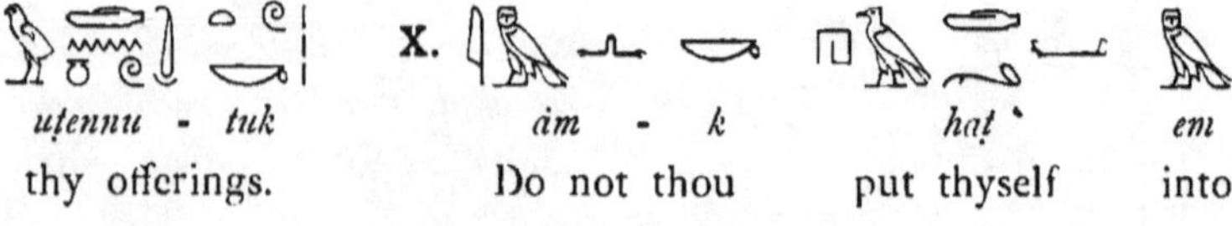

uṭennu - tuk X. *àm - k haṭ em*

thy offerings. Do not thou put thyself into

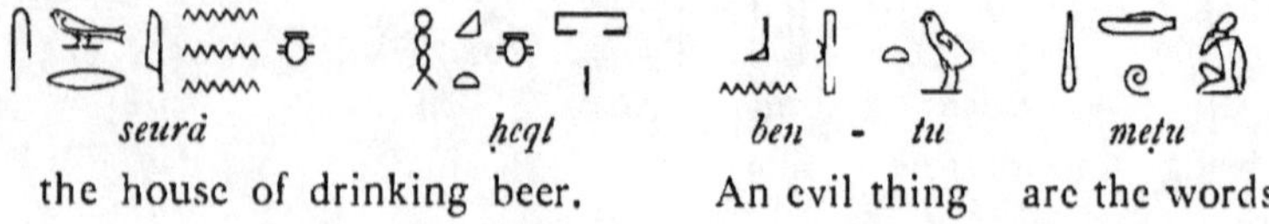

seurà ḥeqt ben - tu meṭu

the house of drinking beer. An evil thing are the words

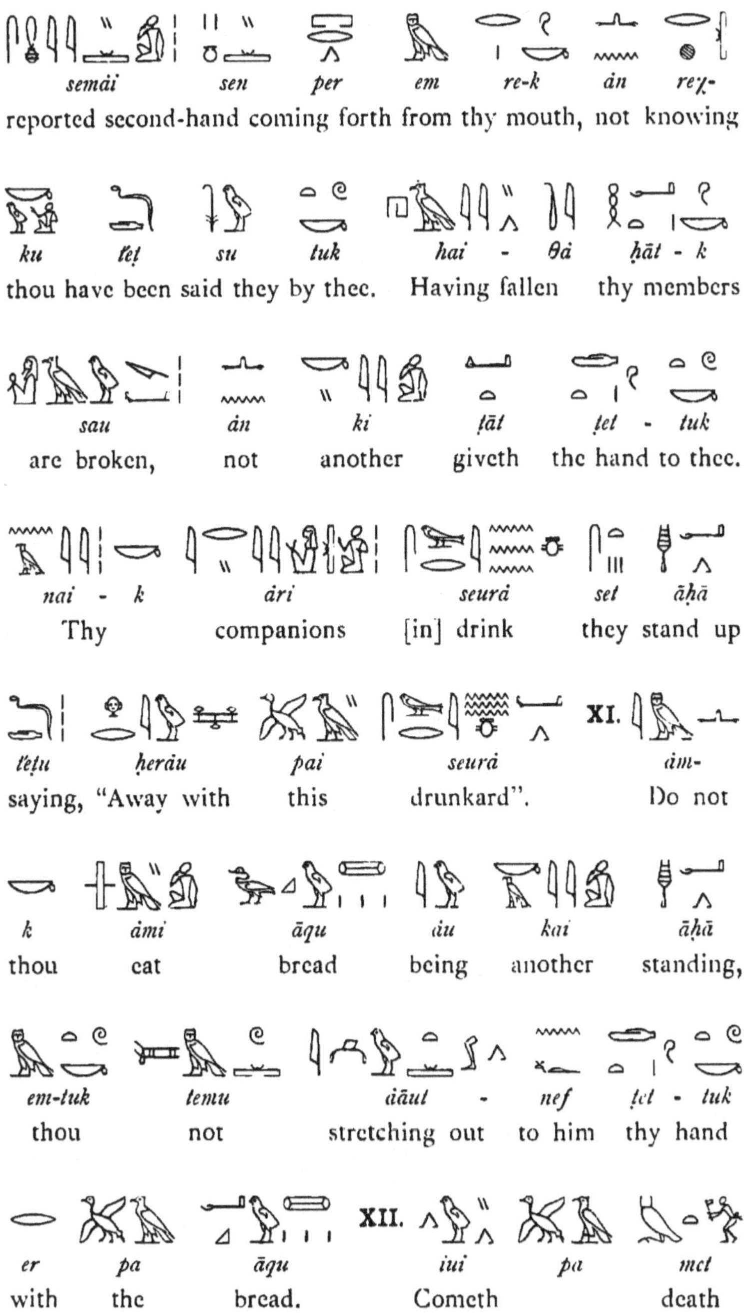
semäi sen per em re-k än reχ-
reported second-hand coming forth from thy mouth, not knowing
ku ṭeṭ su tuk hai - θä ḥāt - k
thou have been said they by thee. Having fallen thy members
sau än ki ṭāt ṭet - tuk
are broken, not another giveth the hand to thee.
nai - k äri seurä set āḥā
Thy companions [in] drink they stand up
ṭeṭu ḥeräu pai seurä äm-
saying, "Away with this drunkard". Do not
k ämi āqu äu kai āḥā
thou eat bread being another standing,
em-tuk temu däut - nef ṭet - tuk
thou not stretching out to him thy hand
er pa āqu iui pa met
with the bread. Cometh death
XI.
XII.

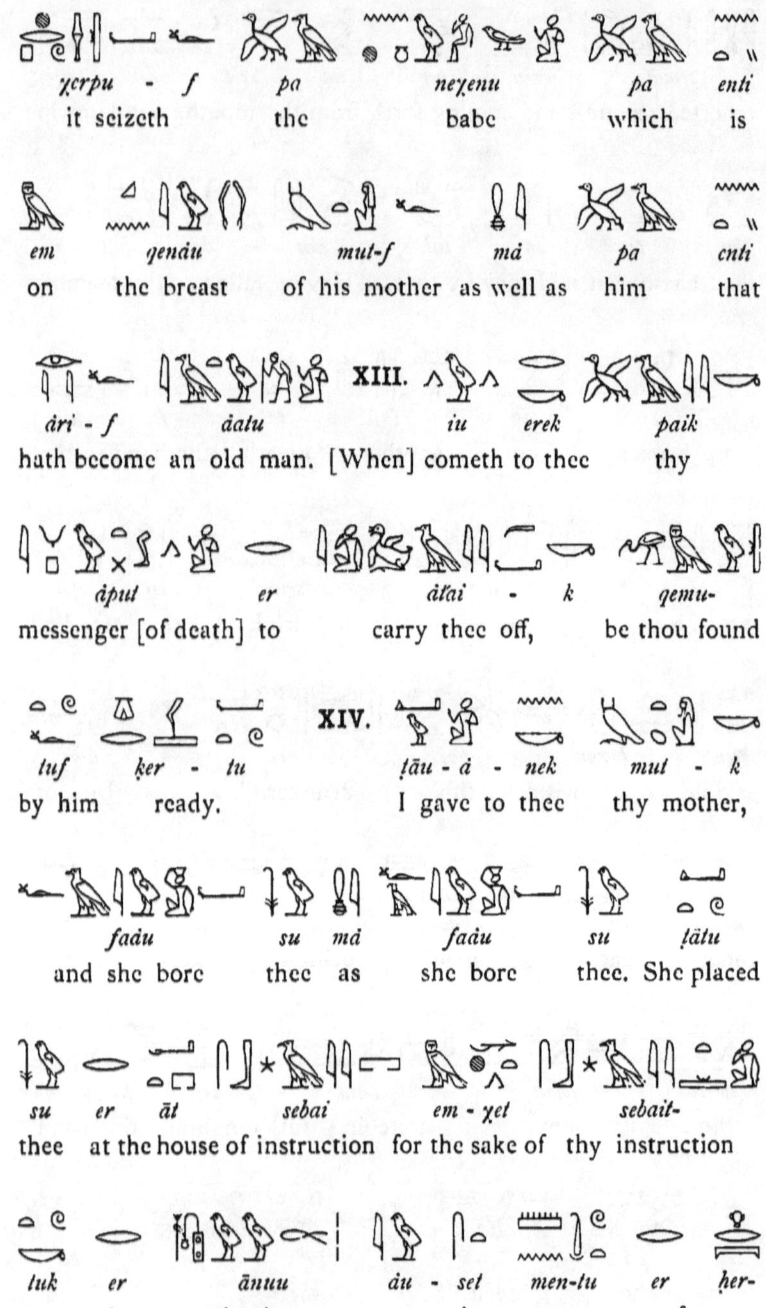

χerpu - f pa neχenu pa enti
it seizeth the babe which is

em qenȧu mut-f mȧ pa enti
on the breast of his mother as well as him that

XIII.

ȧri - f ȧatu iu erek paik
hath become an old man. [When] cometh to thee thy

ȧput er ȧťai - k qemu-
messenger [of death] to carry thee off, be thou found

XIV.

tuf ḳer - tu ṭāu - ȧ - nek mut - k
by him ready. I gave to thee thy mother,

faȧu su mȧ faȧu su ṭātu
and she bore thee as she bore thee. She placed

su er āt sebai em - χet sebait-
thee at the house of instruction for the sake of thy instruction

tuk er ānuu ȧu - set men-tu er ḥer-
in books, was she constant for

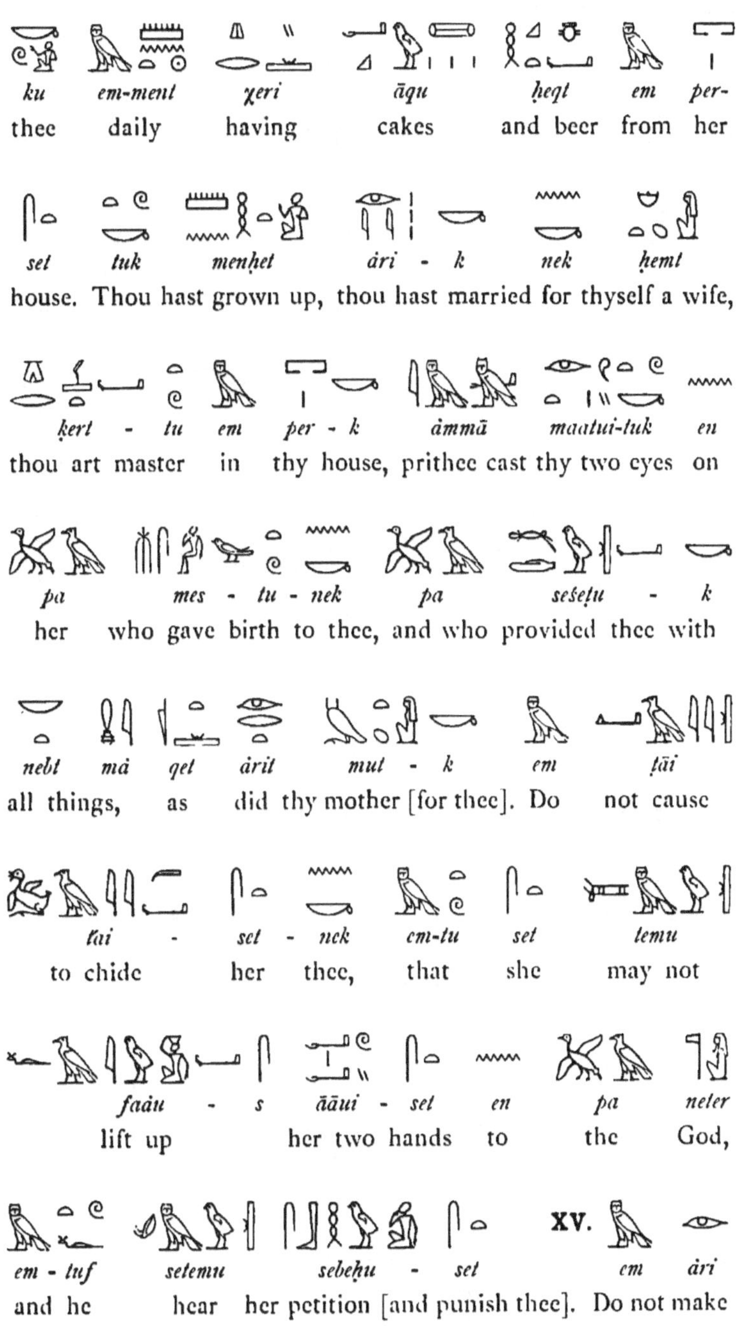

ku em-ment χeri āqu ḥeqt em per-
thee daily having cakes and beer from her

set tuk menḥet ȧri - k nek ḥemt
house. Thou hast grown up, thou hast married for thyself a wife,

ḳert - tu em per - k ȧmmā maatui-tuk en
thou art master in thy house, prithee cast thy two eyes on

pa mes - tu - nek pa seśeṭu - k
her who gave birth to thee, and who provided thee with

nebt mȧ qet ȧrit mut - k em ṭāi
all things, as did thy mother [for thee]. Do not cause

ṭai - set - nek em-tu set temu
to chide her thee, that she may not

faȧu - s āāui - set en pa neter
lift up her two hands to the God,

em - tuf setemu sebeḥu - set XV. em ȧri
and he hear her petition [and punish thee]. Do not make

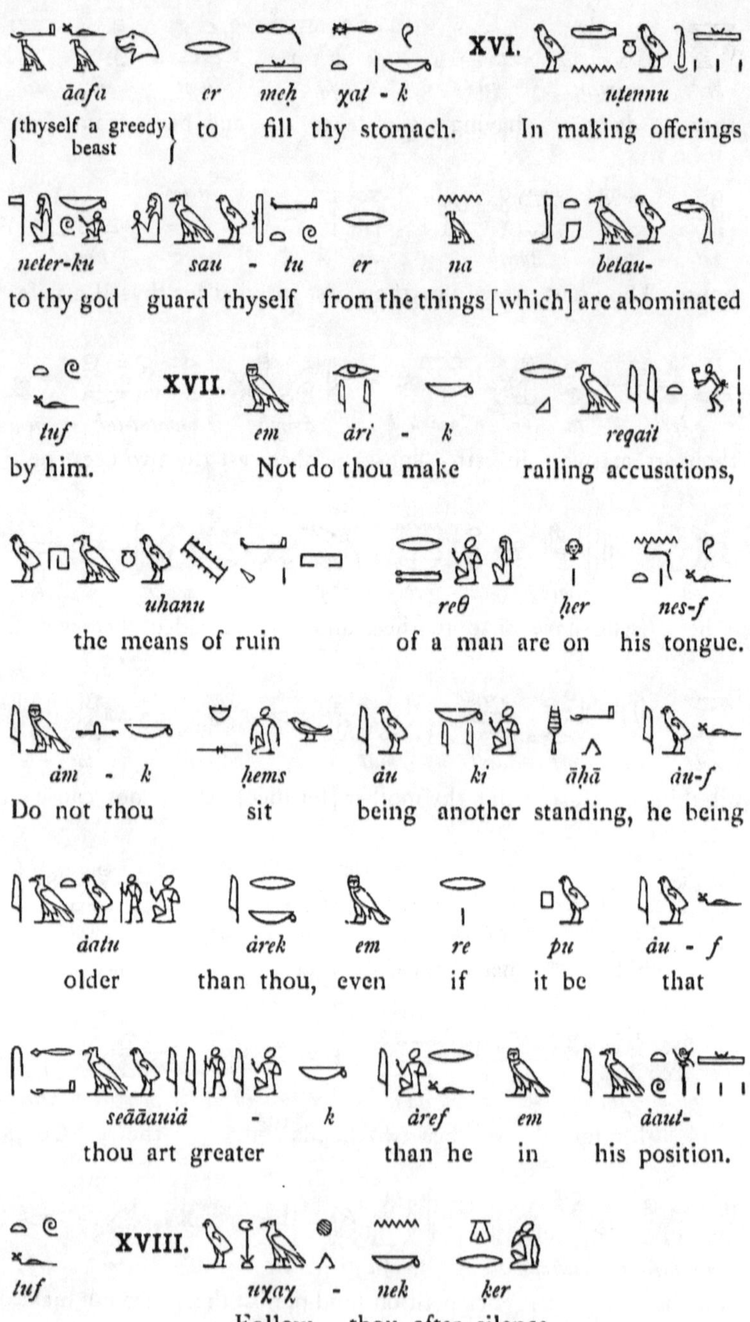
āafa er meḥ χat - k XVI. uṭennu
{thyself a greedy beast} to fill thy stomach. In making offerings
neter-ku sau - tu er na betau-
to thy god guard thyself from the things [which] are abominated
tuf XVII. em ȧri - k reqait
by him. Not do thou make railing accusations,
uhanu reθ ḥer nes-f
the means of ruin of a man are on his tongue.
ȧm - k ḥems ȧu ki āḥā ȧu-f
Do not thou sit being another standing, he being
ȧatu ȧrek em re pu ȧu - f
older than thou, even if it be that
seāāauiȧ - k ȧref em ȧaut-
thou art greater than he in his position.
tuf XVIII. uχaχ - nek ḳer
Follow thou after silence.

HYMN TO OSIRIS.

[XVIIIth dynasty.]

ȧnet' ḥrȧ - k Ȧusȧr neb ḥeḥ suten neteru

Homage to thee, Osiris, lord of eternity, king of the gods,

āšt rennu ṫeser χeperu šeta ȧru em erperu

of many names, holy of form, hidden of attribute in the temples,

šepses ka pu χent Ṭeṭṭeṭ ur χert

the sacred of *ka* is he, dwelling in Tattu, (*i. e.*, Mendes) {the mighty one} contained

2 *em Seχem neb hennu em Ȧti*

in the shrine Sekhem, the lord of praises in the nome of Ati,

χent ṫef em Ȧnnu neb seχau em

at the head {of what is produced} in Annu, (*i. e.*, Heliopolis) the lord {of whom mention is made} in

Maāti ba šeta neb Qerert ṫeser em

Maāti, the soul hidden, the lord of Qerert, the holy one in

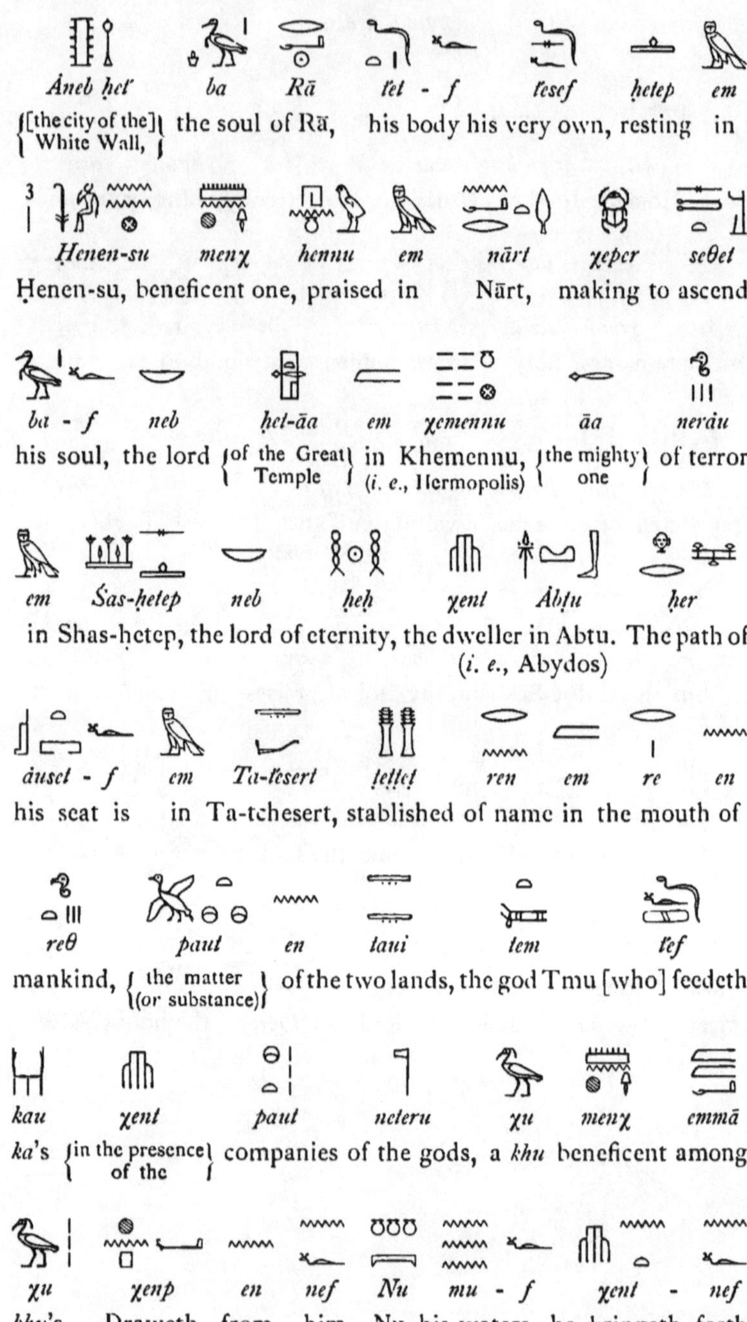

Åneb ḥet' ba Rā t'et - f t'esef ḥetep em
[[the city of the] White Wall,] the soul of Rā, his body his very own, resting in

3 *Ḥenen-su menχ ḥennu em nārt χeper seθet*
Ḥenen-su, beneficent one, praised in Nārt, making to ascend

ba - f neb ḥet-āa em χemennu āa nerāu
his soul, the lord {of the Great Temple} in Khemennu, (*i. e.*, Hermopolis) {the mighty one} of terror

em Śas-ḥetep neb ḥeḥ χent Åbṭu ḥer
in Shas-ḥetep, the lord of eternity, the dweller in Abtu. The path of (*i. e.*, Abydos)

åuset - f em Ta-t'esert ṭetṭet ren em re en
his seat is in Ta-tchesert, stablished of name in the mouth of

reθ paut en taui tem t'ef
mankind, {the matter (or substance)} of the two lands, the god Tmu [who] feedeth

kau χent paut neteru χu menχ emmā
ka's {in the presence of the} companies of the gods, a *khu* beneficent among

χu χenp en nef Nu mu - f χent - nef
khu's. Draweth from him Nu his waters, he bringeth forth

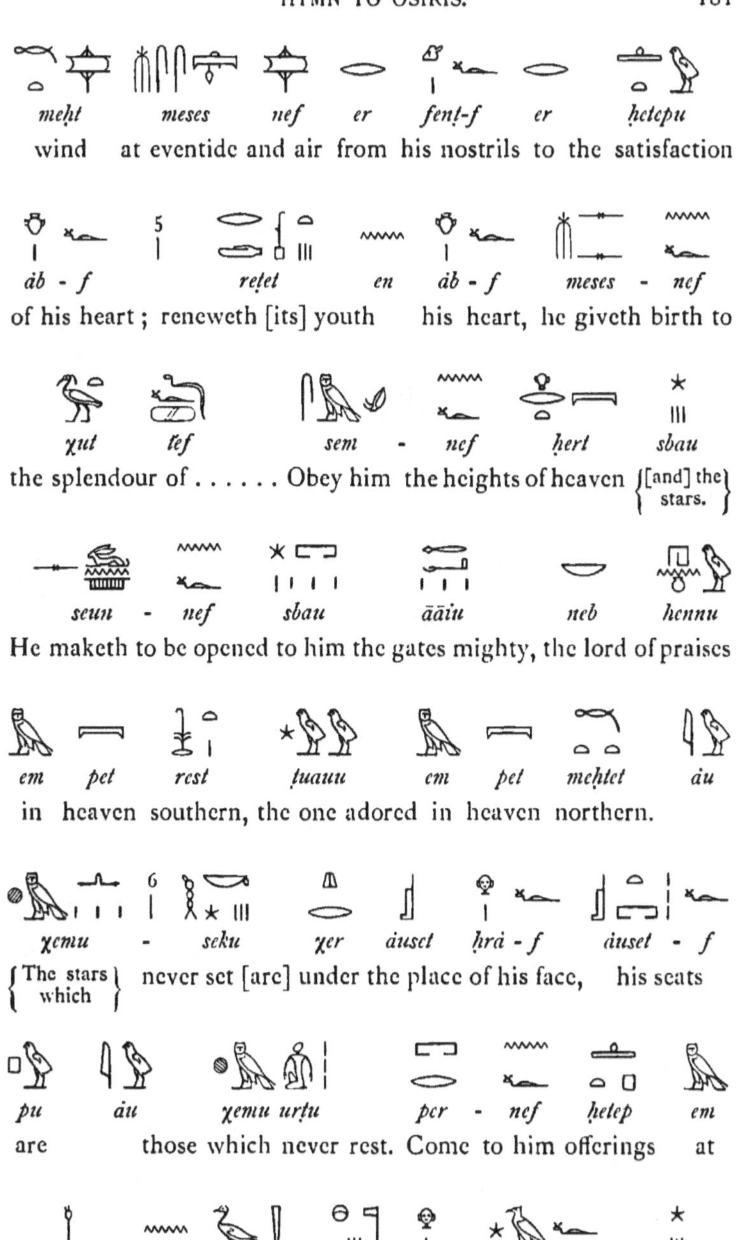

meḥt meses nef er fenṭ-f er ḥetepu
wind at eventide and air from his nostrils to the satisfaction

åb - f reṭet en åb - f meses - nef
of his heart; reneweth [its] youth his heart, he giveth birth to

χut ṭef sem - nef ḥert sbau
the splendour of . . . . . . Obey him the heights of heaven {[and] the stars.}

seun - nef sbau āāiu neb hennu
He maketh to be opened to him the gates mighty, the lord of praises

em pet rest ṭuaau em pet meḥtet åu
in heaven southern, the one adored in heaven northern.

χemu - seku χer åuset ḥrå - f åuset - f
{The stars which} never set [are] under the place of his face, his seats

pu åu χemu urṭu per - nef ḥetep em
are those which never rest. Come to him offerings at

utu en Seb pautti ḥer ṭua - f sbau
the command of Seb. {The divine companies are} for praising him, the stars

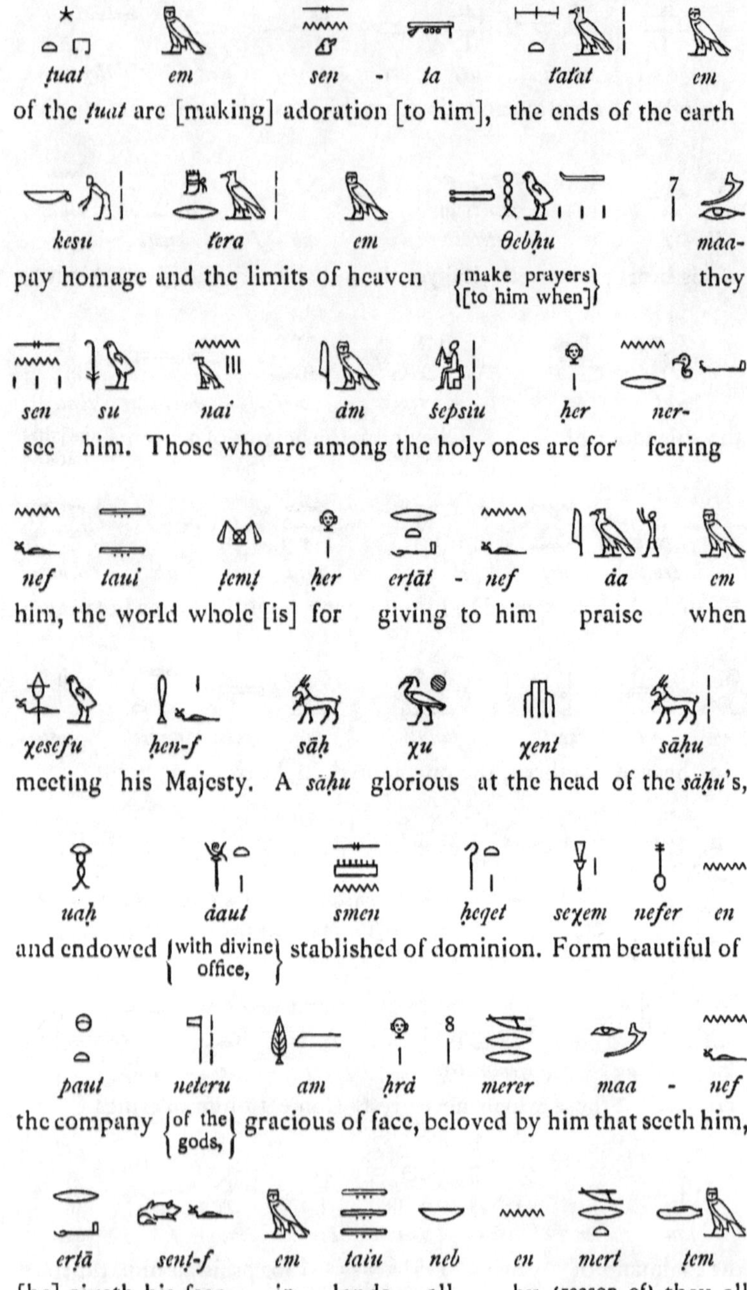

ṭuat *em* *sen* - *ta* *ṫaṫat* *em*

of the *ṭuat* are [making] adoration [to him], the ends of the earth

kesu *ṫera* *em* *θebḥu* *maa-*

pay homage and the limits of heaven {make prayers [to him when]} they

sen *su* *nai* *àm* *šepsiu* *ḥer* *ner-*

see him. Those who are among the holy ones are for fearing

nef *taui* *ṭemṭ* *ḥer* *erṭāt* - *nef* *àa* *em*

him, the world whole [is] for giving to him praise when

χesefu *ḥen-f* *sāḥ* *χu* *χent* *sāḥu*

meeting his Majesty. A *sāḥu* glorious at the head of the *sāḥu*'s,

uaḥ *àaut* *smen* *ḥeqet* *seχem* *nefer* *en*

and endowed {with divine office,} stablished of dominion. Form beautiful of

paut *neteru* *am* *ḥrà* *merer* *maa* - *nef*

the company {of the gods,} gracious of face, beloved by him that seeth him,

erṭā *senṭ-f* *em* *taiu* *neb* *en* *mert* *ṭem*

[he] giveth his fear in lands all by {reason of [his] love,} they all

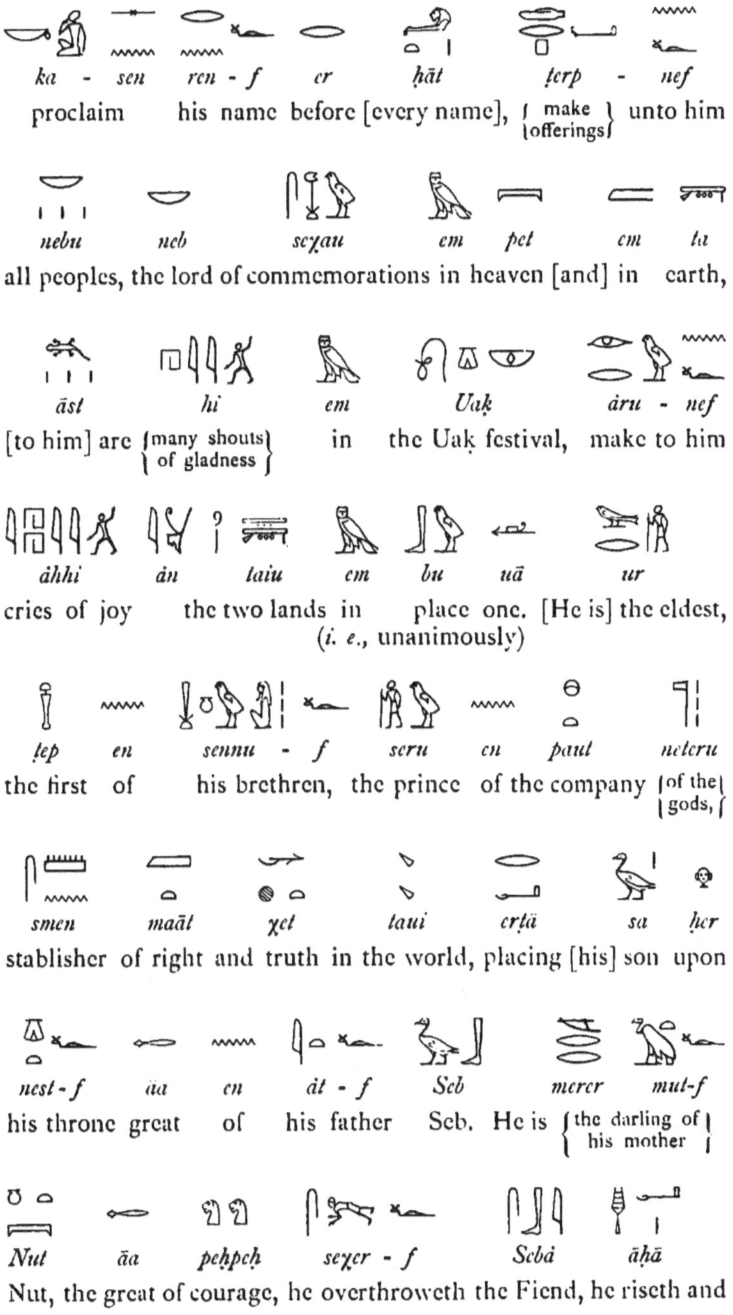

ka - sen ren - f er ḥāt ṭerp - nef

proclaim his name before [every name], {make offerings} unto him

nebu neb seχau em pet em ta

all peoples, the lord of commemorations in heaven [and] in earth,

āst hi em Uaḳ àru - nef

[to him] are {many shouts of gladness} in the Uaḳ festival, make to him

àhhi àn taiu em bu uā ur

cries of joy the two lands in place one. [He is] the eldest,

(*i. e.*, unanimously)

ṭep en sennu - f seru en paut neteru

the first of his brethren, the prince of the company {of the gods,}

smen maāt χet taui erṭā sa ḥer

stablisher of right and truth in the world, placing [his] son upon

nest - f äa en àt - f Seb merer mut-f

his throne great of his father Seb. He is {the darling of his mother}

Nut āa peḥpeḥ seχer - f Sebà āḥā

Nut, the great of courage, he overthroweth the Fiend, he riseth and *sma - f* 10 *χeft - f erṭā senṭ - f em χeru - f*

slaughtereth his enemy, he placeth his fear in his adversary,

àn ťeru . . . . men àb reṭ-

[he] carrieth off the boundaries . . . . . ., [he is] fixed of heart, his legs

f seθet (?) āuāu Seb sutenit taui

are raised up; [he is] the heir of Seb {and of the kingdom} of the world.

maa - f χu - f seutu - nef nef sem

He hath seen his powers, he hath given command to him to direct

11 *taiu en em ā er uaḥ en sep*

the lands by [his] hand as long as the abiding of {times and seasons.}

àri - nef ta pen em ā - f mu - f nef - f

He hath made earth this with his hand, its waters, its air,

sem - f menment - f nebt paìt nebt

its vegetation, its cattle all, [its] birds all,

χepanen nebt ťetfet - f āut - f

[its] fishes all, its creeping things [all], its four-footed beasts [all].

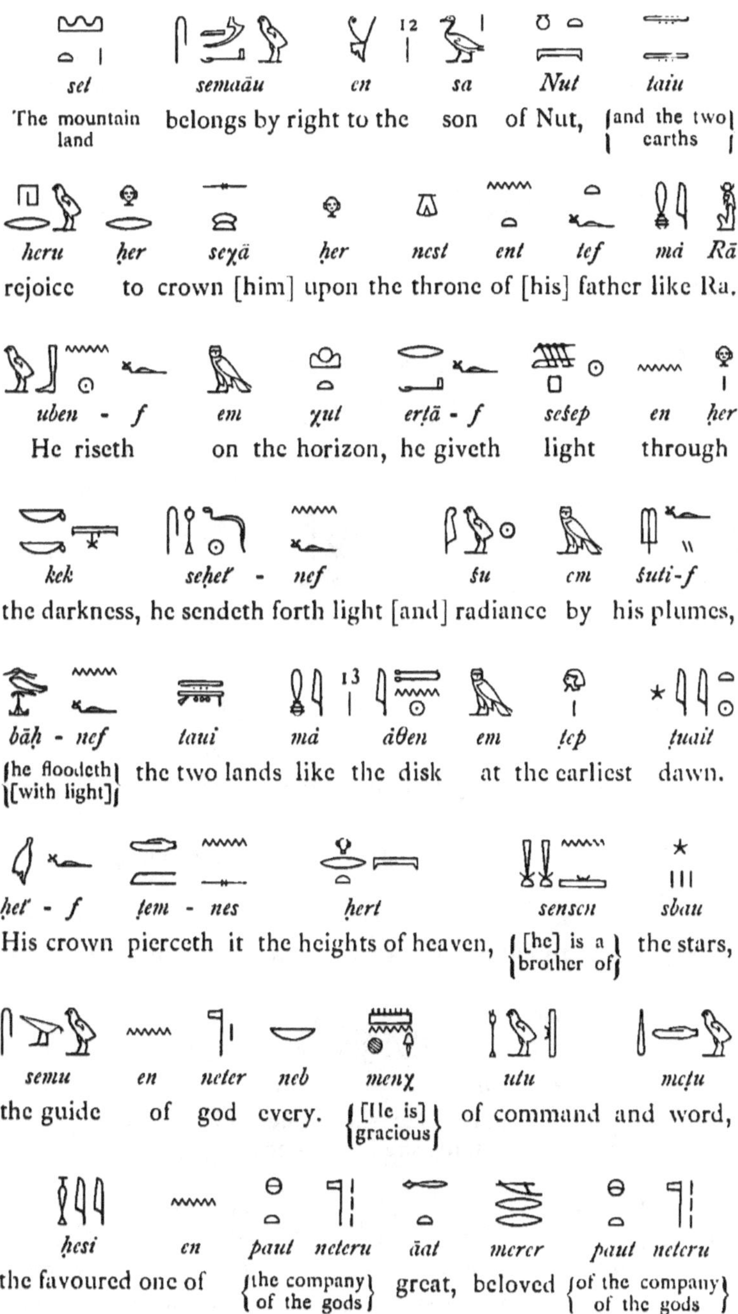

set *semaāu* *en* 12 *sa* *Nut* *taiu*
The mountain land belongs by right to the son of Nut, {and the two earths}

heru *ḥer* *seχā* *ḥer* *nest* *ent* *tef* *mā* *Rā*
rejoice to crown [him] upon the throne of [his] father like Ra.

uben - f *em* *χut* *ertā - f* *sešep* *en* *ḥer*
He riseth on the horizon, he giveth light through

kek *seḥet' - nef* *šu* *em* *šuti-f*
the darkness, he sendeth forth light [and] radiance by his plumes,

bāḥ - nef *taui* *mā* 13 *āθen* *em* *tep* *tuait*
{he floodeth [with light]} the two lands like the disk at the earliest dawn.

ḥet' - f *tem - nes* *hert* *sensen* *sbau*
His crown pierceth it the heights of heaven, {[he] is a brother of} the stars,

semu *en* *neter* *neb* *menχ* *utu* *metu*
the guide of god every. {[He is] gracious} of command and word,

ḥesi *en* *paut* *neteru* *āat* *merer* *paut* *neteru*
the favoured one of {the company of the gods} great, beloved {of the company of the gods}

neťeset àri en sent - f māket - f seḥerit
little. Hath made his sister protection for him, driving away

χeru 14 *seḥemet sepu seśeṭ χeru em*
[his] enemies, turning back evil hap, pronouncing the word with

χu re - s àqert nes àn uh en
the strength of her mouth, strong of tongue, not fallible in

meṭu semenχet utu meṭu Àuset
speech. Acting beneficently by command and word [is] Isis,

χut neťet sen - s ḥeḥet su àtet
the mighty one, the avenger of her brother. Seeking him without

beḳeḳ 15 *reret ta pen em ḥai àn*
rest, going round earth this with cries of grief, not

χen - nes àn qemtu - s su àrit śut
alighted she not had she found him. Making light
(*i. e.*, until she had found)

em śut - s χepert nefu em ṭenḥ àrit hennu
with her hair, {making to become} air by [her] wings, making cries

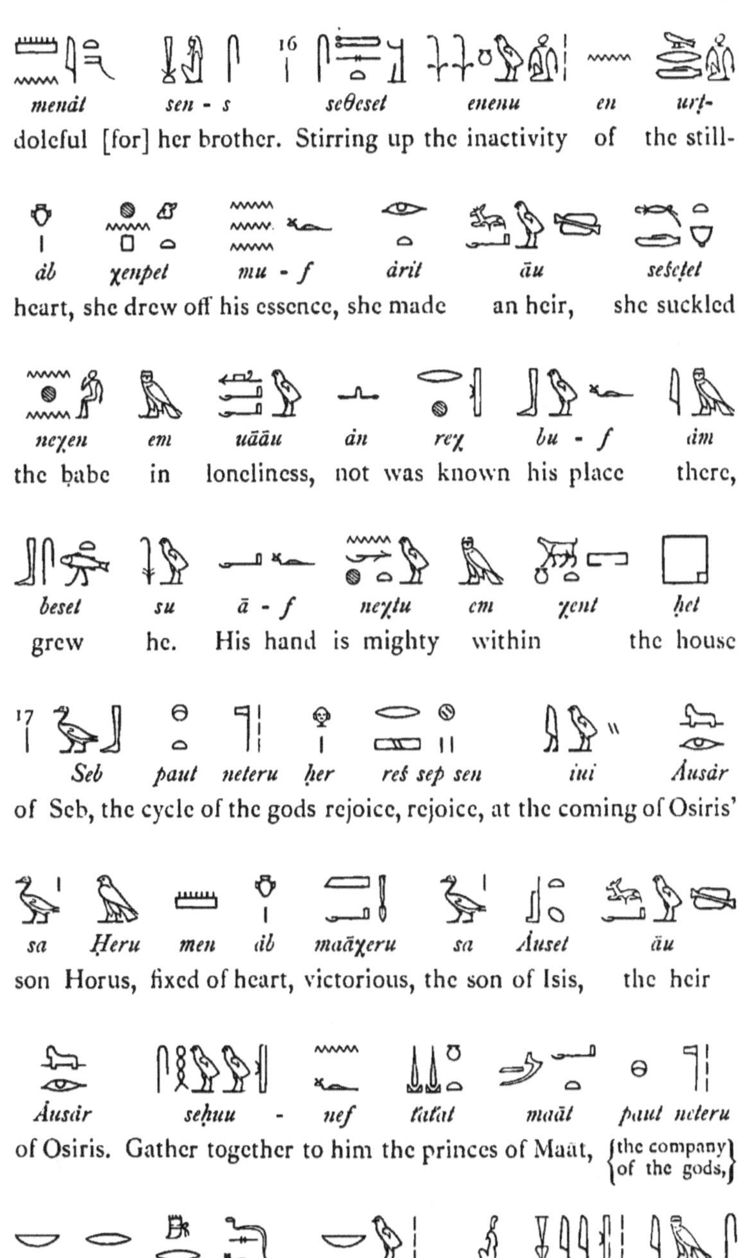

menȧt sen - s 16 *seθeset enenu en urṭ-*
doleful [for] her brother. Stirring up the inactivity of the still-

ȧb χenpet mu - f ȧrit āu seśeṭet
heart, she drew off his essence, she made an heir, she suckled

neχen em uāāu ȧn reχ bu - f ȧm
the babe in loneliness, not was known his place there,

beset su ā - f neχtu em χent ḥet
grew he. His hand is mighty within the house

17 *Seb paut neteru ḥer reś sep sen iui Ȧusȧr*
of Seb, the cycle of the gods rejoice, rejoice, at the coming of Osiris'

sa Ḥeru men ȧb maāχeru sa Ȧuset āu
son Horus, fixed of heart, victorious, the son of Isis, the heir

Ȧusȧr seḥuu - nef ṭaṭat maāt paut neteru
of Osiris. Gather together to him the princes of Maāt, {the company of the gods,}

Neb - er - ṭer ṭesef nebu Maāt sami ȧm - s
and Neb-er-tcher himself, and the lords of Maat, assemble therein,

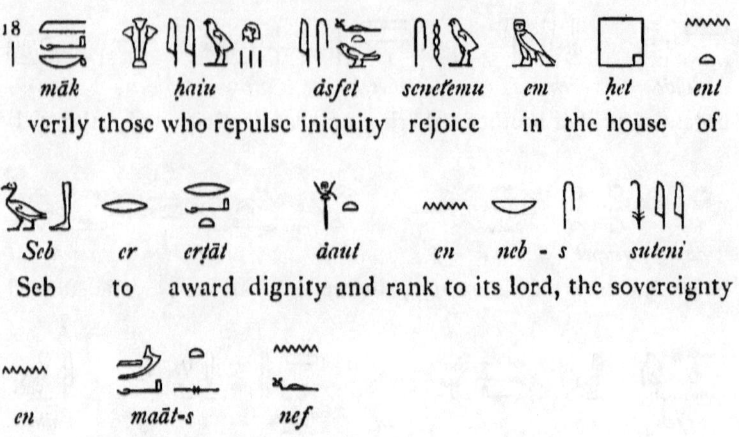

18 *māk* *ḥaiu* *ȧsfet* *seneťemu* *em* *ḥet* *ent*

verily those who repulse iniquity rejoice in the house of

Seb *er* *erṭāt* *ȧaut* *en* *neb - s* *suteni*

Seb to award dignity and rank to its lord, the sovereignty

en *maāt-s* *nef*

of its right and truth is to him.

FROM THE STELE OF TEḤUTI-NEFER.

[XVIIIth dynasty.]

I. *suten ḥetep tā Ȧmen-Rā neb nest*

May a royal oblation give Amen-Rā, the lord of the thrones

taiu pautti en sep tep χent Ȧptet

of the world, the matter of time primeval, dweller in the Apts,

seχem šeps χeper t'esef Neb-er-t'er em ȧuset-f

form sacred, creator of himself and Neb-er-tcher in seat his

nebt tā - f ānχ en mer - nef ȧaut en

every. May he give life to him that loveth him, and old age to him

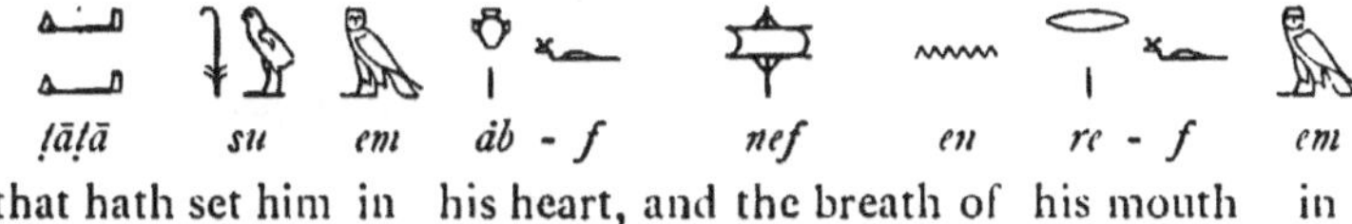

ṭāṭā su em ȧb - f nef en re - f em

that hath set him in his heart, and the breath of his mouth in

ḥesut - f ȧn feχ - nef χer t'etta maa - f neter

his favoured one, not may he decay for ever. May he see the god,

àtef tememu Àmen men χet nebt

father of mankind Amen, the stablisher of thing every.

uś - f ta ḥet' āāui - f āb er

May he eat bread white, may his two hands be pure in

ṭuat en ṭua reχit àri - f ḥemset

the underworld in adoring celestial beings, may he make his seat

em āāiut χenemes - f ābu

in the hall of columns, may he be associated with the priests and

neter ḥenu ṭā - sen nef āut em sti

prophets, may they give to him food offerings with drink offerings,

re mest er trà en χaiu

and bread and cakes for the season of the night.

àm - f śens en un - ḥrà bābā - f

May he eat the bread of the "Opening of the Face", may he converse

ḥenā àmtu àbeṭ seśep - f sent em ment

with those who are in [their] month. May he receive cakes daily

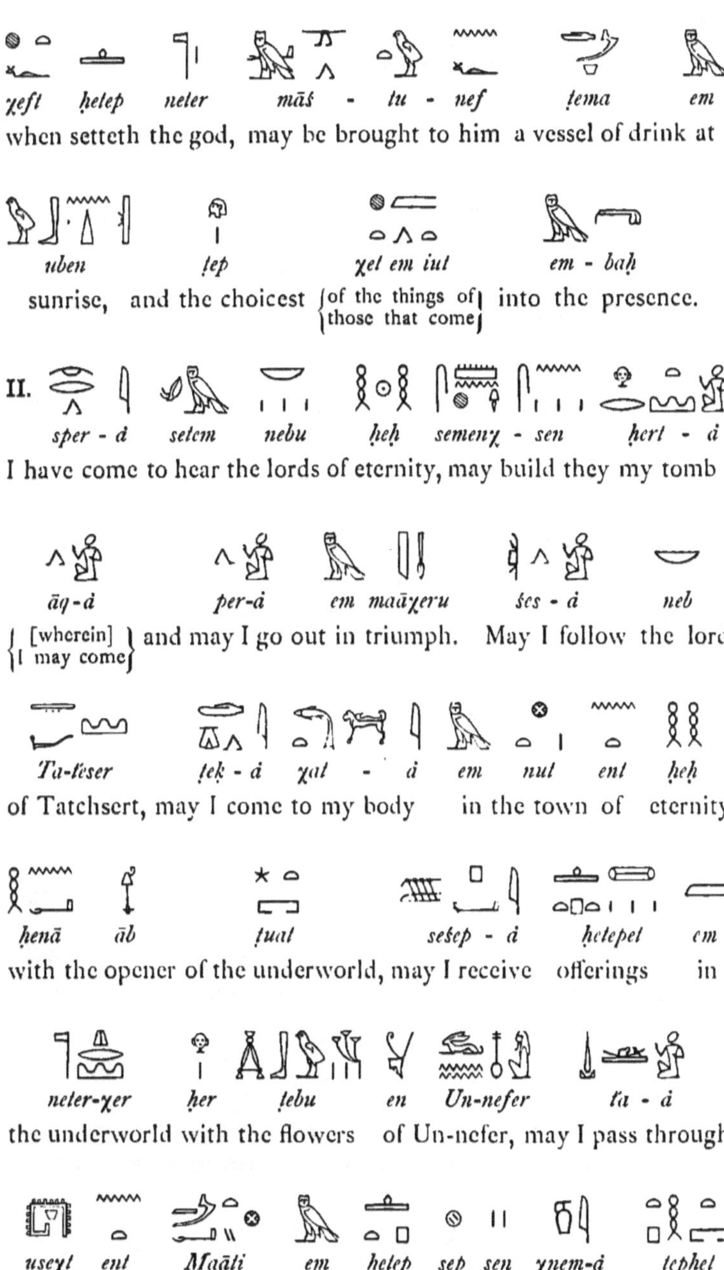

χeft ḥetep neter māś - tu - nef ṭema em
when setteth the god, may be brought to him a vessel of drink at

uben ṭep χet em iut em - baḥ
sunrise, and the choicest {of the things of / those that come} into the presence.

II. *sper - ȧ setem nebu ḥeḥ semenχ - sen ḥert - ȧ*
I have come to hear the lords of eternity, may build they my tomb

āq-ȧ per-ȧ em maāχeru śes - ȧ neb
{[wherein] / I may come} and may I go out in triumph. May I follow the lord

Ta-ṫeser ṭek - ȧ χat - ȧ em nut ent ḥeḥ
of Tatchsert, may I come to my body in the town of eternity

ḥenā āb ṭuat seśep - ȧ ḥetepet em
with the opener of the underworld, may I receive offerings in

neter-χer ḥer ṭebu en Un-nefer ṫa - ȧ
the underworld with the flowers of Un-nefer, may I pass through

useχt ent Maāti em ḥetep sep sen χnem-ȧ tepḥet
the hall of two-fold Maāt in peace; twice. May I attain {to the shrine}

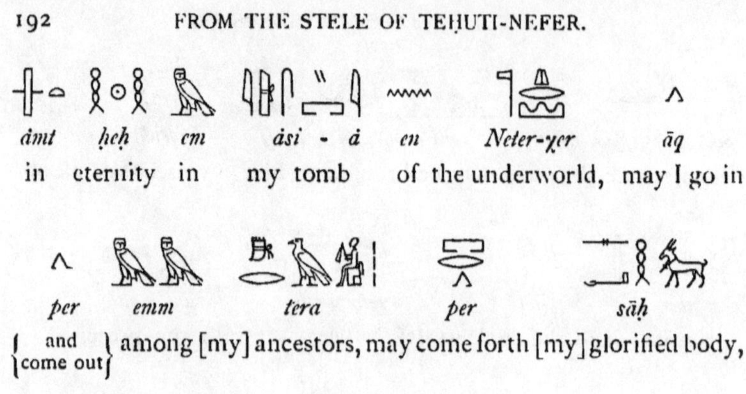

àmt ḥeḥ em àsi - à en Neter-χer āq

in eternity in my tomb of the underworld, may I go in

per emm ṭera per sāḥ

{and come out} among [my] ancestors, may come forth [my] glorified body,

šes - f Ḥennu ṭerp - tuf em

may it follow Hennu, may be offered to it from

menṭiu Ḥeru ta ḥeqt àrp ḥer àrt

the breasts of Horus cakes, ale, wine and milk

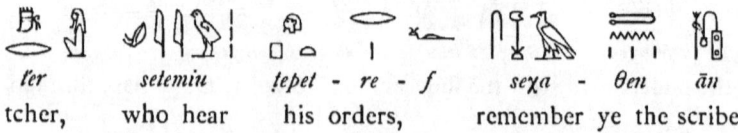

em ment ent hru neb

daily day every.

III. *à neteru àmu Neter-χert ḥemsiu er ḳes Neb-er-*

Hail gods in the underworld, who sit near Neb-er-

ṭer setemiu ṭepet - re - f seχa - θen ān

tcher, who hear his orders, remember ye the scribe

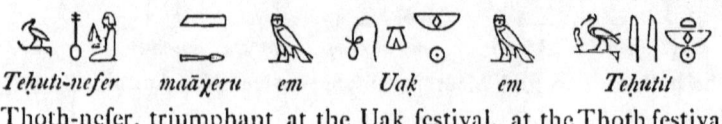

Teḥuti-nefer maāχeru em Uaḳ em Teḥutit

Thoth-nefer, triumphant at the Uaḳ festival, at the Thoth festival,

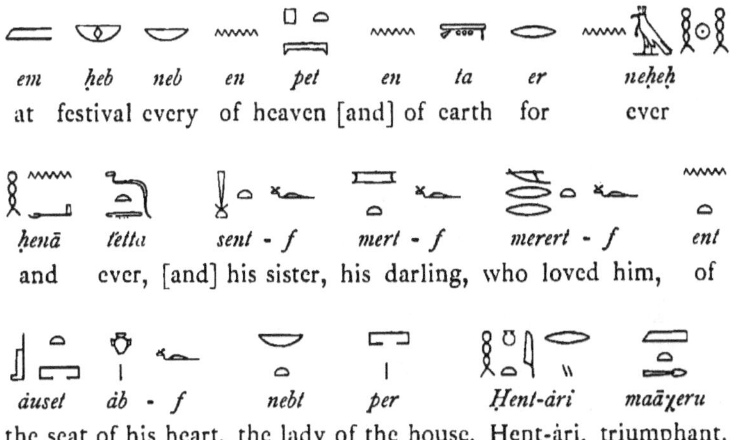

em ḥeb neb en pet en ta er neḥeḥ
at festival every of heaven [and] of earth for ever

ḥenā t'etta sent - f mert - f merert - f ent
and ever, [and] his sister, his darling, who loved him, of

àuset àb - f nebt per Ḥent-àri maāχeru
the seat of his heart, the lady of the house, Ḥent-àri, triumphant.

FROM THE STELE OF TCHANNI, A SCRIBE.

[XVIIIth dynasty.]

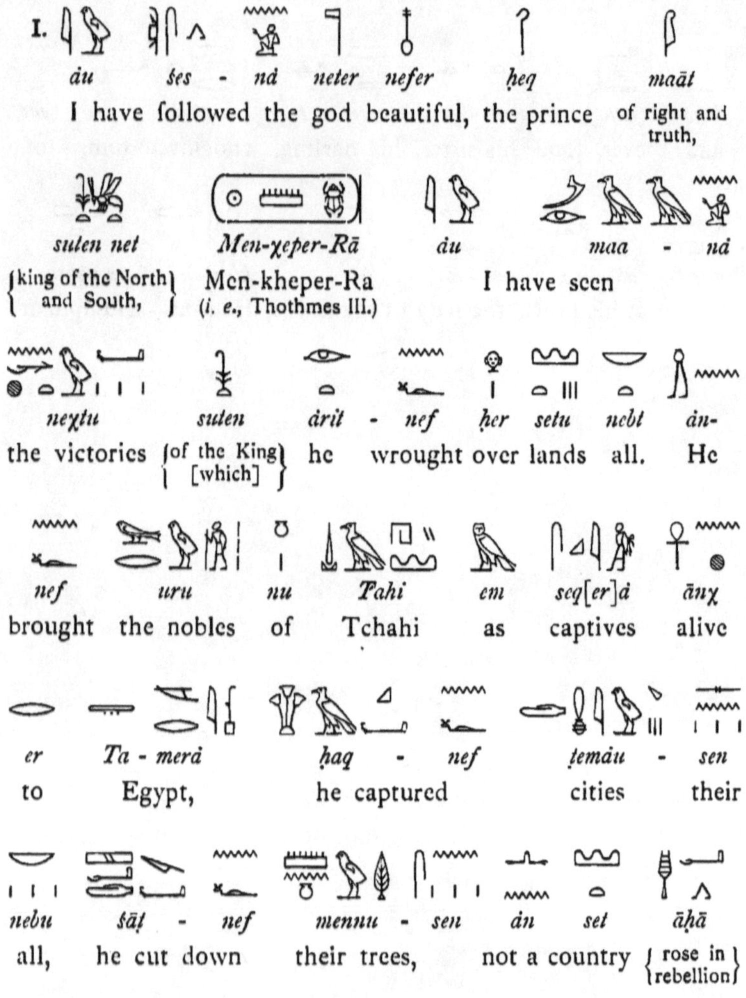

I. *àu šes - nà neter nefer ḥeq maāt*
I have followed the god beautiful, the prince of right and truth,

suten net Men-χeper-Rā àu maa - nà
{king of the North and South,} Men-kheper-Ra (*i. e.*, Thothmes III.) I have seen

neχtu suten àrit - nef ḥer setu nebt àn-
the victories {of the King [which]} he wrought over lands all. He

nef uru nu Tahi em seq[er]à ānχ
brought the nobles of Tchahi as captives alive

er Ta - merà ḥaq - nef ṭemàu - sen
to Egypt, he captured cities their

nebu šāṭ - nef mennu - sen àn set āḥā
all, he cut down their trees, not a country {rose in rebellion}

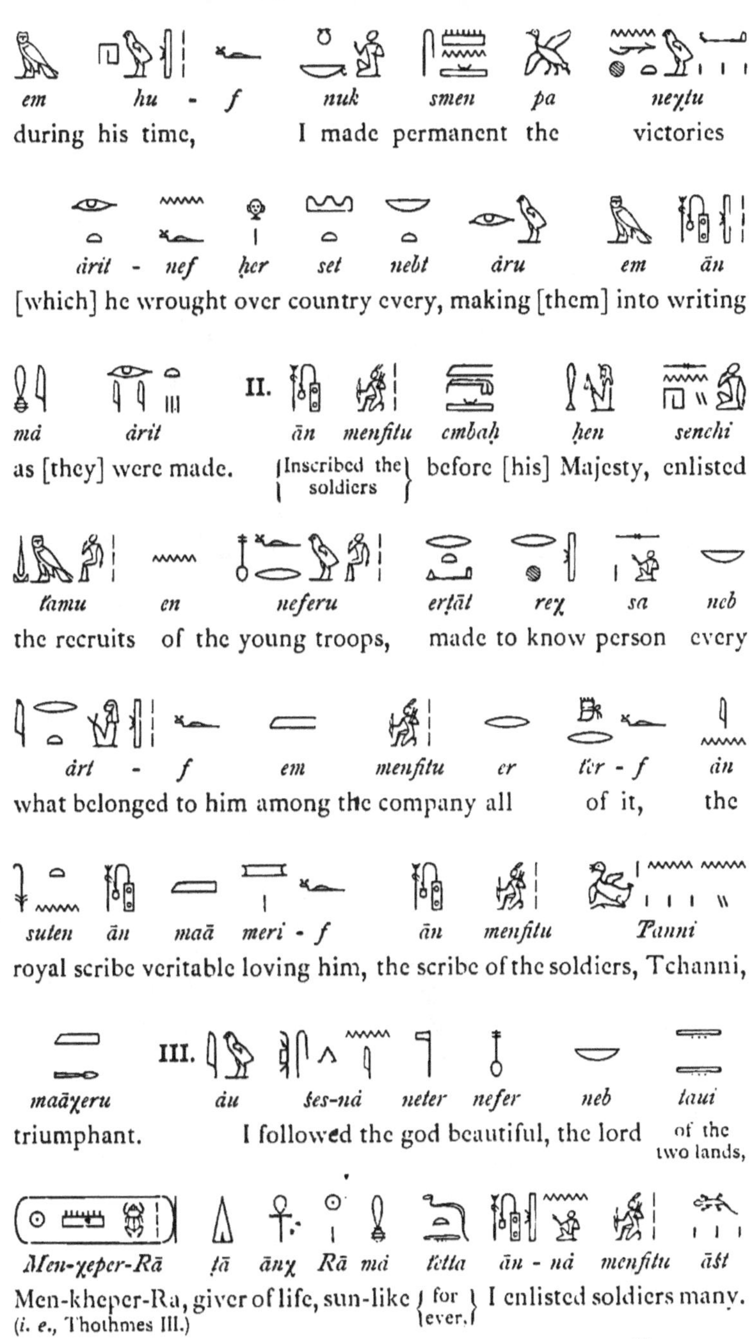

em hu - f nuk smen pa neχtu
during his time, I made permanent the victories

ȧrit - nef ḥer set nebt ȧru em ān
[which] he wrought over country every, making [them] into writing

mȧ ȧrit II. *ān menfitu cmbaḥ ḥen senchi*
as [they] were made. {Inscribed the soldiers} before [his] Majesty, enlisted

ṫamu en neferu erṭāt reχ sa neb
the recruits of the young troops, made to know person every

ȧrt - f em menfitu er ṫer - f ȧn
what belonged to him among the company all of it, the

suten ān maā meri - f ān menfitu Tanni
royal scribe veritable loving him, the scribe of the soldiers, Tchanni,

maāχeru III. *ȧu šes-nȧ neter nefer neb taui*
triumphant. I followed the god beautiful, the lord of the two lands,

Men-χeper-Rā ṭā ānχ Rā mȧ ṫetta ān - nȧ menfitu āšt
Men-kheper-Ra, giver of life, sun-like {for ever,} I enlisted soldiers many.
(*i. e.*, Thothmes III.)

FROM THE STELE OF SESH, A SCRIBE.

[XVIIIth dynasty.]

i - nȧ χer - k Un-neferu maa - ȧ

I have come to you, Un-neferu, that I may see

tuau - ȧ neferu-k ȧu šes - nȧ neter nefer

and that I may adore thy beauties. I have followed the god beautiful,

ȧn ḥet' - ȧ utu - nef nebt per - nȧ χer

not {have I done contrary} to what he commanded all. I have come forth with

ḥesut en ḥesi - f ȧn ḥesi

the favoured ones of his praise, not is praised

χebṭ - nef nuk bak χu en neb - f

the doer of evil by him. I am a servant noble of his lord,

meḥ - ȧb en ȧmi ḥet-ā neχen - ȧ er

filling the heart of him that is in the palace. {I passed my childhood} in

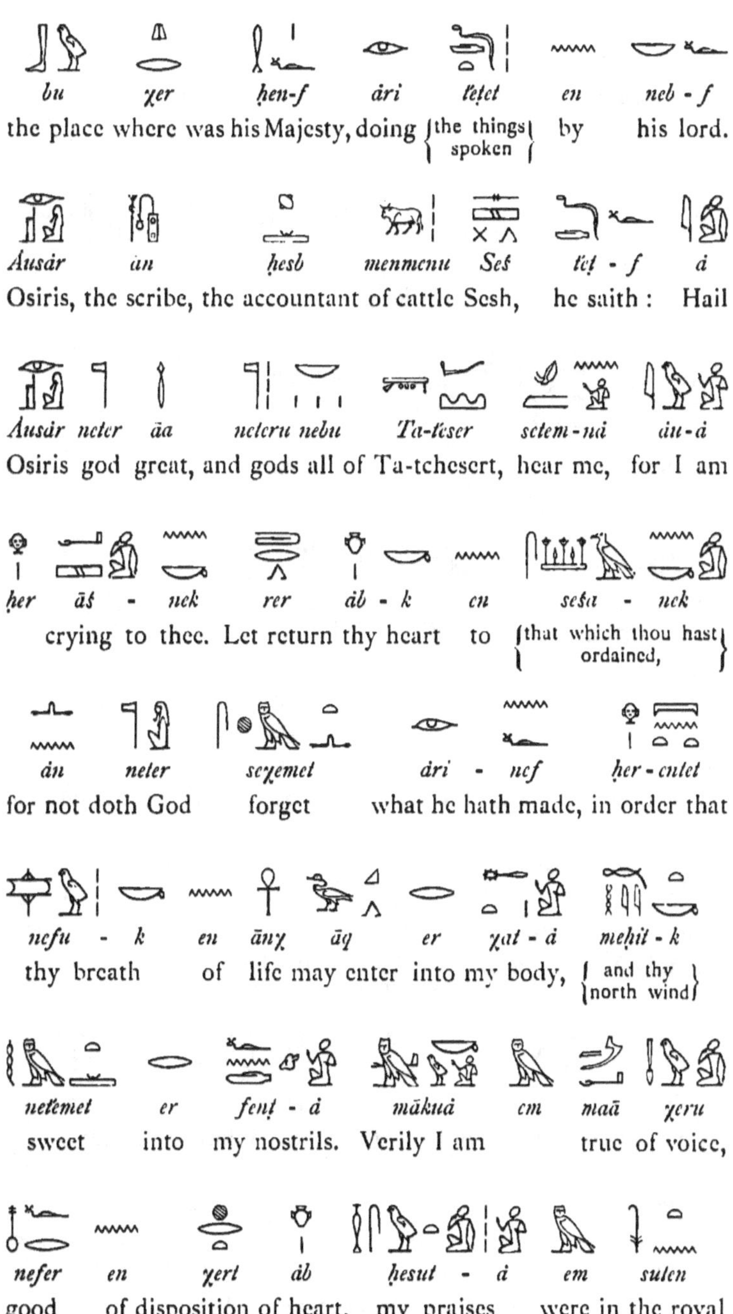

bu χer ḥen-f ȧri ṭeṭet en neb-f

the place where was his Majesty, doing {the things spoken} by his lord.

Ȧusȧr ȧn ḥesb menmenu Seš ṭeṭ-f ȧ

Osiris, the scribe, the accountant of cattle Sesh, he saith: Hail

Ȧusȧr neter āa neteru nebu Ta-ṭeser setem-nȧ ȧu-ȧ

Osiris god great, and gods all of Ta-tchesert, hear me, for I am

ḥer āš-nek rer ȧb-k en seša-nek

crying to thee. Let return thy heart to {that which thou hast ordained,}

ȧn neter seχemet ȧri-nef ḥer-entet

for not doth God forget what he hath made, in order that

nefu-k en ānχ āq er χat-ȧ meḥit-k

thy breath of life may enter into my body, {and thy north wind}

neṭemet er fenṭ-ȧ mākuȧ em maā χeru

sweet into my nostrils. Verily I am true of voice,

nefer en χert ȧb ḥesut-ȧ em suten

good of disposition of heart, my praises were in the royal

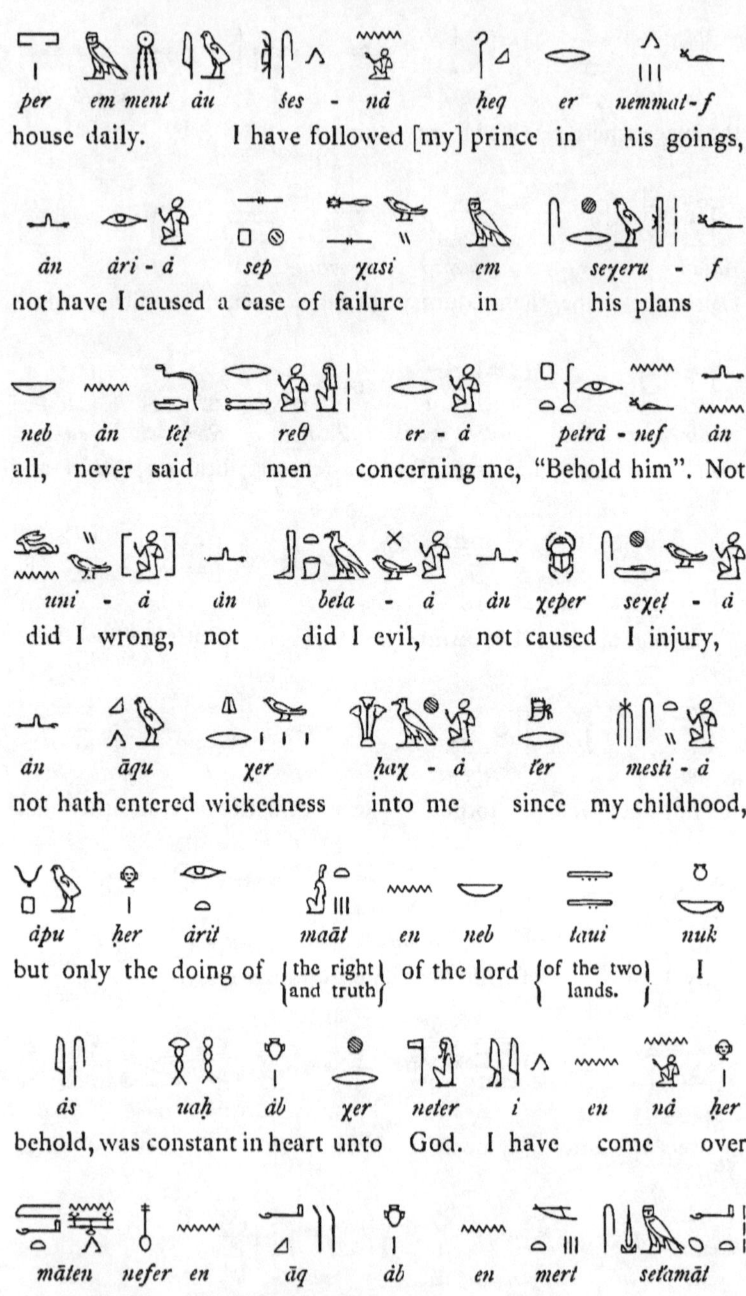

per em ment àu šes - nà ḥeq er nemmat-f

house daily. I have followed [my] prince in his goings,

àn àri - à sep χasi em seχeru - f

not have I caused a case of failure in his plans

neb àn t'eṭ reθ er - à petrà - nef àn

all, never said men concerning me, "Behold him". Not

uni - à àn beta - à àn χeper seχeṭ - à

did I wrong, not did I evil, not caused I injury,

àn āqu χer ḥaχ - à t'er mesti - à

not hath entered wickedness into me since my childhood,

àpu ḥer àrit maāt en neb taui nuk

but only the doing of {the right and truth} of the lord {of the two lands.} I

às uaḥ àb χer neter i en nà ḥer

behold, was constant in heart unto God. I have come over

māten nefer en āq àb en mert set'amāt

the path fair of straightness of heart, and of the love of virtues (?) (*i. e.*, justice)

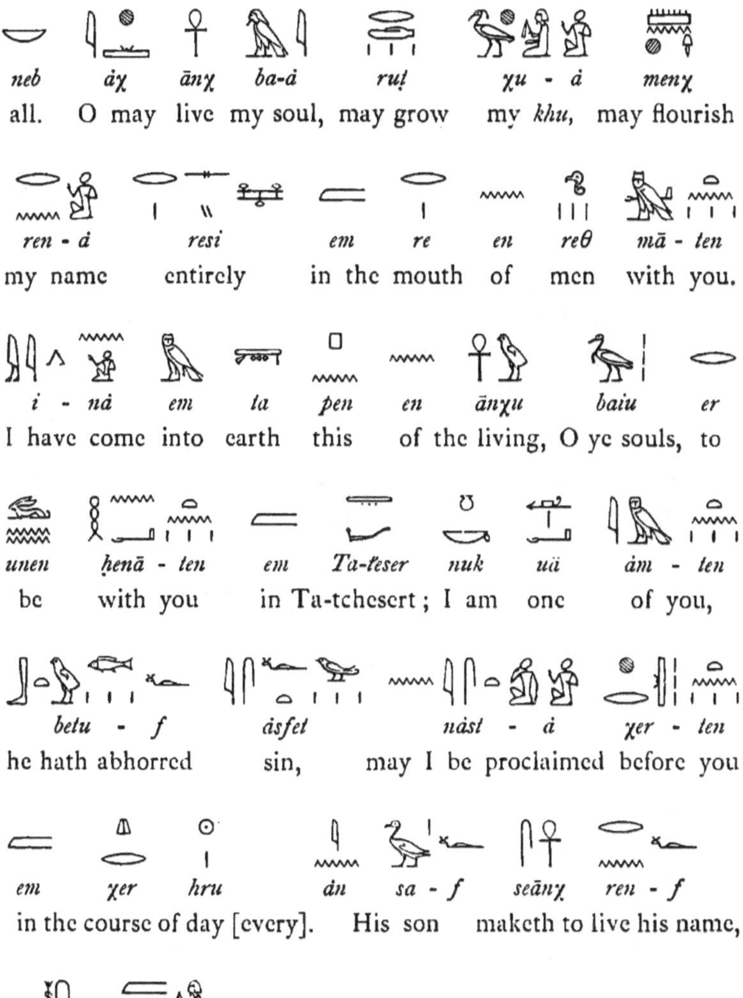

neb ȧχ ānχ ba-ȧ ruṭ χu - ȧ menχ
all. O may live my soul, may grow my *khu*, may flourish

ren - ȧ resi em re en reθ mā - ten
my name entirely in the mouth of men with you.

i - nȧ em ta pen en ānχu baiu er
I have come into earth this of the living, O ye souls, to

unen ḥenā - ten em Ta-t̄eser nuk uā ȧm - ten
be with you in Ta-tchesert; I am one of you,

betu - f ȧsfet nȧst - ȧ χer - ten
he hath abhorred sin, may I be proclaimed before you

em χer hru ȧn sa - f seānχ ren - f
in the course of day [every]. His son maketh to live his name,

ān Meḥu
the scribe Mehu.

FROM A SEPULCHRAL STELE.

[XVIIIth dynasty (?).]

suten ṭā ḥetep Ȧusȧr ḥeq ťetta neter āa neb

Royal may give oblation Osiris, prince of eternity, god great, lord

Ȧbṭu Ȧp-uat qemā Ȧp-uat meḥt Ȧnpu ȧm

of Abydos, Ap-uat of the south, Ap-uat of the north, Anubis dweller

ut Ptaḥ-Seker neb šeta - θȧ ȧt ṭā - sen

{in the town of embalmment,} Ptaḥ-Seker, lord of the hidden place, may they give

χu em pet us[r] em ta maāχeru em Neter-χert

glory in heaven, strength upon earth, triumph in Neter-khert,

O(sic)

pert āq er ȧsi - ȧ qebḥ - ȧ šuit - f (sic)

{and a coming forth from and} a going in to my tomb. May I refresh my shadow,

surȧ - ȧ mu em mer - ȧ hru neb uať

may I drink water from my pool day every, may flourish

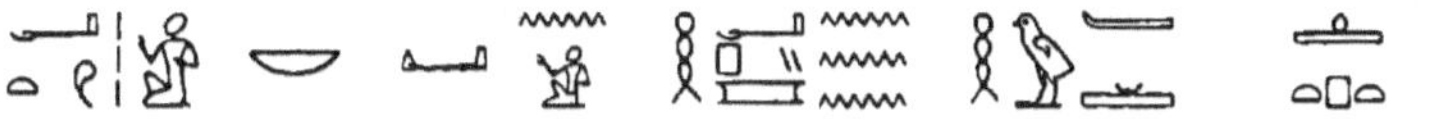

āt - à neb ṭā - nà Ḥāpi ḥu ḥetepet

my limbs all, may give me the Nile food, and offerings,

renpit er trà - s setuut - à ḥer maā

and flowers at its season. May I walk by the side

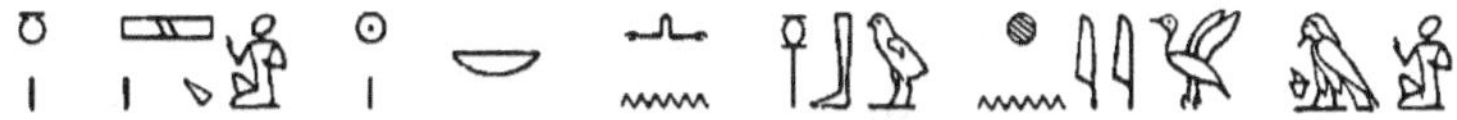

nu še - à hru neb àn àbu χeni ba - à

of my lake day every without ceasing. May alight my soul

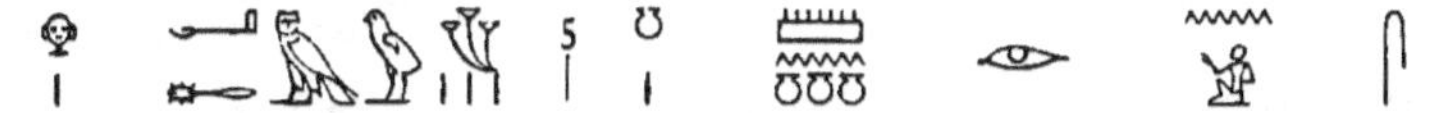

ḥer āχamu nu mennu àri - nà - s

upon the branches of the trees [which] I have made them, (*i. e.*, planted)

seqebḥ - à ḥer χeru neh - à àm-à tau

may I cool myself under my sycamores, may I eat the bread

en ṭāṭā - sen àu - nà re er meṭ - à

of their giving, may be to me a mouth that I may speak

àm - f mà Ḥeru - šesu peru - à χer ṭes

with it like the Horus followers, may I come forth bearing a vase

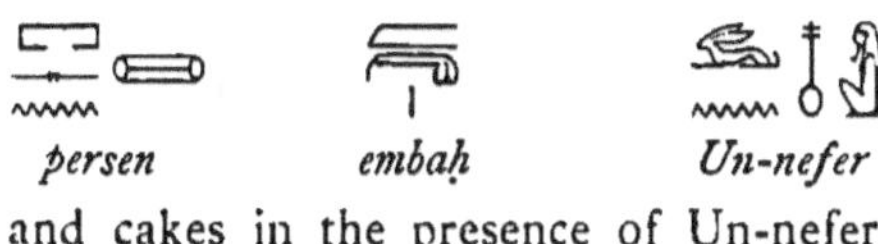

persen embaḥ Un-nefer

and cakes in the presence of Un-nefer.

THE STELE OF ȦMEN-ḤETEP, A ROYAL SCRIBE AT MEMPHIS.

[XVIIIth dynasty (?).]

un - nek pet un - nek ta

May be opened to thee heaven, may be opened to thee earth,

un - nek uat em Neter-χert per - k

may be opened to thee a way in the underworld. {Mayest thou come forth,}

āq - k ḥenā Rā usten - k mȧ

mayest thou go in with Rā, mayest thou walk like

nebu ḥeḥ sešep - k sennu em āāui - k

the lords of eternity, mayest thou receive cakes in thy hands,

ḥeptet āb ḥer χaut Ḥeru ānχ ba - k

and bread pure upon the altar of Horus. May live thy soul,

ruṭ metu - k āb ḥrȧ - k em uat

{may germinate thy sinews and muscles,} may pierce thy face into the way

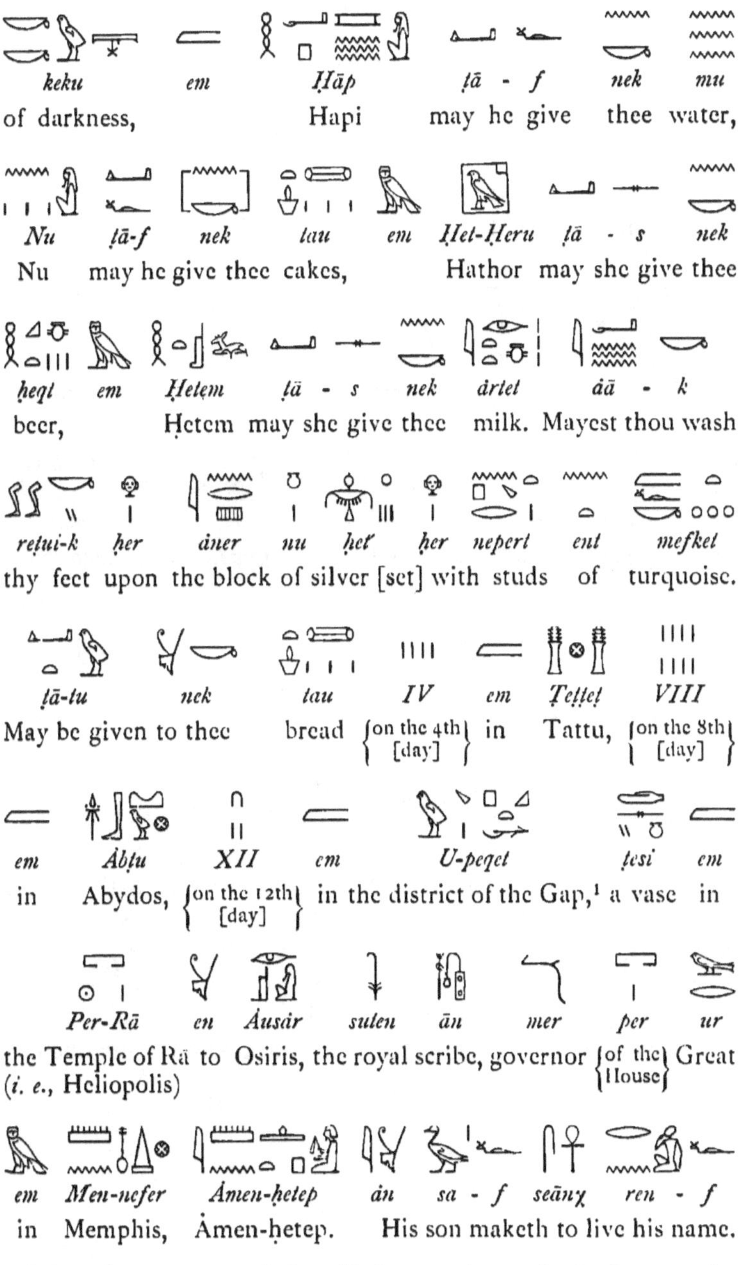

keku em Ḥāp ṭā - f nek mu
of darkness, Hapi may he give thee water,

Nu ṭā-f nek tau em Ḥet-Ḥeru ṭā - s nek
Nu may he give thee cakes, Hathor may she give thee

ḥeqt em Ḥetem ṭā - s nek årtet āā - k
beer, Ḥetem may she give thee milk. Mayest thou wash

reṭui-k ḥer åner nu ḥet' ḥer nepert ent mefket
thy feet upon the block of silver [set] with studs of turquoise.

ṭā-tu nek tau IV em Ṭeṭṭeṭ VIII
May be given to thee bread {on the 4th [day]} in Tattu, {on the 8th [day]}

em Åbṭu XII em U-peqet ṭesi em
in Abydos, {on the 12th [day]} in the district of the Gap,[1] a vase in

Per-Rā en Åusår suten ān mer per ur
the Temple of Rā (*i. e.*, Heliopolis) to Osiris, the royal scribe, governor {of the House} Great

em Men-nefer Åmen-ḥetep ån sa - f seānχ ren - f
in Memphis, Åmen-ḥetep. His son maketh to live his name.

[1] *I. e.*, the country round about Abydos near the opening in the mountains through which souls were supposed to pass into the next world.

FROM A HYMN TO ḤĀPI, THE GOD OF THE NILE.

[XVIIIth or XIXth dynasty.]

ṭuauu en Ḥāpi ȧneṭet ḥrȧ - k
A Hymn of praise of Ḥāpi. Homage to thee

Ḥāpi per - nek em ta pen it
Ḥāpi! Thou comest forth in land this, coming

em ḥetep er seānχu Qemt ȧmen
in peace to make to live Egypt, hidden one,

semu keku em hru ḥes nu
guide of the darkness on the day [when] it is [his] pleasure to

semu āui seχet qemamu
guide it, waterer of the fields which hath created

Rā seānχu ȧb nebt sesurȧ set
Rā, making to live animals all, making to drink the land

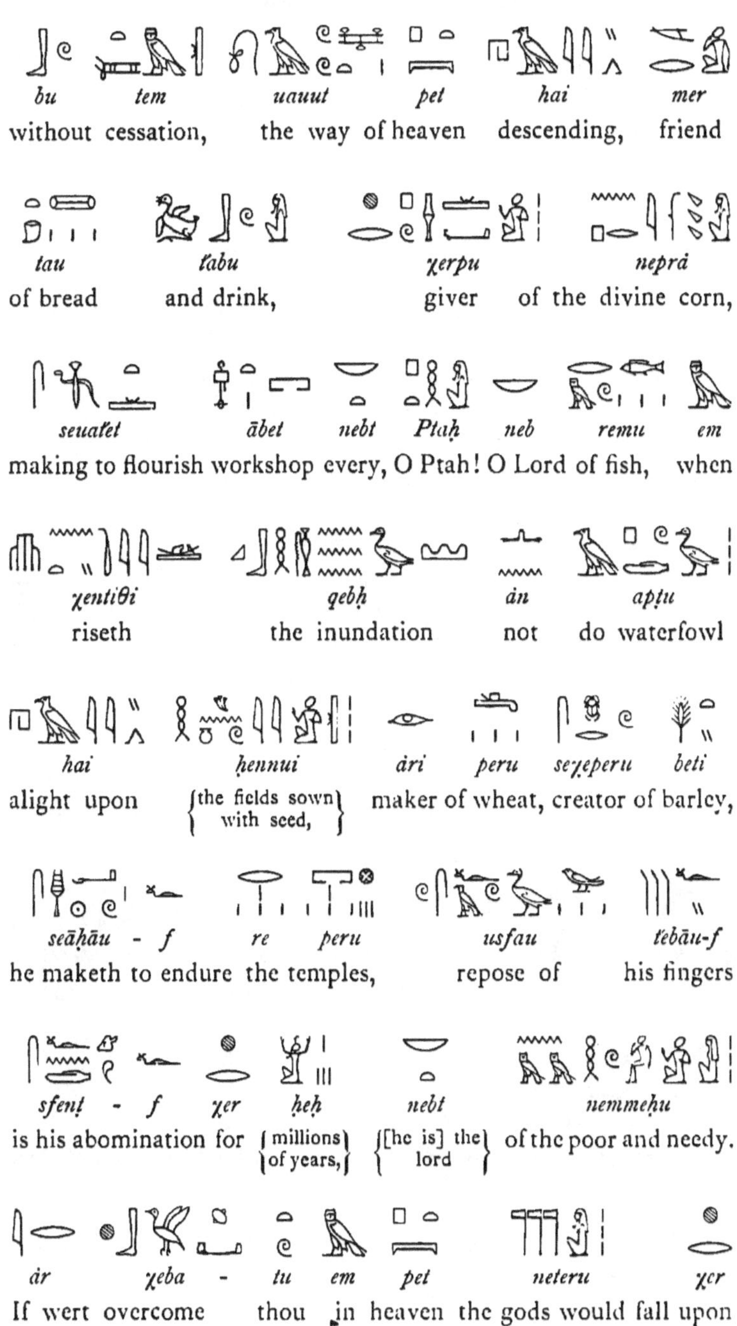

bu tem uauut pet hai mer
without cessation, the way of heaven descending, friend

tau t'abu χerpu neprà
of bread and drink, giver of the divine corn,

seuat'et ābet nebt Ptaḥ neb remu em
making to flourish workshop every, O Ptah! O Lord of fish, when

χentiθi qebḥ àn apṭu
riseth the inundation not do waterfowl

hai ḥennui àri peru seχeperu beti
alight upon {the fields sown with seed,} maker of wheat, creator of barley,

seāḥāu - f re peru usfau t'ebāu-f
he maketh to endure the temples, repose of his fingers

sfenṭ - f χer ḥeḥ nebt nemmeḥu
is his abomination for {millions of years,} {[he is] the lord} of the poor and needy.

àr χeba - tu em pet neteru χer
If wert overcome thou in heaven the gods would fall upon

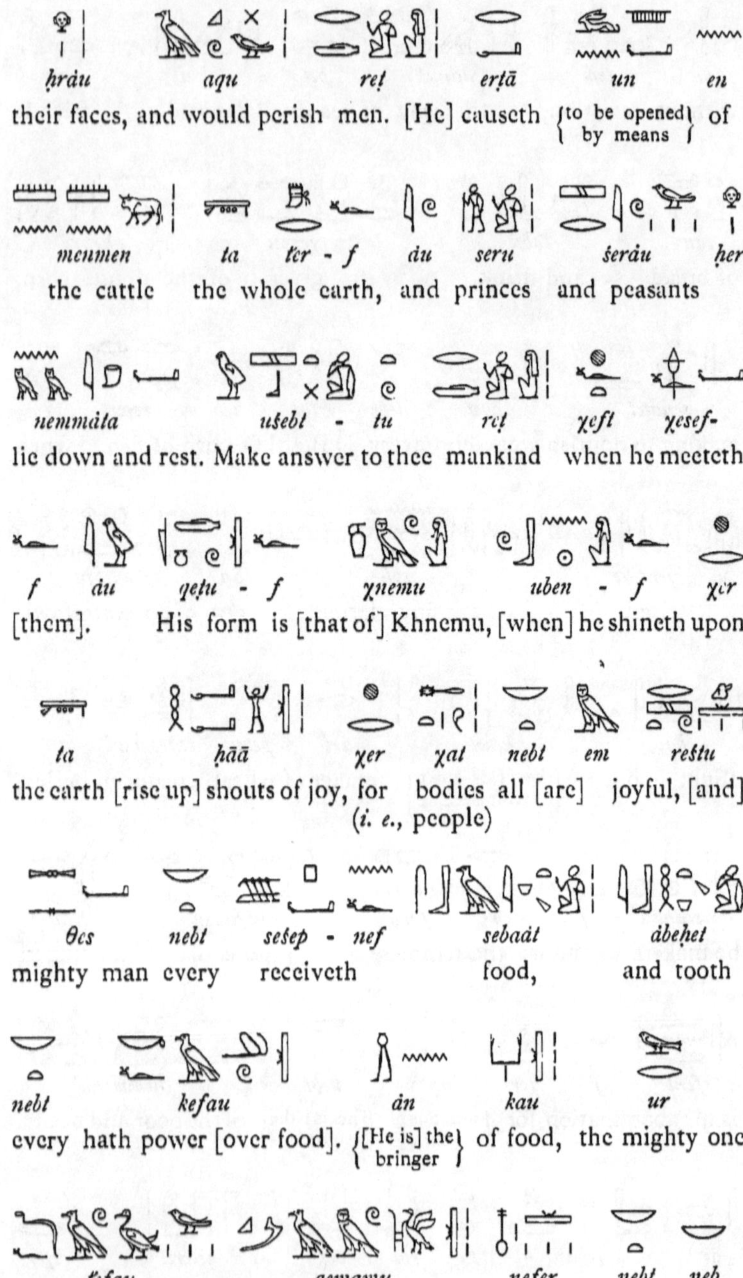

ḥrȧu aqu reṭ erṭā un en

their faces, and would perish men. [He] causeth {to be opened by means} of

menmen ta ṫer - f ȧu seru šerȧu ḥer

the cattle the whole earth, and princes and peasants

nemmȧta ušebt - tu reṭ χeft χesef-

lie down and rest. Make answer to thee mankind when he meeteth

f ȧu qeṭu - f χnemu uben - f χer

[them]. His form is [that of] Khnemu, [when] he shineth upon

ta ḥāā χer χat nebt em reštu

the earth [rise up] shouts of joy, for bodies all [are] joyful, [and]
(*i. e.*, people)

θes nebt sešep - nef sebaȧt ȧbeḥet

mighty man every receiveth food, and tooth

nebt kefau ȧn kau ur

every hath power [over food]. {[He is] the bringer} of food, the mighty one

ṫefau qemamu nefer nebt neb

of provisions, the creator of good things all, the lord

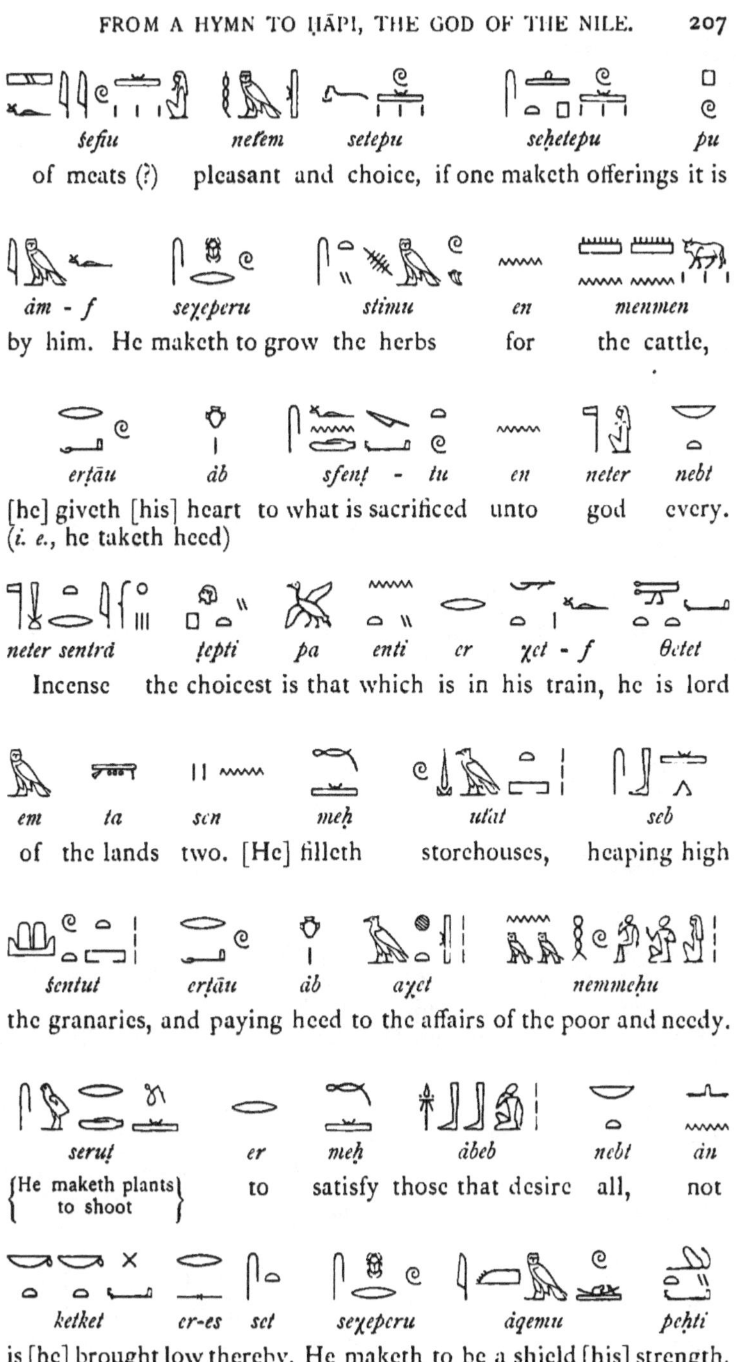

šefiu neṭem setepu seḥetepu pu
of meats (?) pleasant and choice, if one maketh offerings it is

àm-f seχeperu stimu en menmen
by him. He maketh to grow the herbs for the cattle,

erṭāu àb sfenṭ-tu en neter nebt
[he] giveth [his] heart to what is sacrificed unto god every.
(*i. e.*, he taketh heed)

neter sentrà ṭepti pa enti er χet-f θetet
Incense the choicest is that which is in his train, he is lord

em ta sen meḥ utàt seb
of the lands two. [He] filleth storehouses, heaping high

šentut erṭāu àb aχet nemmeḥu
the granaries, and paying heed to the affairs of the poor and needy.

seruṭ er meḥ àbeb nebt àn
{He maketh plants to shoot} to satisfy those that desire all, not

ketket er-es set seχeperu àqemu peḥti
is [he] brought low thereby. He maketh to be a shield [his] strength,

àn meḥu en àner tut ḥer uaḥ - set
Not can [he] be figured in stone, in the images on which are set

seχet ārat àn qemḥu entuf àn
{the double crown [with] uraei,} not to be seen is he, neither

bakà àn χerpu - tuf àn seše ṭ - tuf
works nor offerings can be made to him, not {can he be brought out}

em šettau àn reχ - tu bu entuf àn
from [his] secret places, not is known the place where he is, not

qem tepḥet ànu àn nāit enti
is [he] found [in] shrines inscribed, not is there a habitation which is

tennu - f àn semu em àb - k
sufficiently large for him, not can he be depicted in thy heart.

nehamu - nek ťamu - k χareṭu - k tu
Thou hast rejoiced thy peoples [and] thy children.

neť χet tuk em qemā ment hapu
Thou art a protector in the south, stablished are [thy] laws

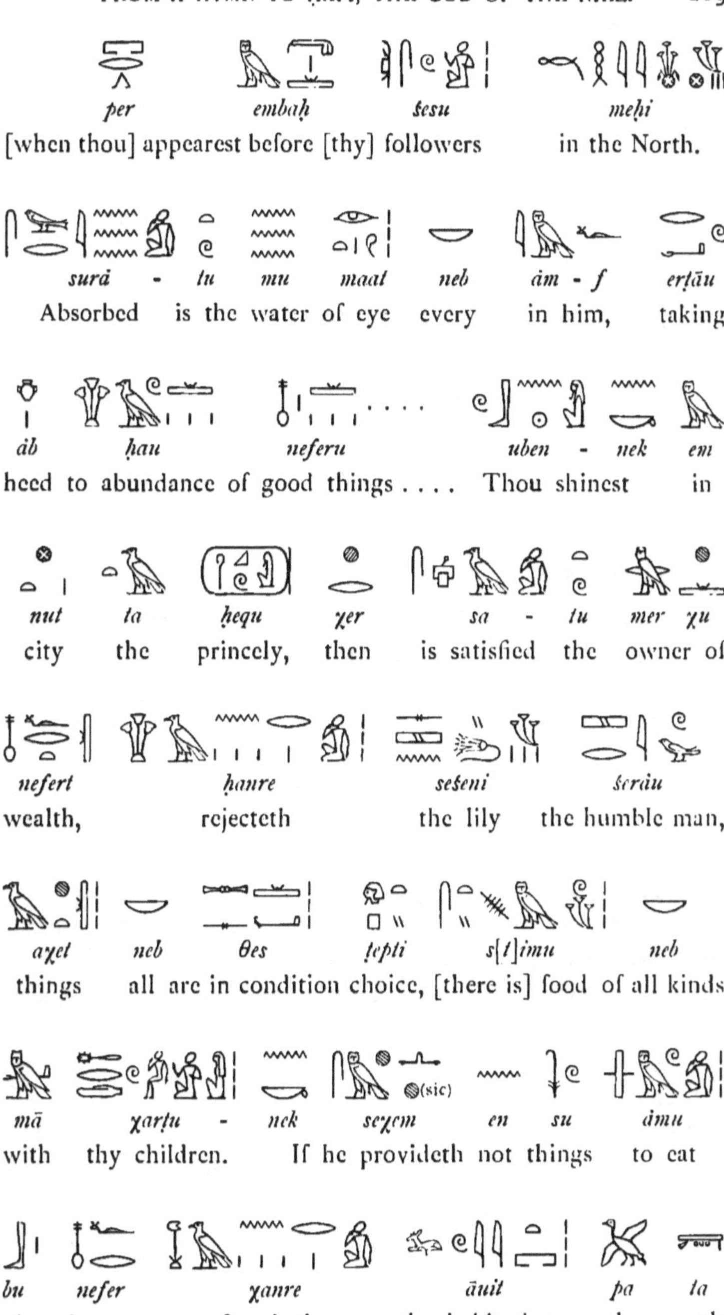

per *embaḥ* *šesu* *meḥi*
[when thou] appearest before [thy] followers in the North.

surā - *tu* *mu* *maat* *neb* *àm* - *f* *erṭāu*
Absorbed is the water of eye every in him, taking

àb *ḥau* *neferu* *uben* - *nek* *em*
heed to abundance of good things .... Thou shinest in

nut *ta* *ḥequ* *χer* *sa* - *tu* *mer* *χu*
city the princely, then is satisfied the owner of

nefert *ḥanre* *sešeni* *šerāu*
wealth, rejecteth the lily the humble man,

aχet *neb* *θes* *ṭepti* *s*[*t*]*imu* *neb*
things all are in condition choice, [there is] food of all kinds

mā *χarṭu* - *nek* *seχem* *en* *su* *àmu*
with thy children. If he provideth not things to eat

bu *nefer* *χanre* *āuit* *pa* *ta*
happiness forsaketh the habitations, the earth

14

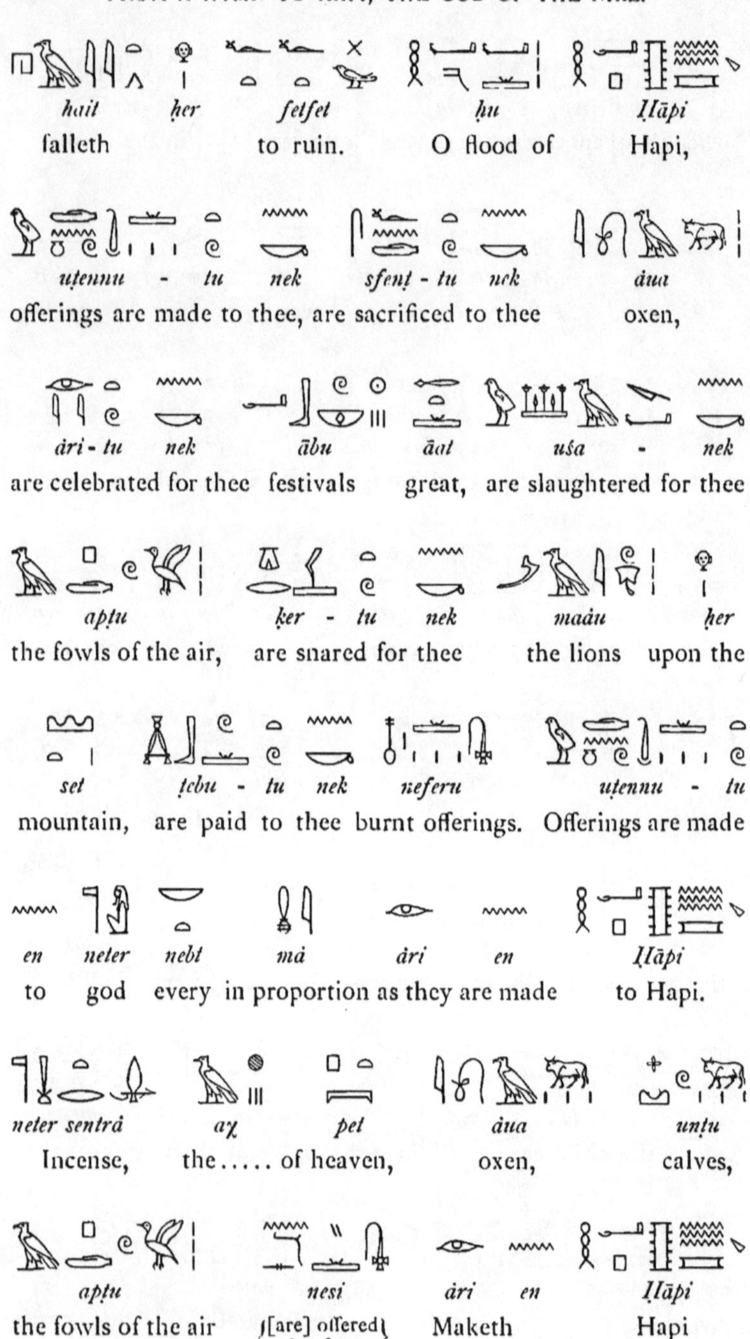
hait *ḥer* *fetfet* *ḥu* *Ḥāpi*
falleth to ruin. O flood of Hapi,
uṭennu - tu nek sfenṭ - tu nek àua
offerings are made to thee, are sacrificed to thee oxen,
àri - tu nek ābu āat uśa - nek
are celebrated for thee festivals great, are slaughtered for thee
apṭu ḳer - tu nek maàu ḥer
the fowls of the air, are snared for thee the lions upon the
set ṭebu - tu nek neferu uṭennu - tu
mountain, are paid to thee burnt offerings. Offerings are made
en neter nebt mà àri en Ḥāpi
to god every in proportion as they are made to Hapi.
neter sentrà aχ pet àua unṭu
Incense, the..... of heaven, oxen, calves,
apṭu nesi àri en Ḥāpi
the fowls of the air [are] offered by fire. Maketh Hapi

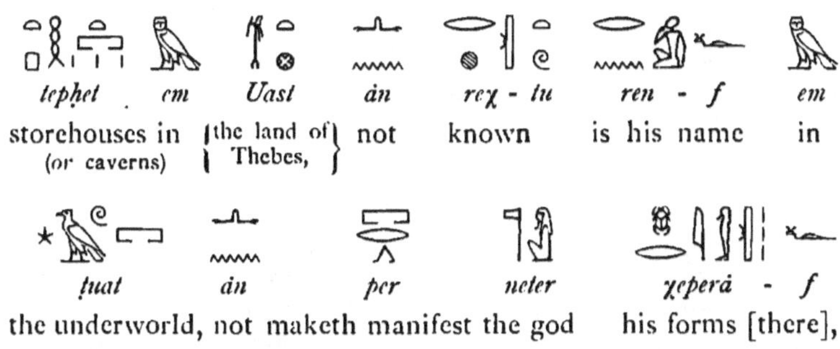

tephet em Uast ȧn reχ-tu ren-f em

storehouses (or caverns) in {the land of Thebes,} not known is his name in

ṭuat ȧn per neter χeperȧ-f

the underworld, not maketh manifest the god his forms [there],

usfa seχeru

idle [are] imaginings [concerning them].

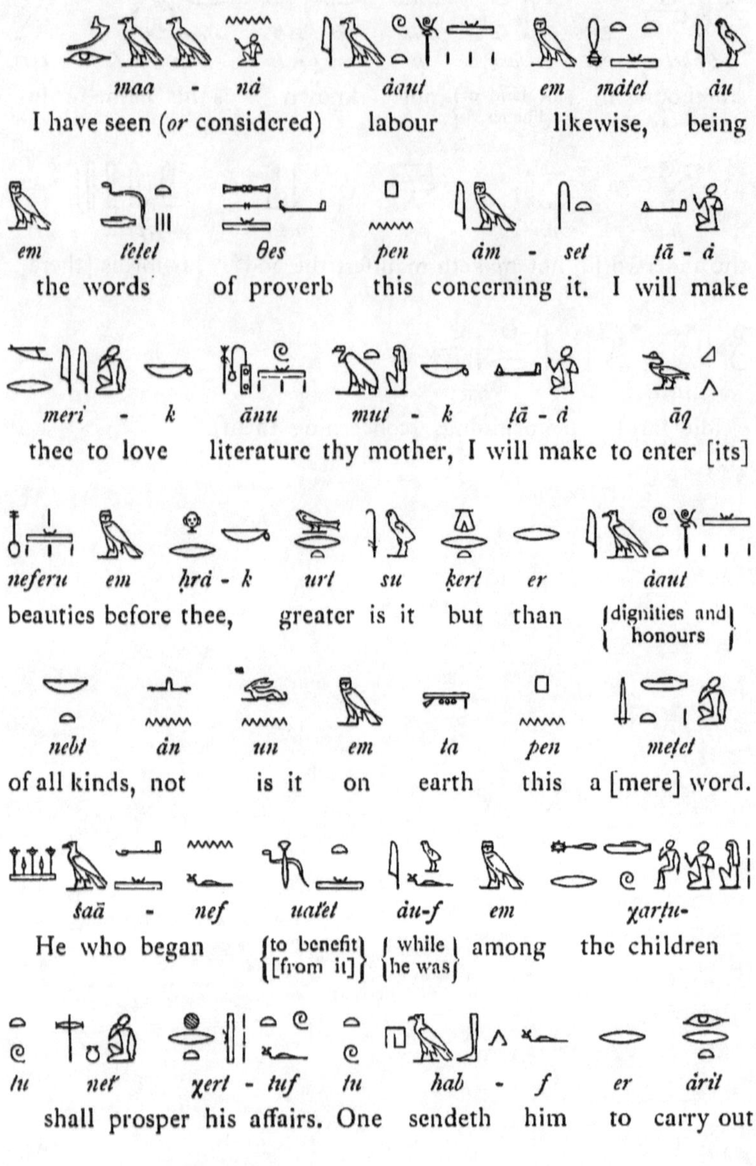

maa - nȧ ȧaut em mȧtet ȧu

I have seen (*or* considered) labour likewise, being

em t'et'et θes pen ȧm - set tā - ȧ

the words of proverb this concerning it. I will make

meri - k ānu mut - k tā - ȧ āq

thee to love literature thy mother, I will make to enter [its]

neferu em ḥrȧ - k urt su ḳert er ȧaut

beauties before thee, greater is it but than {dignities and honours}

nebt ȧn un em ta pen met'et

of all kinds, not is it on earth this a [mere] word.

śaā - nef uat'et ȧu-f em χarṭu-

He who began {to benefit [from it]} {while he was} among the children

tu net' χert - tuf tu hab - f er ȧrit

shall prosper his affairs. One sendeth him to carry out

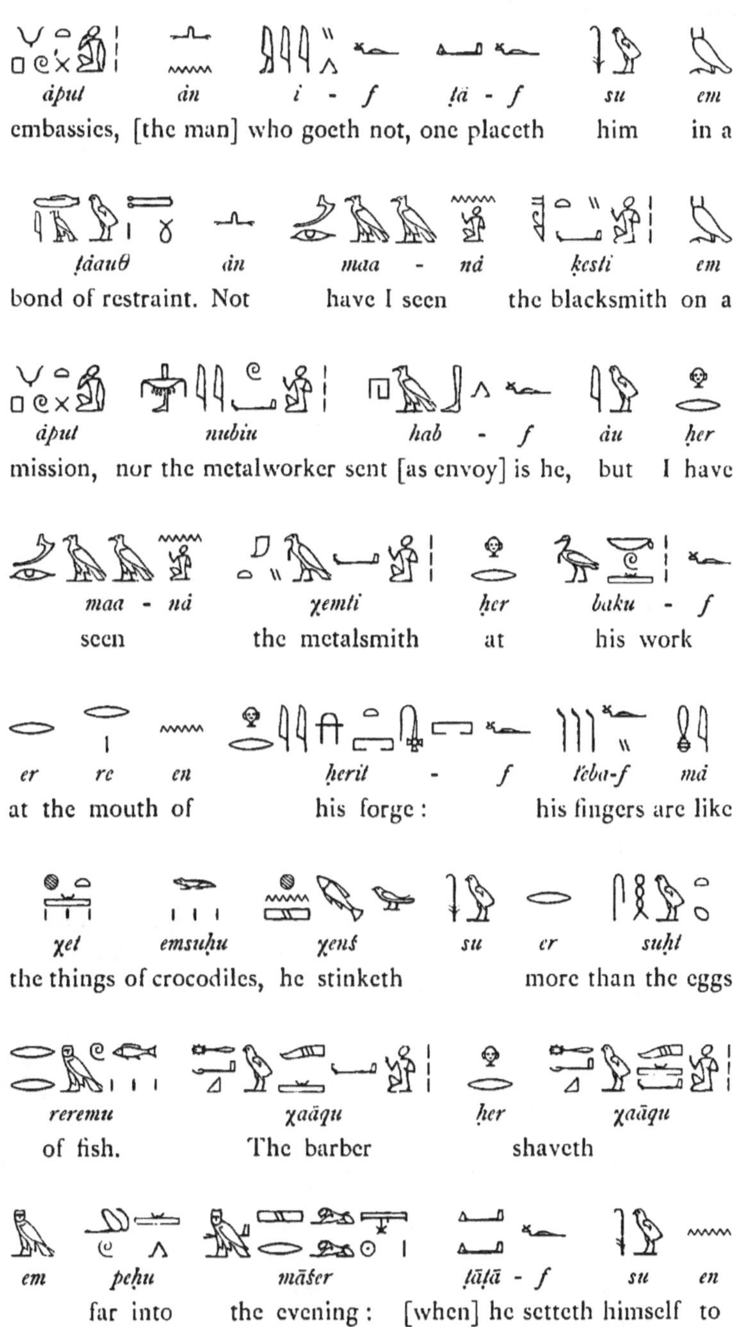

ȧput ȧn i - f ṭā - f su em
embassies, [the man] who goeth not, one placeth him in a

ṭȧauθ ȧn maa - nȧ ḳesti em
bond of restraint. Not have I seen the blacksmith on a

ȧput nubiu hab - f ȧu ḥer
mission, nor the metalworker sent [as envoy] is he, but I have

maa - nȧ χemti ḥer baku - f
seen the metalsmith at his work

er re en ḥerit - f ťeba-f mȧ
at the mouth of his forge: his fingers are like

χet emsuḥu χenś su er suḥt
the things of crocodiles, he stinketh more than the eggs

reremu χaāqu ḥer χaāqu
of fish. The barber shaveth

em peḥu māśer ṭāṭā - f su en
far into the evening: [when] he setteth himself to

āmāit *ṭāṭā - f* *su* *ḥer* *qāḥāt - f*
eat he placeth himself upon his elbow (*or* shoulder).

ṭāṭā - f *su* *er* *mert* *er* *mert* *er*
He betaketh himself from house (?) to house to

nχaχ *er* *χaāqu - f* *qenen - f*
seek after his men who need shaving, he worketh violently

āāui-f *er* *meḥ* *χat - f* *mà* *net* (or *bàt*) *àmi*
his two arms to fill his belly, even as bees eat

er *kat - set* *qennuiu* *em* *χennu*
from their labours. A weaver within

nait *bàn* *su* *er* *set ḥemt* *masti - f*
the factory, wretched is he more than a woman. His legs

àm - f *er* *re* *en* *àb - f* *àn* *tepà - nef* *nifu*
are under him at the door of his heart, not breatheth he the air.

àr *χeba - nef* *em* *hru* *em* *seχet - tu*
If he fail for a day in weaving,

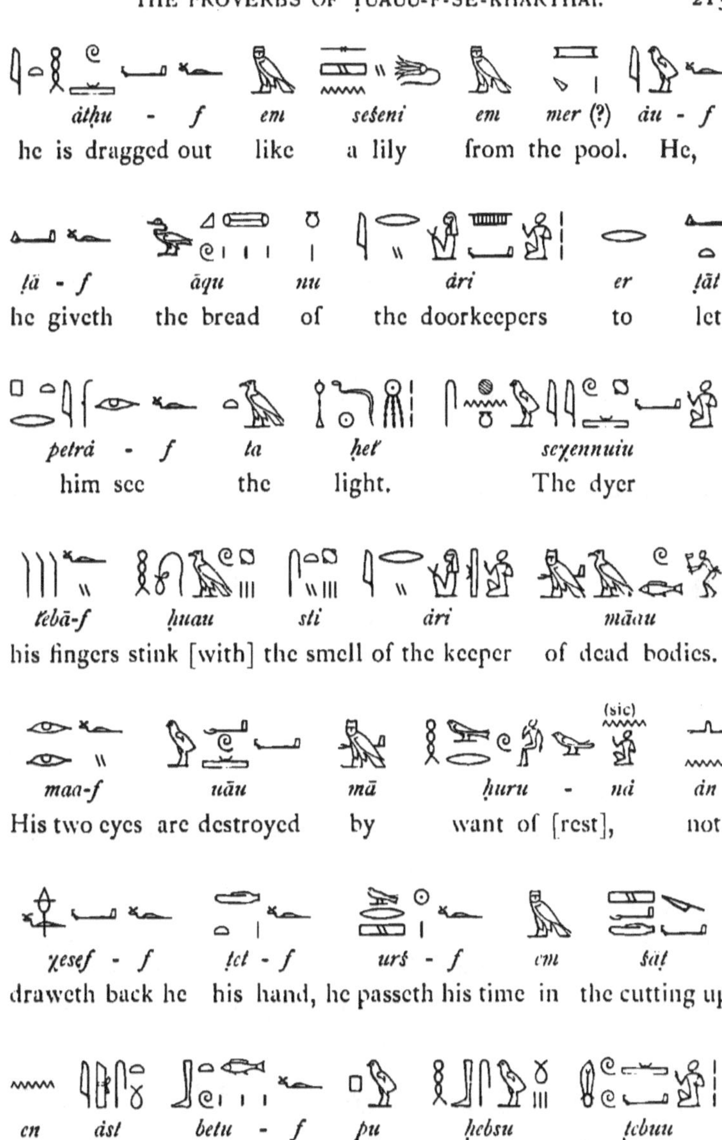

àtḥu - f em sešeni em mer (?) àu - f

he is dragged out like a lily from the pool. He,

ṭā - f āqu nu àri er ṭāt

he giveth the bread of the doorkeepers to let

petrà - f ta ḥet' seχennuiu

him see the light. The dyer

t'ebā-f ḥuau sti àri māau

his fingers stink [with] the smell of the keeper of dead bodies.

maa-f uāu mā ḥuru - nà (sic) àn

His two eyes are destroyed by want of [rest], not

χesef - f ṭet - f urš - f em šāṭ

draweth back he his hand, he passeth his time in the cutting up

en àst betu - f pu ḥebsu ṭebuu

of garments, an abomination is he [in his] clothes. The shoemaker

bàn su er si χer ṭebḥet - f

unfortunate is he most of all, for he chattereth

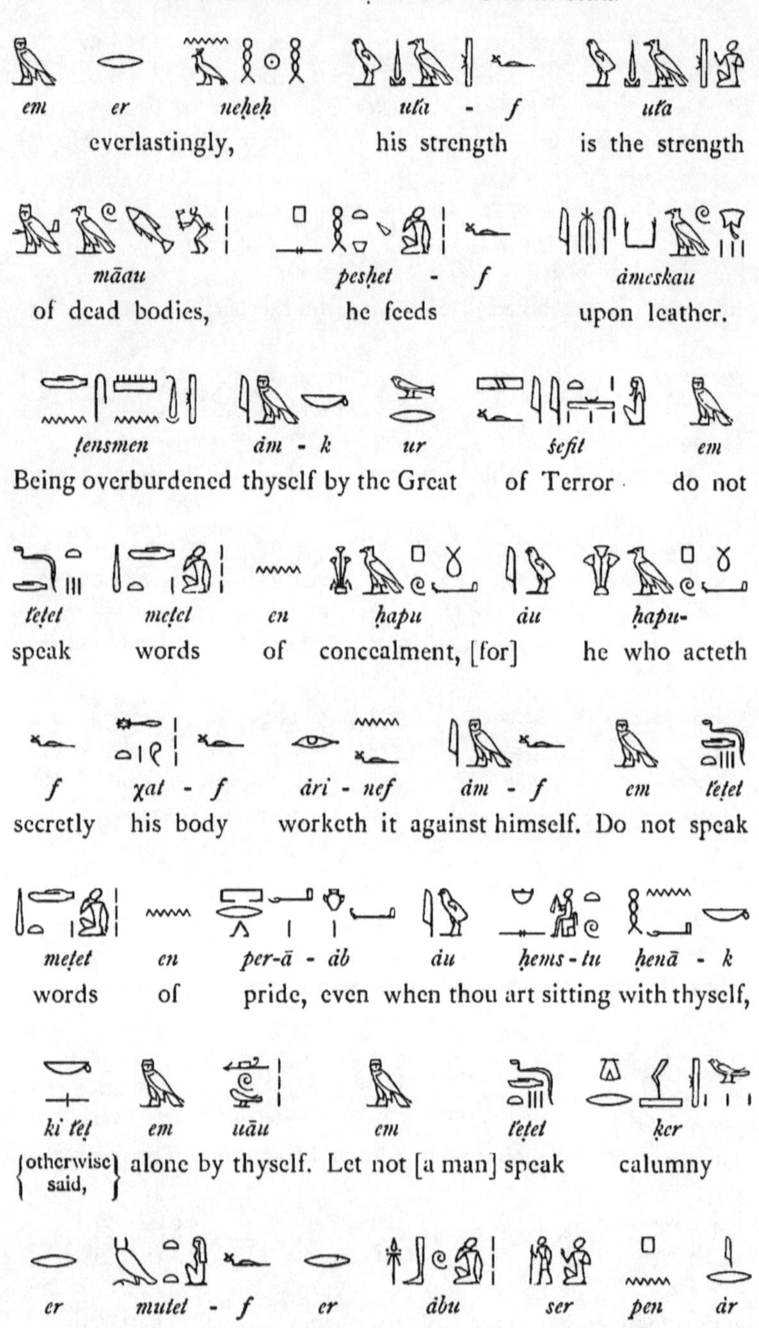

em er neḥeḥ uʈa - f uʈa

everlastingly, his strength is the strength

māau pesḥet - f àmeskau

of dead bodies, he feeds upon leather.

ṭensmen àm - k ur šefit em

Being overburdened thyself by the Great of Terror do not

ʈeṭet meṭet en ḥapu àu ḥapu-

speak words of concealment, [for] he who acteth

f χat - f àri - nef àm - f em ʈeṭet

secretly his body worketh it against himself. Do not speak

meṭet en per-ā - àb àu ḥems - tu ḥenā - k

words of pride, even when thou art sitting with thyself,

ki ʈeṭ em uāu em ʈeṭet ḳer

{otherwise said,} alone by thyself. Let not [a man] speak calumny

er mutet - f er àbu ser pen àr

against his mother for the sake of Chief this.

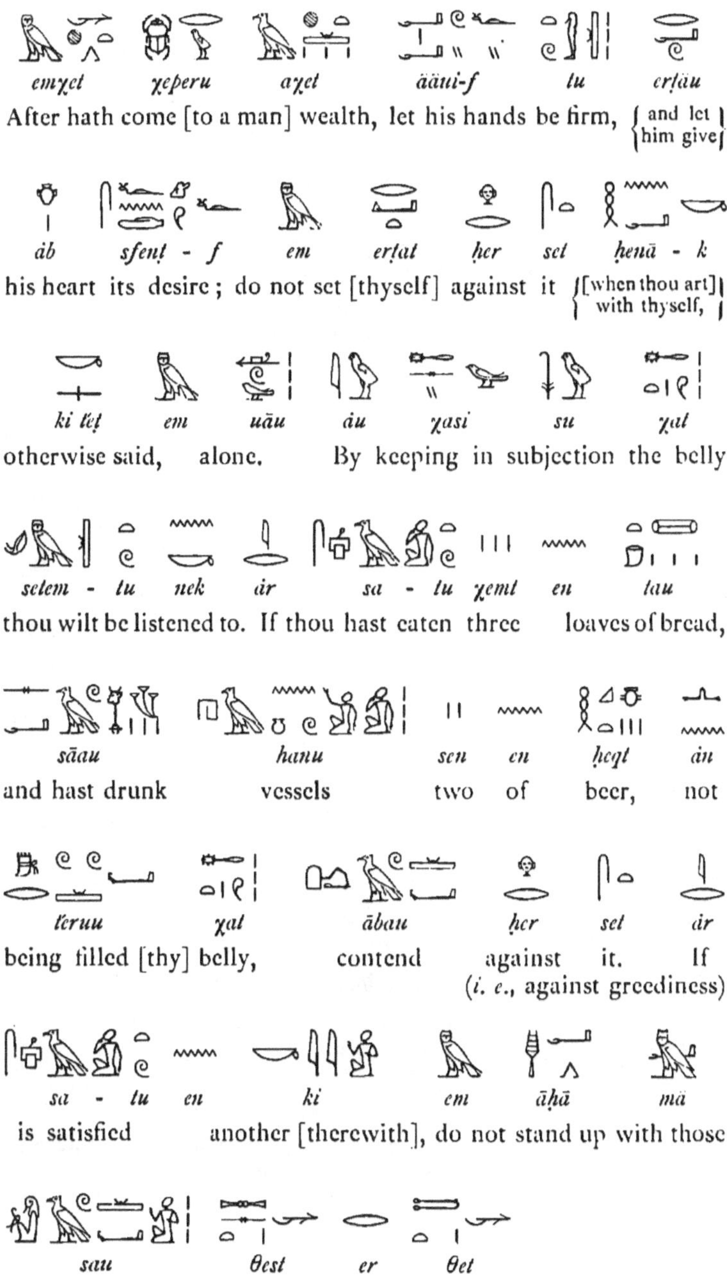

emχet χeperu aχet ääui-f tu erṭàu

After hath come [to a man] wealth, let his hands be firm, {and let him give}

àb sfenṭ - f em erṭat ḥer set ḥenā - k

his heart its desire; do not set [thyself] against it {[when thou art] with thyself,}

ki ṭeṭ em uāu àu χasi su χat

otherwise said, alone. By keeping in subjection the belly

setem - tu nek àr sa - tu χemt en tau

thou wilt be listened to. If thou hast eaten three loaves of bread,

sāau hanu sen en ḥeqt àn

and hast drunk vessels two of beer, not

ṭeruu χat ābau ḥer set àr

being filled [thy] belly, contend against it. If (*i. e.*, against greediness)

sa - tu en ki em āḥā mä

is satisfied another [therewith], do not stand up with those

sau θest er θet

who break a board upon a stake.

THE DESTRUCTION OF MANKIND.

[XIXth dynasty.]

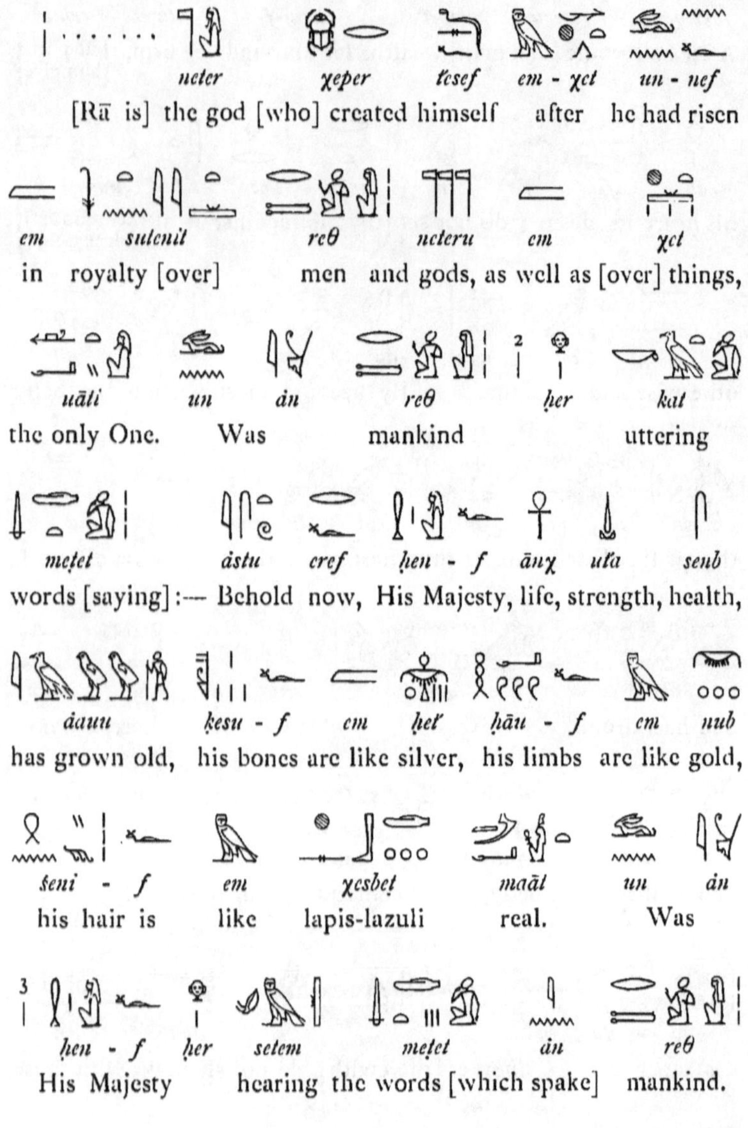

neter χeper t'esef em - χet un - nef
[Rā is] the god [who] created himself after he had risen
em sutenit reθ neteru em χet
in royalty [over] men and gods, as well as [over] things,
uāti un ȧn reθ 2 ḥer kat
the only One. Was mankind uttering
meṭet ȧstu eref ḥen - f ānχ uṭa senb
words [saying]:— Behold now, His Majesty, life, strength, health,
ȧauu ḳesu - f em ḥet' ḥāu - f em nub
has grown old, his bones are like silver, his limbs are like gold,
šeni - f em χesbeṭ maāt un ȧn
his hair is like lapis-lazuli real. Was
3 ḥen - f ḥer setem meṭet ȧn reθ
His Majesty hearing the words [which spake] mankind.

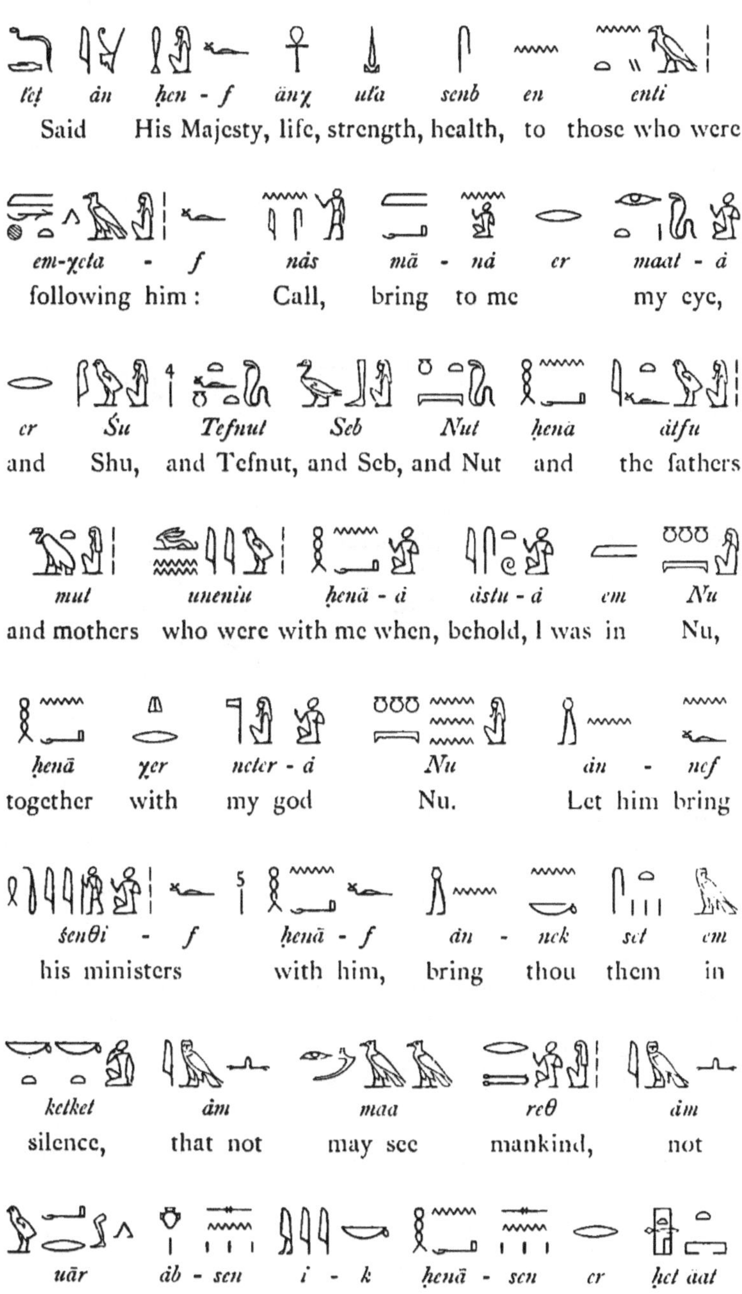

t'eṭ ȧn ḥen - f ānχ ut'a senb en enti

Said His Majesty, life, strength, health, to those who were

em-χeta - f nȧs mā - nȧ er maat - ȧ

following him: Call, bring to me my eye,

er Śu Tefnut Seb Nut ḥenā ȧtfu

and Shu, and Tefnut, and Seb, and Nut and the fathers

mut uneniu ḥenā - ȧ ȧstu - ȧ em Nu

and mothers who were with me when, behold, I was in Nu,

ḥenā χer neter - ȧ Nu ȧn - nef

together with my god Nu. Let him bring

śenθi - f ḥenā - f ȧn - nek set em

his ministers with him, bring thou them in

ketket ȧm maa reθ ȧm

silence, that not may see mankind, not

uār ȧb - sen i - k ḥenā - sen er ḥet āat

may flee their hearts. Come thou with them into the temple,

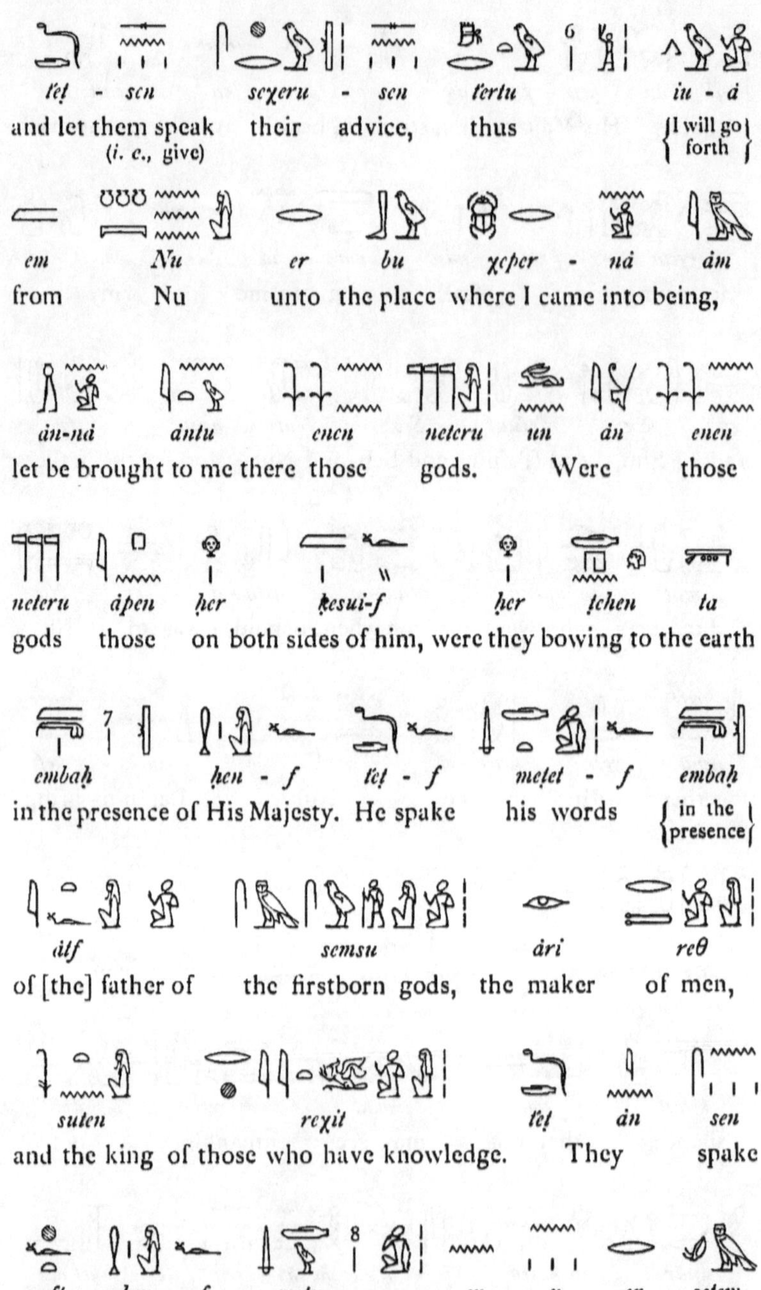

ṭeṭ - sen seχeru - sen ṭertu iu - à

and let them speak (*i. e.*, give) their advice, thus {I will go forth}

em Nu er bu χeper - nà àm

from Nu unto the place where I came into being,

àn-nà àntu enen neteru un àn enen

let be brought to me there those gods. Were those

neteru àpen ḥer ḳesui-f ḥer ṭehen ta

gods those on both sides of him, were they bowing to the earth

embaḥ ḥen - f ṭeṭ - f meṭet - f embaḥ

in the presence of His Majesty. He spake his words {in the presence}

àtf semsu àri reθ

of [the] father of the firstborn gods, the maker of men,

suten reχit ṭeṭ àn sen

and the king of those who have knowledge. They spake

χeft ḥen - f meṭu en n er setem-

before His Majesty :— Speak to us, for we are

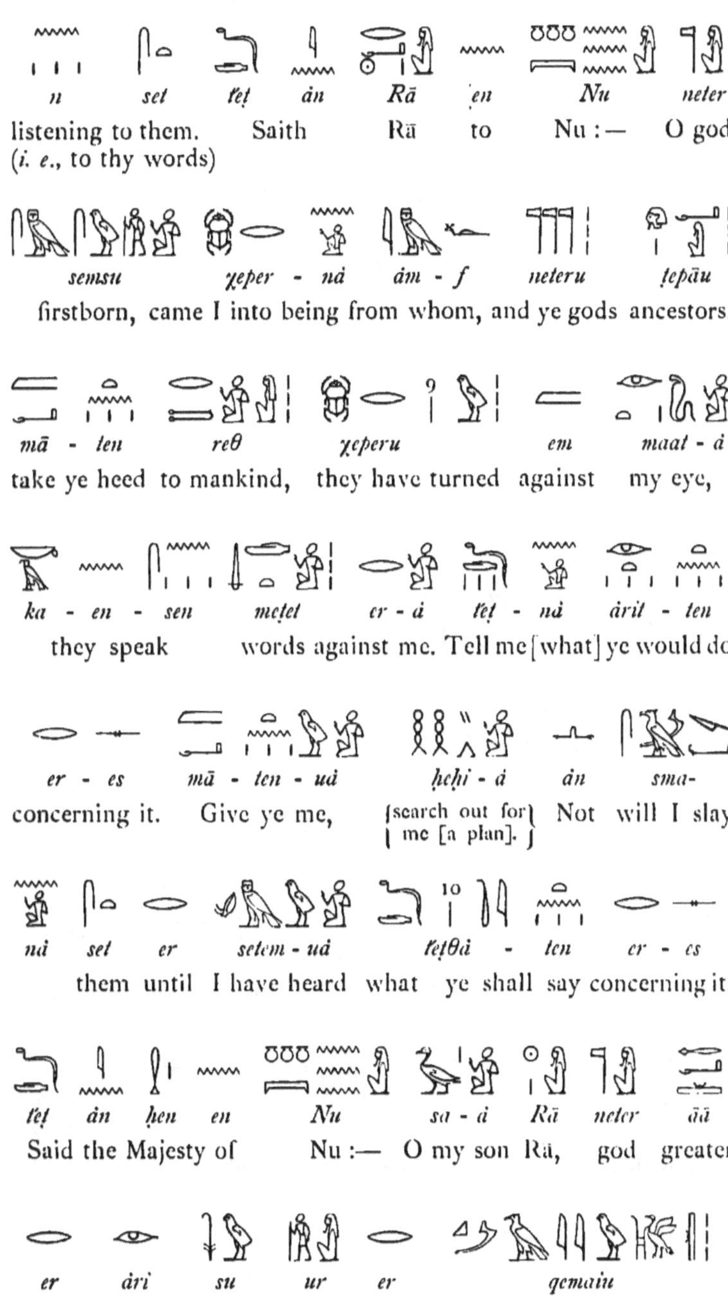

n set ṭeṭ ȧn Rā ˌen Nu neter

listening to them. Saith Rā to Nu :— O god
(*i. e.*, to thy words)

semsu χeper - nȧ ȧm - f neteru ṭepāu

firstborn, came I into being from whom, and ye gods ancestors,

mā - ten reθ χeperu em maat - ȧ

take ye heed to mankind, they have turned against my eye,

ka - en - sen meṭet er - ȧ ṭeṭ - nȧ ȧrit - ten

they speak words against me. Tell me [what] ye would do

er - es mā - ten - uȧ ḥeḥi - ȧ ȧn sma-

concerning it. Give ye me, {search out for me [a plan].} Not will I slay

nȧ set er setem - uȧ ṭeṭθȧ - ten er - es

them until I have heard what ye shall say concerning it.

ṭeṭ ȧn ḥen en Nu sa - ȧ Rā neter āā

Said the Majesty of Nu :— O my son Rā, god greater

er ȧri su ur er qemaiu

than [he] that made him, older than those divine beings who created

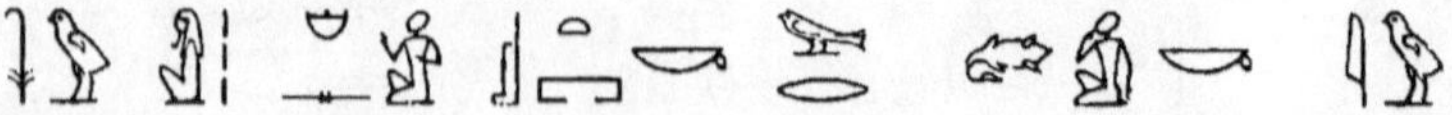

su ḥems ȧuset - k ur senṭ - k ȧu

him! fixed is thy throne, great is the fear of thee; let

maat - k er uaiu ȧm - k ṭeṭ

thine eye be upon those who have blasphemed against thee. Saith

ȧn ḥen en Rā mā - ten set uār

the Majesty of Rā :— Behold ye them fleeing

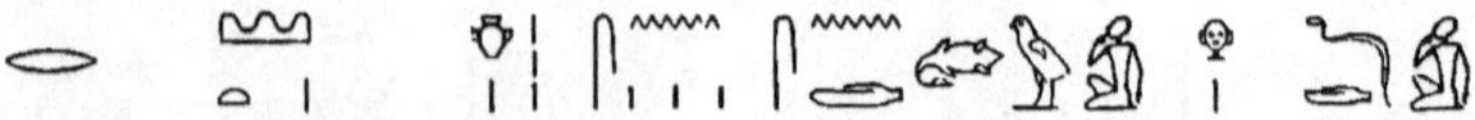

er set ȧbu - sen senṭu ḥer ṭeṭ-

unto the mountains, their hearts are afraid by reason of what they

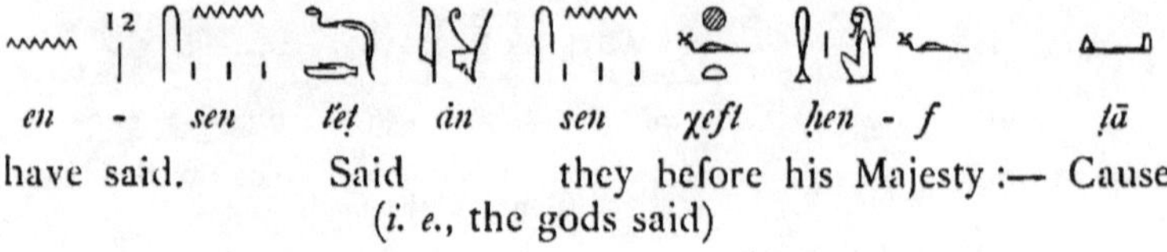

en - sen ṭeṭ ȧn sen χeft ḥen - f ṭā

have said. Said they before his Majesty :— Cause
(*i. e.*, the gods said)

šem maat - k ḥau - s - nek set

to go forth thine eye, [and] let it destroy for thee those [who]

ua em ṭu ȧn maat χenti

blaspheme [thee] with wickedness. Not an eye existeth

ȧm - s er ḥu - k set ha - s em

among them which can resist thee [when] it descendeth in

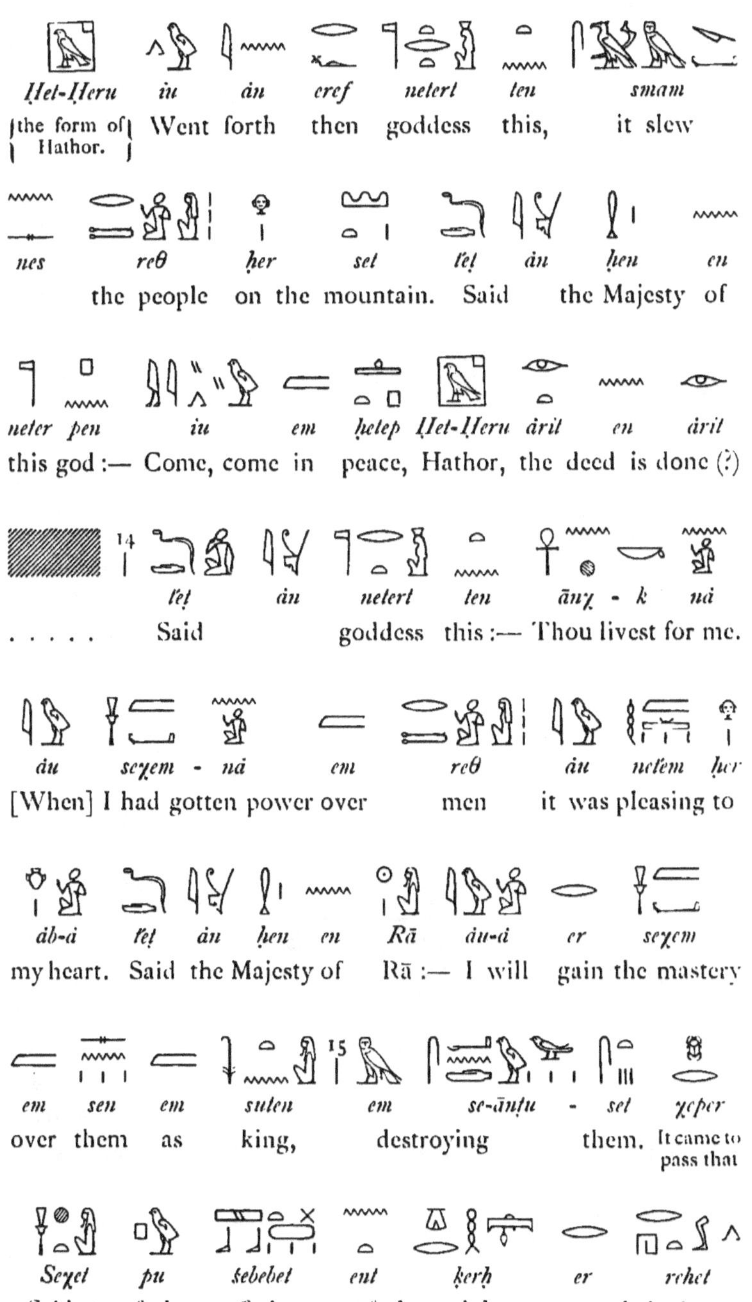

Ḥet-Ḥeru iu ȧn eref netert ten smam
{the form of Hathor.} Went forth then goddess this, it slew

nes reθ ḥer set ṭeṭ ȧn ḥen en
the people on the mountain. Said the Majesty of

neter pen iu em ḥetep Ḥet-Ḥeru ȧrit en ȧrit
this god :— Come, come in peace, Hathor, the deed is done (?)

14 *ṭeṭ ȧn netert ten ānχ - k nȧ*
. . . . . Said goddess this :— Thou livest for me.

ȧu seχem - nȧ em reθ ȧu neṭem ḥer
[When] I had gotten power over men it was pleasing to

ȧb-ȧ ṭeṭ ȧn ḥen en Rā ȧu-ȧ er seχem
my heart. Said the Majesty of Rā :— I will gain the mastery

em sen em suten 15 *em se-āntu - set χeper*
over them as king, destroying them. It came to pass that

Seχet pu ṡebebet ent ḳerḥ er rehet
Sekhet of the offerings of the night waded about

ḥer snef - sen śaā em Suten-ḥenen

in their blood beginning in Suten-ḥenen.

ṭeṭ àn Rā nàs mā - nà àputi

Said Rā :— Call, bring me messengers

χau sànnu seχs - sen śut

swift and speedy, they [who] can run like the wind

en χat àn àn tu enen àputi

of the body. One brought these messengers

àpen ḥer āāui ṭeṭ àn ḥen en neter pen

these straightway. Said the Majesty of god this :—

śa - sen er Ābu àn - nà ṭāṭāāt er

Let them go to Elephantine [and] bring me mandrakes in

ur àn àn tu nef enen ṭāṭāāt

great number. One brought to him these mandrakes,

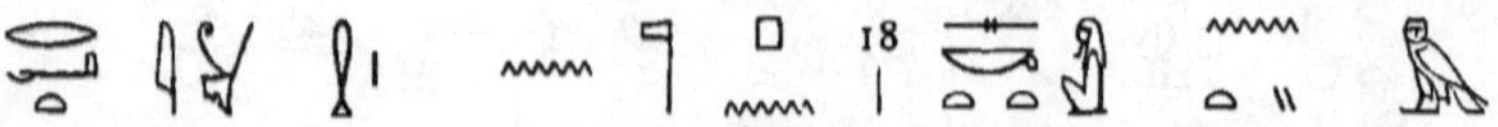

erṭā àn ḥen en neter pen Sektet enti em

[and] gave the majesty of god this to Sektet who is in

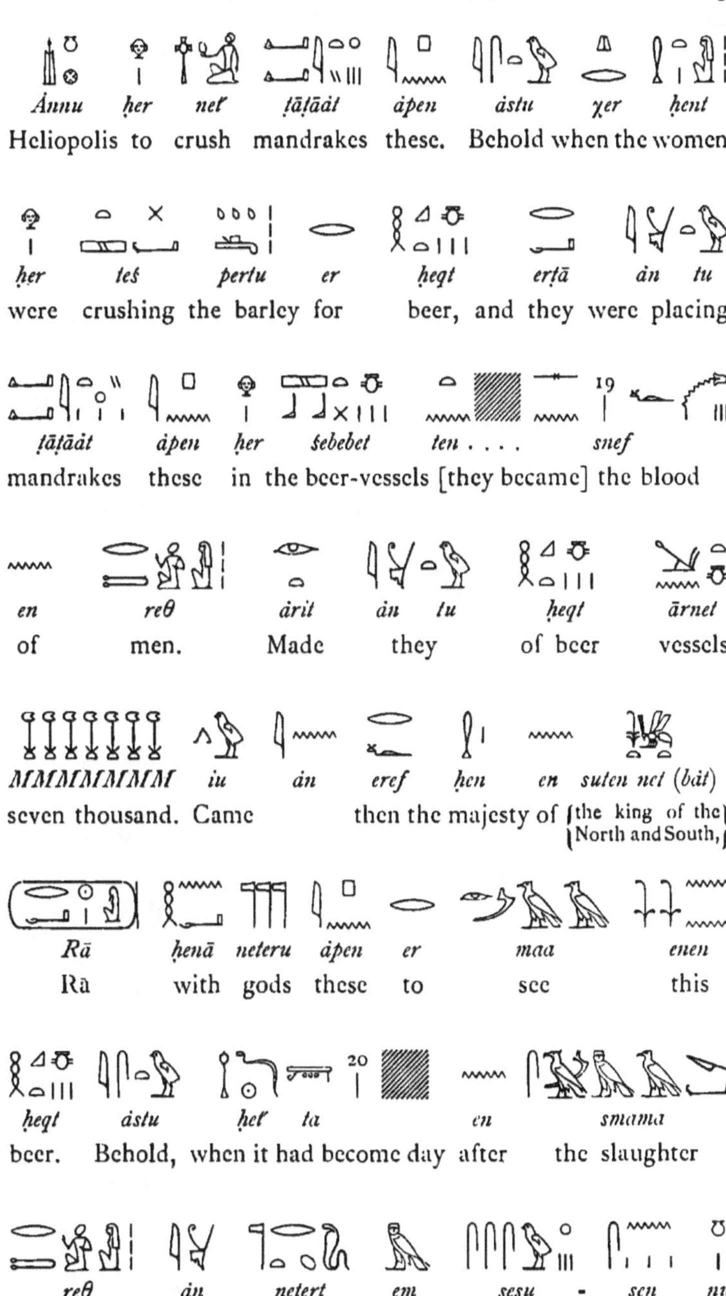

Ånnu ḥer neṭ ṭāṭāāt åpen åstu χer ḥent
Heliopolis to crush mandrakes these. Behold when the women

ḥer teš pertu er ḥeqt erṭā ån tu
were crushing the barley for beer, and they were placing

ṭāṭāāt åpen ḥer šebebet ten . . . . snef
mandrakes these in the beer-vessels [they became] the blood

en reθ årit ån tu ḥeqt ārnet
of men. Made they of beer vessels

MMMMMMM iu ån eref ḥen en suten net (båt)
seven thousand. Came then the majesty of {the king of the North and South,}

Rā ḥenā neteru åpen er maa enen
Rā with gods these to see this

ḥeqt åstu ḥeṭ ta en smama
beer. Behold, when it had become day after the slaughter

reθ ån netert em sesu - sen nu
of men by the goddess during their period (?) of

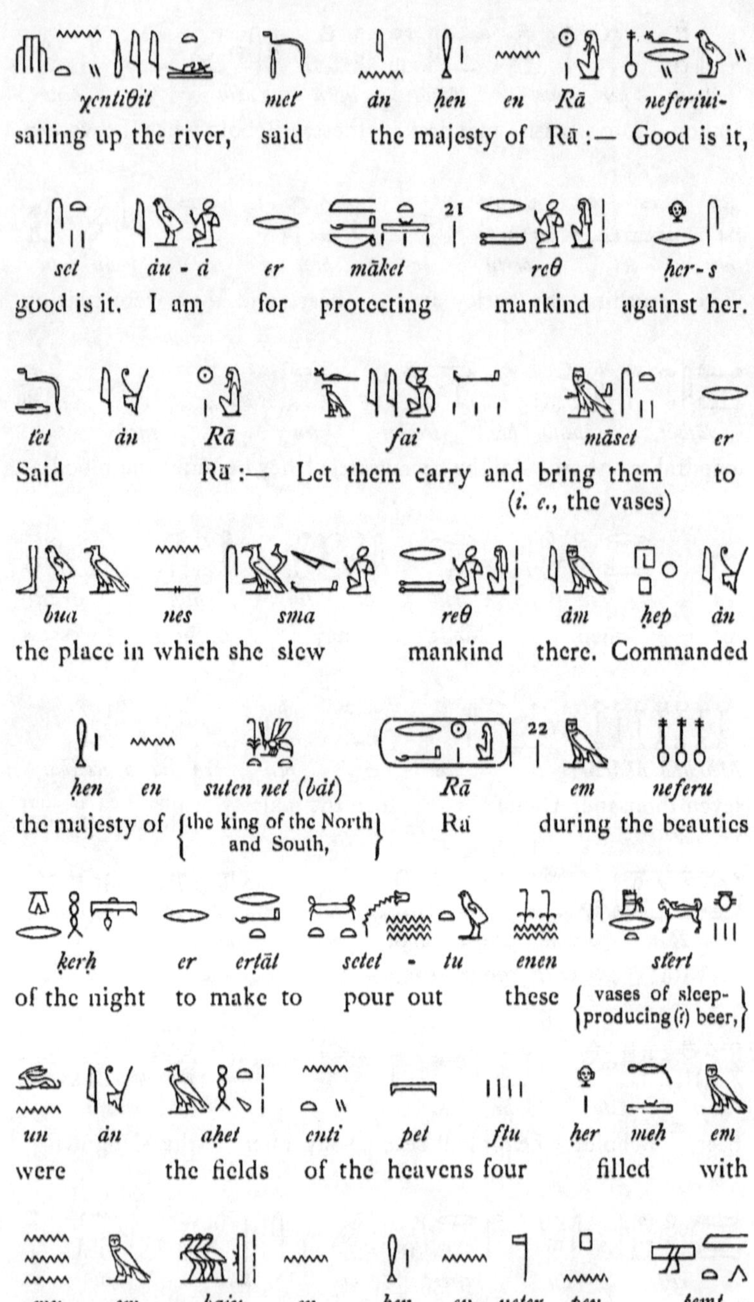

χentiθit *met'* *àn* *ḥen* *en* *Rā* *neferiui-*
sailing up the river, said the majesty of Rā :— Good is it,

set *àu - à* *er* *māket* 21 *reθ* *ḥer - s*
good is it. I am for protecting mankind against her.

t'et *àn* *Rā* *fai* *māset* *er*
Said Rā :— Let them carry and bring them to
(*i. e.*, the vases)

bua *nes* *sma* *reθ* *àm* *ḥep* *àn*
the place in which she slew mankind there. Commanded

ḥen *en* *suten net (bàt)* *Rā* 22 *em* *neferu*
the majesty of {the king of the North and South,} Rā during the beauties

ḳerḥ *er* *erṭāl* *setet - tu* *enen* *sḍert*
of the night to make to pour out these {vases of sleep-producing (?) beer,}

un *àn* *aḥet* *enti* *pet* *fṭu* *ḥer* *meḥ* *em*
were the fields of the heavens four filled with

mu *em* *baiu* *en* *ḥen* *en* *neter* *pen* *šemt*
liquid by the Will of the majesty of god this. Came

àn *netert* *ten* *em* *ṭuaiu* *qem* - *nes*

goddess this in the morning, found she
(*i. e.*, Sekhet)

enen *ḥer* *meḥt* *nefer* *àn* *ḥrà* - *set* *àm*

this [heaven] flooded, joyful became her face thereby,

un *àn* *set* *ḥer* *seurà* *nefer* *ḥer* *àb* - *set*

was she drinking [thereof], pleasing [was it] to her heart,

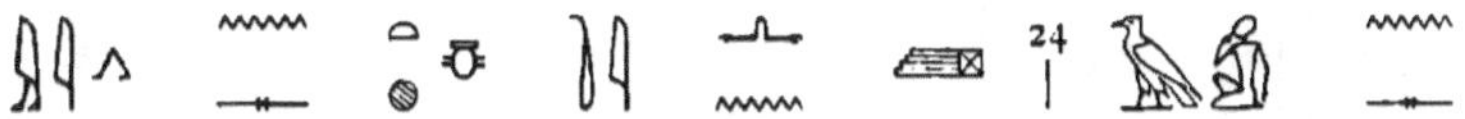

i - *nes* *teχ* - *θà* *àn* *saa* - *nes*

she came being drunk, not knew she

reθ *ṭeṭ* *àn* *ḥen* *en* *Rā* *en* *netert*

mankind [again]. Said the majesty of Ra to goddess

ten *it* - *iu* *em* *ḥetep* *amit* *χeper*

this :— Come, come, in peace, {O gracious goddess, [and henceforth]} there were

nefert *em* *Amem* *ṭeṭ* *àn* *ḥen* *en* *Rā*

beautiful women in Amem. Said the majesty of Rā

en *netert* *ten* *àri* *en* *set* *sṭertet*

to goddess this :— Let be made for her {vases of sleep-producing drink}

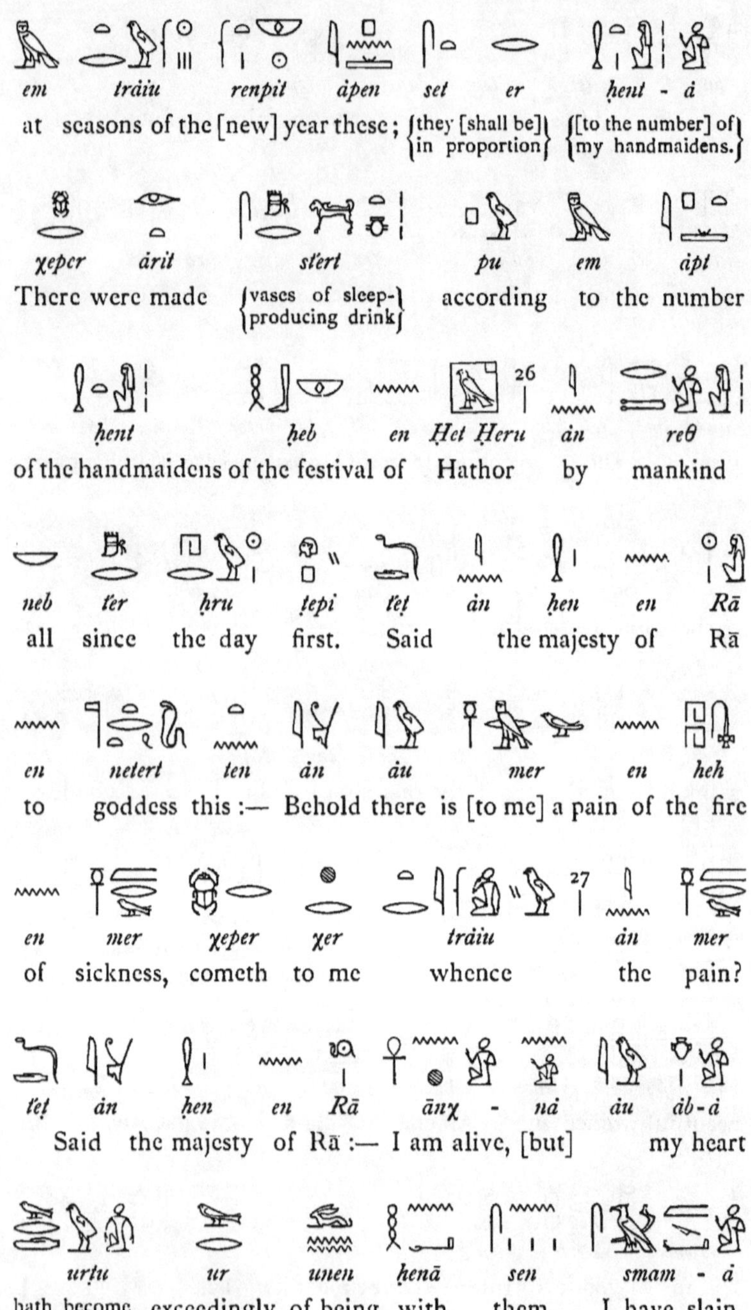

em trȧiu renpit ȧpen set er ḥent - ȧ

at seasons of the [new] year these; {they [shall be] in proportion} {[to the number] of my handmaidens.}

χeper ȧrit sḳert pu em ȧpt

There were made {vases of sleep-producing drink} according to the number

ḥent ḥeb en Ḥet Ḥeru 26 *ȧn reθ*

of the handmaidens of the festival of Hathor by mankind

neb ṭer ḥru ṭepi ṭeṭ ȧn ḥen en Rā

all since the day first. Said the majesty of Rā

en netert ten ȧn ȧu mer en heh

to goddess this:— Behold there is [to me] a pain of the fire

en mer χeper χer trȧiu 27 *ȧn mer*

of sickness, cometh to me whence the pain?

ṭeṭ ȧn ḥen en Rā ānχ - nȧ ȧu ȧb - ȧ

Said the majesty of Rā:— I am alive, [but] my heart

urṭu ur unen ḥenā sen smam - ȧ

hath become weary exceedingly of being with them. (*i. e.*, with men) I have slain

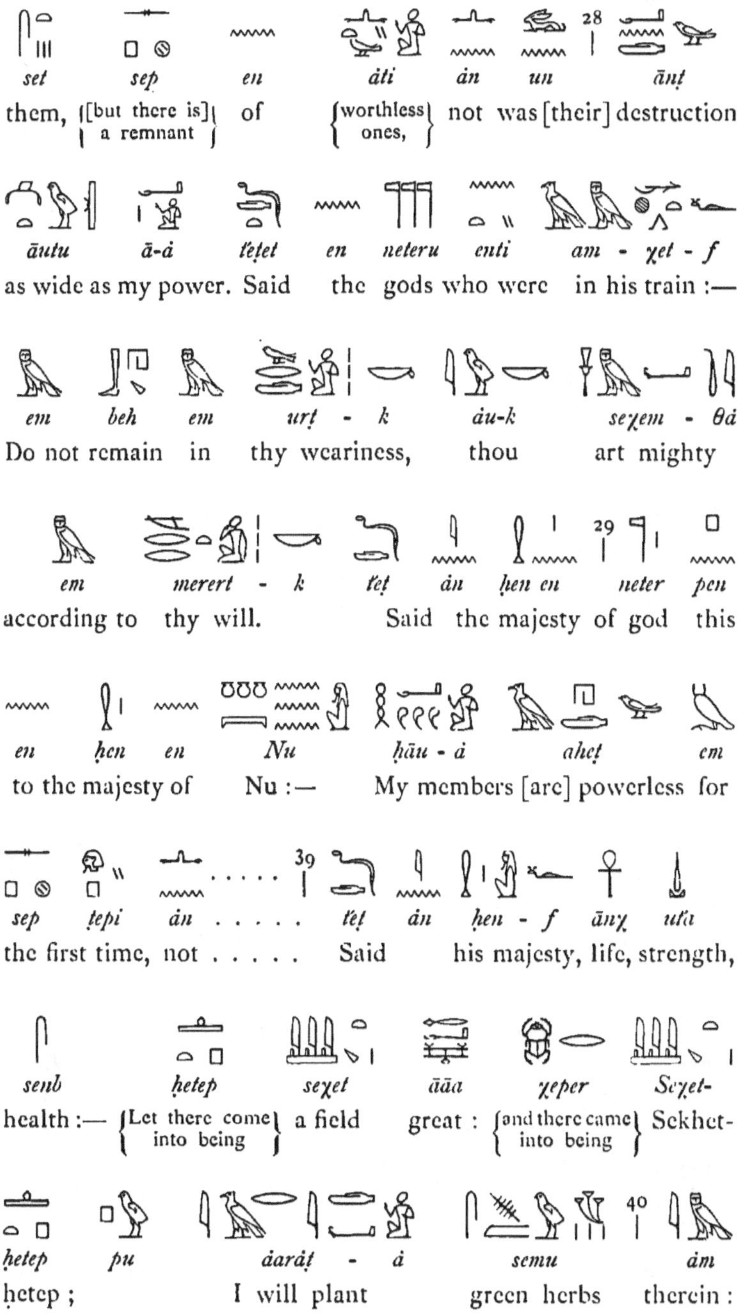

set sep en àti àn un 28 *ānṭ*
them, {[but there is] a remnant} of {worthless ones,} not was [their] destruction

āutu ā-à ṭeṭet en neteru enti am - χet - f
as wide as my power. Said the gods who were in his train :—

em beh em urṭ - k àu-k seχem - θà
Do not remain in thy weariness, thou art mighty

em merert - k ṭeṭ àn ḥen en 29 *neter pen*
according to thy will. Said the majesty of god this

en ḥen en Nu ḥāu - à aheṭ em
to the majesty of Nu :— My members [are] powerless for

sep ṭepi àn . . . . . 39 *ṭeṭ àn ḥen - f ānχ uṭa*
the first time, not . . . . . Said his majesty, life, strength,

senb ḥetep seχet āāa χeper Seχet-
health :— {Let there come into being} a field great : {and there came into being} Sekhet-

ḥetep pu àaràṭ - à semu 40 *àm*
ḥetep ; I will plant green herbs therein :

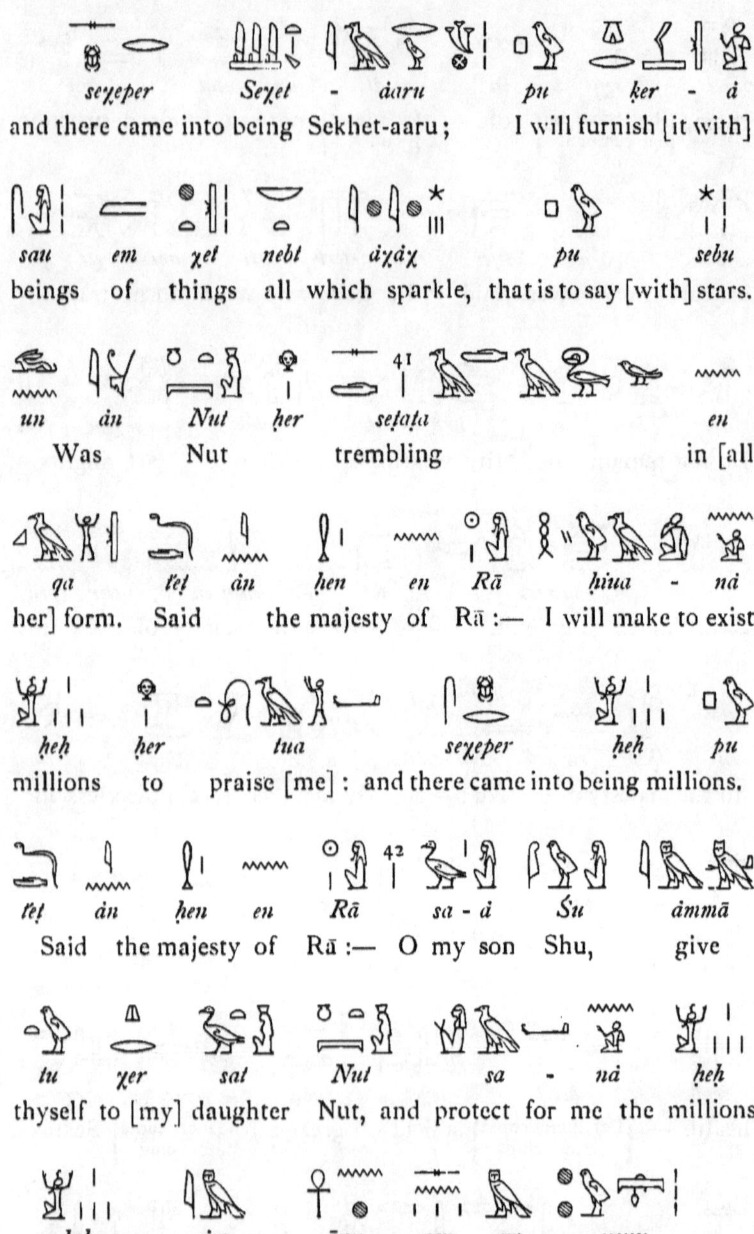

seχeper Seχet - åaru pu ḳer - å

and there came into being Sekhet-aaru; I will furnish [it with]

sau em χet nebt åχåχ pu sebu

beings of things all which sparkle, that is to say [with] stars.

un ån Nut ḥer seṭaṭa en

Was Nut trembling in [all

qa t'eṭ ån ḥen en Rā ḥiua - nå

her] form. Said the majesty of Rā :— I will make to exist

ḥeḥ ḥer tua seχeper ḥeḥ pu

millions to praise [me] : and there came into being millions.

t'eṭ ån ḥen en Rā sa - å Śu åmmā

Said the majesty of Rā :— O my son Shu, give

tu χer sat Nut sa - nå ḥeḥ

thyself to [my] daughter Nut, and protect for me the millions

ḥeḥ åm ānχ - sen em χeχu

of millions [who are] there, they live in darkness.

THE WAR OF RAMESES II AGAINST THE KHETA.

[XIXth dynasty.]

I. *neter nefer χerp peḥ peḥ āā neχtu*

The god beautiful, the Power, doubly mighty, great of strength,

ḥeṭ set nebt suten net (bȧt) Usr-maāt-Rā-setep-en-Rā

subduer of foreign lands all, {king of the North and South} {Usr-maāt-Rā-setep-en-Rā,}

sa Rā Rā-meses meri Ȧmen pa āḥā ȧri en

son of the Sun, Rameses, beloved of Ȧmen. The halt [which] made

ḥen - f ȧu-f ḥems ḥer meḥt ȧment Qeṭeš

his majesty. He was encamped at the north-west of Kadesh,

ȧu-f ḥer āq em χennu pa χeru āā en

he was going in among the enemy mighty of

na en χeru en Χeta ȧu-f uāu ḥer ṭep - f

those of the wretched ones of Kheta. He was alone by himself, *àn* *ki* *ḥenā-f* *qem-nef* *ànḥu* *su*

not another [was] with him, he found surrounding him

MM + *D* *en ā* *en* *ḥetrāu* *em* *fṭet* *χat*

two thousand five hundred horsemen in four companies

em *uat-f* *nebt* *àu-f* *ḥer* *āuāu* - *sen* *àr-u*

on his path every. Was he smiting them making them

em *àniu* *χer* *ḥāt* *sesemut* - *f* *àu-f* *ḥer*

into corpses before his horses. Was he

χaṭeb *uru* *neb* *en* *set* *neb* *na* *senu*

slaying the princes all of foreign lands all, the brethren

en *pa* *χer* *en* *χeta* *ḥenā* *naif* *seru*

of the wretched one of Kheta together with his nobles

āau *naif* *menfitu* *taif* *neθḥetr* *àu-f* *ḥer*

mighty, his soldiers, his cavalry. Was he

ḳebḳeb - *set* *χer* *ḥer* *ḥrà* - *sen* *àu-f* *ḥer*

casting down them throwing [them] upon their faces. Was he

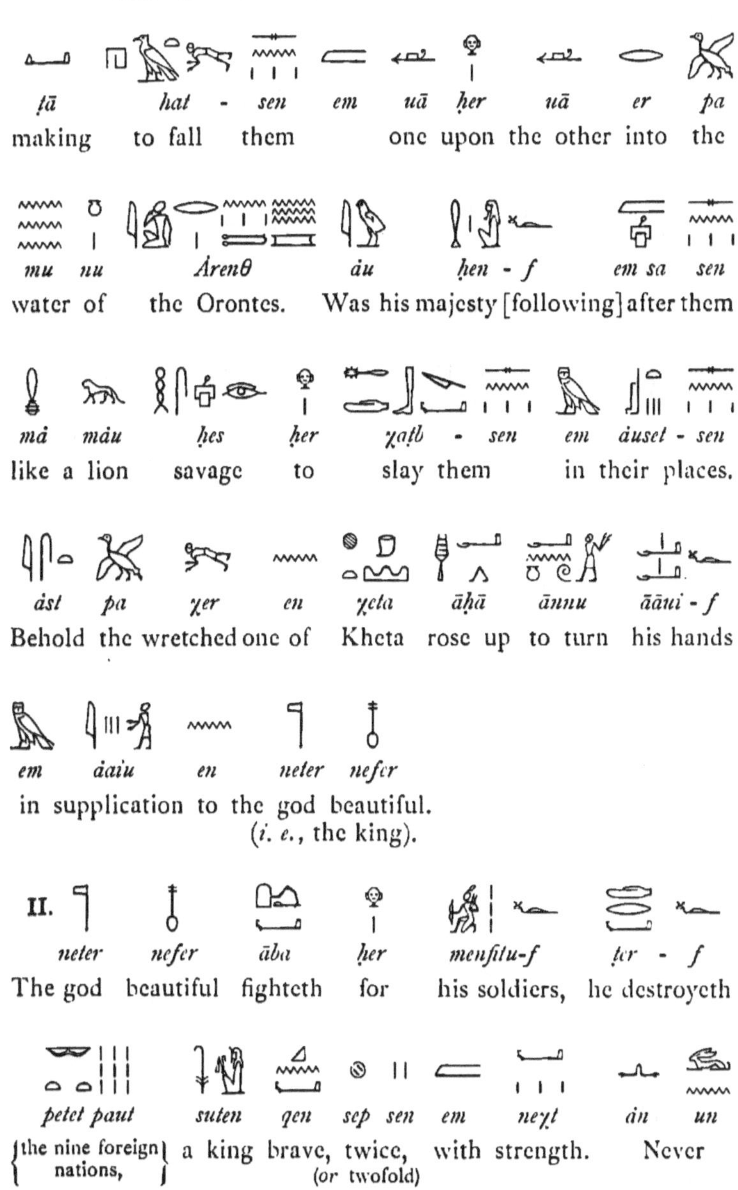

ṭā hat - sen em uā ḥer uā er pa
making to fall them one upon the other into the

mu nu Ȧrenθ ȧu ḥen - f em sa sen
water of the Orontes. Was his majesty [following] after them

mȧ mȧu ḥes ḥer χaṭb - sen em ȧuset - sen
like a lion savage to slay them in their places.

ȧst pa χer en χeta āḥā ānnu āāui - f
Behold the wretched one of Kheta rose up to turn his hands

em ȧaȧu en neter nefer
in supplication to the god beautiful.
(*i. e.*, the king).

II. *neter nefer āba ḥer menfitu-f ṭer - f*
The god beautiful fighteth for his soldiers, he destroyeth

petet paut suten qen sep sen em neχt ȧn un
{the nine foreign nations,} a king brave, twice, (or twofold) with strength. Never

ȧri - nef sen āq em āšt
hath been made [his] second. Going in among the multitudes

menfitu en set neb àrit - sen em

of the soldiers of foreign lands all [he] was making them into

tebtebet ḥebs àrit ḥer - f em metet

dead men. A reckoning was made for him of the *phalli*

ur en χeta ṭeṭ en Neherina

of the chiefs of Kheta [and] the hands of Mesopotamia.

HYMN TO RĀ BY HUNEFER.

[British Museum papyrus No. 9901.]

[XIXth dynasty.]

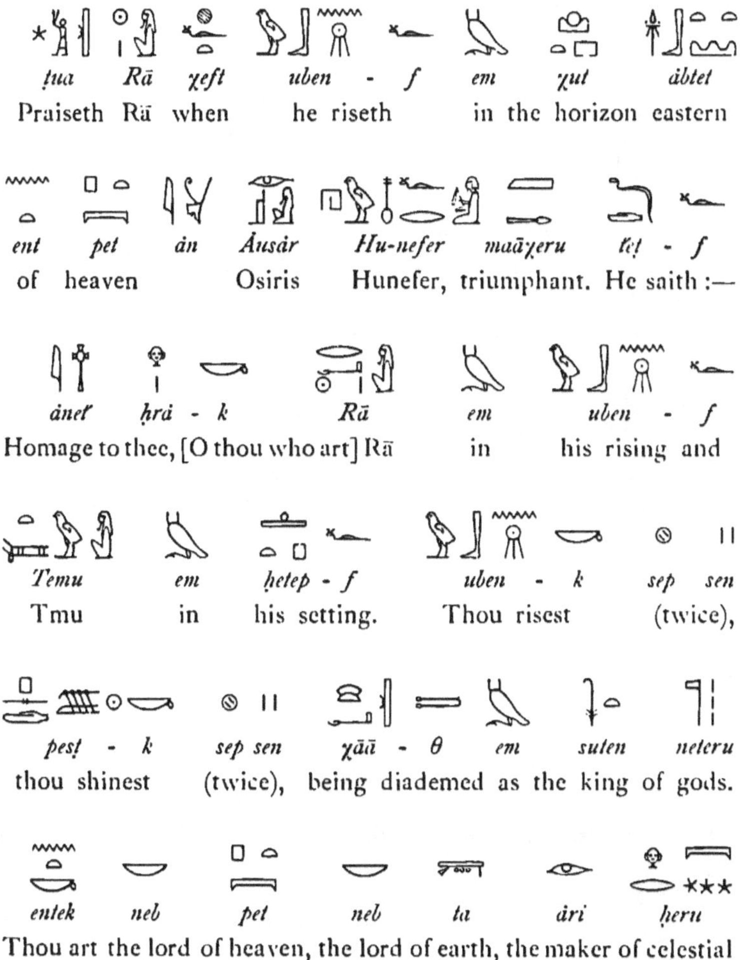
ṭua Rā χeft uben - f em χut ȧbtet
Praiseth Rā when he riseth in the horizon eastern
ent pet ȧn Ȧusȧr Ḥu-nefer maāχeru ṭeṭ - f
of heaven Osiris Hunefer, triumphant. He saith :—
ȧnet' ḥrȧ - k Rā em uben - f
Homage to thee, [O thou who art] Rā in his rising and
Temu em ḥetep - f uben - k sep sen
Tmu in his setting. Thou risest (twice),
pesṭ - k sep sen χāā - θ em suten neteru
thou shinest (twice), being diademed as the king of gods.
entek neb pet neb ta ȧri ḥeru
Thou art the lord of heaven, the lord of earth, the maker of celestial

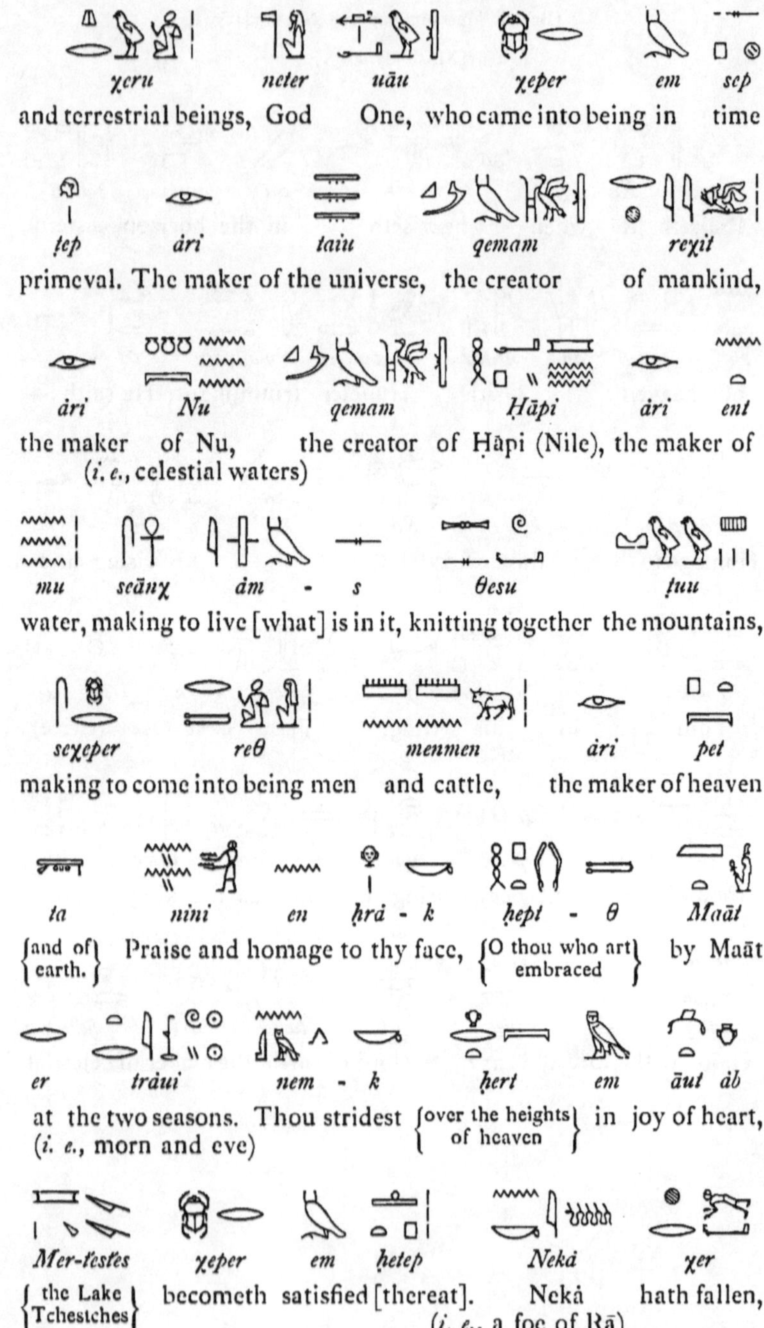

χeru *neter* *uāu* *χeper* *em* *sep*
and terrestrial beings, God One, who came into being in time

ṭep *ȧri* *taiu* *qemam* *reχit*
primeval. The maker of the universe, the creator of mankind,

ȧri *Nu* *qemam* *Ḥāpi* *ȧri* *ent*
the maker of Nu, (*i. e.*, celestial waters) the creator of Ḥāpi (Nile), the maker of

mu *seānχ* *ȧm* - *s* *θesu* *ṭuu*
water, making to live [what] is in it, knitting together the mountains,

seχeper *reθ* *menmen* *ȧri* *pet*
making to come into being men and cattle, the maker of heaven

ta *nini* *en* *ḥrȧ* - *k* *ḥept* - *θ* *Maāt*
{and of earth.} Praise and homage to thy face, {O thou who art embraced} by Maāt

er *trȧui* *nem* - *k* *ḥert* *em* *āut* *ȧb*
at the two seasons. (*i. e.*, morn and eve) Thou stridest {over the heights of heaven} in joy of heart,

Mer-ṭesṭes *χeper* *em* *ḥetep* *Nekȧ* *χer*
{the Lake Tchestches} becometh satisfied [thereat]. Nekȧ (*i. e.*, a foe of Rā) hath fallen,

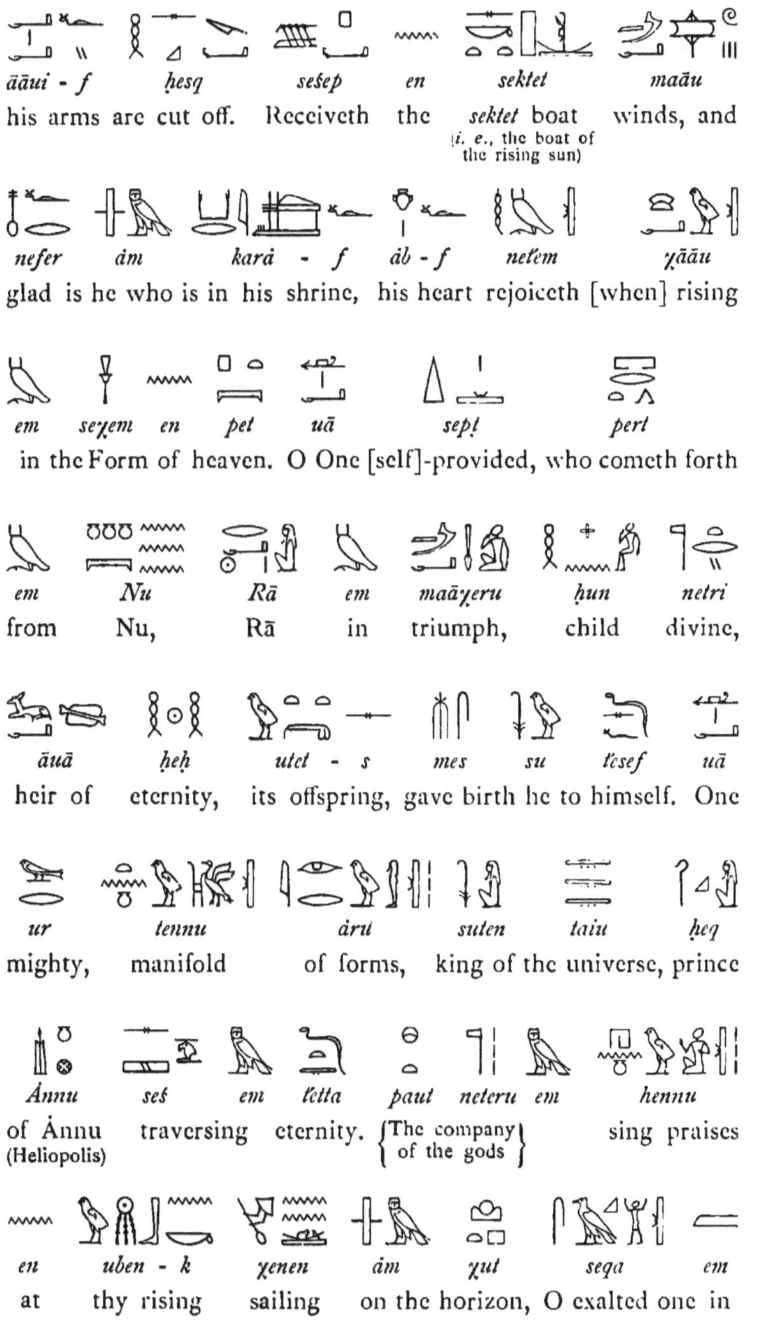

āāui - f ḥesq seśep en sektet maāu
his arms are cut off. Receiveth the *sektet* boat (*i. e.*, the boat of the rising sun) winds, and

nefer àm karà - f àb - f neṭem χāāu
glad is he who is in his shrine, his heart rejoiceth [when] rising

em seχem en pet uā sepṭ pert
in the Form of heaven. O One [self]-provided, who cometh forth

em Nu Rā em maāχeru ḥun netri
from Nu, Rā in triumph, child divine,

āuā ḥeḥ utet - s mes su ṭesef uā
heir of eternity, its offspring, gave birth he to himself. One

ur tennu àru suten taiu ḥeq
mighty, manifold of forms, king of the universe, prince

Ànnu seś em ṭetta paut neteru em hennu
of Ànnu (Heliopolis) traversing eternity. {The company of the gods} sing praises

en uben - k χenen àm χut seqa em
at thy rising sailing on the horizon, O exalted one in

sektet *ȧnet' ḥrȧ-k* *Ȧmen-Rā* *ḥetep* *ḥer* *maāt*

{the *sektet* boat.} Homage to thee Ȧmen-Rā, resting upon *maāt*, (*i. e.*, thou art governed by unchanging laws).

ṭa - k *ḥert* *ȧu* *ḥrȧ* *neb* *maa - nek*

Thou passest over the upper regions, doth face every see thee;

ruṭ - k *seqeṭeṭ* *ḥen - k* *satu - k*

thou germinatest, strideth on thy majesty, thy rays are

em *ḥrȧu*

upon [all] faces.

FROM THE PAPYRUS OF RAMESES III.

[XXth dynasty.]

nerāu	*I*	*ḥet'*	*em*	*qeḥqeḥ*	*annu*	*II*
Goat,	one.	Silver	in	beaten	tablets,	two.

nenibu	*III*	*χemti*	*em*	*qeḥqeḥ*	*ānnu*	*IV*
Trees,	three.	Bronze	in	beaten	tablets,	four.

qemā nefer	*ṭu*	*V*	*θeḥennu*	*hennu*	*X*	*χet*
Linen fine	garments,	five.	Crystal,	measures	ten.	Wood

en	*ānti*	*XV*	*ānti*	*hannu*	*XX*
of	*ānti* unguent,	fifteen.	*Ānti* unguent,	measures	twenty.

ḥet'et	*mesθȧ*	*L*	*reθ*	*100*	*māfek*
Plants,	measures	fifty.	Men,	one hundred.	Turquoise,

χeperȧ	*200 + 20 + 4*	*θeḥen*	*χetem*	*1000 + 500 + 50*
scarabs,	224.	Crystal,	rings,	1550.

tau nefer ȧuf šāi 9000 + 800 + 40 + 5

Nefer bread, flesh, cakes, 9845.

tau nefer tau berber 40,000 + 6000 + 500

Nefer bread, loaves of pyramid form, 46,500.

tau nefer tau ḥeṭ en uṭennu

Nefer bread, loaves white for offerings

100,000 × 5 + 70,000 + 2000 ḥetep tau nefer āqu

572,000. Total, *nefer* bread, cakes

šeben 100,000 × 28 + 40,000 + 4000 + 300 + 50 + 7

various 2,844,357.

THE LEGEND OF RĀ AND ISIS.

[XXth dynasty.]

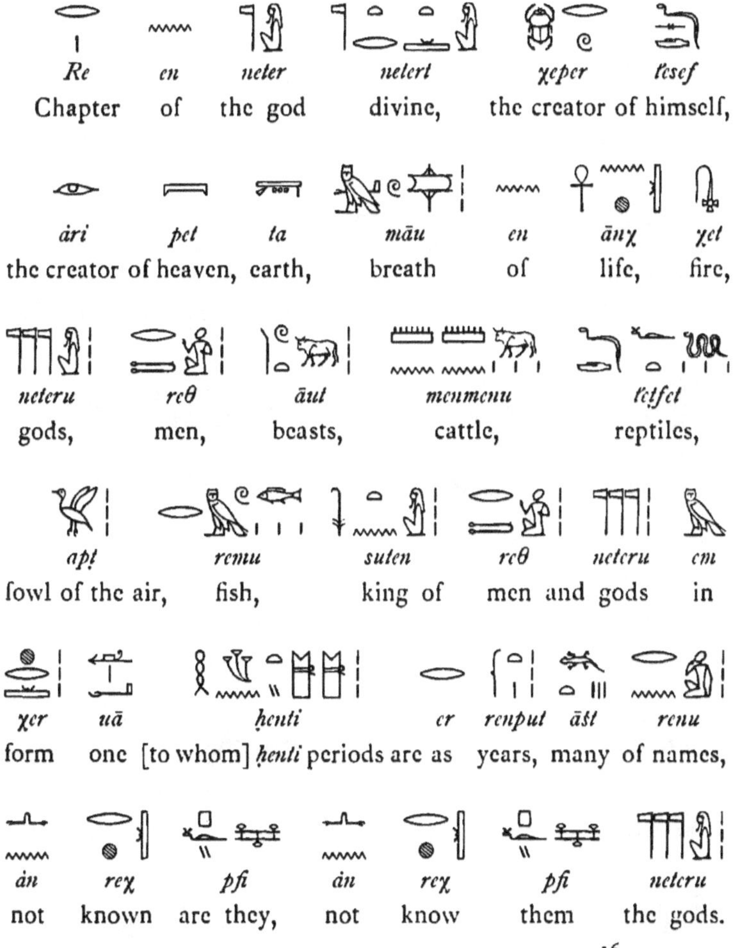

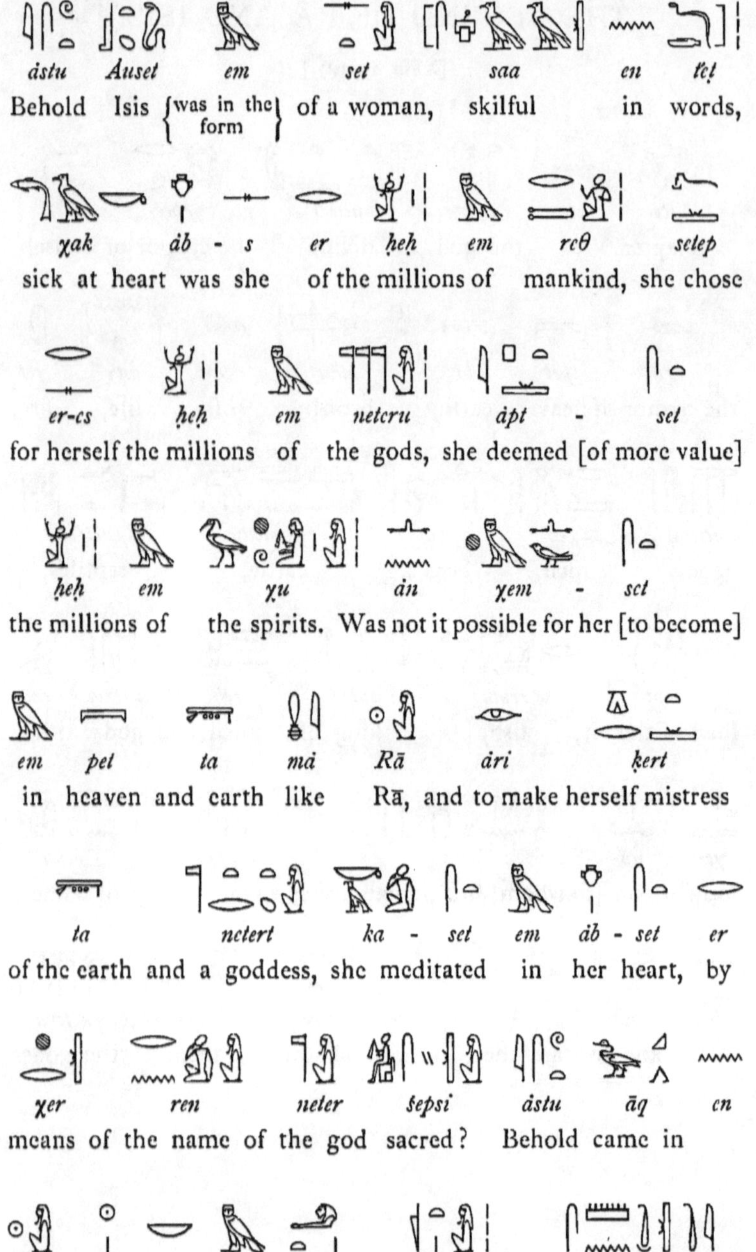

àstu Àuset em set saa en ṭeṭ
Behold Isis {was in the form} of a woman, skilful in words,

χak àb - s er ḥeḥ em reθ setep
sick at heart was she of the millions of mankind, she chose

er-es ḥeḥ em neteru àpt - set
for herself the millions of the gods, she deemed [of more value]

ḥeḥ em χu àn χem - set
the millions of the spirits. Was not it possible for her [to become]

em pet ta mà Rā àri ḳert
in heaven and earth like Rā, and to make herself mistress

ta netert ka - set em àb - set er
of the earth and a goddess, she meditated in her heart, by

χer ren neter šepsi àstu āq en
means of the name of the god sacred? Behold came in

Rā hru neb em ḥāt qet smen - θà
Rā day every at the head of [his] sailors, and was stablished

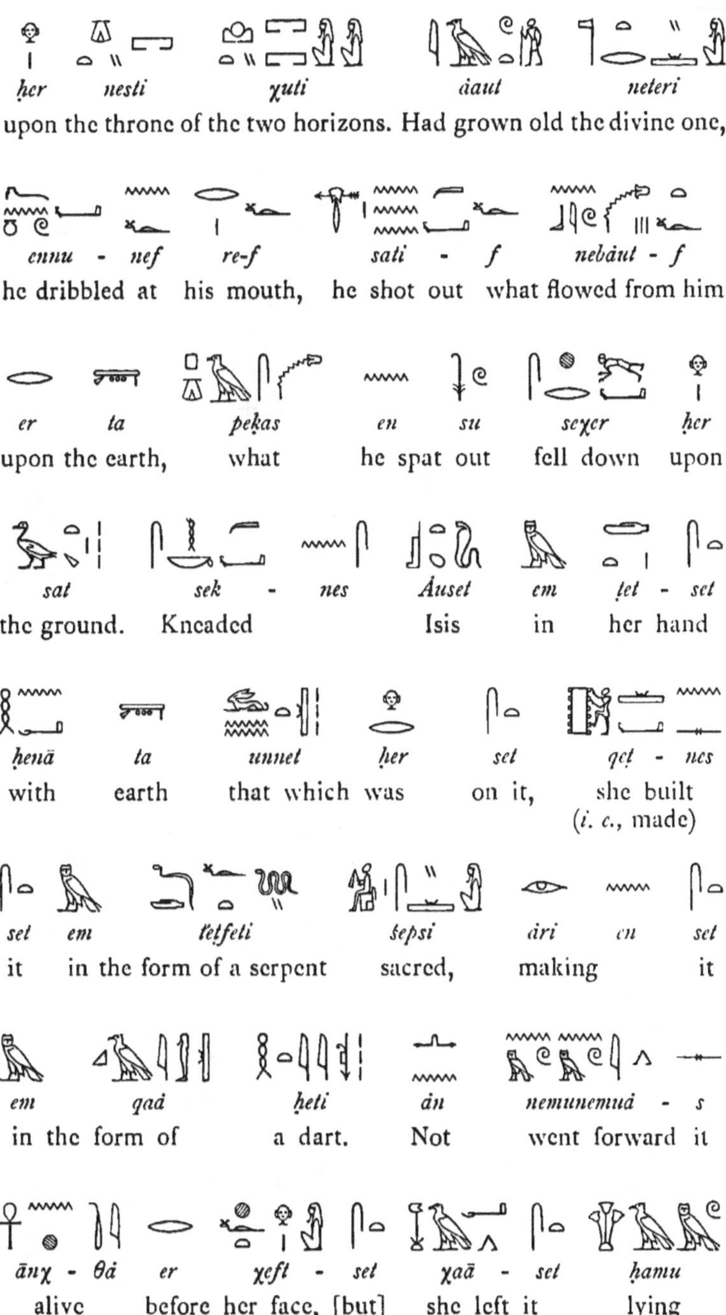

ḥer nesti χuti ȧaut neteri
upon the throne of the two horizons. Had grown old the divine one,

ennu - nef re-f sati - f nebȧut - f
he dribbled at his mouth, he shot out what flowed from him

er ta peḳas en su seχer ḥer
upon the earth, what he spat out fell down upon

sat sek - nes Ȧuset em ṭet - set
the ground. Kneaded Isis in her hand

ḥenā ta unnet ḥer set qeṭ - nes
with earth that which was on it, she built (*i. e.*, made)

set em ṭetfeti ṡepsi ȧri en set
it in the form of a serpent sacred, making it

em qaȧ ḥeti ȧn nemunemuȧ - s
in the form of a dart. Not went forward it

ānχ - θȧ er χeft - set χaā - set ḥamu
alive before her face, [but] she left it lying

ḥer ual āpep neter āa ḥer set er àba - f
on the path went the god great along it according to his wish

emχet taui-f neter šepsi χāā - f er
in his two lands. The god sacred rose [and came]

ḥa neteru em Āa-perti ānχ uťa
forth, the gods of the great double house, life, strength,

senb emχet - f sefetsefet - f mà hru neb
health, following him; he strode on as [he did] day every.

unχu - set em ťetfet šepsi χet
Shot out its fang the serpent sacred, and the fire

ānχet per - θà àm - f ťesef ťer - nes
of life was going out from his own body, it destroyed

àmi na āšu neter neteri - f
the dweller among the cedars, the god divine he opened

re - f χeru en ḥen - f ānχ uťa senb
his mouth, the cry of his Majesty, life, strength, health,

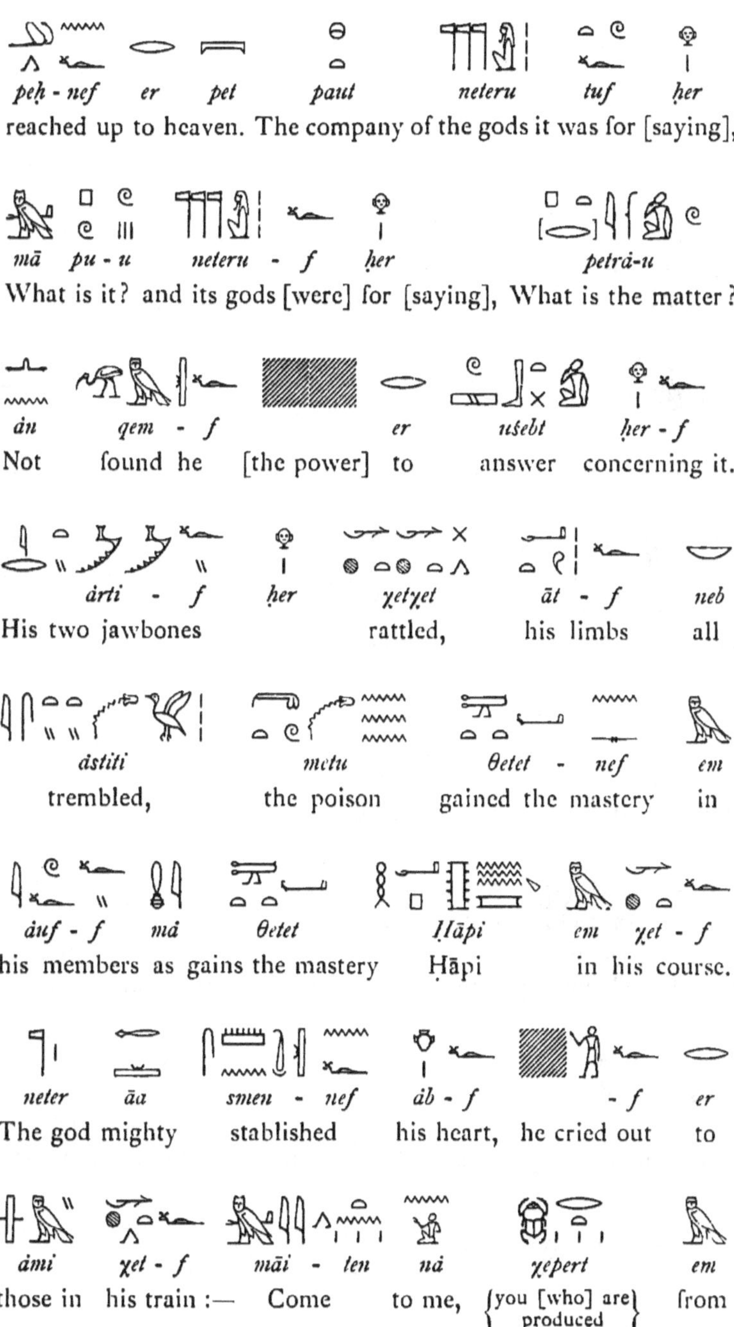

peḥ - nef er pet paut neteru tuf ḥer
reached up to heaven. The company of the gods it was for [saying],

mā pu - u neteru - f ḥer petrȧ-u
What is it? and its gods [were] for [saying], What is the matter?

ȧn qem - f er usebt ḥer - f
Not found he [the power] to answer concerning it.

ȧrti - f ḥer χetχet āt - f neb
His two jawbones rattled, his limbs all

ȧstiti metu θetet - nef em
trembled, the poison gained the mastery in

ȧuf - f mȧ θetet Ḥāpi em χet - f
his members as gains the mastery Ḥāpi in his course.

neter āa smen - nef ȧb - f - f er
The god mighty stablished his heart, he cried out to

ȧmi χet - f māi - ten nȧ χepert em
those in his train :— Come to me, {you [who] are produced} from

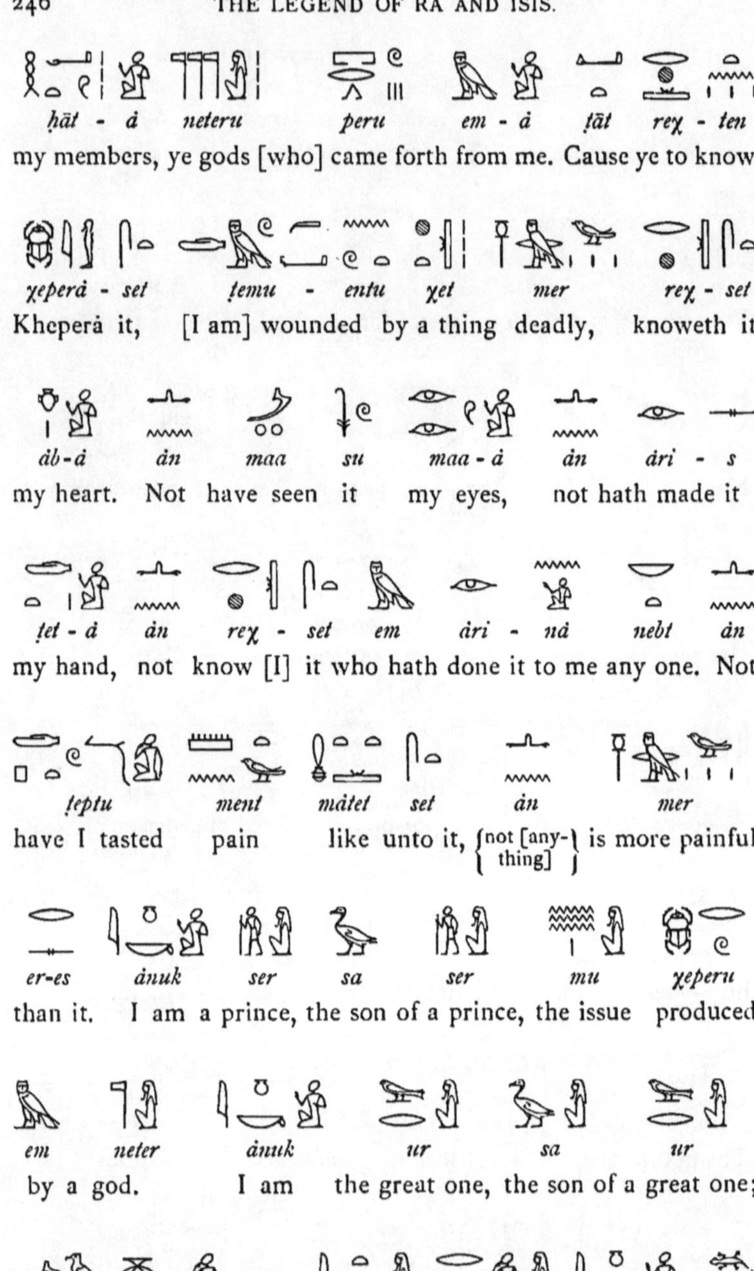

ḥāt - ȧ neteru peru em - ȧ ṭāt reχ - ten

my members, ye gods [who] came forth from me. Cause ye to know

χeperȧ - set ṭemu - entu χet mer reχ - set

Kheperȧ it, [I am] wounded by a thing deadly, knoweth it

ȧb - ȧ ȧn maa su maa - ȧ ȧn ȧri - s

my heart. Not have seen it my eyes, not hath made it

ṭet - ȧ ȧn reχ - set em ȧri - nȧ nebt ȧn

my hand, not know [I] it who hath done it to me any one. Not

ṭeptu ment mȧtet set ȧn mer

have I tasted pain like unto it, {not [any-thing]} is more painful

er-es ȧnuk ser sa ser mu χeperu

than it. I am a prince, the son of a prince, the issue produced

em neter ȧnuk ur sa ur

by a god. I am the great one, the son of a great one;

maut en ȧtf - ȧ ren - ȧ ȧnuk āšt

hath thought out my father my name. I am of many

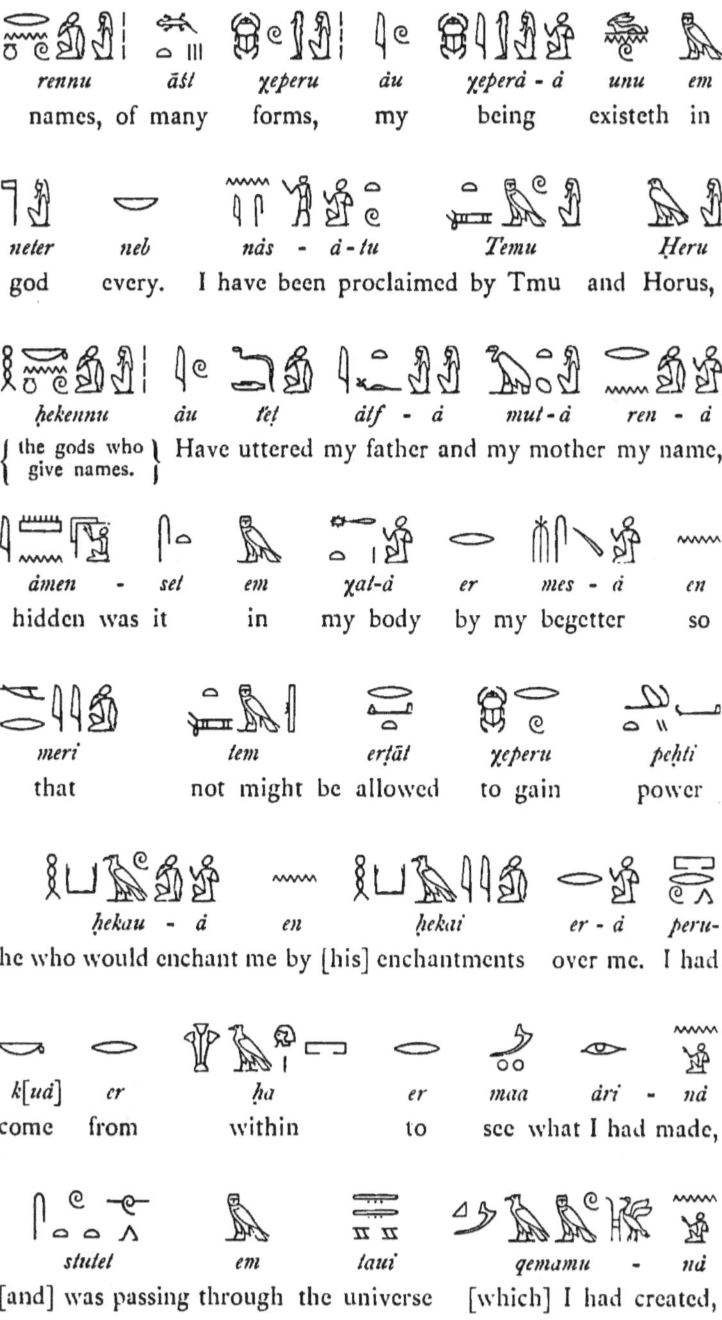

rennu āšt χeperu ȧu χeperȧ - ȧ unu em
names, of many forms, my being existeth in

neter neb nȧs - ȧ - tu Temu Ḥeru
god every. I have been proclaimed by Tmu and Horus,

ḥekennu ȧu ṭeṭ ȧtf - ȧ mut - ȧ ren - ȧ
{the gods who give names.} Have uttered my father and my mother my name,

ȧmen - set em χat-ȧ er mes - ȧ en
hidden was it in my body by my begetter so

meri tem erṭāt χeperu peḥti
that not might be allowed to gain power

ḥekau - ȧ en ḥekai er - ȧ peru-
he who would enchant me by [his] enchantments over me. I had

k[uȧ] er ḥa er maa ȧri - nȧ
come from within to see what I had made,

stutet em taui qemamu - nȧ
[and] was passing through the universe [which] I had created,

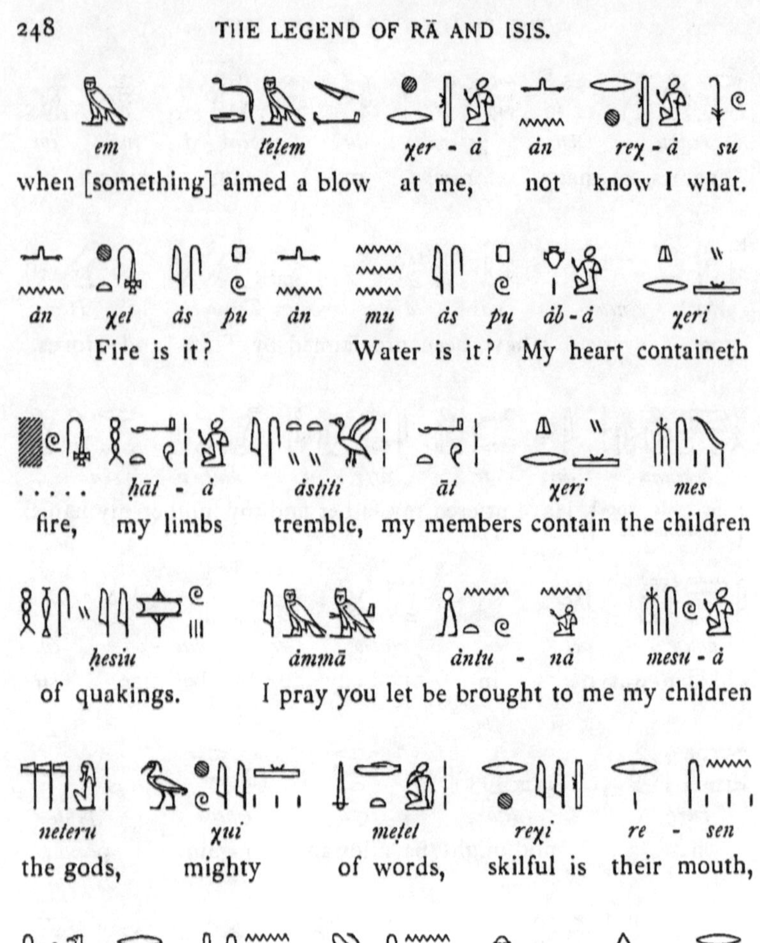

em *ṭeṭem* *χer - à* *àn* *reχ - à* *su*

when [something] aimed a blow at me, not know I what.

àn *χet* *às* *pu* *àn* *mu* *às* *pu* *àb - à* *χeri*

Fire is it? Water is it? My heart containeth

. . . . . *ḥāt - à* *àstiti* *āt* *χeri* *mes*

fire, my limbs tremble, my members contain the children

ḥesiu *àmmā* *àntu - nà* *mesu - à*

of quakings. I pray you let be brought to me my children

neteru *χui* *meṭet* *reχi* *re - sen*

the gods, mighty of words, skilful is their mouth,

sarṭ - sen *peḥ - sen* *ḥer* *iu* *er-ef*

their powers they reach to heaven. Came to him

mesu *neter* *neb* *àm* *χeri* *àkebu - nef*

[his] children, god every there with his cries of weeping.

iu *en* *Àuset* *χeri* *χut - set* *àuset* *re-*

Came Isis with her powerful words, the place of

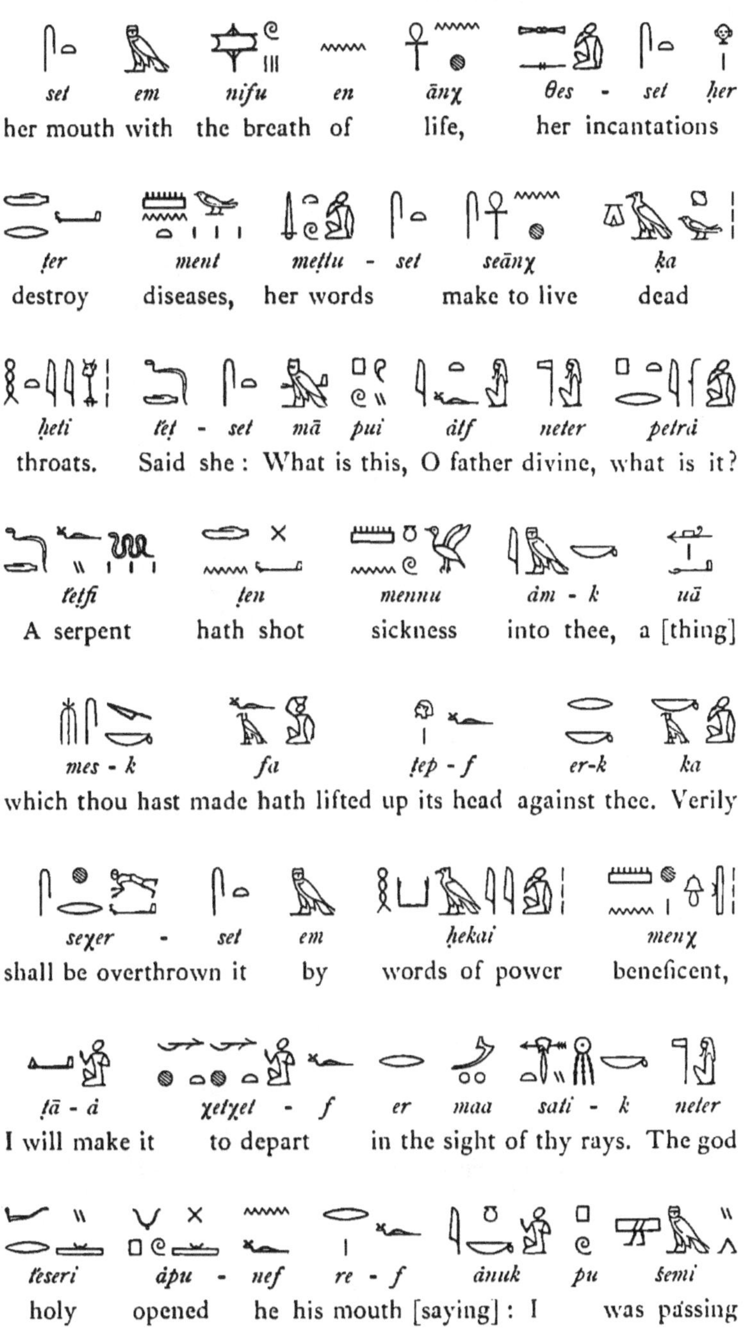

set em nifu en ānχ θes - set ḥer
her mouth with the breath of life, her incantations

ṭer ment meṭtu - set seānχ ḳa
destroy diseases, her words make to live dead

ḥeti ṭeṭ - set mā pui àtf neter petrà
throats. Said she: What is this, O father divine, what is it?

ṭetfi ṭen mennu àm - k uā
A serpent hath shot sickness into thee, a [thing]

mes - k fa ṭep - f er-k ka
which thou hast made hath lifted up its head against thee. Verily

seχer - set em ḥekai menχ
shall be overthrown it by words of power beneficent,

ṭā - à χetχet - f er maa sati - k neter
I will make it to depart in the sight of thy rays. The god

ṭeseri àpu - nef re - f ànuk pu šemi
holy opened he his mouth [saying]: I was passing

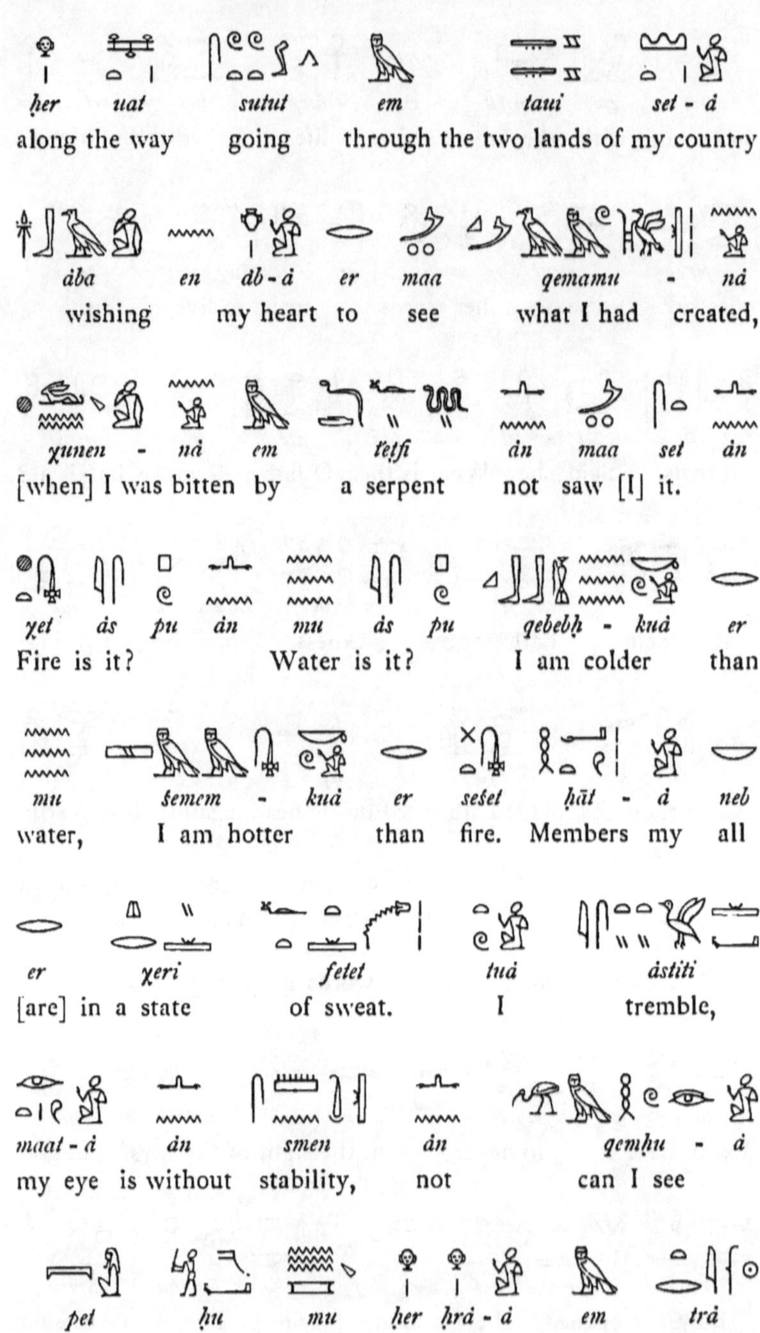

ḥer uat sutut em taui set - à
along the way going through the two lands of my country

àba en àb - à er maa qemamu - nà
wishing my heart to see what I had created,

χunen - nà em ṫeṭfi àn maa set àn
[when] I was bitten by a serpent not saw [I] it.

χet às pu àn mu às pu qebebḥ - kuà er
Fire is it? Water is it? I am colder than

mu šemem - kuà er sešet ḥāt - à neb
water, I am hotter than fire. Members my all

er χeri fetet tuà àstiti
[are] in a state of sweat. I tremble,

maat - à àn smen àn qemḥu - à
my eye is without stability, not can I see

pet ḥu mu ḥer ḥrà - à em trà
the heavens. Riseth water on my face [as] in the time

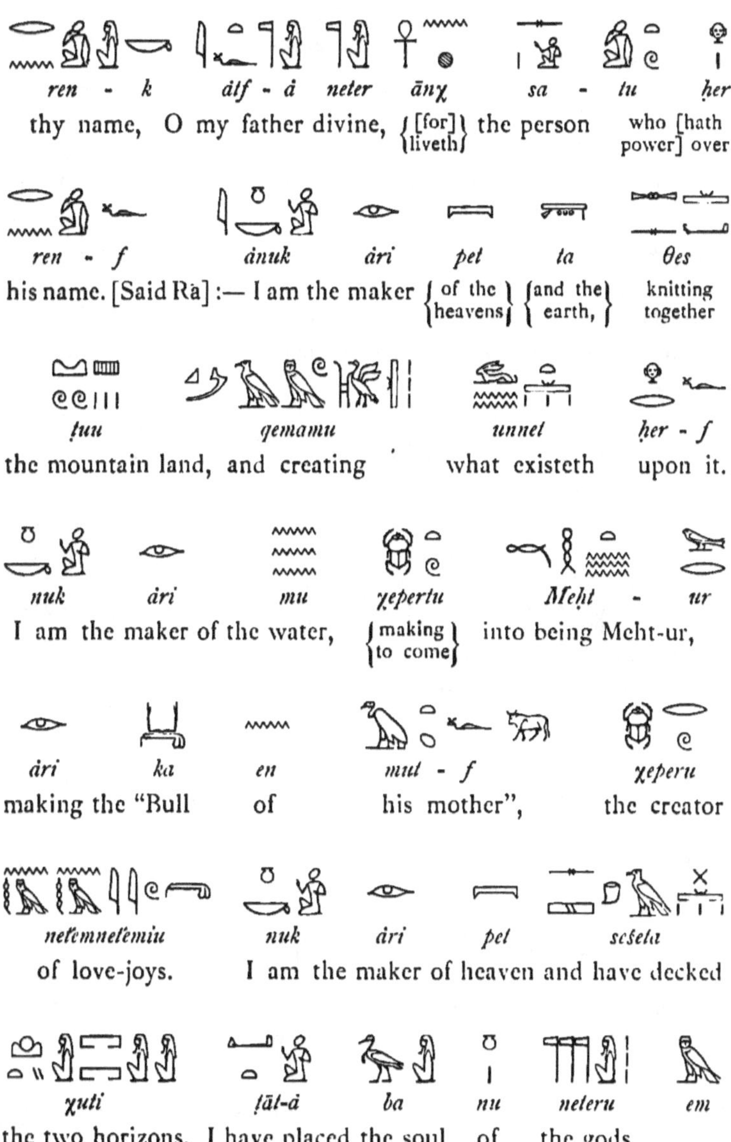

ren - k *àtf - à* *neter* *ānχ* *sa - tu* *ḥer*
thy name, O my father divine, {[for] liveth} the person who [hath power] over

ren - f *ànuk* *àri* *pet* *ta* *θes*
his name. [Said Rā] :— I am the maker {of the heavens} {and the earth,} knitting together

ṭuu *qemamu* *unnet* *ḥer - f*
the mountain land, and creating what existeth upon it.

nuk *àri* *mu* *χepertu* *Meḥt - ur*
I am the maker of the water, {making to come} into being Meht-ur,

àri *ka* *en* *mut - f* *χeperu*
making the "Bull of his mother", the creator

neṭemneṭemiu *nuk* *àri* *pet* *seśeta*
of love-joys. I am the maker of heaven and have decked

χuti *ṭāt-à* *ba* *nu* *neteru* *em*
the two horizons, I have placed the soul of the gods

χennu - set ȧnuk un maaui-f χeperu
within it. I am [he who when he] opens his eyes becometh

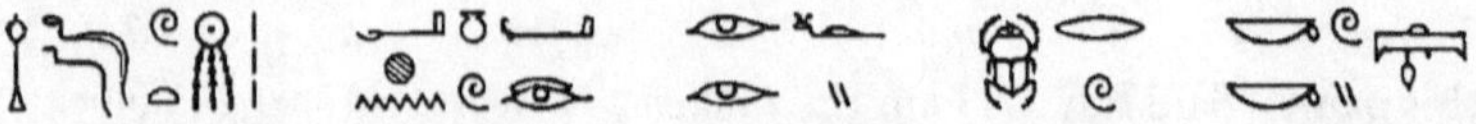

ḥeṭeṭu āχennu maaui-f χeperu kekui
light, [when he] shutteth his two eyes becometh darkness.

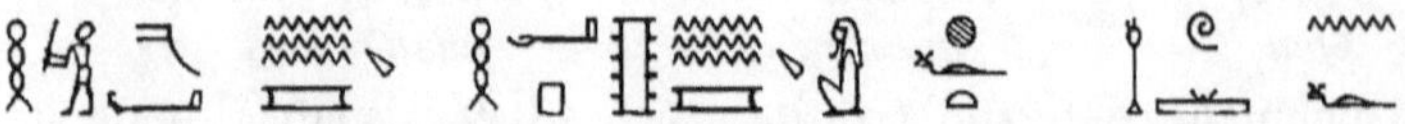

ḥu mu Ḥāpi χeft utu - nef
Rise the waters of the Nile when he giveth the order,

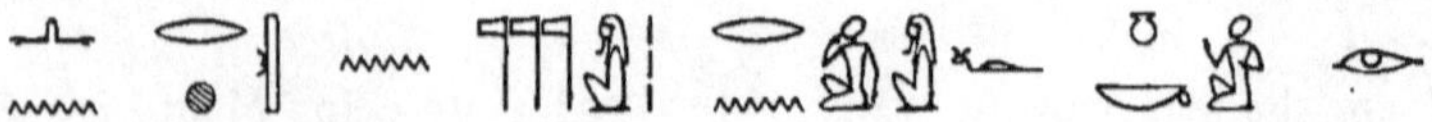

ȧn reχ en neteru ren - f nuk ȧri
not know the gods his name. I am the maker

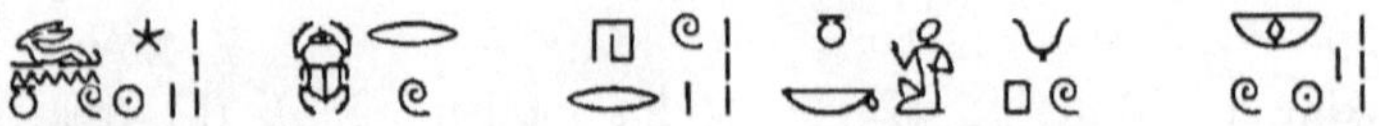

unnu χeperu hru nuk ȧpu ḥebu
of the hours, the creator of the days. I am the opener of the festivals

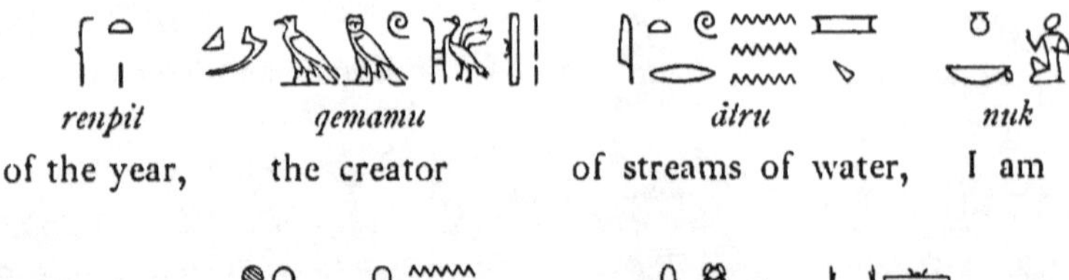

renpit qemamu ȧtru nuk
of the year, the creator of streams of water, I am

ȧri χet ānχet er seχeperu kat en
the maker of the fire living making to be done the works of

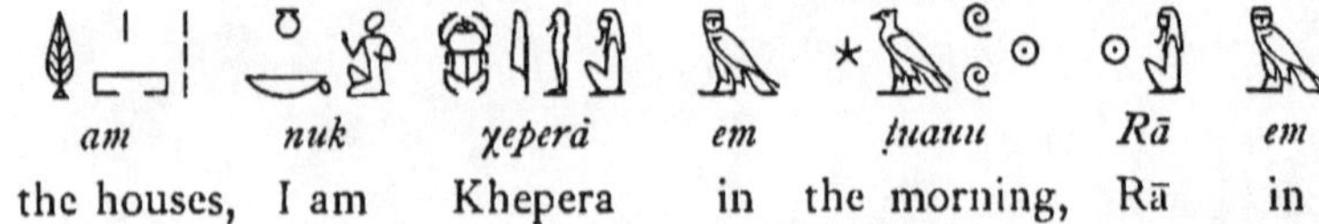

am nuk χeperȧ em ṭuauu Rā em
the houses, I am Khepera in the morning, Rā in

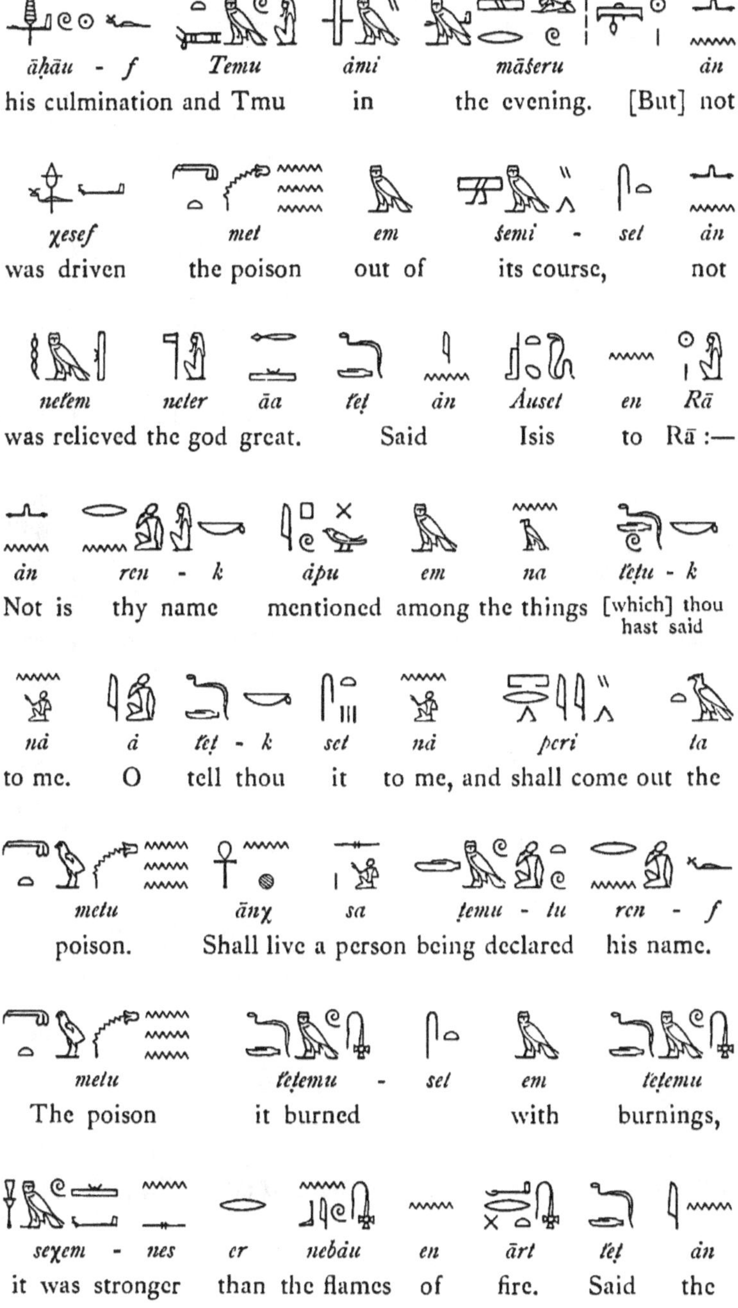

āḥāu - f Temu ȧmi māšeru ȧn
his culmination and Tmu in the evening. [But] not

χesef met em šemi - set ȧn
was driven the poison out of its course, not

net'em neter āa t'et ȧn Ȧuset en Rā
was relieved the god great. Said Isis to Rā :—

ȧn ren - k ȧpu em na t'eṭu - k
Not is thy name mentioned among the things [which] thou hast said

nȧ ȧ t'eṭ - k set nȧ peri ta
to me. O tell thou it to me, and shall come out the

metu ānχ sa ṭemu - tu ren - f
poison. Shall live a person being declared his name.

metu t'eṭemu - set em t'eṭemu
The poison it burned with burnings,

seχem - nes er nebȧu en ārt t'eṭ ȧn
it was stronger than the flames of fire. Said the

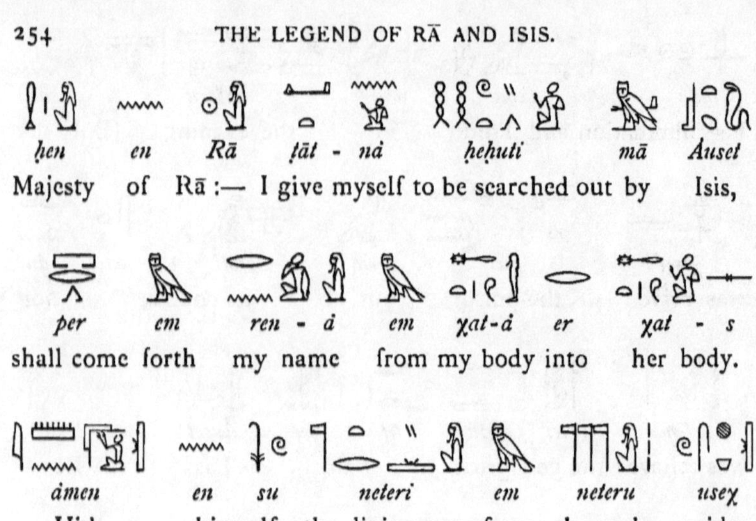

ḥen en Rā ṭāt - nȧ ḥeḥuti mā Ȧuset

Majesty of Rā :— I give myself to be searched out by Isis,

per em ren - ȧ em χat - ȧ er χat - s

shall come forth my name from my body into her body.

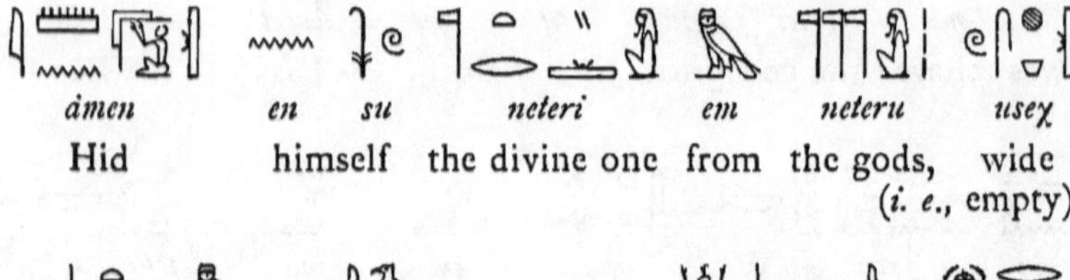

ȧmen en su neteri em neteru useχ

Hid himself the divine one from the gods, wide (*i. e.*, empty)

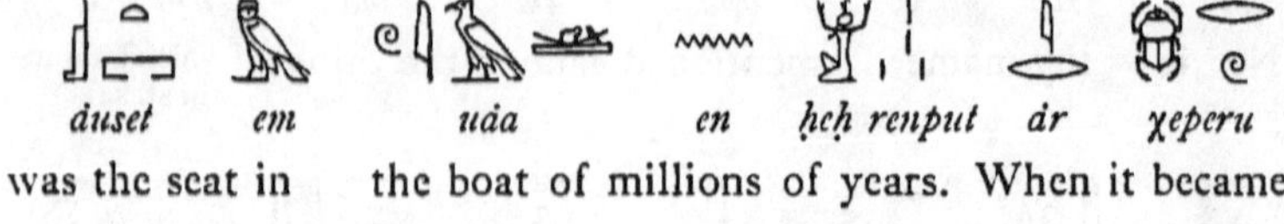

ȧuset em uȧa en ḥeḥ renput ȧr χeperu

was the seat in the boat of millions of years. When it became

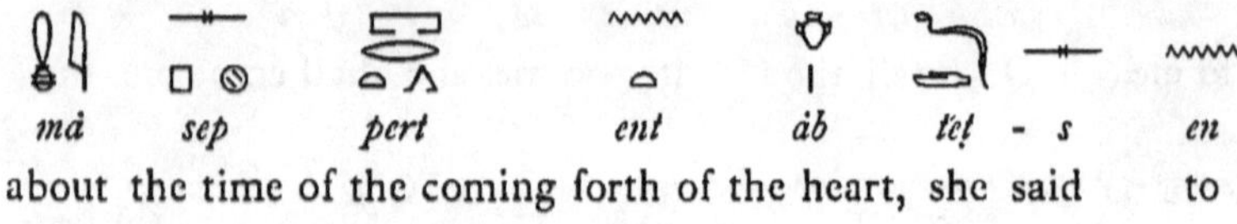

mȧ sep pert ent ȧb ṭeṭ - s en

about the time of the coming forth of the heart, she said to

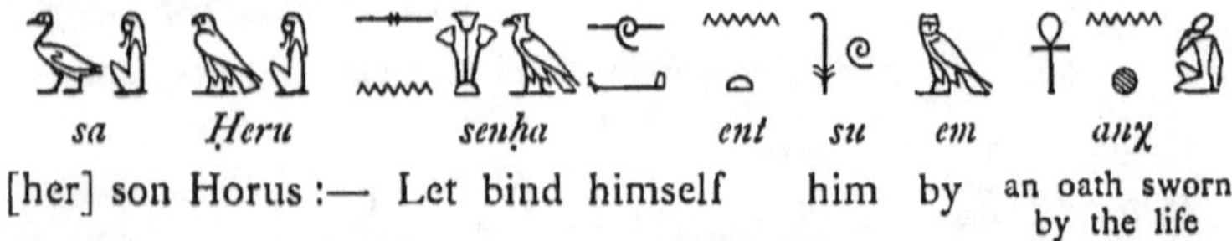

sa Ḥeru senḥa ent su em ānχ

[her] son Horus :— Let bind himself him by an oath sworn by the life

neter erṭāt neter maaui - f neter āat

of the god, that may give the god his two eyes. The god great

uθes - nef ḥer ren - f Ȧuset ur

was taken from him his name, [and] Isis the great lady

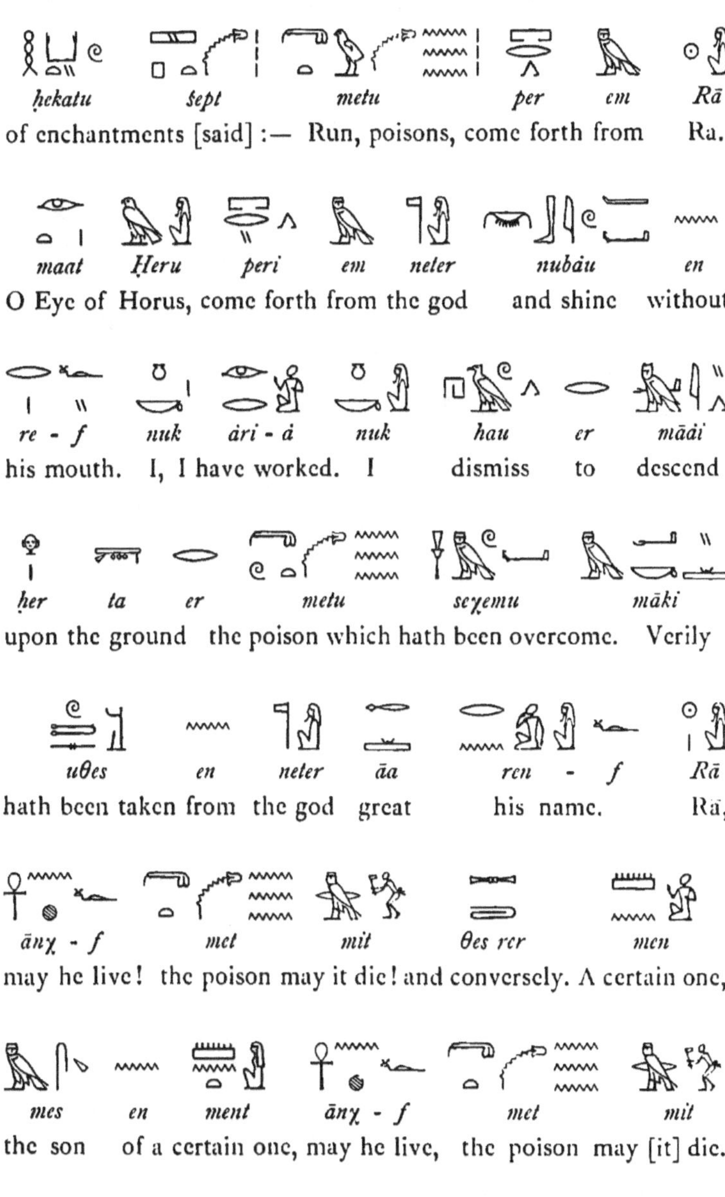

ḥekatu šept metu per em Rā

of enchantments [said]:— Run, poisons, come forth from Ra.

maat Ḥeru peri em neter nubȧu en

O Eye of Horus, come forth from the god and shine without

re - f nuk ȧri - ȧ nuk hau er māȧi

his mouth. I, I have worked. I dismiss to descend

ḥer ta er metu seχemu mākí

upon the ground the poison which hath been overcome. Verily

uθes en neter āa ren - f Rā

hath been taken from the god great his name. Rā,

ānχ - f met mit θes rer men

may he live! the poison may it die! and conversely. A certain one,

mes en ment ānχ - f met mit

the son of a certain one, may he live, the poison may [it] die.

ṭeṭ en Auset ur ḥent neteru

[This] said Isis, the mighty lady, the mistress of the gods,

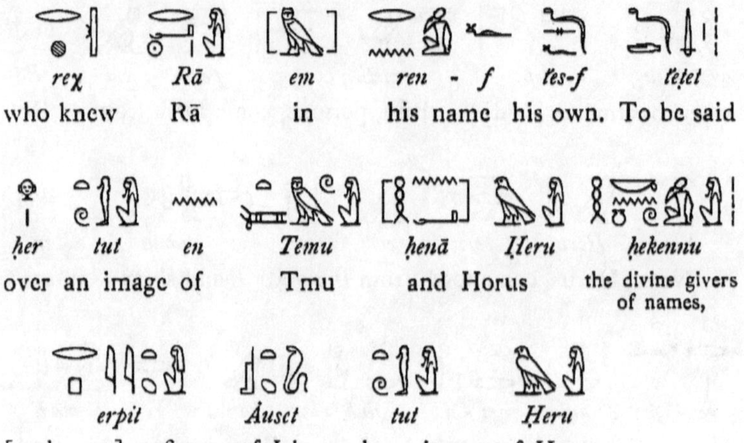

reχ Rā em ren - f t̆es-f t̆eṭet

who knew Rā in his name his own. To be said

ḥer tut en Temu ḥenā Ḥeru ḥekennu

over an image of Tmu and Horus the divine givers of names,

erpit Àuset tut Ḥeru

[and over] a figure of Isis, and an image of Horus.

FROM THE MONUMENT OF UAḤ-ÀB-RĀ EM KHU.

[XXVIth dynasty.]

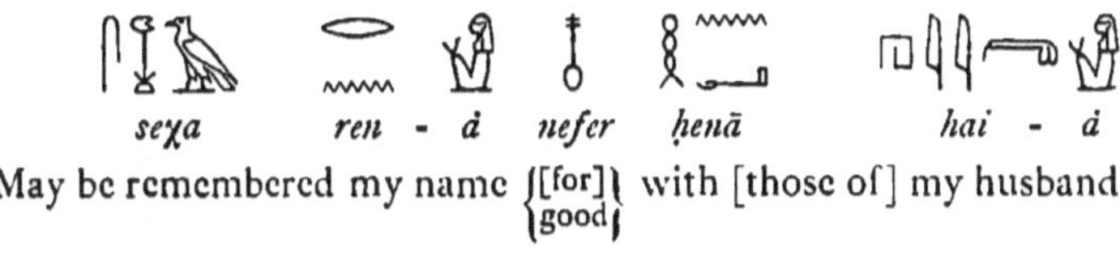

seχa *ren - à* *nefer* *ḥenā* *hai - à*

May be remembered my name {[for] good} with [those of] my husband

mesu - à *er-ḳes* *neteru* *àmu* *χa*

and my children by the gods dwelling in the nome of Mendes.

TEXTS FROM THE SARCOPHAGUS OF PAṬEPEP.

[XXVIth dynasty.]

1. *peseš - s* *māt - k* *Nut* *ḥer - k* *em* *ren - s*

Spreadeth she thy mother Nut over thee in her name

en *šeta*

of "Hidden".

2. 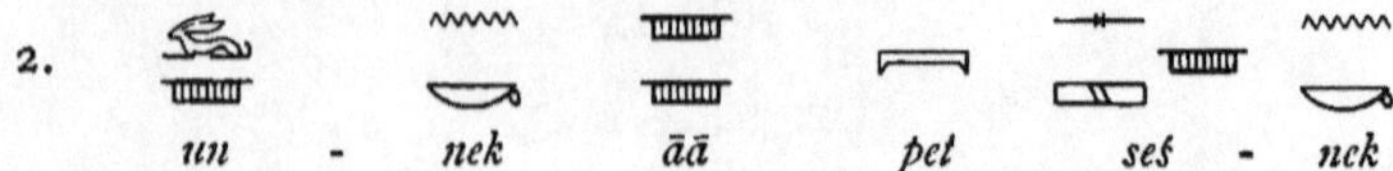

un - nek āā pet seś - nek

Shall be opened to thee the doors of heaven, shall be unbolted for thee

āā seḥef sesep - θ mut-k nut

the doors of the stars of light, shall receive thee thy mother Nut.

3. *meṭ àn Ṭep - ṭu - f χent neter ḥet àm*

Saith he who is on his hill, the chief {of the divine house,} who is

Ut neb Ta-teser neter āa neb qeres

in Ut, the lord {of Ta-tcheser,} the god great, the lord of the sarcophagus,

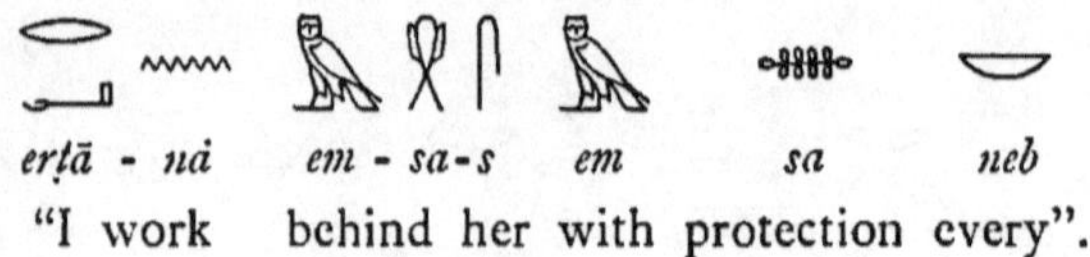

erṭā - nà em - sa - s em sa neb

"I work behind her with protection every".

4. 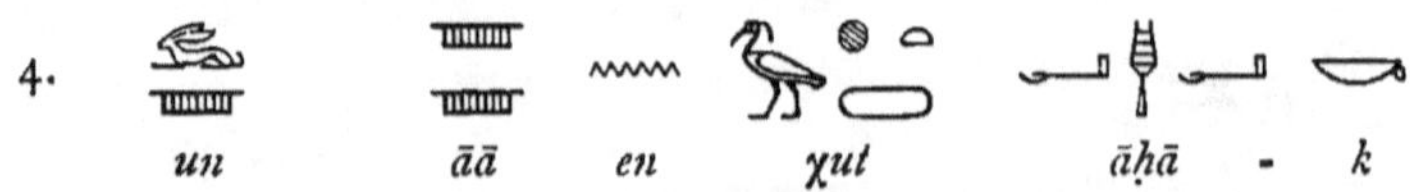

un āā en χut āḥā - k

Shall be opened the doors of the horizon, thou shalt stand up

àref ta pen per em Tem

then on earth this coming forth as Tem.

5. 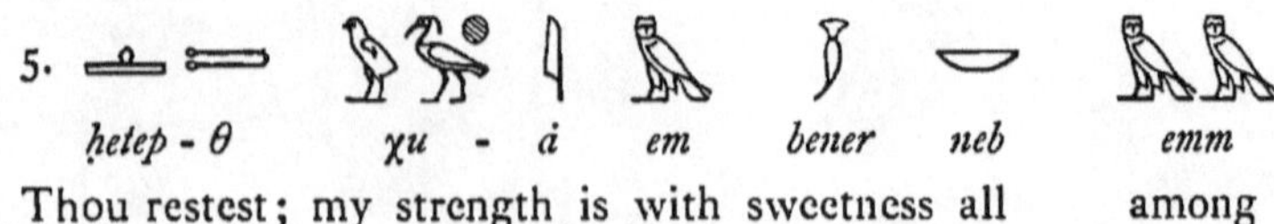

ḥetep - θ χu - à em bener neb emm

Thou restest; my strength is with sweetness all among

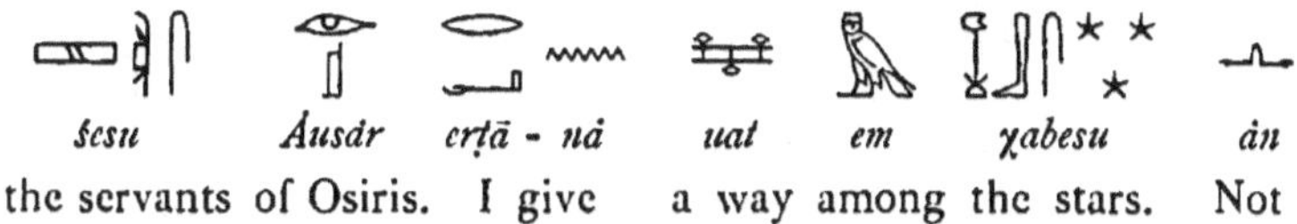

šesu *Ȧusȧr* *erṭā - nȧ* *uat* *em* *χabesu* *ȧn*

the servants of Osiris. I give a way among the stars. Not

mit - k *ṭetta*

shalt thou die for ever.

6. *ha* *Ȧusȧr* *erṭāt* *en* *Ḥeru* *ṭemṭ - θu*

Hail Osiris! Granteth Horus [that] thou shalt be gathered together.

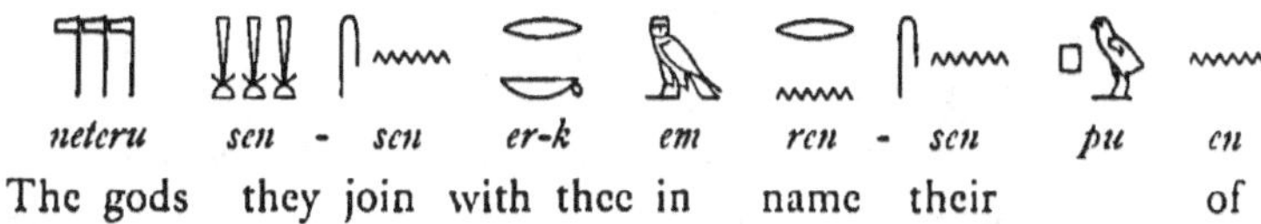

neteru *sen - sen* *er-k* *em* *ren - sen* *pu* *en*

The gods they join with thee in name their of

sen *ent* *ȧteruit*

"Brethren of the shrines of the North and South".

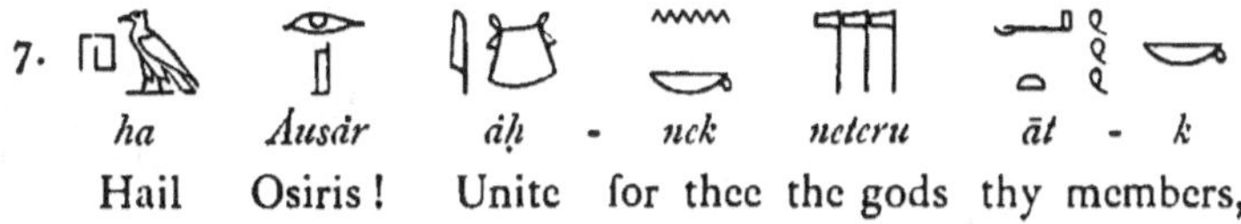

7. *ha* *Ȧusȧr* *ȧḥ - nek* *neteru* *āt - k*

Hail Osiris! Unite for thee the gods thy members,

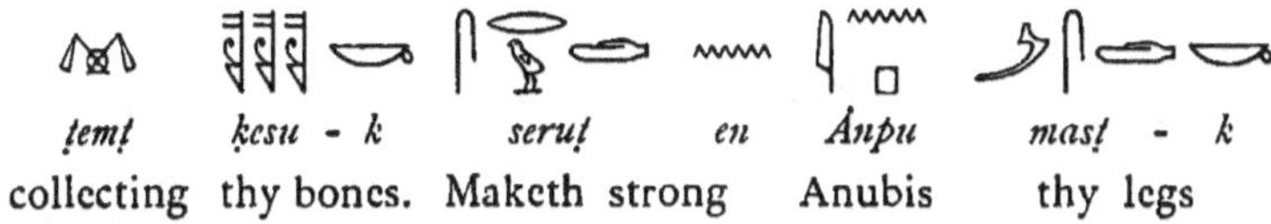

ṭemṭ *ḳesu - k* *seruṭ* *en* *Ȧnpu* *masṭ - k*

collecting thy bones. Maketh strong Anubis thy legs

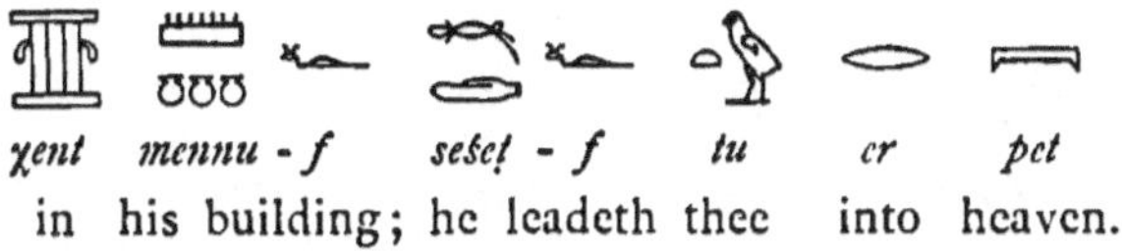

χent *mennu - f* *sešeṭ - f* *tu* *er* *pet*

in his building; he leadeth thee into heaven.

8. 

ha Ȧusȧr ȧn - nek Ḥeru ȧbu neteru nebu em

Hail Osiris! {Bringeth to thee} Horus {the hearts} of gods all at

sep ȧn bȧu ȧm - sen mā - f nem ānχ

once, not is there evil in them {in respect of him,} {[O thou who] again} livest!

9. *renp - k mȧ qet - k Ȧusetet uben - s em*

Thou becomest young as thou wast. Isis she shineth in

pet en ȧb - k θes-s ṭet - k χu - s

heaven at thy wish, she raiseth up thy body, she strengtheneth

ḥāu - k ṭetta

thy members for eternity.

10. *erṭā - nȧ uben - k em χu ȧḥā - k*

I have granted that shalt shine thou, in splendour shall be thy limbs;

ȧm - k āš seḥetep - nek ka - k

not shalt thou lament; thou art at peace with thy Ka,

seḥetep - f - θu ṭetta

it shall be at peace with thee for ever.

THE LEGEND OF THE SEVEN YEARS' FAMINE IN THE REIGN OF TCHESER.

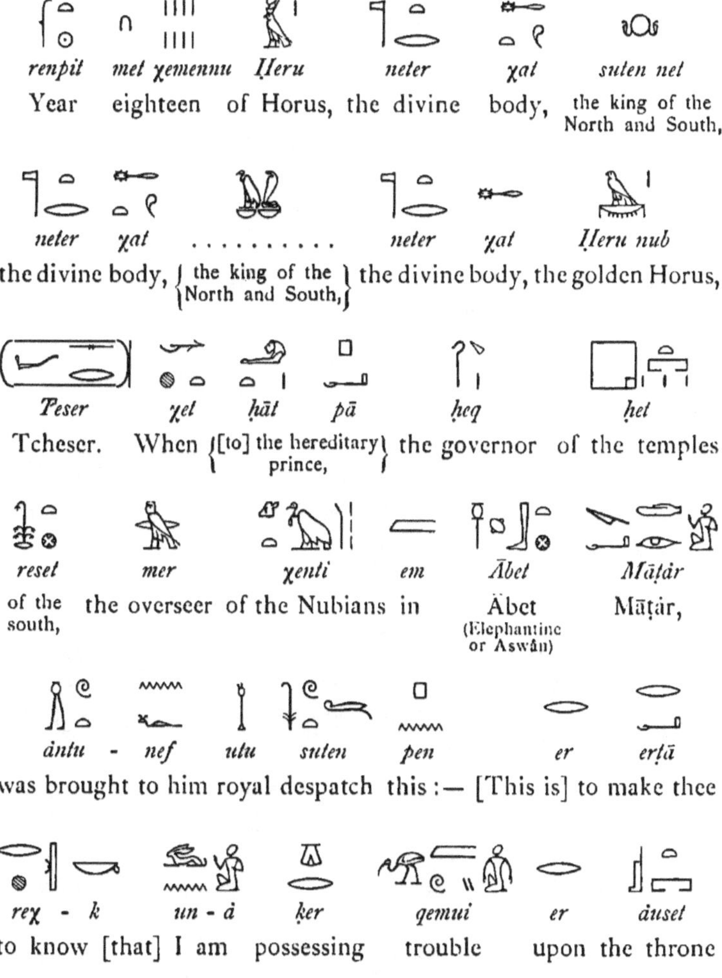
renpit met χemennu Ḥeru neter χat suten net
Year eighteen of Horus, the divine body, the king of the North and South,
neter χat . . . . neter χat Ḥeru nub
the divine body, the king of the North and South, the divine body, the golden Horus,
Ṭeser χet ḥāt pā ḥeq ḥet
Tcheser. When [to] the hereditary prince, the governor of the temples
reset mer χenti em Ābet Māṭār
of the south, the overseer of the Nubians in Ābet (Elephantine or Aswân) Māṭār,
ȧntu - nef utu suten pen er ertā
was brought to him royal despatch this :— [This is] to make thee
reχ - k un - ȧ ḳer qemui er ȧuset
to know [that] I am possessing trouble upon the throne

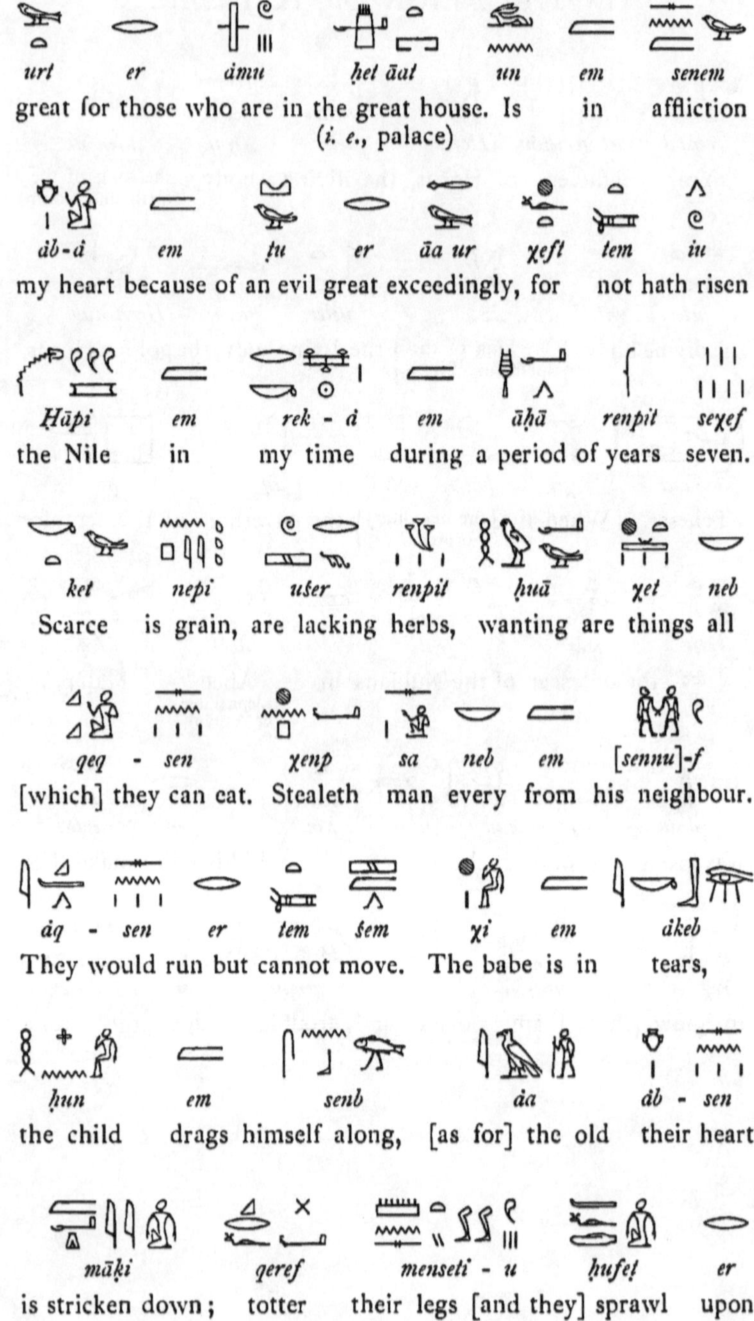

urt er ȧmu ḥet āat un em senem

great for those who are in the great house (*i. e.*, palace). Is in affliction

ȧb-ȧ em ṭu er āa ur χeft tem iu

my heart because of an evil great exceedingly, for not hath risen

Ḥāpi em rek - ȧ em āḥā renpit seχef

the Nile in my time during a period of years seven.

ket nepi user renpit ḥuā χet neb

Scarce is grain, are lacking herbs, wanting are things all

qeq - sen χenp sa neb em [sennu]-f

[which] they can eat. Stealeth man every from his neighbour.

ȧq - sen er tem śem χi em ȧkeb

They would run but cannot move. The babe is in tears,

ḥun em senb ȧa ȧb - sen

the child drags himself along, [as for] the old their heart

māḳi qeref menseti - u ḥufeṭ er

is stricken down; totter their legs [and they] sprawl upon

ta āāui-u er χen-u sennu em
the earth, their hands [lie] upon their bosoms. The nobles are

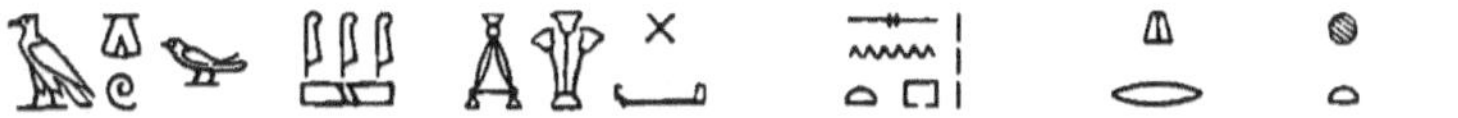

aḳu sešu ṭebḥa sent χer χet
empty of counsel, is broken open the treasury, instead of money

per nefui unui neb em qem maāu
cometh forth wind. Beings all are in distress. Hath meditated

àb-à ān er ḥāt neť un àm-à
my heart going back to the aforetime upon the deliverer who was in my place

tràt neteru heb χer heb ḥer ṭep I-em-ḥetep
in the time of the gods, {the ibis-god,} the *kher-ḥeb* in chief, (*i. e.*, the chief reader) I-em-ḥetep (*i. e.*, Imouthis)

sa Ptaḥ Res-àneb-f seb àuset mes
the son of Ptaḥ of his South Wall (*i. e.*, of Memphis). Where is the place of the birth

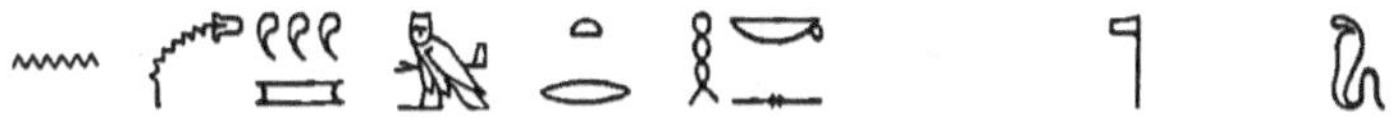

en Ḥāpi mā trà ḥek-s neter netert
of the Nile? Who then is its guardian? [What] god [or] goddess

àm-s pe-trà-tu seχem-f un-f smen àp-
is in it? What then is his form? Is it he who hath announced

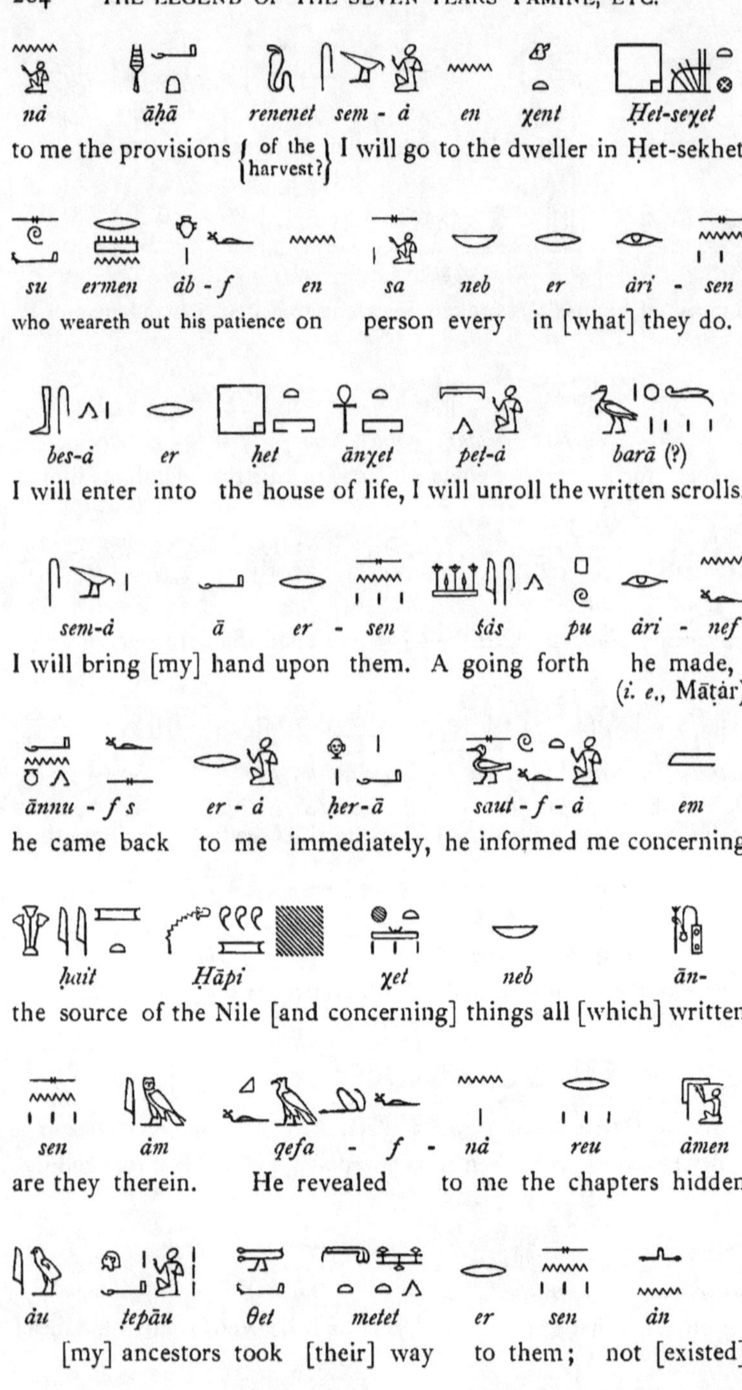

nȧ āḥā renenet sem - ȧ en χent Ḥet-seχet

to me the provisions {of the harvest?} I will go to the dweller in Ḥet-sekhet

su ermen ȧb - f en sa neb er ȧri - sen

who weareth out his patience on person every in [what] they do.

bes-ȧ er ḥet ānχet peṭ-ȧ barā (?)

I will enter into the house of life, I will unroll the written scrolls,

sem-ȧ ā er - sen šās pu ȧri - nef

I will bring [my] hand upon them. A going forth he made, (*i. e.*, Māṭȧr)

ānnu - f s er - ȧ ḥer - ā saut - f - ȧ em

he came back to me immediately, he informed me concerning

ḥait Ḥāpi χet neb ān-

the source of the Nile [and concerning] things all [which] written

sen ȧm qefa - f - nȧ reu ȧmen

are they therein. He revealed to me the chapters hidden

ȧu ṭepāu θet metet er sen ȧn

[my] ancestors took [their] way to them; not [existed]

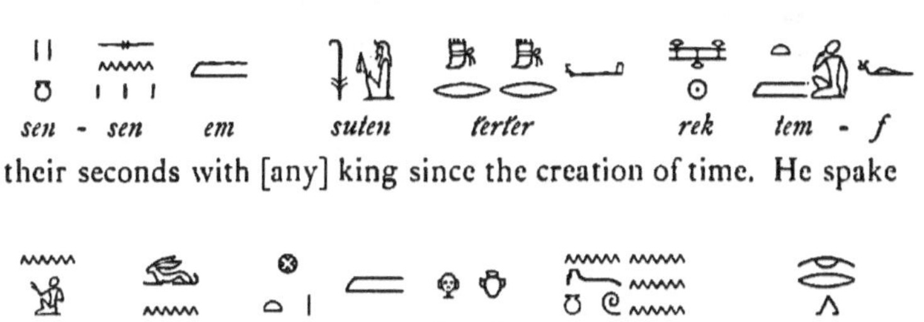

sen - sen em suten ṭerṭer rek tem - f

their seconds with [any] king since the creation of time. He spake

nà un nut em ḥer-àb ennu sper

to me :— There is a town in the midst of the stream, cometh forth

Ḥāp [àm-s] Ābet pu ren - f ḥā ḥāt pu

Ḥāpi from it ; Ābet is its name, {at the beginning} {the first town} was it.

II. (sic)

seneṭemṭem àb - à ṭer setem - à enen āq

Was doubly glad my heart when I heard this. [I] went in,

seš meru unχ àri

revealed [to me] the superintendents what was sealed. Was made

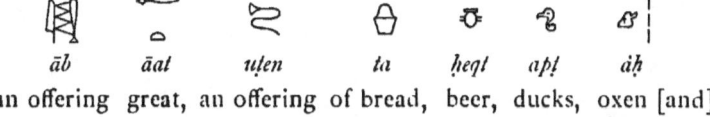

āb àri sem šeta àri

the libation, was made the celebration of the mysteries, was made

āb āat uṭen ta ḥeqt apṭ àḥ

an offering great, an offering of bread, beer, ducks, oxen [and]

χet neb nefer en neteru neteret àmu

things all good to the gods [and] goddesses who are in

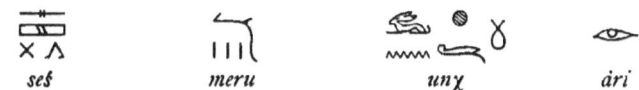

Ābet *tem - tu* *ren - sen* *em* *ḳes*
Elephantine, are proclaimed their names in the place [called]

sťer *àb* *em* *ānχ* *usr* *qem - à* *neter* *āḥā*
"Resteth the heart in life and strength". I found the god standing

em *senk-à* *seḥetep - nef* *em* *ṭua* *semeḥ-*
before my sight, he was gratified at [my] adoration, and I made

s *embaḥ - f* *ābi* *maat - f* *ser* *àb - f*
supplication before him. Opening his eyes, was moved his heart,

uaťet *χeru - f* *nuk* *χnemu* *nub - k* *āāui-à*
spake his voice, {[saying]: I am} Khnemu thy creator. My two hands

ḥaui - k *er* *seqa* *ťet - k* *er* *snib*
were upon thee to knit together thy body, to make healthy

āḥāu - k *ut-à* *àb - nek* *āat* *χer* *āat*
thy members; I gave a heart to thee. Stones [lie] upon stones

. . . . *ťer* *baḥ* *àn* *àri* *kat* *àm - sen*
. . . from times of old, {[but] no one hath} done work with them

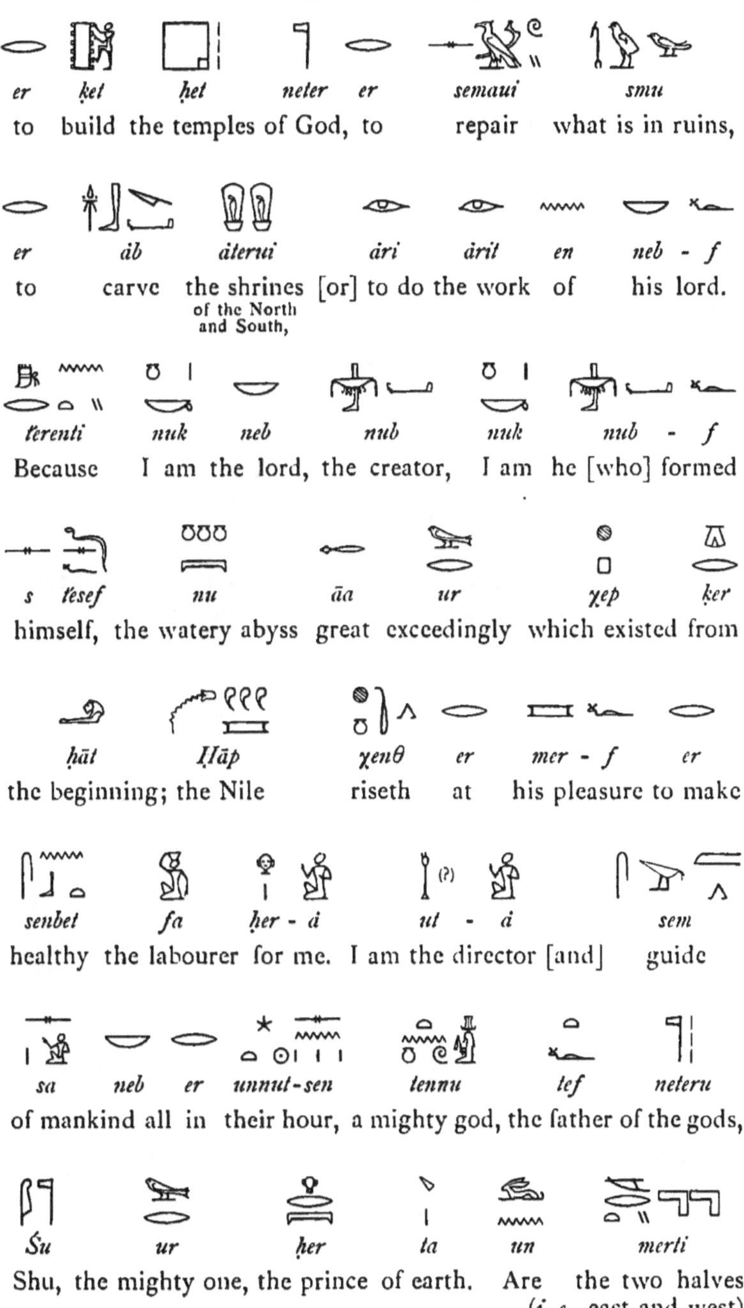

er ḳet ḥet neter er semaui smu
to build the temples of God, to repair what is in ruins,

er ȧb ȧterui ȧri ȧrit en neb - f
to carve the shrines of the North and South, [or] to do the work of his lord.

ṫerenti nuk neb nub nuk nub - f
Because I am the lord, the creator, I am he [who] formed

s ṫesef nu āa ur χep ḳer
himself, the watery abyss great exceedingly which existed from

ḥāt Ḥāp χenθ er mer - f er
the beginning; the Nile riseth at his pleasure to make

senbet fa ḥer - ȧ ut - ȧ sem
healthy the labourer for me. I am the director [and] guide

sa neb er unnut-sen tennu tef neteru
of mankind all in their hour, a mighty god, the father of the gods,

Śu ur ḥer ta un merti
Shu, the mighty one, the prince of earth. Are the two halves (*i. e.*, east and west)

em ṭebt ḳer - à χnemut - nà sefeχ

of heaven {the abode [which]} I possess. A fountain is to me, to open (?) it

reχ - à Ḥāp seχen-tef er seχet seχen-tef

I know, Hapi (Nile) he embraceth the fields, his embrace

seχ ānχ fent neb mà seχen-nt

maketh abundant {[the means] of life} for nose every, (*i. e.*, all people) according to [his] embrace

er seχet er neχeχ seχer bes - à nek

of the fields. . . . . I will make to flow for thee

Ḥāp àn renpit àb enen er ta

Ḥāp (Nile), without a year of need, subsiding upon land

neb reṭ semu neb en χertu χer neṫ

the whole. {Shall shoot up} vegetation all, {shall bend [the plants]} [which] bear grain,

ārāt (?) χent χet neb sepa χet

the goddess shall be over things all, shall increase things

neb em ḥeḥ er meḥ renpit

all by millions according to the cubit of the year.

INSCRIPTION OF THE REIGN OF PTOLEMY V.

[Gizeh Museum, No. 5576.]

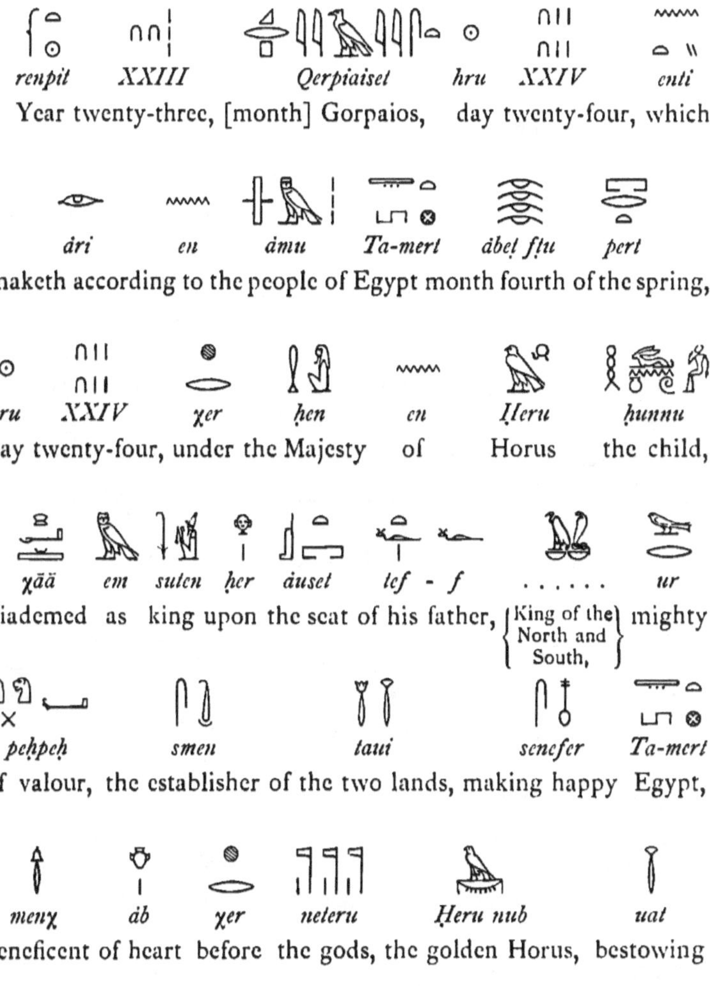

renpit *XXIII* *Qerpiaiset* *hru* *XXIV* *enti*
Year twenty-three, [month] Gorpaios, day twenty-four, which

àri *en* *àmu* *Ta-mert* *àbeṭ fṭu* *pert*
maketh according to the people of Egypt month fourth of the spring,

hru *XXIV* *χer* *ḥen* *en* *Ḥeru* *ḥunnu*
day twenty-four, under the Majesty of Horus the child,

χāā *em* *suten* *ḥer* *àuset* *tef - f* . . . . . . *ur*
diademed as king upon the seat of his father, {King of the North and South,} mighty

peḥpeḥ *smen* *taui* *senefer* *Ta-mert*
of valour, the establisher of the two lands, making happy Egypt,

menχ *àb* *χer* *neteru* *Ḥeru nub* *uat*
beneficent of heart before the gods, the golden Horus, bestowing

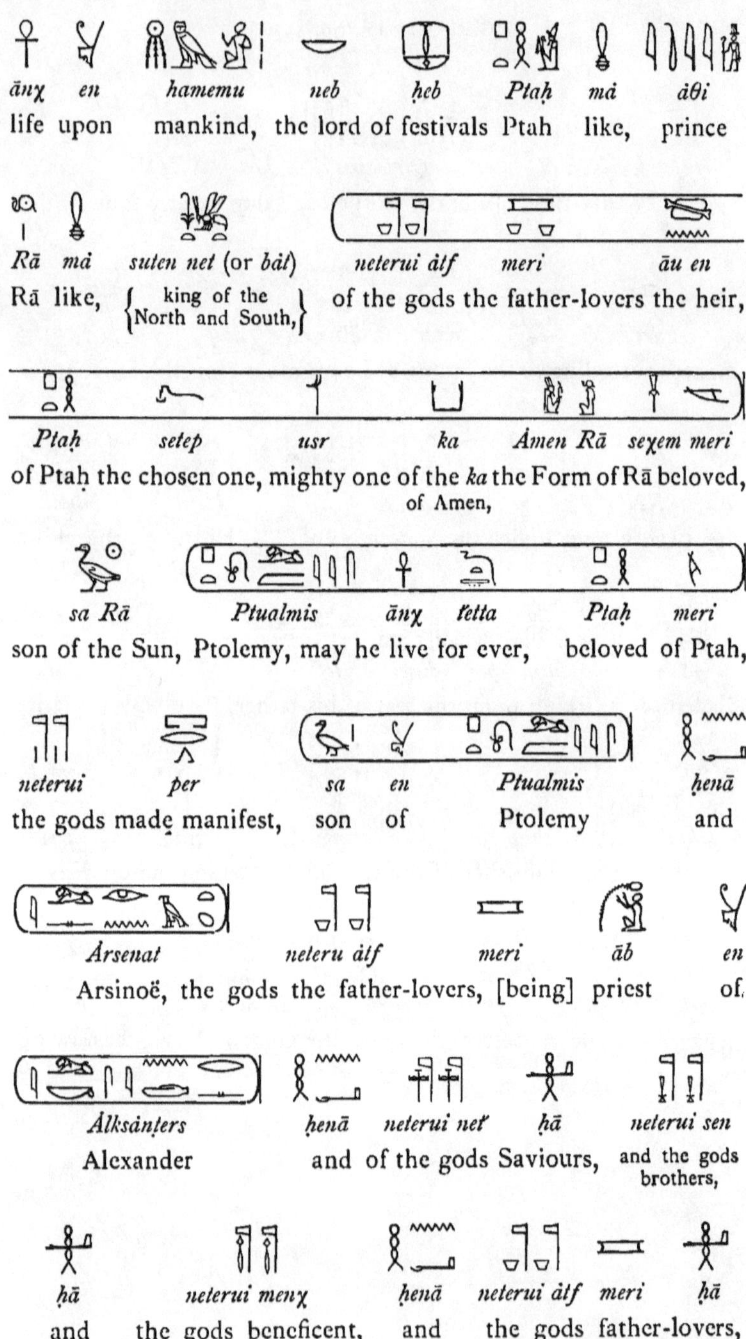

ānχ en hamemu neb ḥeb Ptaḥ mȧ ȧθi

life upon mankind, the lord of festivals Ptah like, prince

Rā mȧ suten net (or *bȧt*) *neterui ȧtf meri āu en*

Rā like, {king of the North and South,} of the gods the father-lovers the heir,

Ptaḥ setep usr ka Ȧmen Rā seχem meri

of Ptaḥ the chosen one, mighty one of the *ka* the Form of Rā beloved, of Amen,

sa Rā Ptualmis ānχ ṫetta Ptaḥ meri

son of the Sun, Ptolemy, may he live for ever, beloved of Ptah,

neterui per sa en Ptualmis ḥenā

the gods made manifest, son of Ptolemy and

Ȧrsenat neteru ȧtf meri āb en

Arsinoë, the gods the father-lovers, [being] priest of

Ȧlksȧnṭers ḥenā neterui neṫ ḥā neterui sen

Alexander and of the gods Saviours, and the gods brothers,

ḥā neterui menχ ḥenā neterui ȧtf meri ḥā

and the gods beneficent, and the gods father-lovers,

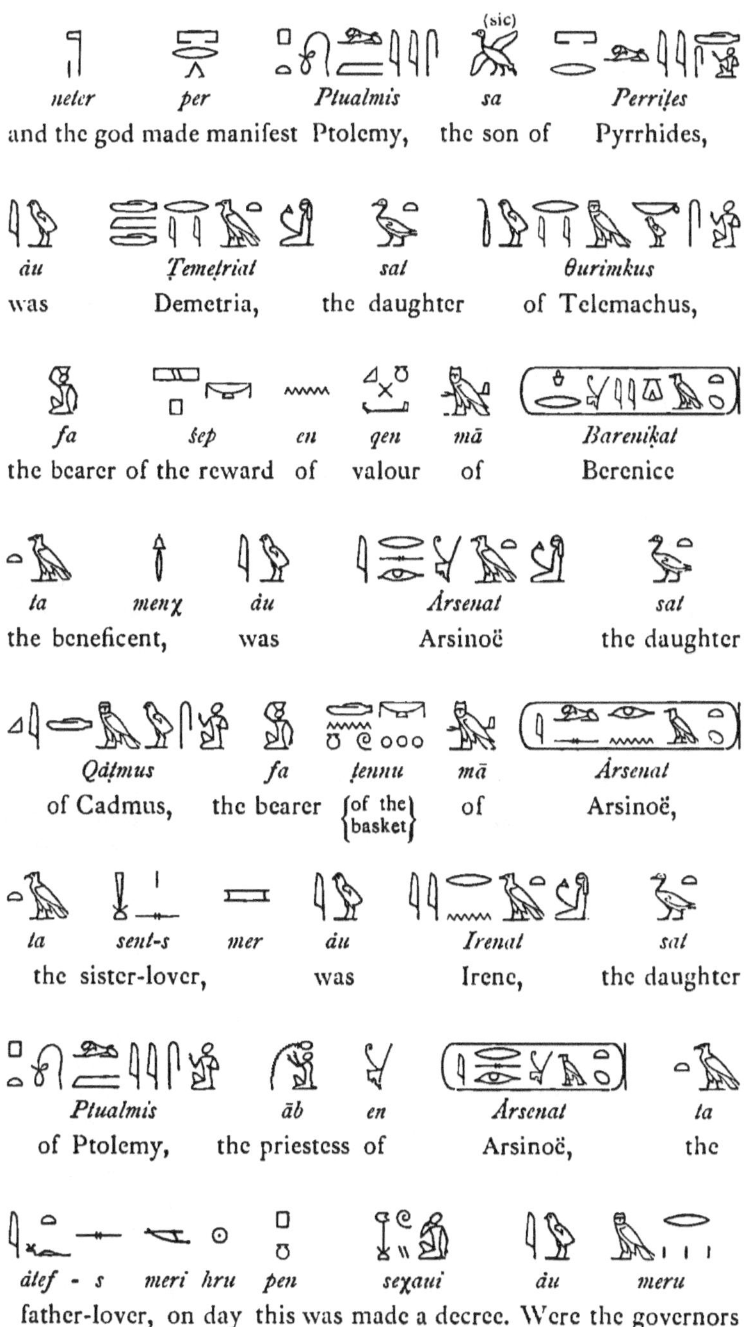

(sic)

neter per Ptualmis sa Perrițes

and the god made manifest Ptolemy, the son of Pyrrhides,

àu Țemețriat sat θurimkus

was Demetria, the daughter of Telemachus,

fa šep en qen mā Bareniķat

the bearer of the reward of valour of Berenice

ta menχ àu Ȧrsenat sat

the beneficent, was Arsinoë the daughter

Qàțmus fa țennu mā Ȧrsenat

of Cadmus, the bearer {of the basket} of Arsinoë,

ta sent-s mer àu Irenat sat

the sister-lover, was Irene, the daughter

Ptualmis āb en Ȧrsenat ta

of Ptolemy, the priestess of Arsinoë, the

àtef - s meri hru pen seχaui àu meru

father-lover, on day this was made a decree. Were the governors

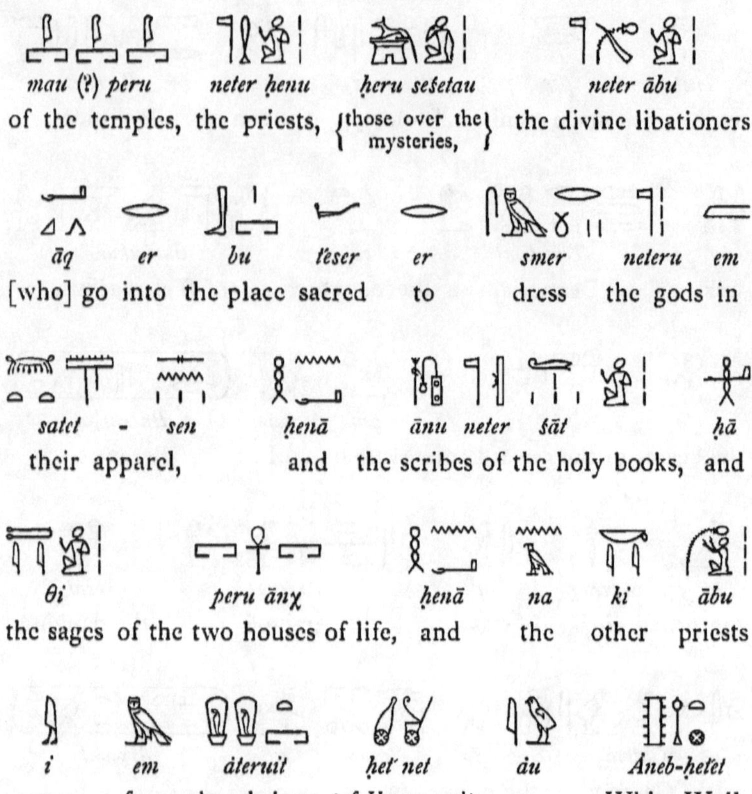

mau (?) peru neter ḥenu ḥeru seśetau neter ābu
of the temples, the priests, {those over the mysteries,} the divine libationers
āq er bu t'eser er smer neteru em
[who] go into the place sacred to dress the gods in
satet - sen ḥenā ānu neter śāt ḥā
their apparel, and the scribes of the holy books, and
θi peru ānχ ḥenā na ki ābu
the sages of the two houses of life, and the other priests
i em àteruit ḥet' net àu Àneb-ḥet'et
come from the shrines {of Upper and Lower Egypt} to White Wall. (Memphis)

TEXTS

TO BE TRANSLITERATED AND TRANSLATED

Titles of Usertsen III., King of Egypt.

Address to the gods of Judgment.

[From the Papyrus of Nebseni.]

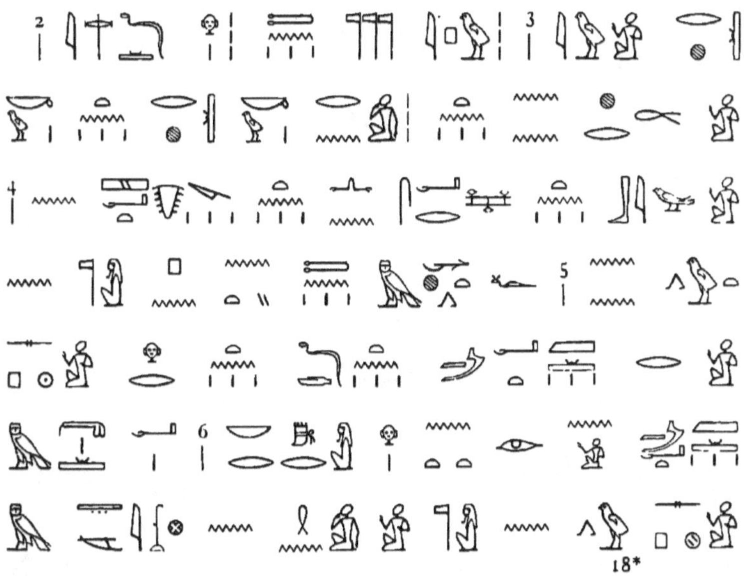

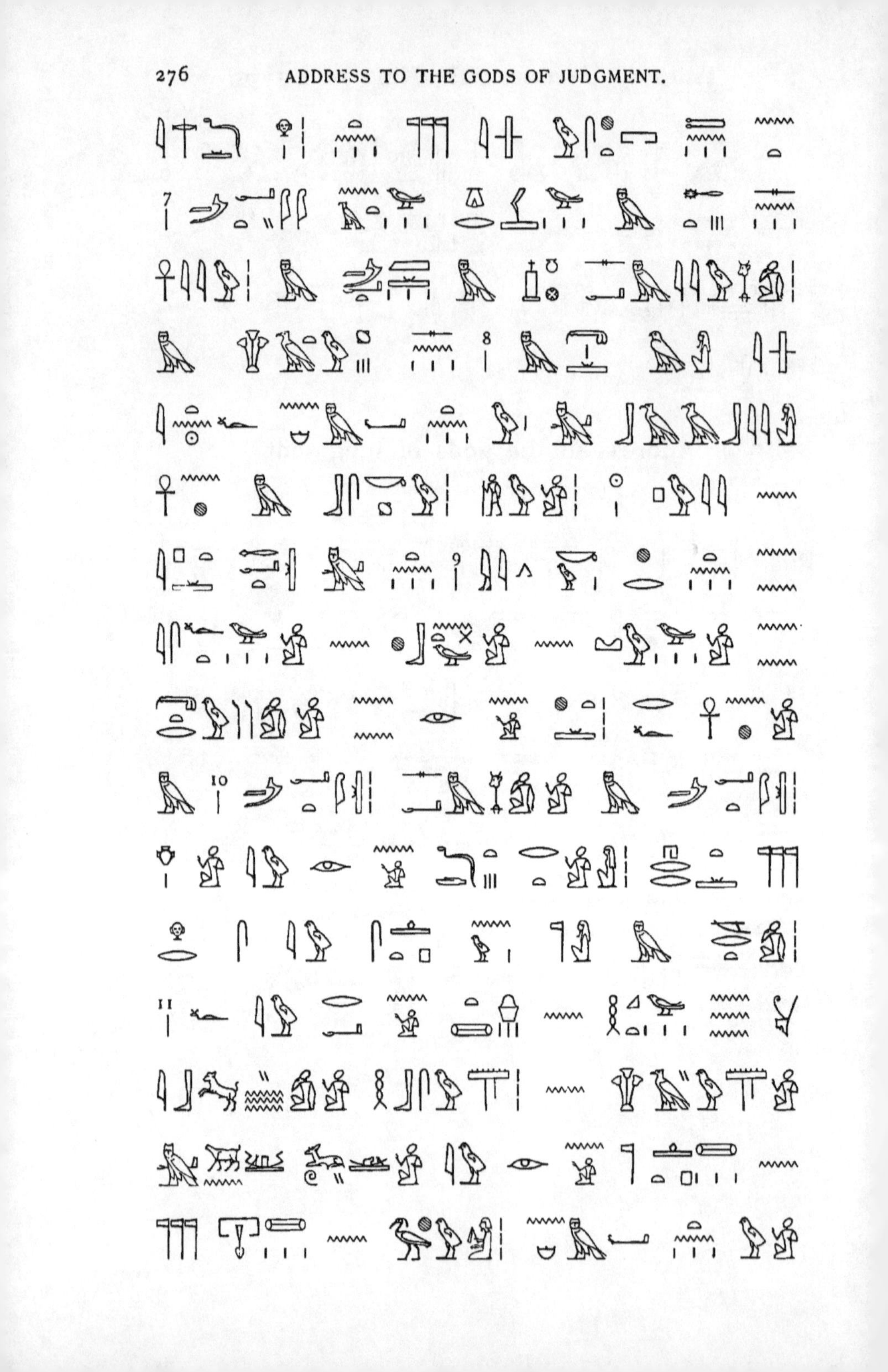

A prayer to the gods of the Underworld.

[From the Papyrus of Ani.]

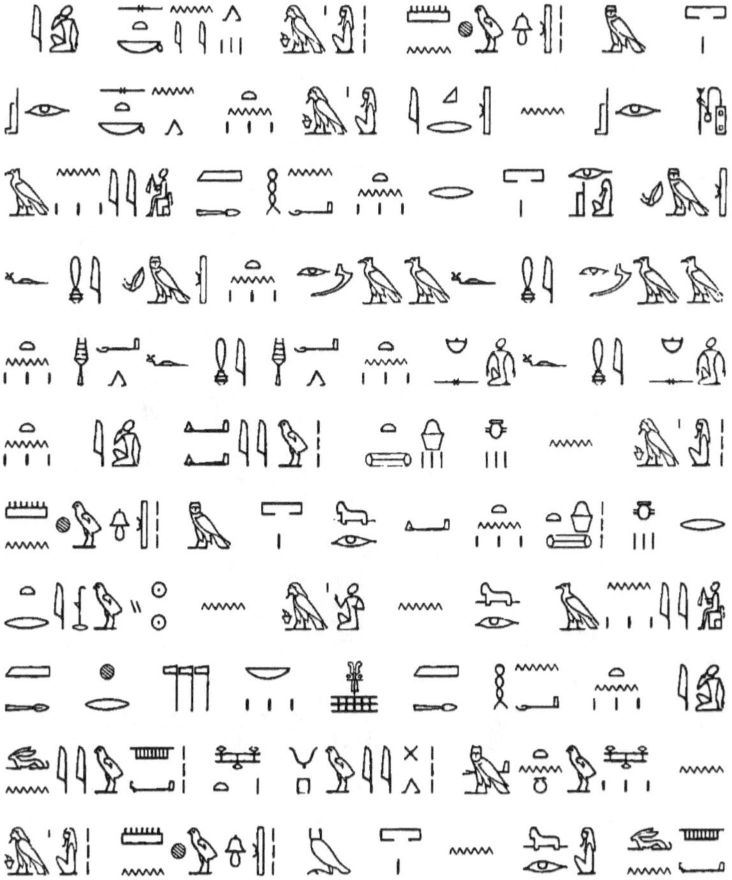

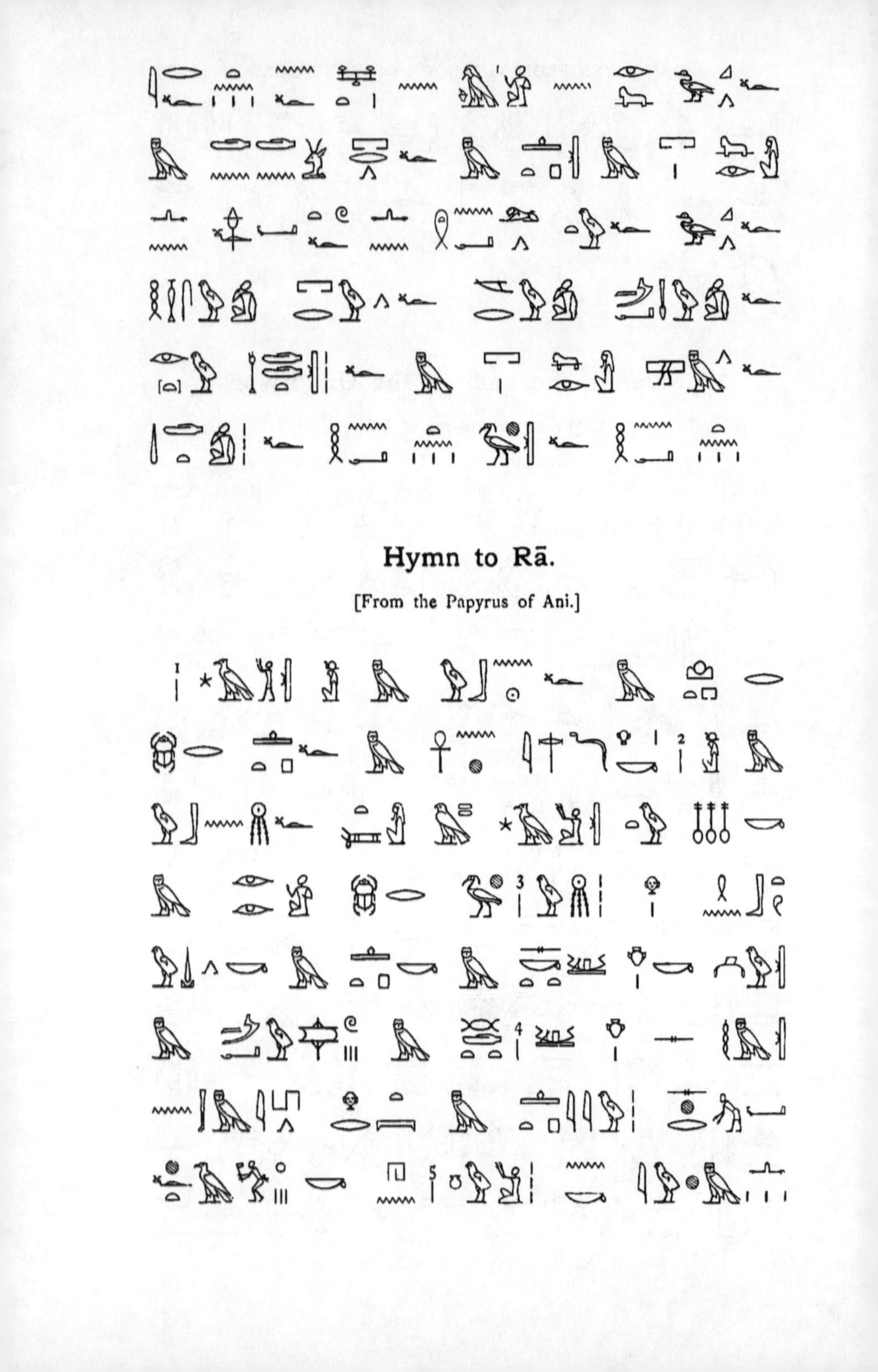

Hymn to Rā.

[From the Papyrus of Ani.]

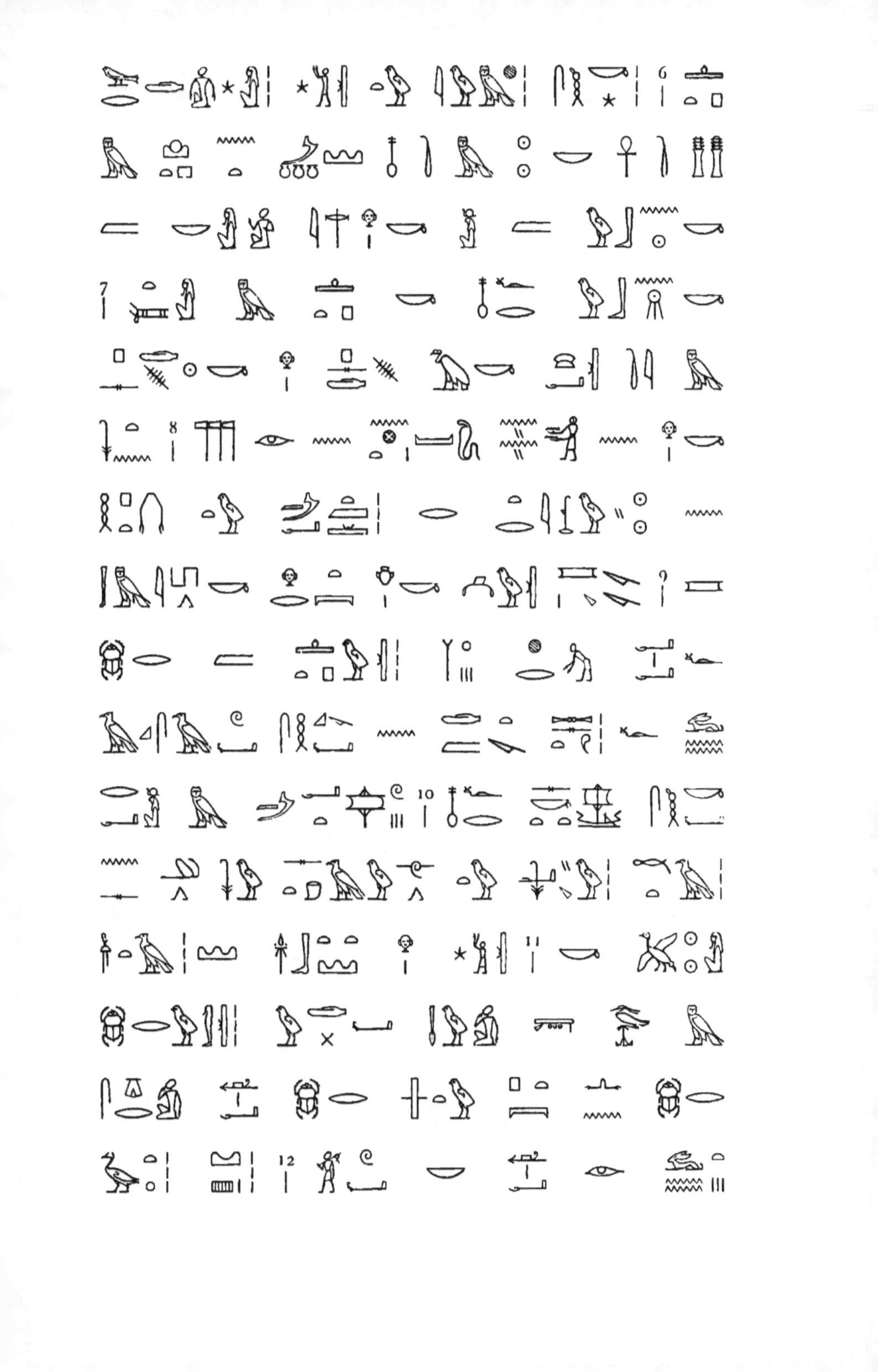

[illegible] 6 [illegible]

[illegible]

[illegible]

7 [illegible]

[illegible]

[illegible] 8 [illegible]

[illegible]

[illegible]

[illegible]

[illegible]

[illegible] 10 [illegible]

[illegible]

[illegible] 11 [illegible]

[illegible]

[illegible]

[illegible] 12 [illegible]

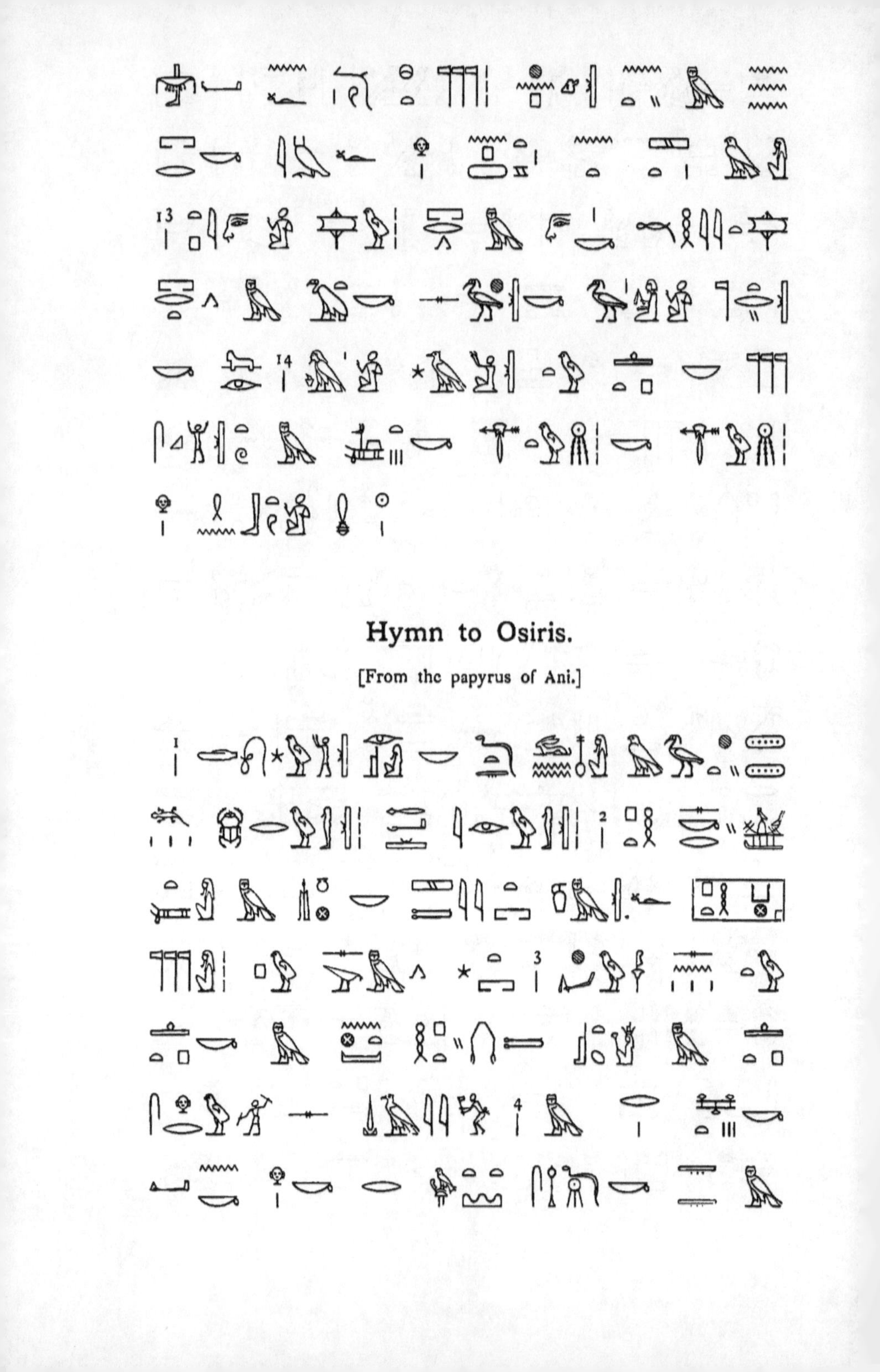

Hymn to Osiris.

[From the papyrus of Ani.]

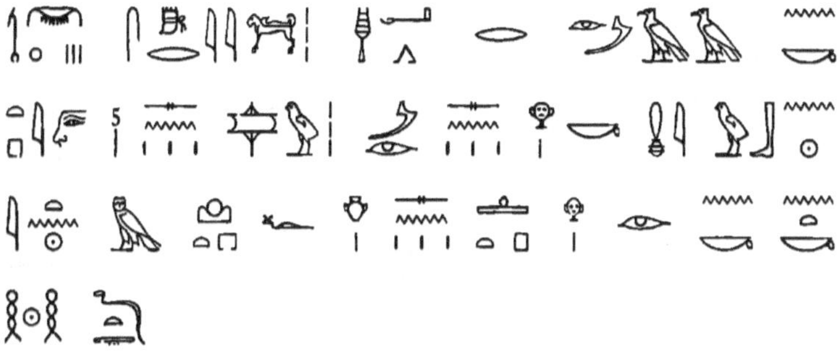

A Litany.

[From the Papyrus of Ani.]

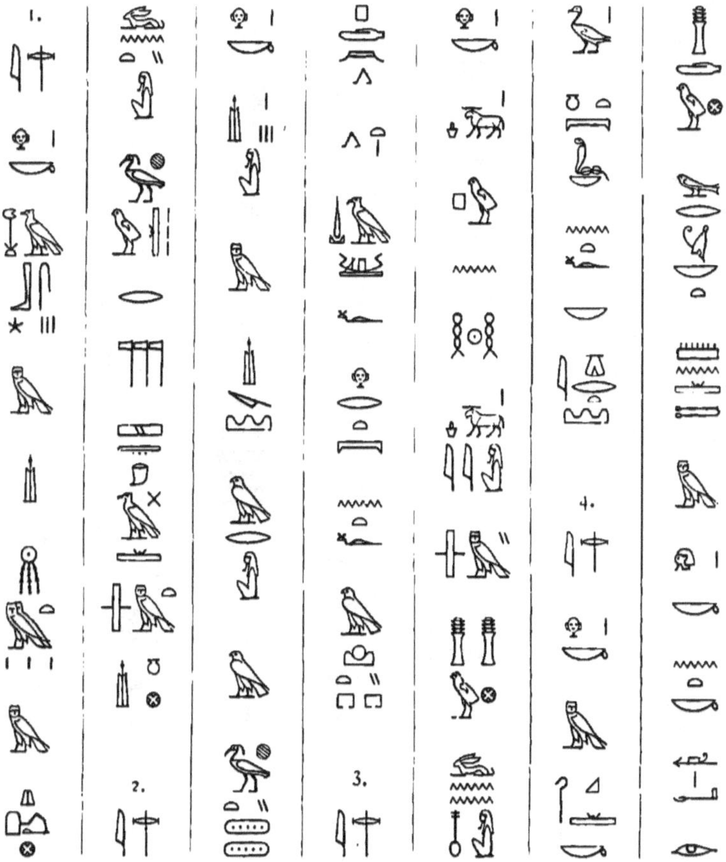

5.

6.

7.

8.

9.

A Prayer of Ani.

[From the Papyrus of Ani.]

Inscription of Seti I. King of Egypt.

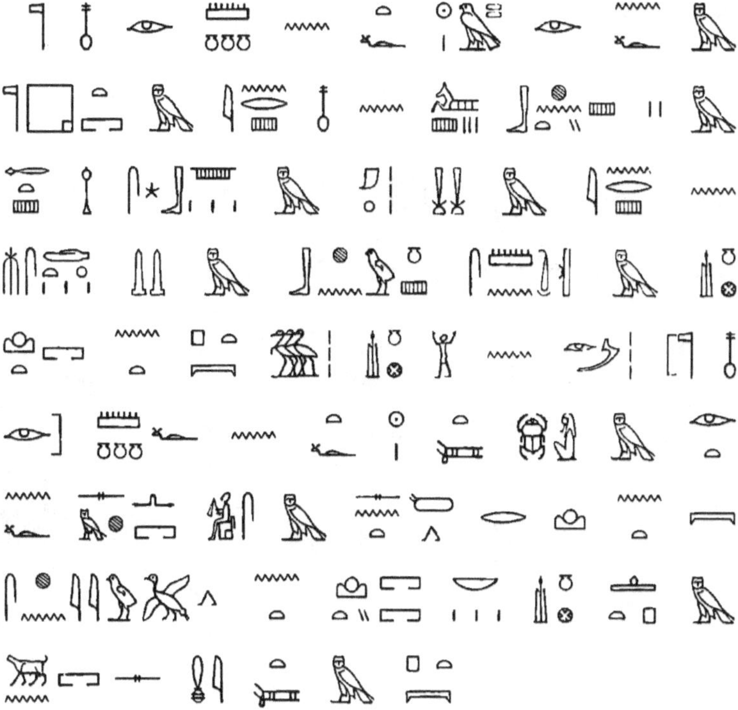

Inscriptions of the scribe Pai.

I.

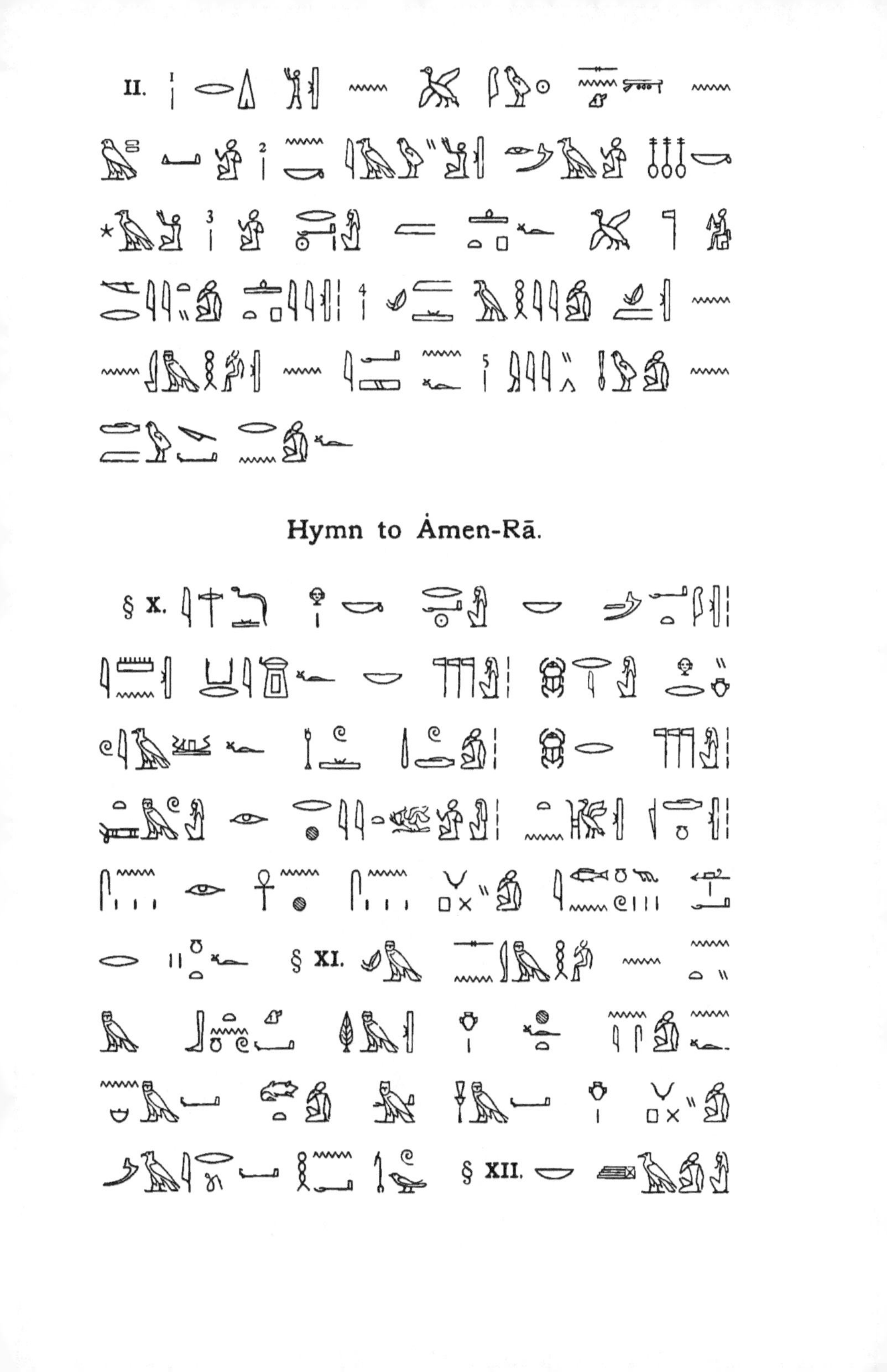

II. 1 2 3 4 5

Hymn to Ȧmen-Rā.

§ X.

§ XI.

§ XII.

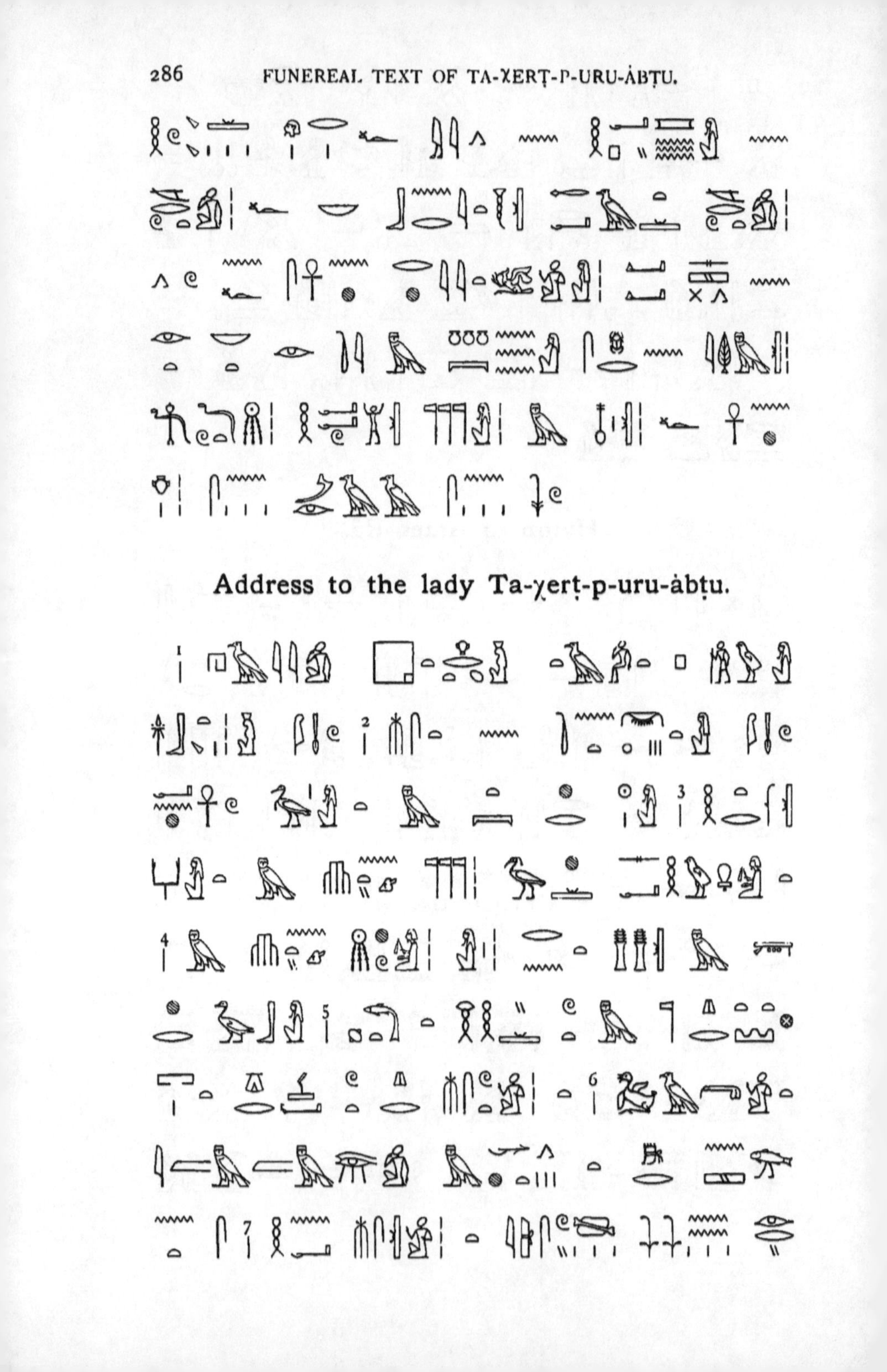

Address to the lady Ta-χerṭ-p-uru-àbṭu.

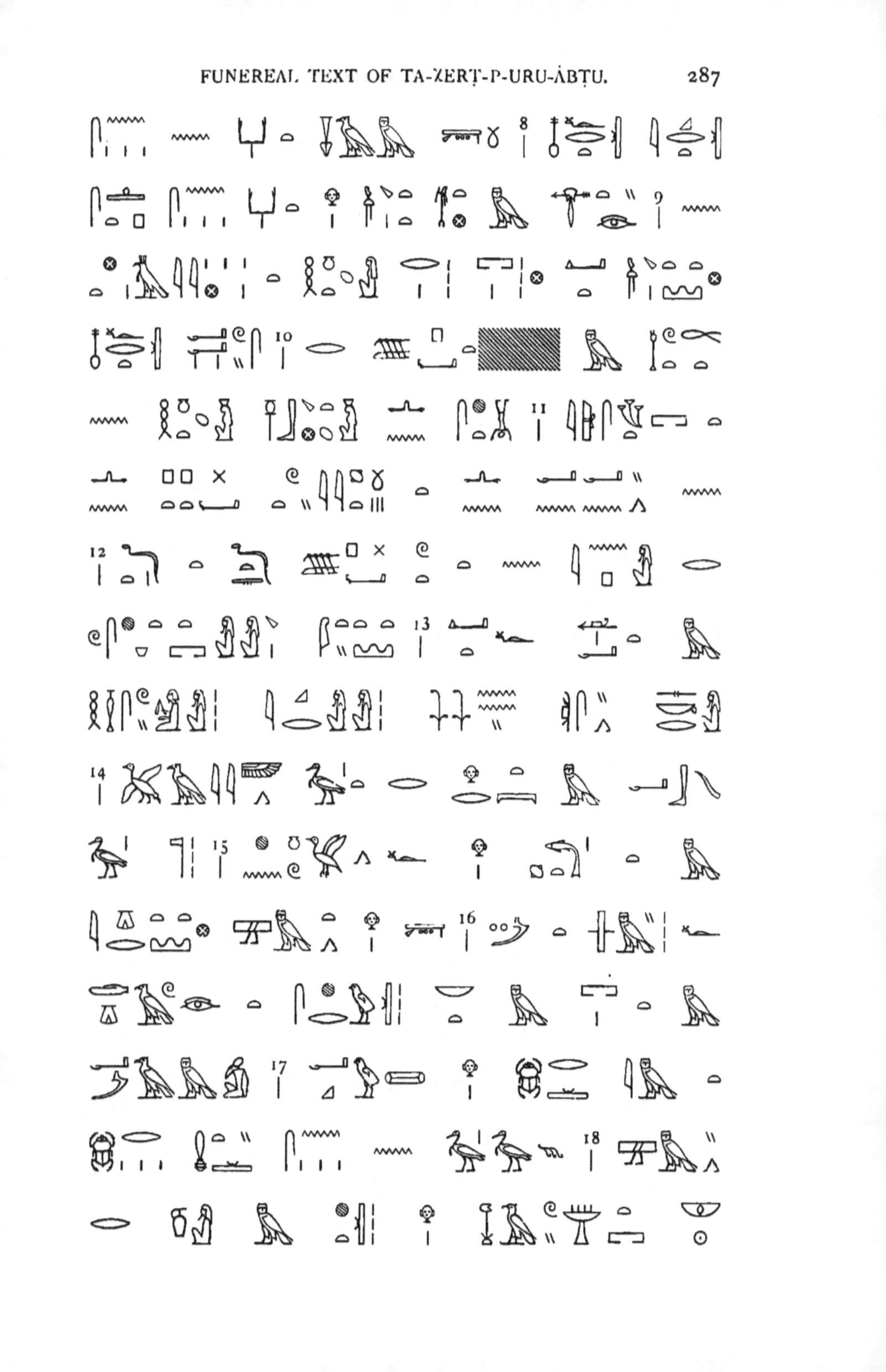

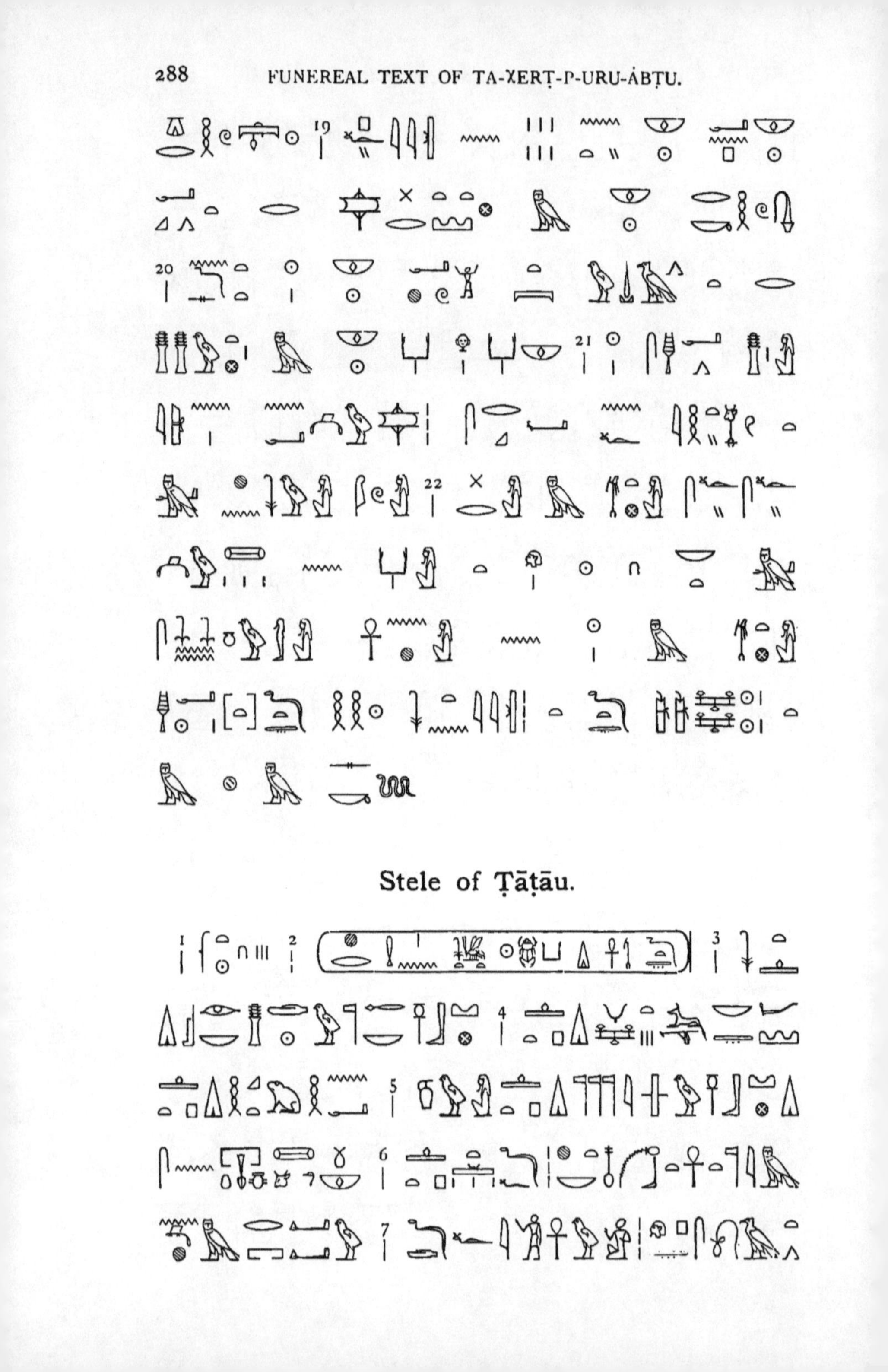

Stele of Ṭāṭāu.

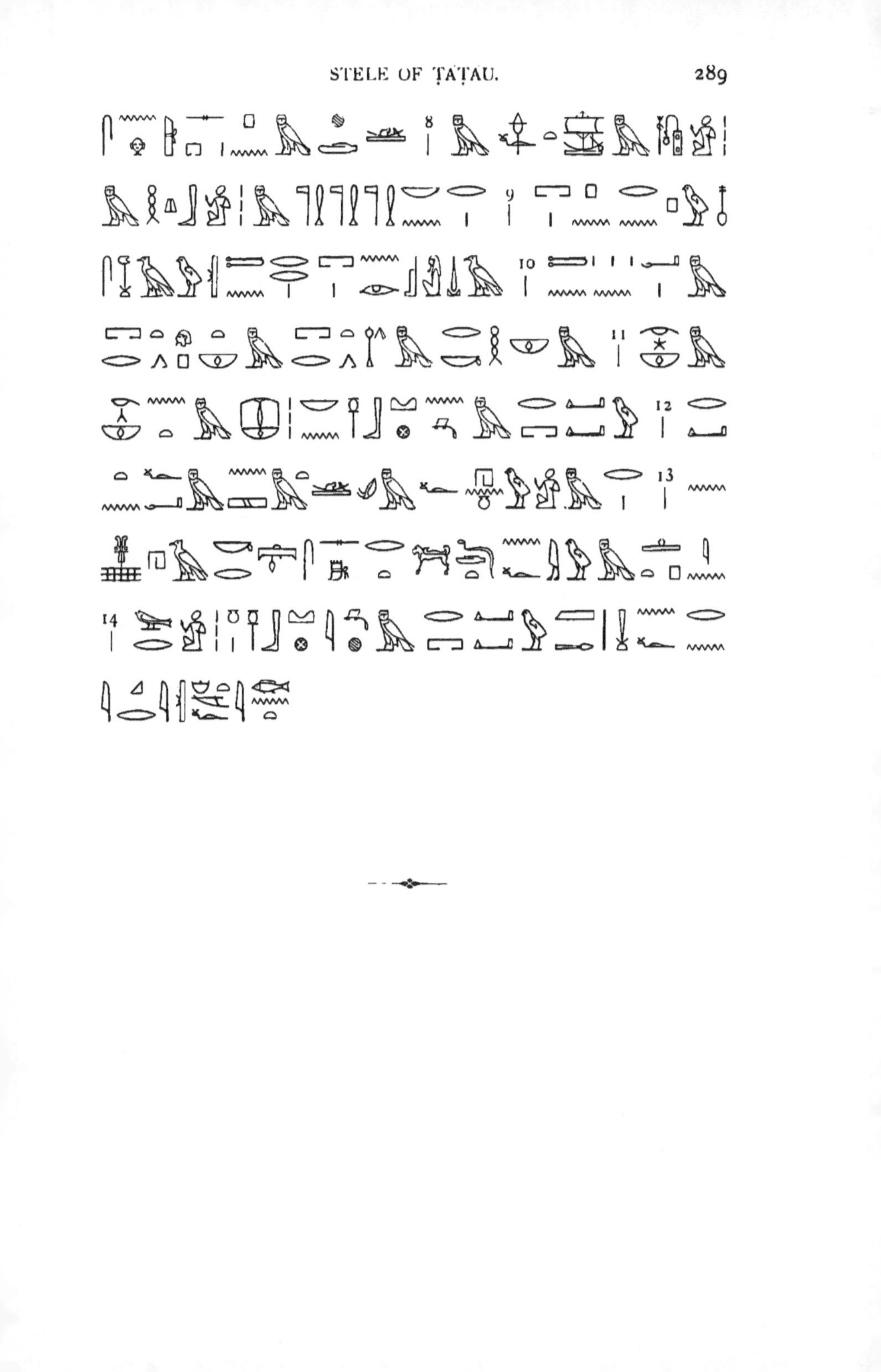

GLOSSARY.

A

Ani	a proper name
aqesau	to cut off
atet	moment

Ȧ

ȧ	I, me
ȧ	I, me
ȧ	O
ȧ	O
ȧau	old age
ȧaui	praise, adoration
ȧāš	to cry out
ȧu	to be
ȧuχemu	those who do not
Ȧusȧr	Osiris
Ȧuset	Isis

	ȧuset	place
	ȧb	heart
	ȧbu	hearts
	ȧbi	thirsty man
	Ȧbṭu	nome of Abydos
	Ȧbṭu	city of Abydos
	Ȧbtet	funeral mountain of Abydos
	Ȧbtet	the lady of Abydos
	ȧbeṭ	monthly festival
	ȧpi	to decree, judge
	ȧpt	judgment
	ȧpui	messengers, openers
	ȧpu	those
	Ȧp-uat	"opener of ways" *i. e.*, the name of a god
	ȧm	in, on, among, from, out of
	ȧmi	the one in
	ȧmiu / *ȧmu*	those dwelling in
	ȧmtu	in
	ȧm	gracious
	ȧm	delights

àmemmem	to weep
àmen	hidden
Àmenta	the hidden place, the West
Àmentaiu	those in the West
Àmentet	the funeral mountain or city on the west bank of the Nile
àmaχ	venerated
Àmsu	name of a god or star
àn	not, without, destitute of
àn	by
àn	to bring, carry
Àn	name of a god
Ànnu	Heliopolis
Ànpu	Anubis
ànnu	skin, colour
àner	stone
Ànt	name of a female
Àn-ṭes	a mythological place
ànet' ḥrà	homage to thee!
àr	then
àri	to make, maker, to do

àrit	work
àritu	made
àru	forms
àref	therefore
àḥti	throat
às	tomb
àst	tomb
àsiu	those who are rewarded with something
àsfet	sins, faults
àsn	breath of air
àten	disk
àtebui	the two banks of the celestial Nile
àqer	to be perfect
àqert	a perfect thing
àqeru	perfected divine beings
Àḳertet	a name of the underworld
Àḳert	a name of the underworld

Ā

ā	hand, power
āāui	the two hands
āa	great

āāt	great, mighty
āā	mighty one
āu	dilatation
āut ȧb	joy, pleasure
āu ḥetep	plenitude of peace
āu	food, cakes
āui	shipwrecked man
āb	to meet
āb	pure
ābt	
āmam	to eat
ān	scribe
ānāni	to break into
ānp	name of a festival
ānχ	to live, live!, life
ānχ	to live
ānχu	
ānχ-θ	living
ānχi	

ānχu *ānχiu*	living beings
ānχ	land of life
āḥā	to stand
āḥā	period of existence
āχu	to lift up, to support
āš	many
āat	a kind of stone
āṭtet	name of a boat of the sun
āq	just, true, equal
āq	to enter, to go in
āqu	food

I

i	to come
iu	to come

U

u	they, them
uat	way, road, path
uat	roads

uaḥi	to be permanent
Uast	Thebes
Uaṭet	name of a goddess
uȧ	I, me
uȧa	boat
uā	one
uāt	one
uben	to rise (of the sun)
un	to be, to exist
unen	to be, is
unenet	things which are
un	to open
uniu	openers
Un-nefer	a name of Osiris
Unti	a name of a god
ur	great, great one
uru	chiefs
Ur	name of a god
urt	name of a crown
urṭ	those who rest

usu	weak, feeble
usm	electrum (?)
user	to be strong
user	power
Usertsen	a king's name
useχt	a hall
useχtet maātet	hall of double right and truth
utit	mummy bandages
utu	to decree
utut	decree
utḥet	altar of offerings
uṭa	to go forth, set out
uṭat	the eye of the Sun
uṭ	to shoot out
uṭeṭet	commands

B

ba	soul
ba	divine soul
baiu	souls

baiu	divine souls
ba	ram
Bai	the divine Ram
Baba	proper name
Baabi	name of a god
bāḥ	to overflow, inundate to flood
bȧt	wonders, marvels
bȧt	a kind of stone
bȧn	evil, wicked
benerȧt	graciousness
beχenti	pylons
beχennu	a kind of stone
beseku	intestines
betu	to abominate
betennu	oppression

P

p	the
pa	the
Pai	proper name
pai	to fly
paut	company, cycle
pautti	the double company of the gods

pu	is
pui	this
pfi	that
pen	this
per	house
per, *peru*	to come forth
perert	thing which is brought forth
pert	appearance, manifestation
perχeru	sepulchral meals of bread, beer, oxen, fowl, linen bandages, etc.
peḥ	to arrive at, attain to
peḥreru	runner
pesṭ	back
pesṭ	to shine
pet	heaven
petpet	to break open
Ptaḥ	name of a god
Ptaḥ-Sekeri-Tem	the triad of Ptah, Socharis, and Tmu
peṭ	to stretch out, extend

F

f	he, his
fenṭ	nose

M

em	in, among, upon, when, as, with
emm	in
embaḥ	in the presence of, before
emmā	with, from
em reχ	knowingly
em χenti	among
em χet	following
emχetu	followers
em sent	round about, following
em sati	in front of
maa	to see
maati	the two eyes
manu	the mountain of the setting sun
maȧr	to be strong, mighty

	maāt	to be right and true, right and truth
	Maāt	the goddess of right and truth
	Maāti	twofold right and truth
	maā-χeru	one whose word is right and true
	maāu	winds
	mȧ	like, as
	mȧti	like, as
	mȧu	daily
	māχen	boat
	māket	strength, protection
	mātennu	ways, paths
	mu	water
	mut	mother
	men	to stablish
	men	monuments
	menχu	beneficent, perfect
	ment	pain, sickness
	ment	daily
	mer	to love, be loved

meri	loving
meriti	beloved
meru, *mert*	will, wish
mer	superintendent
Mer-ṭesṭes	a mythological locality
meḥit	north wind
meḥta	dwellers in the north
mestu	what is born
mestu	children
mesṭet	a kind of stone
met	ten
meteru	to bear [false] witness
meṭu, *meṭet*	words, speech

N

Hieroglyph note	Transliteration	Meaning
,	*n*	of, to, before, by, with
n =	*àn*	not, without
enen =	*àn*	not, without
	nat	without
	Naà-ruṭ = *Àn-ruṭ-f*, *i. e.*, "nothing grows in it"	a mythological locality,

	nȧ	I, me
	nȧs	to call, invoke, proclaim
	nini	to do homage
	nāāu	winds
	Nārt	name of a god
	nuȧ	I, me
	nuk	I
	Nu	name of a god
	Nut	name of a goddess
	nut	city
	nuti	citizens
	neb	every, all
	neb	lord
	nebu	lords, all
	nebt	all, every, lord, lady
	nub	to form, to mould
	Neb-er-ṭer	name of a god
	nept	inundated land
	nef	him, to him
	nefu	winds
	Nef-urtet	a mythological locality

nefer	to be good, or beautiful, a good thing
nefer-θ	good
nefert	a good thing
neferu	beauties
nemȧ	to stride
nemmȧt	step
nemeḥ	feeble, weak
eneniu	things which, those which
neḥi	suppliant
neḥem	to deliver
Neχen	name of a city
nes	her, it
nes	tongue
neš	to enter
nešemet	boat
nek	thee
ent	of, which
net	thou
neter	god, divine
neteru	gods

neteru	gods
neteri	strong
neter ḥenu	priests
neter ḥet	temple
neter ḥetepu	divine offerings
Neter-χert *Neter-χertet*	the underworld
enti	of, who, which
entef	he, him
entek	thou
neťem	sweet, pleasant
neťesetet	little

R

er	for, from, against, more than, to
er ḥert	upwards
Rā	the Sungod
Rā-Ḥeru-χuti	Rā-Harmachis
Rā-χā-kau	prenomen of Usertsen III.
Rā-χeper-ka	prenomen of Usertsen I.

Rā-Tem-χeperȧ	a triad of gods
re	mouth
re-per	temple
re-peru	temples
eref	therefore
ren	name
Ren-ȧqer	a proper name
renpit	year
renput	years
reχ	to know
reχit	intelligent beings
rekḥ	name of a festival
rekḥu	heat
ret	men and women
reθ	men and women
ruṭ	to grow
erṭāt	to give
erṭā	to give

H

hai	O
haker	name of a festival
hamemet	human beings

hennu	to praise
hennu	praises
hru	day
hereret	what is pleasing

Ḥ

ḥaiu	naked man
ḥatu	foul, filth
ḥu	food
ḥāāu	to rejoice
ḥā	limbs, members
Ḥāpi	the Nile
ḥeb	festival
ḥebu	festivals
ḥebsu	clothing
ḥept	to embrace
ḥems	to sit
ḥemt	wife
ḥen	Majesty, priest
ḥenā	and, with
ḥenti	two periods of 60 years each

ḥent	mistress, lady
ḥer	to, for, on, upon, by
ḥer-àb, *ḥeri-àb*	within
ḥer entet	because
ḥer-s	thereat
Ḥeru	Horus
Ḥeru nub	golden Horus
Ḥeru-χuti	Harpocrates
ḥrà	face
ḥràu	faces
ḥeru	terrors
ḥert	celestial regions
ḥeḥ	eternity
ḥesu	to be pleased
ḥesu, *ḥestu*	favours
ḥesui	favoured ones

ḥetep	to rest, to repose, to be at peace, to set down, peace, to set (of the sun)
ḥetep	offering
ḥetepiu	those who give peace
ḥetepu	offerings
ḥetepet	offerings
ḥetrȧ	to pay something due
Ḥet-ḥert	Hathor
Ḥet-Ptaḥ-ka	Memphis
ḥet'	white
ḥet't'ut	light
ḥeq	to rule
ḥeq	beer, ale
ḥeqert	hungry
Ḥeqt	name of a goddess

χ

χaut	table, altar
χauit	altar

χabesu	stars
χat	dead body
χat	body, bodies
χā	to be crowned
χa-θā	crowned
χā	crown
χu	a spiritual part of a man
χu	to glorify, be glorified, to protect
χu	rays of light
χu	shining, spiritual beings
χut	horizon
χebent	sin, wickedness
χeper	to come into being
χeperu	product, what exists
χeperu	transformations, forms of existence
Χeperā	a god of creation

	χeft	towards, opposite, in face of
	χefta	enemies
	χemt	three
	χemt	copper, bronze
	χnem	to join, to unite
	Χnemu	a god of creation
	χen	interior of
	χen / *χennu*	to alight, to hover over
	χenp	to draw out
	χenti	before, dwelling at
	Χensu	name of a god
	χer	under, to, with
	χer	to cast down, be overthrown
	Χer-āba	a city near Memphis
	χeru	voice, word

χer ḥebu	chief readers
χesef	to meet, to repulse
χeseft	to sail up the river
χet	things
χeṭ	to float down the river

S

s	she, it, her, sign of the causative
sa	son, child
sa Rā	son of the Sun
Sa	the god of intelligence
sam ta	burial
sat	earth
satu	to shine, rays
sȧs	six
sām	to eat
samiu	devourers
sānχ	to vivify
sār	to bring forward
sāḥā	to make to stand up
sȧḥu	the spiritual body

	su	he, him
	suat	to make to travel
	Seb	the god of the earth
	sebu	doors
	sebàu	fiends
	sebi	to pass on
	sep	case, moment, time
	sep sen	twice, duplicity
	sepu	times
	sefisefi	abundance
	smauti (?)	uniter of North and South
	sem	to guide, leader
	smà	to accuse
	smàt (?)	half monthly festival
	smen	to establish
	sen	they, them
	sen	two
	sent	twice
	sen	brother
	sensen	bases of statues
	senb	good health

sennu	image
sen ta	adoration
senṭet	to fear, fear
senṭet	timid man
seru	nobles, chiefs
serq	to make to breathe
seχa	to remember, remembrance
seχu	to glorify
seχeper	to make to come into being
seχem	shrine
seχem	strong
seχeniu	those who make to alight
seχer	to overthrow
seχeru	things which go on, affairs, plans, schemes
seχet	to be overthrown
seḥeru	to drive away
seḥet'	to illuminate
seḥeq	to cut, to sever
seḥetep	to lay to rest, to appease
seš	to pass, motion
sešep	to receive

sek	infinity
sek	to draw on
seku	those who set
Seker	name of a god
seker	name of sacred boat
sektet	a boat of the sun
seqa	to exalt
seḳer	silence
sta	to be towed along
setem	to hear
suten	king, royal
suteni	sovereignty
suten ān	royal scribe
suten net (or *bāt*)	King of the North and South
Suten-ḥenen	Heracleopolis
suten ḥetep ṭā	give a royal offering!
setekeni	those who make to enter
s'ert	a lying down
s'eri	to lie down

SH

šāt	slaughter
Šu	name of a god
šu	light
šeps	sacred, holy
šem	to go
šen	to curse
šenār	to repulse, be repulsed
šenbet	body
šesi	to follow
šet Ḥeru	"Lake of Horus", a mythological locality
šeta	hidden
šeθit	hidden place

T

t	thee, thou
ta	bread, cakes
ta	land, the earth
taui	the lands of the North and South, the world
Ta-merá	a name of Egypt
Ta-ṭesertet	the underworld
tu	thee, mark of the passive

tepȧ	to smell
tepḥet	storehouse
tef	father
Tem / *Temu*	a god of Heliopolis
tem ȧb	strong of heart
temt	sledge
ten	ye, you
ten	how many
trȧui	morning and evening
teχenui	a pair of obelisks

Ṭ

ṭā	to give, giver
ṭāṭāiu	givers
Ṭāṭāu	name of a man
ṭu	mountains
ṭu / *ṭu*	evil, sin
ṭua	a hymn of praise
ṭuau	to praise, adoration

ṭuat	the underworld
ṭep	head, upon, first
ṭept	name of a festival
ṭep re	utterance
ṭemu	to pronounce
ṭemt	knife
ṭenṭen	confidence, boldness
ṭeṭ	the trunk containing the body of Osiris
ṭeṭṭeṭ	to be stable, firm
ṭeṭṭeṭit	duration
Ṭeṭṭeṭu, *Ṭeṭṭu*	name of a town
ṭeḳau	to see

TH

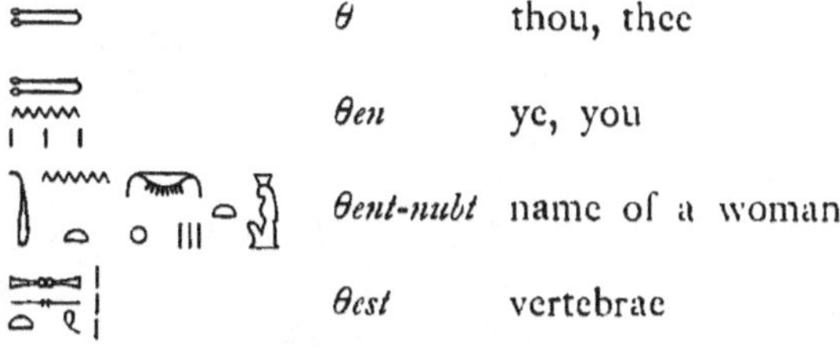

θ	thou, thee
θen	ye, you
θent-nubt	name of a woman
θest	vertebrae

TCH

t'a	to go forth
t'a	husband
t'ai	fiend
t'efau	funeral food or meals
t'et	body
t'etta	eternity, for ever
t'eṭ	to speak, to declare
t'eṭet	words, things said

K

k	thou, thee, thy
ka	the double of a man
kau	doubles
ka	a divine double
karȧ	shrine
kaḥrȧka	a festival
kuȧ	I, me
keḥek	old age

Q

	qemāiu	those in the south
	qereset	burial
	qeṭ	dispositions, natures

Ḳ

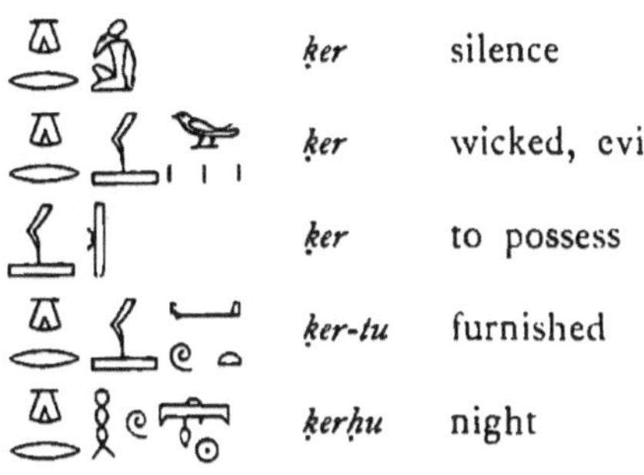

	ḳer	silence
	ḳer	wicked, evil
	ḳer	to possess
	ḳer-tu	furnished
	ḳerḥu	night

www.ingramcontent.com/pod-product-compliance
Lightning Source LLC
Chambersburg PA
CBHW021206230426
43667CB00006B/577

* 9 7 8 3 3 3 7 3 3 0 2 7 9 *